Kiss Me
at the Stroke of
Midnight

0

Rin Mikimoto

I

Contents

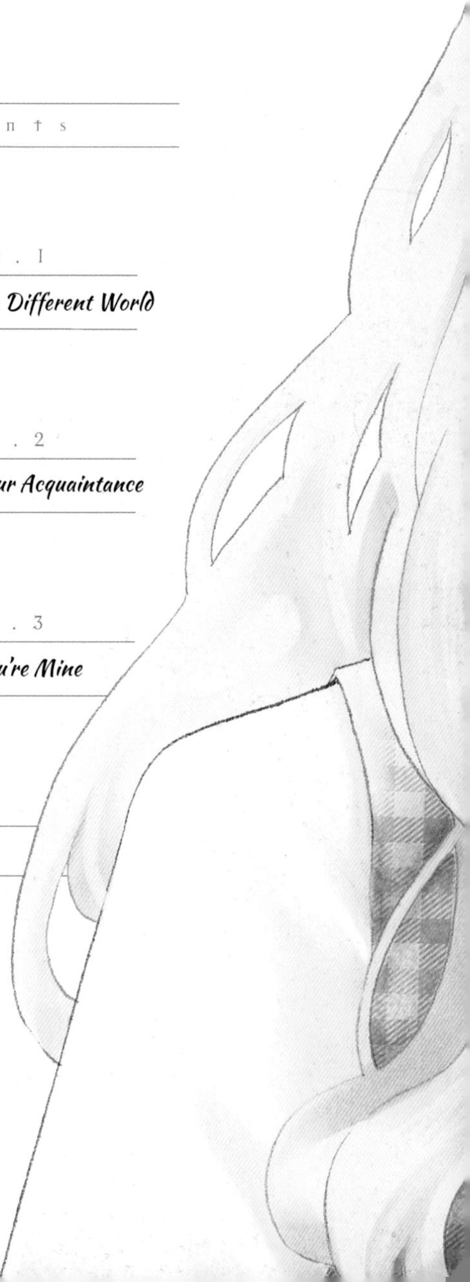

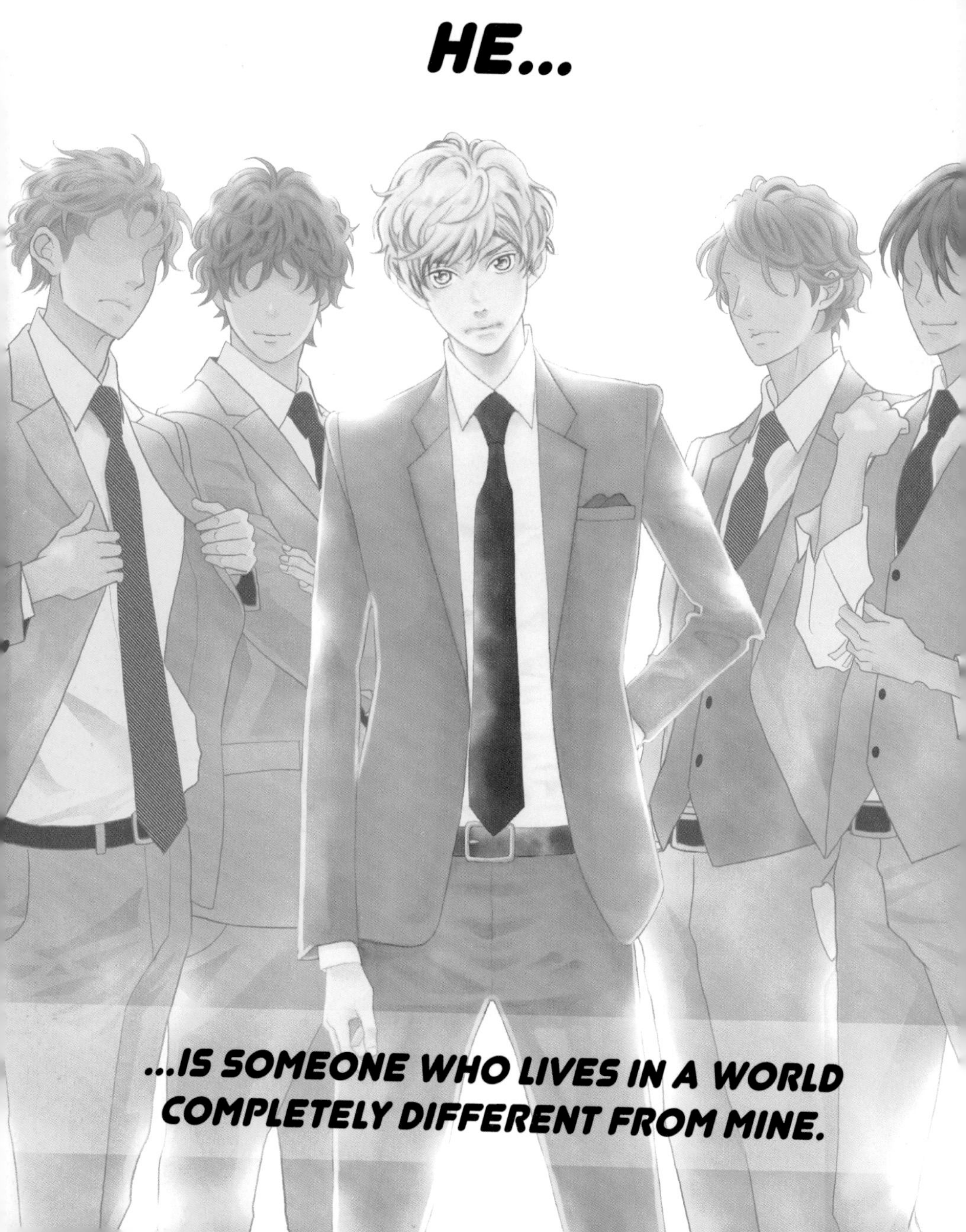
HE...
...IS SOMEONE WHO LIVES IN A WORLD COMPLETELY DIFFERENT FROM MINE.

STORY. I

Someone Who Lives in a Different World

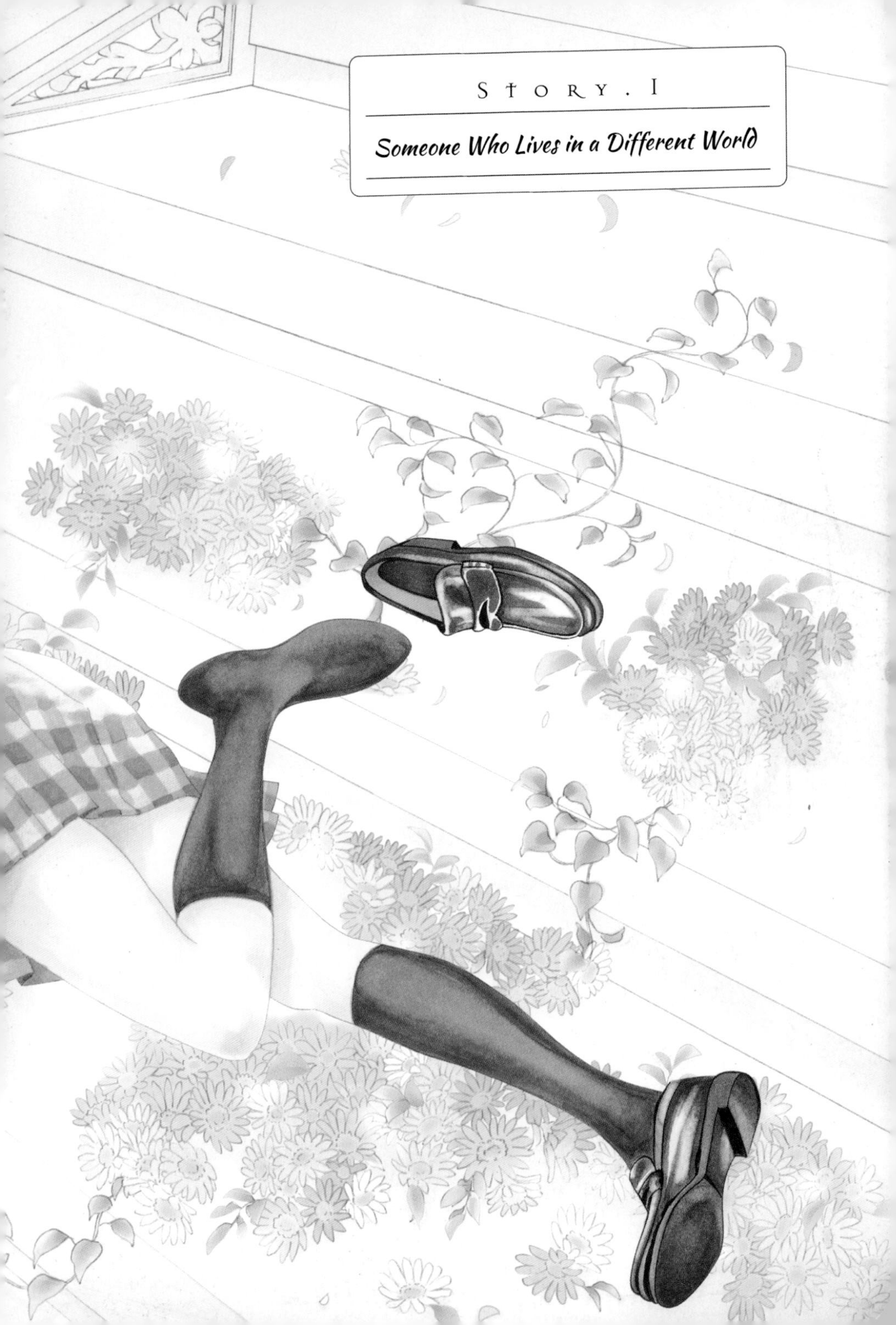

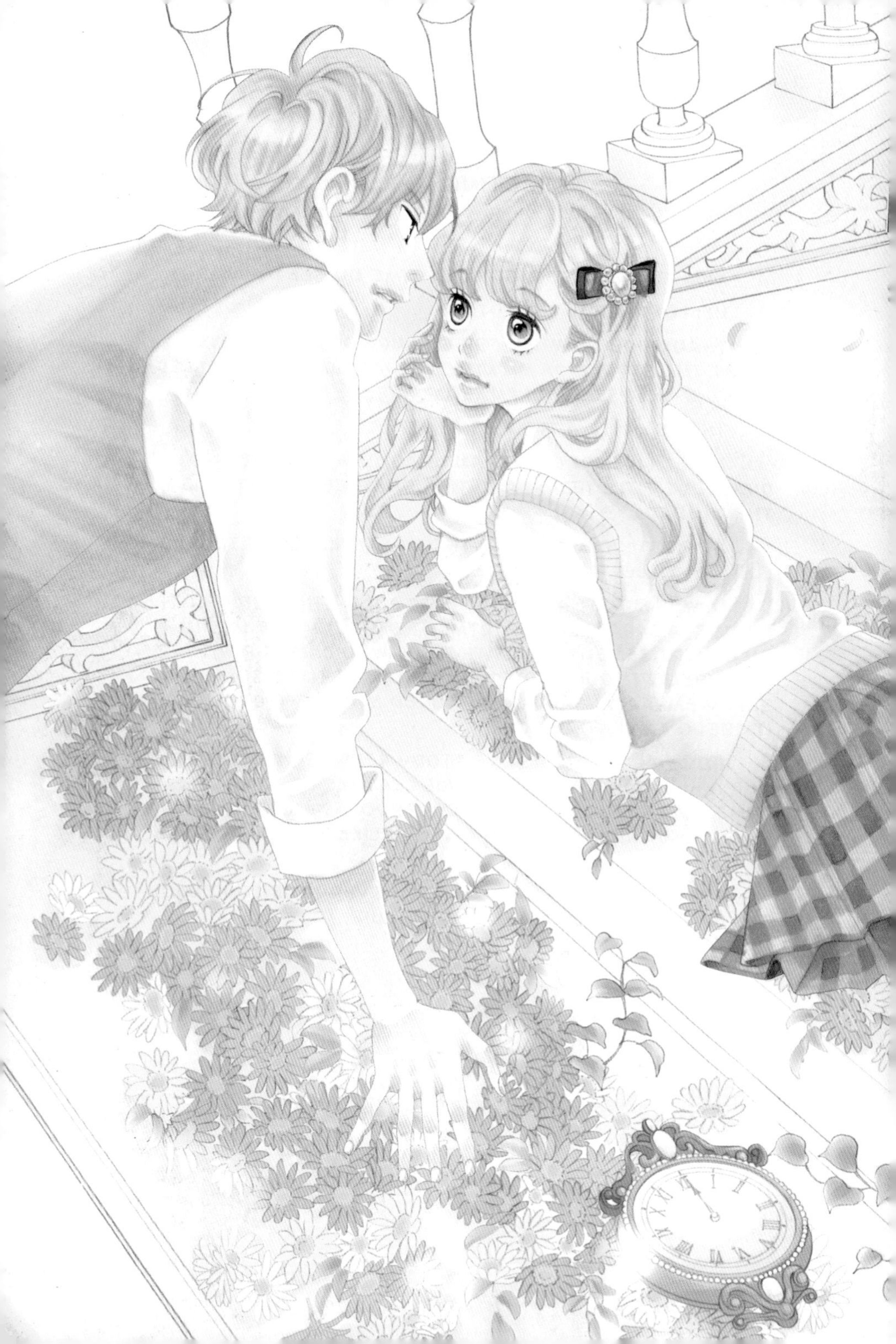

GREETINGS ①

NICE TO MEET YOU, OR LONG TIME NO SEE.

HELLO! I'M RIN MIKIMOTO.

THANK YOU SO MUCH FOR BUYING VOLUME 1 OF *KISS ME AT THE STROKE OF MIDNIGHT*. IN JAPANESE, IT'S CALLED, *GOZEN 0-JI, KISS SHI NI KITEYO*.

THAT'S QUITE A TITLE, ISN'T IT?

I FEEL LIKE MY EDITOR AND I CONSIDERED OVER 50 DIFFERENT TITLE IDEAS. AND THIS UNEXPECTED ONE WAS THE WINNER.

AT FIRST, "CANDY" WAS THE MOST LIKELY CONTENDER FOR THE TITLE.

IT WAS MEANT AS A SARCASTIC JOKE—THE KIND OF TITLE LUMINE (A JAPANESE DEPARTMENT STORE) MIGHT USE IN AN ADVERTISEMENT. I WAS THE ONE WHO CAME UP WITH IT, BUT WHEN I THOUGHT OVER IT AGAIN, THE TITLE SOUNDED SUPER EMBARRASSING! SO I FIGURED MAYBE WE COULD CALL IT "ZERO KISS" FOR SHORT.

ANYWAY, THIS IS A LOVE STORY BETWEEN A CELEBRITY AND A HIGH SCHOOL GIRL—THE BIG LEAGUES OF ROMANTIC COMEDIES! A COUPLE YEARS AGO, I PROBABLY WOULDN'T HAVE EVEN LAID A HAND ON A STORY LIKE THIS. BUT NOW, IT'S JUST PERFECT FOR ME.

I'M GONNA WORK HARD SO THAT EVERYONE CAN ENJOY THE STORY. I HOPE TO SEE YOU AGAIN!

CONTINUED IN ②

MY FAVORITE ACTRESS IS NANA KOMATSU-CHAN. I'M OBSESSED!

I ♥ NANA

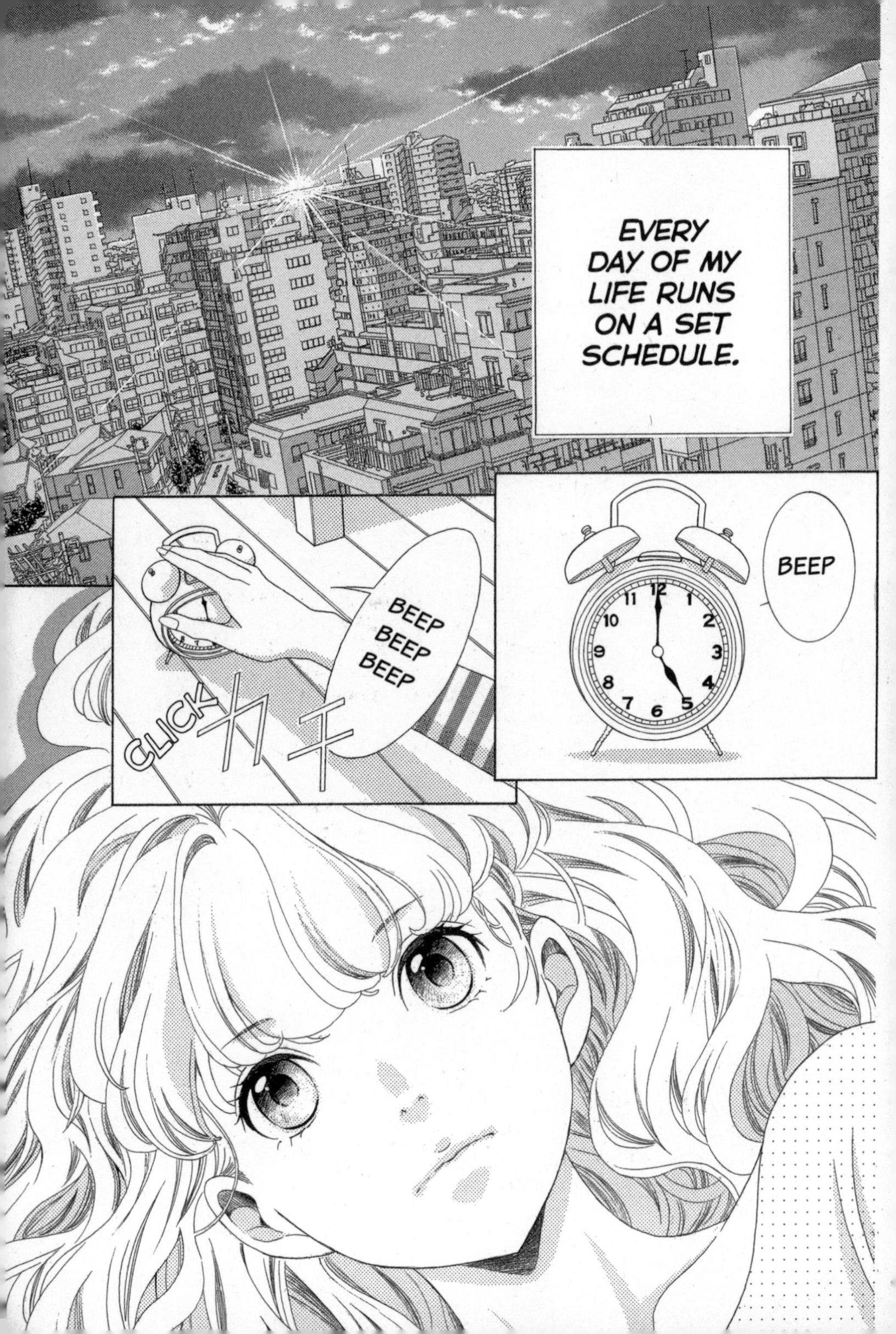
EVERY DAY OF MY LIFE RUNS ON A SET SCHEDULE.
BEEP
BEEP BEEP BEEP
CLICK
カチ

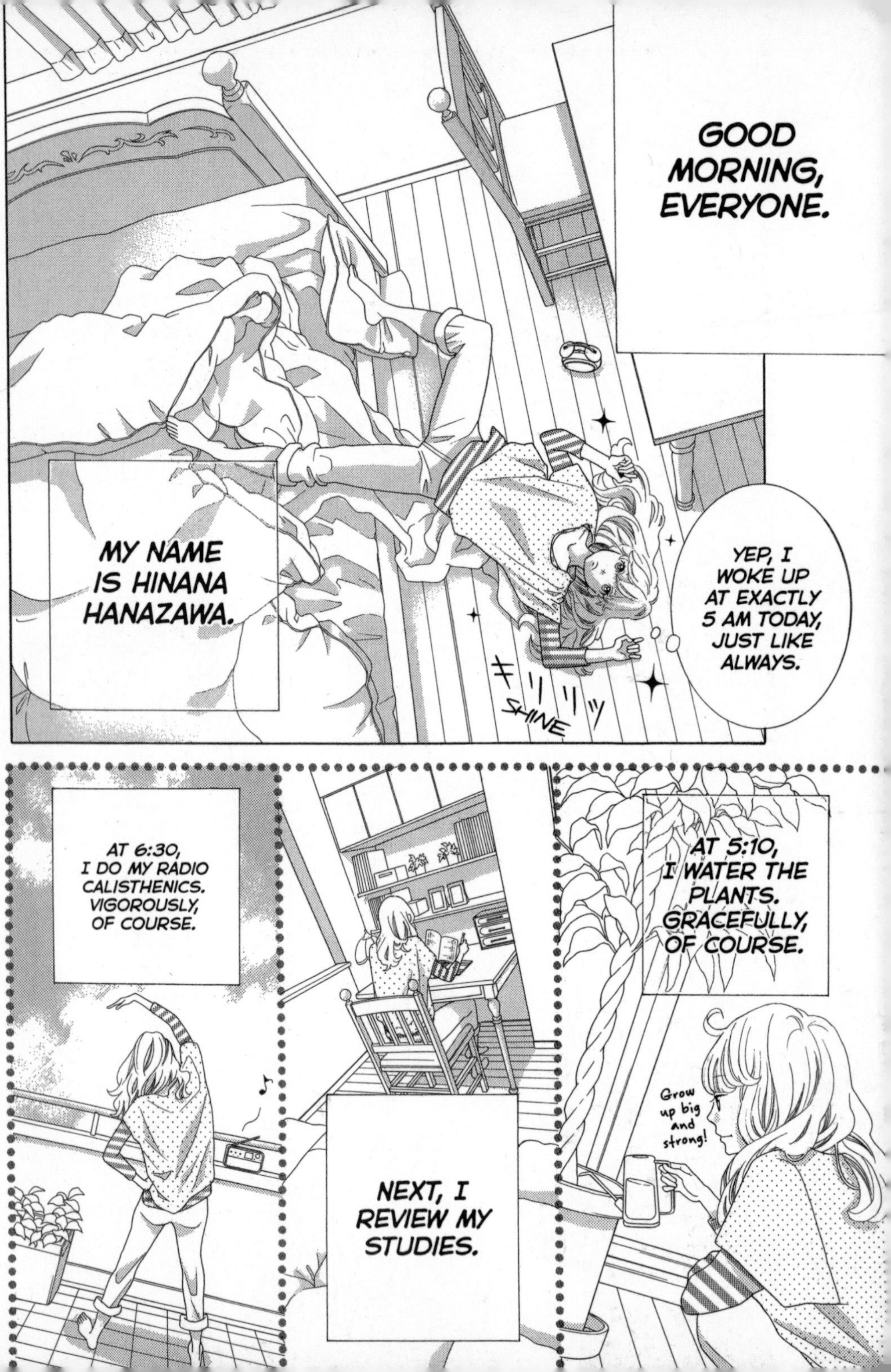
GOOD MORNING, EVERYONE.
YEP, I WOKE UP AT EXACTLY 5 AM TODAY, JUST LIKE ALWAYS.
キリリッ
SHINE
MY NAME IS HINANA HANAZAWA.
AT 5:10, I WATER THE PLANTS. GRACEFULLY, OF COURSE.
Grow up big and strong!
NEXT, I REVIEW MY STUDIES.
AT 6:30, I DO MY RADIO CALISTHENICS. VIGOROUSLY, OF COURSE.

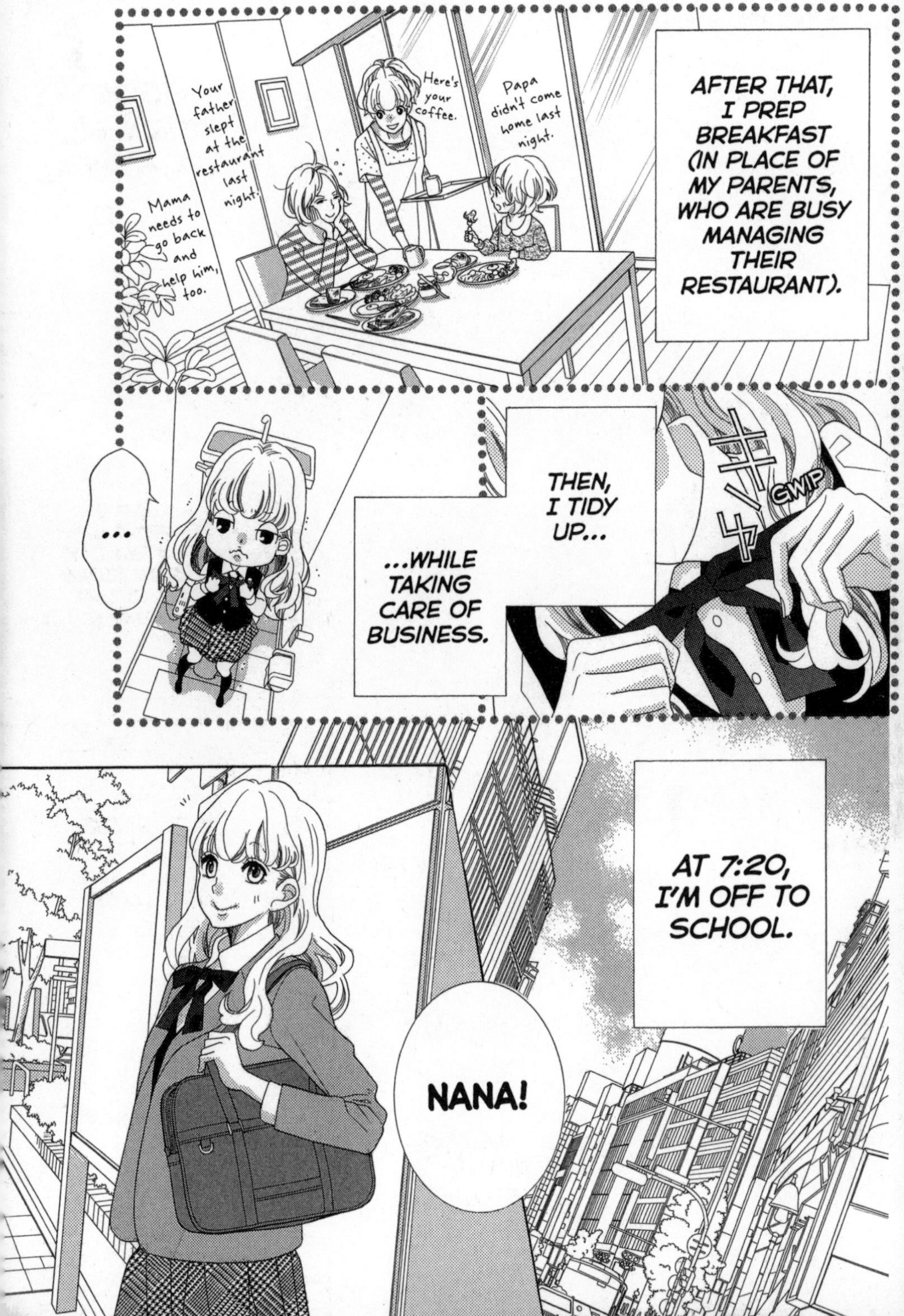
AFTER THAT, I PREP BREAKFAST (IN PLACE OF MY PARENTS, WHO ARE BUSY MANAGING THEIR RESTAURANT).
Papa didn't come home last night.
Here's your coffee.
Your father slept at the restaurant last night.
Mama needs to go back and help him, too.
THEN, I TIDY UP...
GWIP
...WHILE TAKING CARE OF BUSINESS.
...
AT 7:20, I'M OFF TO SCHOOL.
NANA!

MORNIN'!

AH-CHAN! RUN-CHAN!

THANKS FOR WAITING.

Wait. Then you should be joining us all the time.

We're all in different classes, so I can only see you guys during lunch. Of course I'm gonna show up from time to time!

THIS IS A SURPRISE. YOU'RE USUALLY LATER THAN US, RUN-CHAN.

I'VE KNOWN AH-CHAN SINCE CHILDHOOD, AND RUN-CHAN IS MY BEST FRIEND FROM MIDDLE SCHOOL.

THESE TWO ARE MY VERY BEST FRIENDS.

SHUT UP, AKIRA.

SERIOUSLY! RUN IS LIKE THE POSTER-CHILD FOR LATENESS.

LOOK AT THAT!

OH!

AND NEXT UP, HERE'S THE ENTERTAINMENT NEWS. ♪

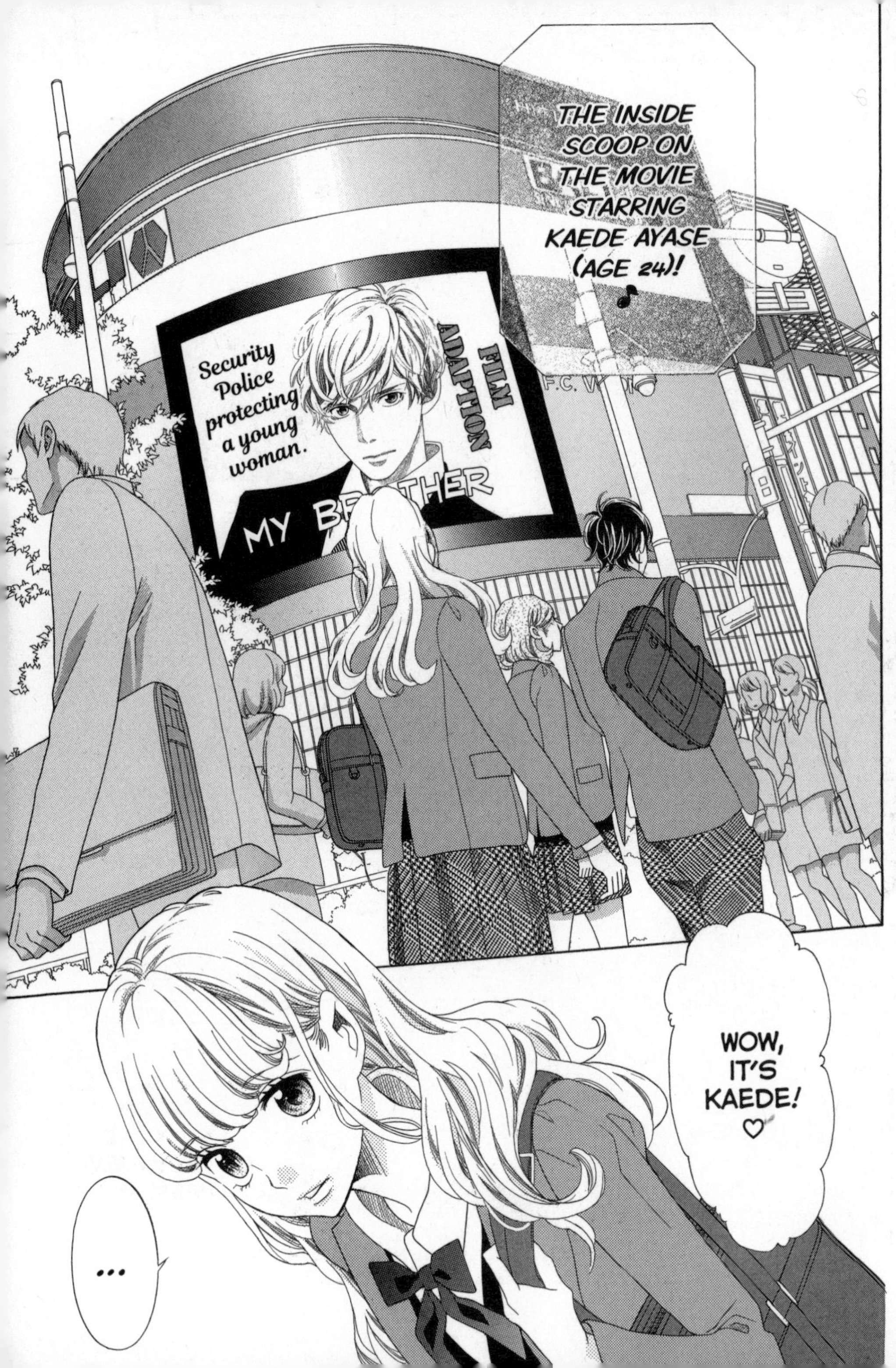
THE INSIDE SCOOP ON THE MOVIE STARRING KAEDE AYASE (AGE 24)! ♪
FILM ADAPTION
Security Police protecting a young woman.
WOW, IT'S KAEDE! ♡
...

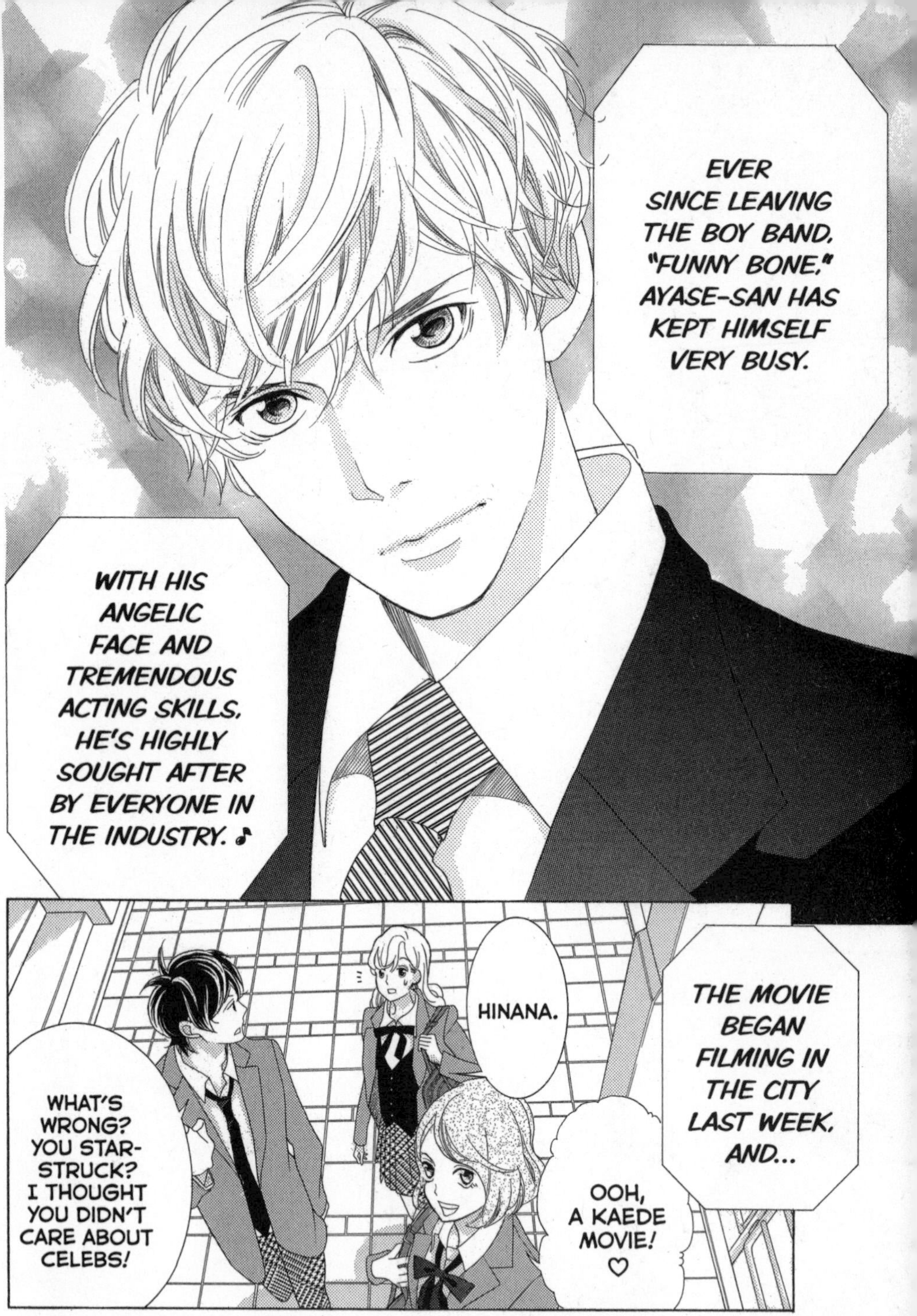
EVER SINCE LEAVING THE BOY BAND, "FUNNY BONE," AYASE-SAN HAS KEPT HIMSELF VERY BUSY.
WITH HIS ANGELIC FACE AND TREMENDOUS ACTING SKILLS, HE'S HIGHLY SOUGHT AFTER BY EVERYONE IN THE INDUSTRY. ♪
THE MOVIE BEGAN FILMING IN THE CITY LAST WEEK, AND...
HINANA.
OOH, A KAEDE MOVIE! ♡
WHAT'S WRONG? YOU STAR-STRUCK? I THOUGHT YOU DIDN'T CARE ABOUT CELEBS!

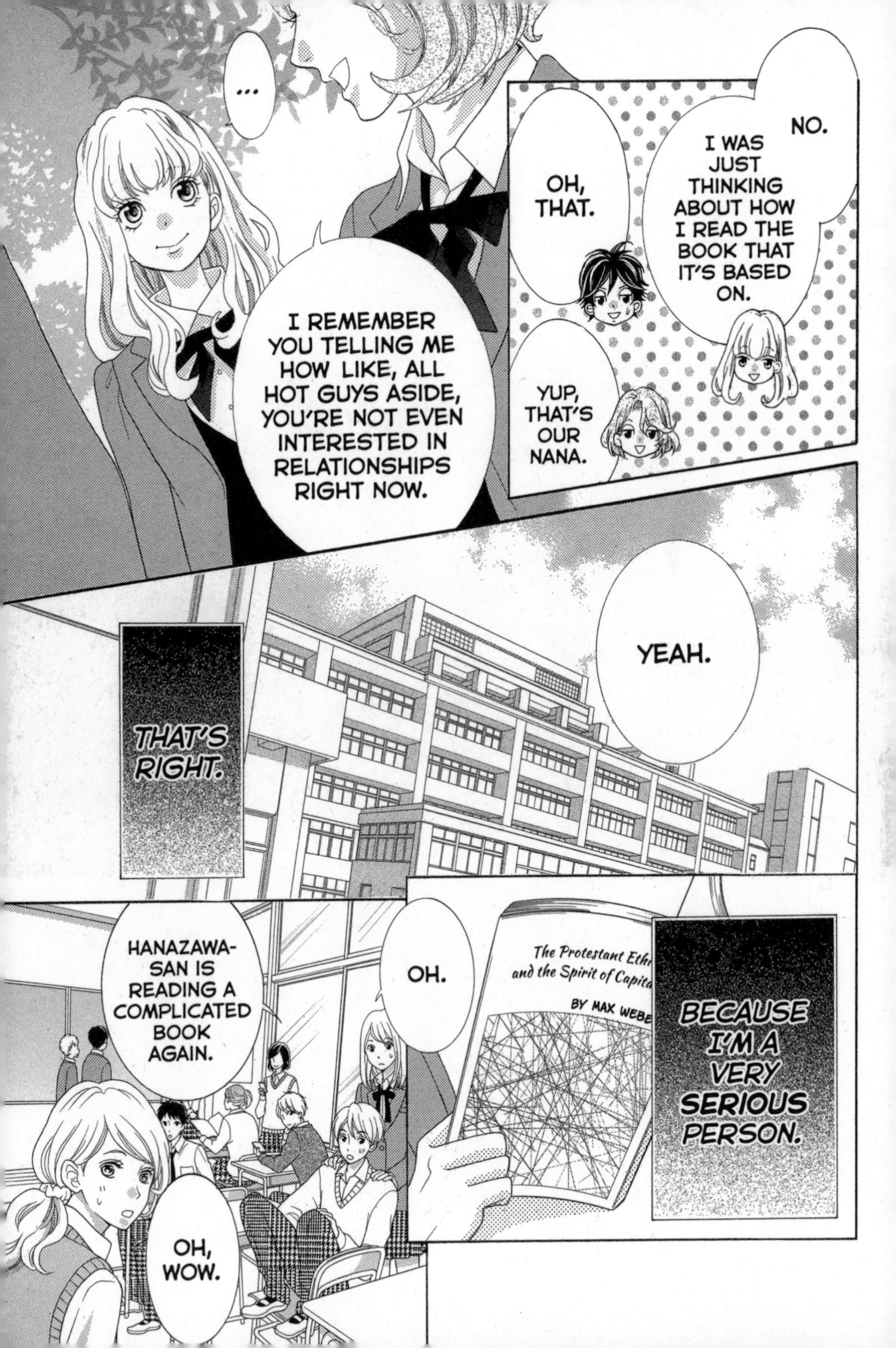
NO.
I WAS JUST THINKING ABOUT HOW I READ THE BOOK THAT IT'S BASED ON.
OH, THAT.
YUP, THAT'S OUR NANA.
...
I REMEMBER YOU TELLING ME HOW LIKE, ALL HOT GUYS ASIDE, YOU'RE NOT EVEN INTERESTED IN RELATIONSHIPS RIGHT NOW.
YEAH.
THAT'S RIGHT.
BECAUSE I'M A VERY SERIOUS PERSON.
OH.
HANAZAWA-SAN IS READING A COMPLICATED BOOK AGAIN.
OH, WOW.

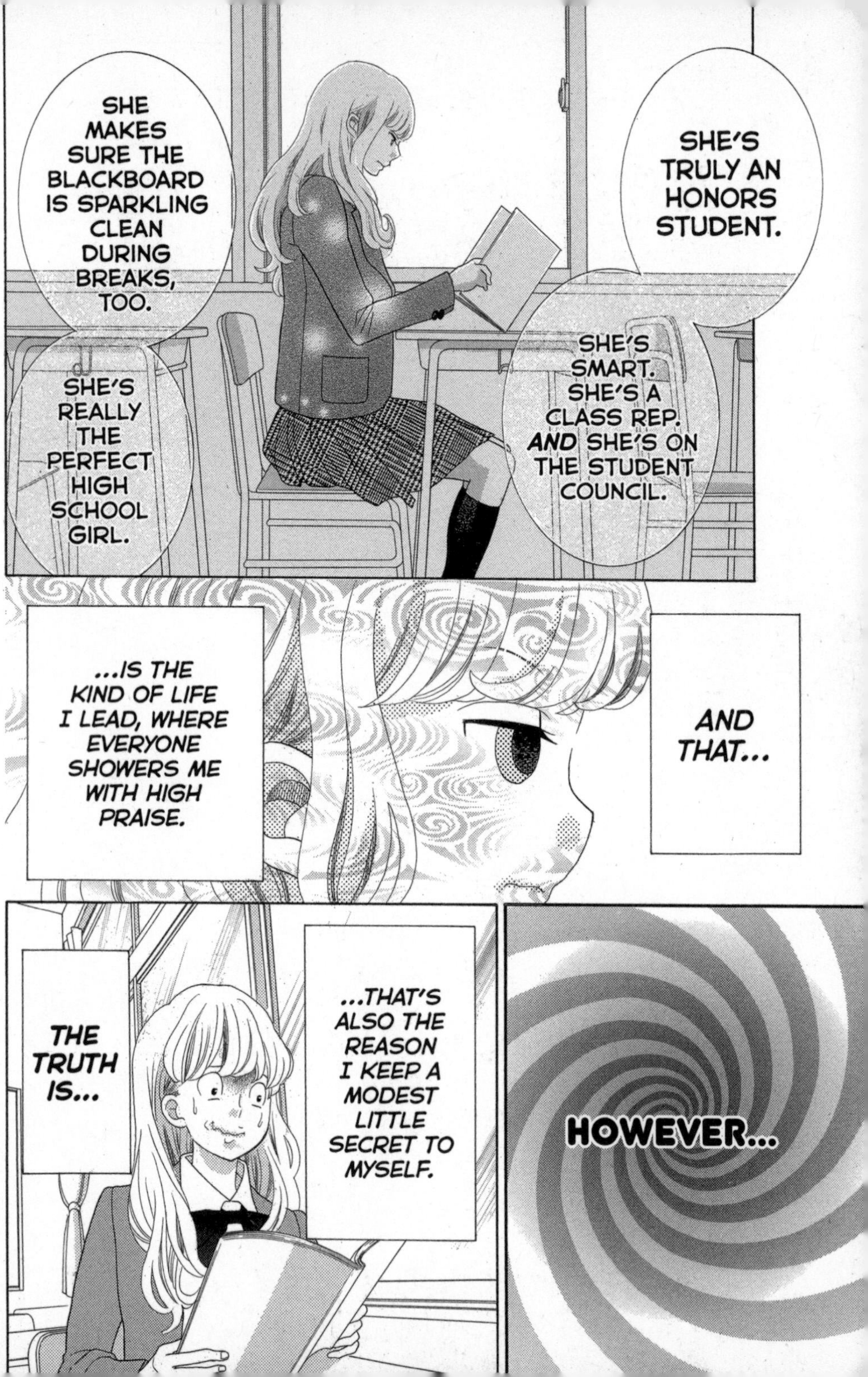
SHE'S TRULY AN HONORS STUDENT.
SHE'S SMART. SHE'S A CLASS REP. *AND* SHE'S ON THE STUDENT COUNCIL.
SHE MAKES SURE THE BLACKBOARD IS SPARKLING CLEAN DURING BREAKS, TOO.
SHE'S REALLY THE PERFECT HIGH SCHOOL GIRL.
AND THAT...
...IS THE KIND OF LIFE I LEAD, WHERE EVERYONE SHOWERS ME WITH HIGH PRAISE.
HOWEVER...
...THAT'S ALSO THE REASON I KEEP A MODEST LITTLE SECRET TO MYSELF.
THE TRUTH IS...

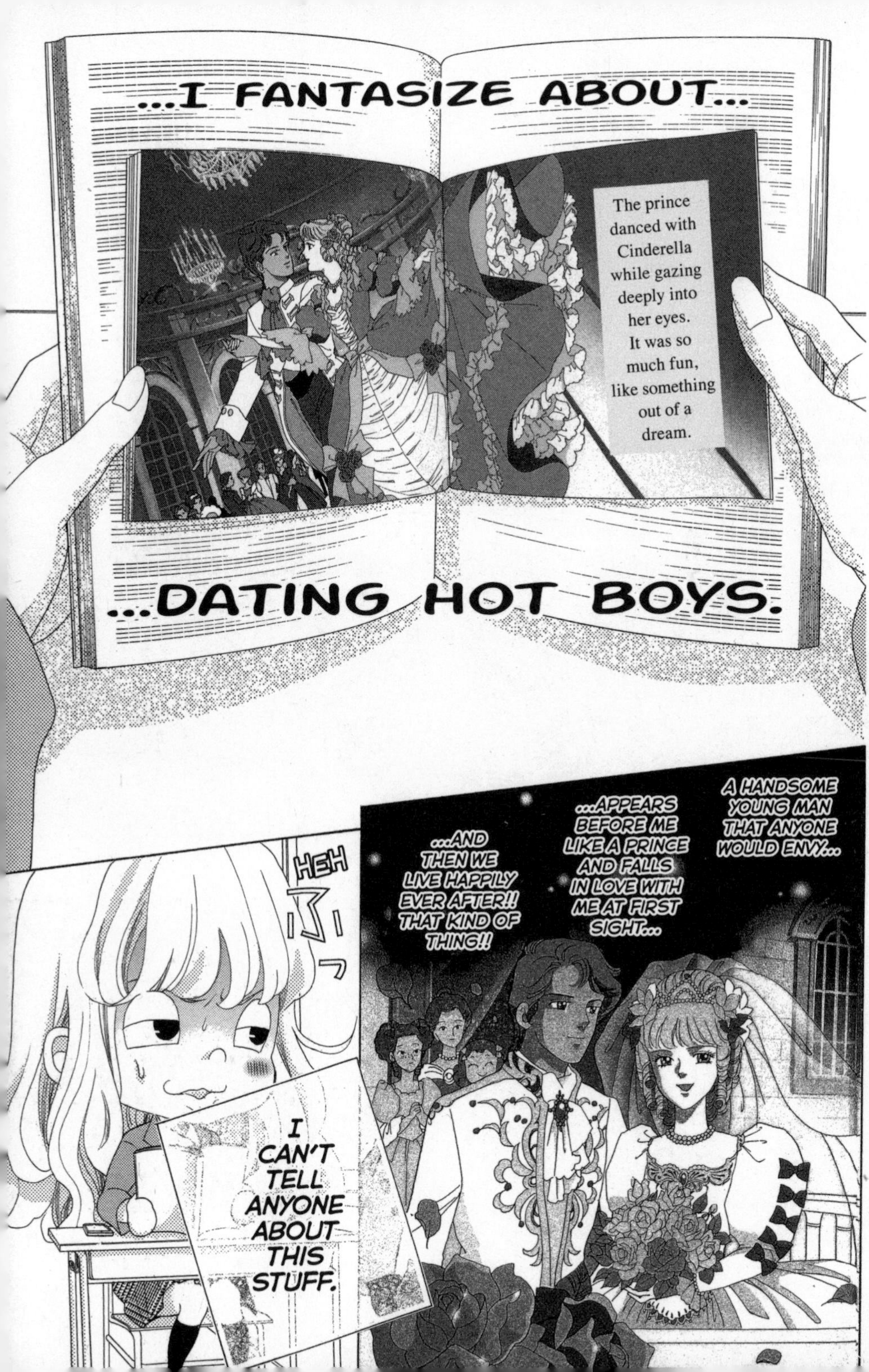
...I FANTASIZE ABOUT...
The prince danced with Cinderella while gazing deeply into her eyes. It was so much fun, like something out of a dream.
...DATING HOT BOYS.
A HANDSOME YOUNG MAN THAT ANYONE WOULD ENVY...
...APPEARS BEFORE ME LIKE A PRINCE AND FALLS IN LOVE WITH ME AT FIRST SIGHT...
...AND THEN WE LIVE HAPPILY EVER AFTER!! THAT KIND OF THING!!
HEH
I CAN'T TELL ANYONE ABOUT THIS STUFF.

Images in book provided by Nagaoka Shoten's "Cinderella" (World Masterpiece Anime Picture Book).

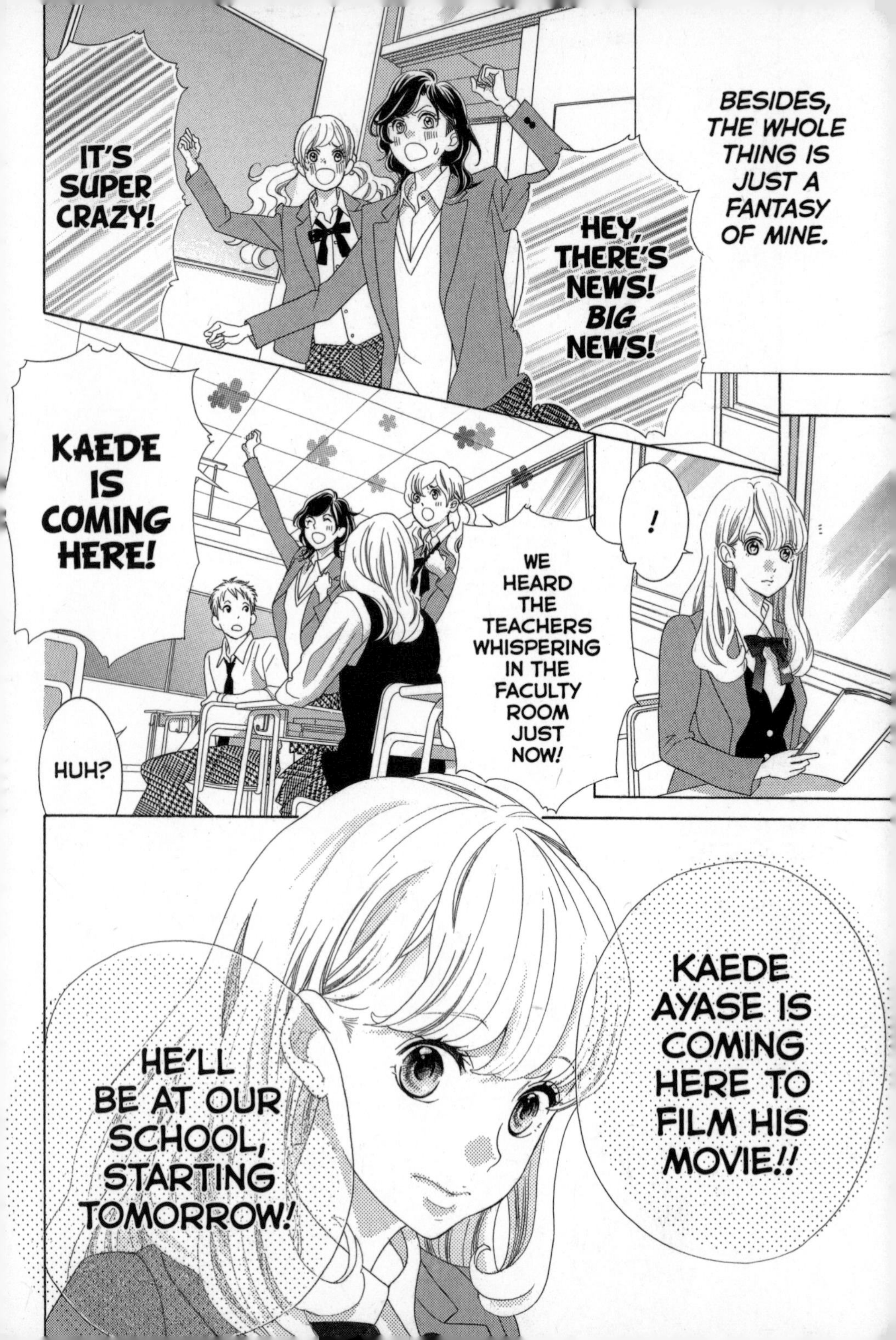
BESIDES, THE WHOLE THING IS JUST A FANTASY OF MINE.
HEY, THERE'S NEWS! BIG NEWS!
IT'S SUPER CRAZY!
!
KAEDE IS COMING HERE!
WE HEARD THE TEACHERS WHISPERING IN THE FACULTY ROOM JUST NOW!
HUH?
KAEDE AYASE IS COMING HERE TO FILM HIS MOVIE!!
HE'LL BE AT OUR SCHOOL, STARTING TOMORROW!

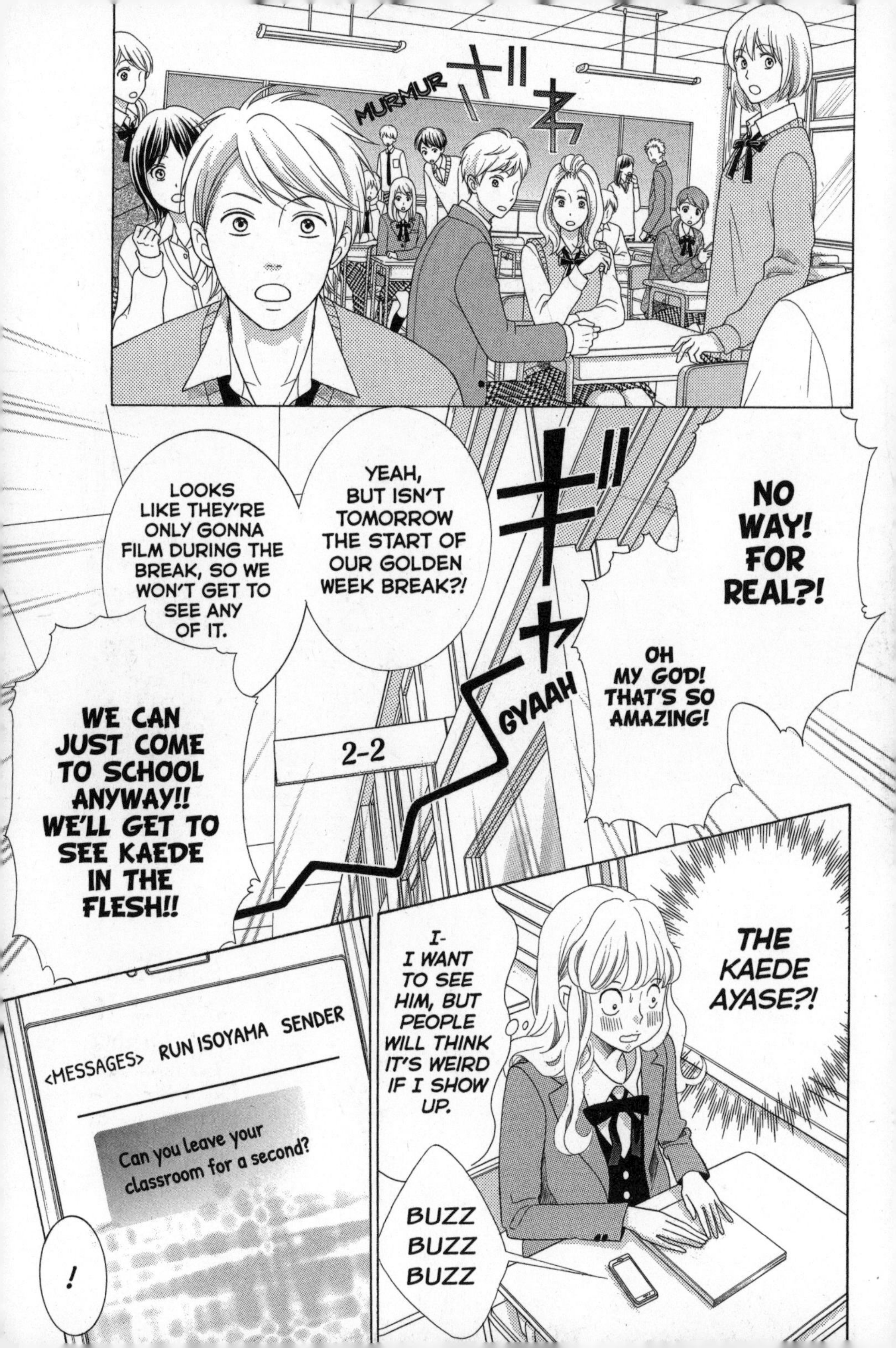
MURMUR
NO WAY! FOR REAL?!
YEAH, BUT ISN'T TOMORROW THE START OF OUR GOLDEN WEEK BREAK?!
LOOKS LIKE THEY'RE ONLY GONNA FILM DURING THE BREAK, SO WE WON'T GET TO SEE ANY OF IT.
OH MY GOD! THAT'S SO AMAZING!
GYAAH
WE CAN JUST COME TO SCHOOL ANYWAY!! WE'LL GET TO SEE KAEDE IN THE FLESH!!
2-2
THE KAEDE AYASE?!
I- I WANT TO SEE HIM, BUT PEOPLE WILL THINK IT'S WEIRD IF I SHOW UP.
BUZZ BUZZ BUZZ
<MESSAGES> RUN ISOYAMA SENDER
Can you leave your classroom for a second?
!

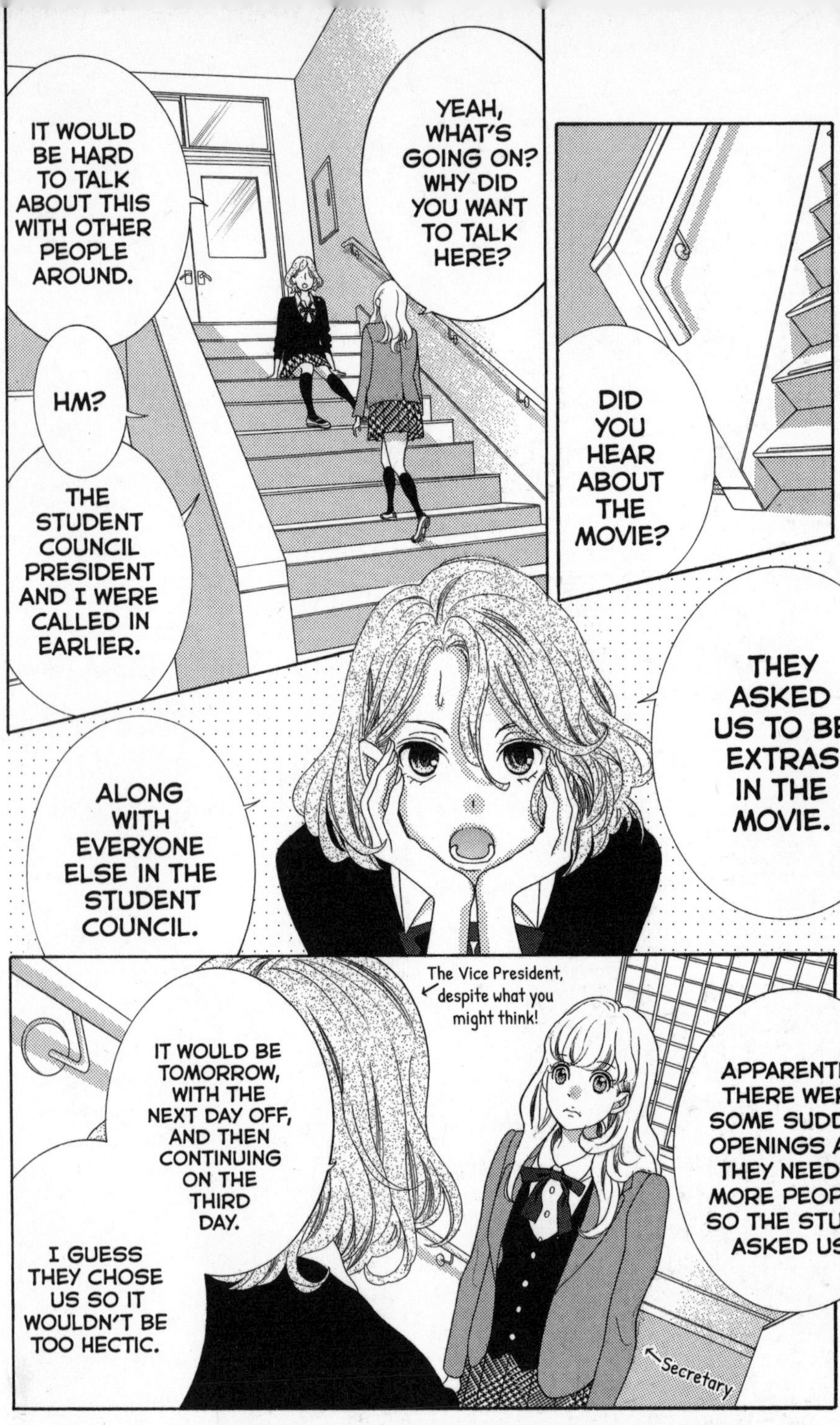
YEAH, WHAT'S GOING ON? WHY DID YOU WANT TO TALK HERE?
IT WOULD BE HARD TO TALK ABOUT THIS WITH OTHER PEOPLE AROUND.
HM?
THE STUDENT COUNCIL PRESIDENT AND I WERE CALLED IN EARLIER.
DID YOU HEAR ABOUT THE MOVIE?
THEY ASKED US TO BE EXTRAS IN THE MOVIE.
ALONG WITH EVERYONE ELSE IN THE STUDENT COUNCIL.
APPARENTLY, THERE WERE SOME SUDDEN OPENINGS AND THEY NEEDED MORE PEOPLE, SO THE STUDIO ASKED US.
The Vice President, despite what you might think!
IT WOULD BE TOMORROW, WITH THE NEXT DAY OFF, AND THEN CONTINUING ON THE THIRD DAY.
I GUESS THEY CHOSE US SO IT WOULDN'T BE TOO HECTIC.
Secretary

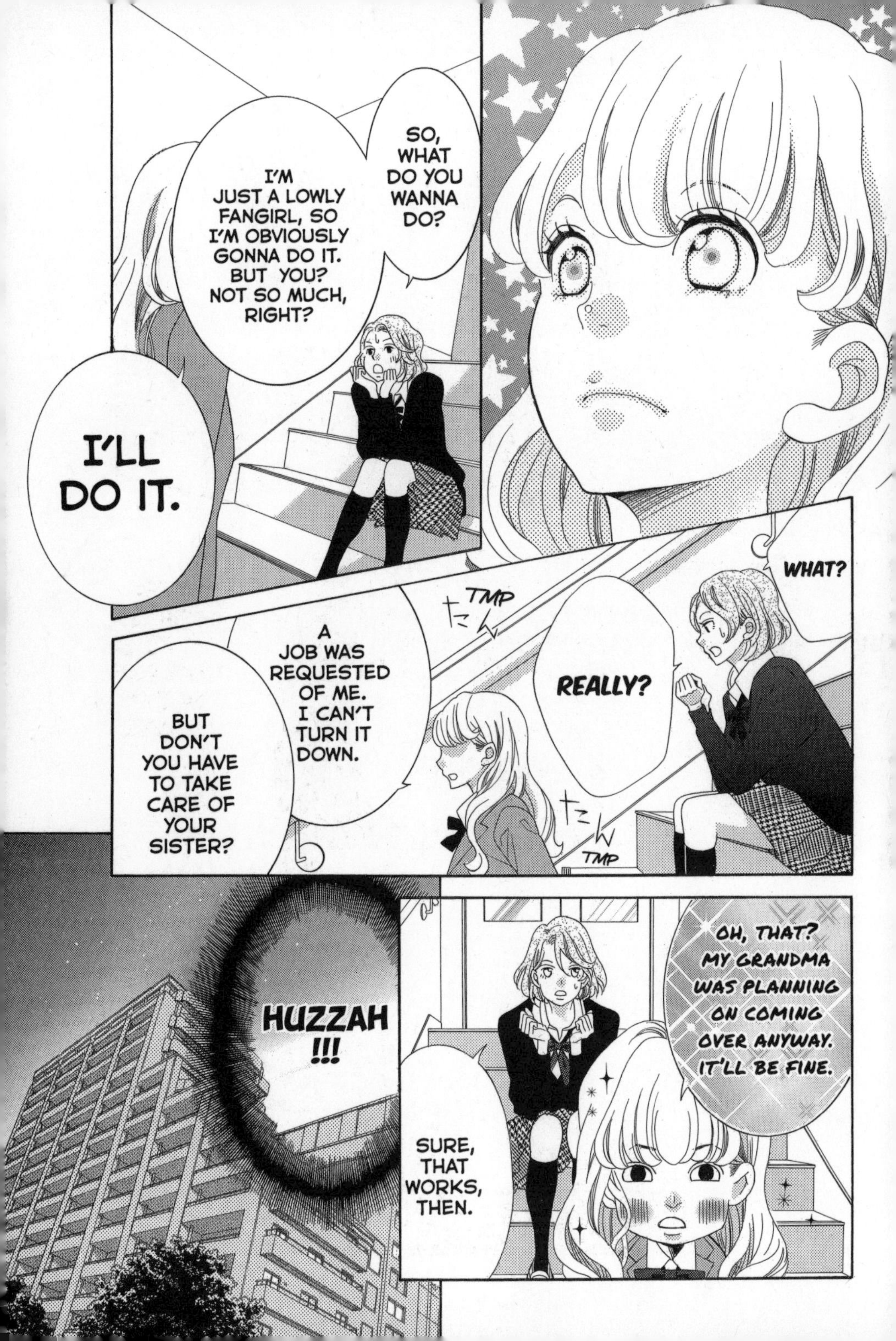
SO, WHAT DO YOU WANNA DO?
I'M JUST A LOWLY FANGIRL, SO I'M OBVIOUSLY GONNA DO IT. BUT YOU? NOT SO MUCH, RIGHT?
I'LL DO IT.
WHAT?
REALLY?
たん TMP
A JOB WAS REQUESTED OF ME. I CAN'T TURN IT DOWN.
BUT DON'T YOU HAVE TO TAKE CARE OF YOUR SISTER?
たん TMP
OH, THAT? MY GRANDMA WAS PLANNING ON COMING OVER ANYWAY. IT'LL BE FINE.
SURE, THAT WORKS, THEN.
HUZZAH !!!

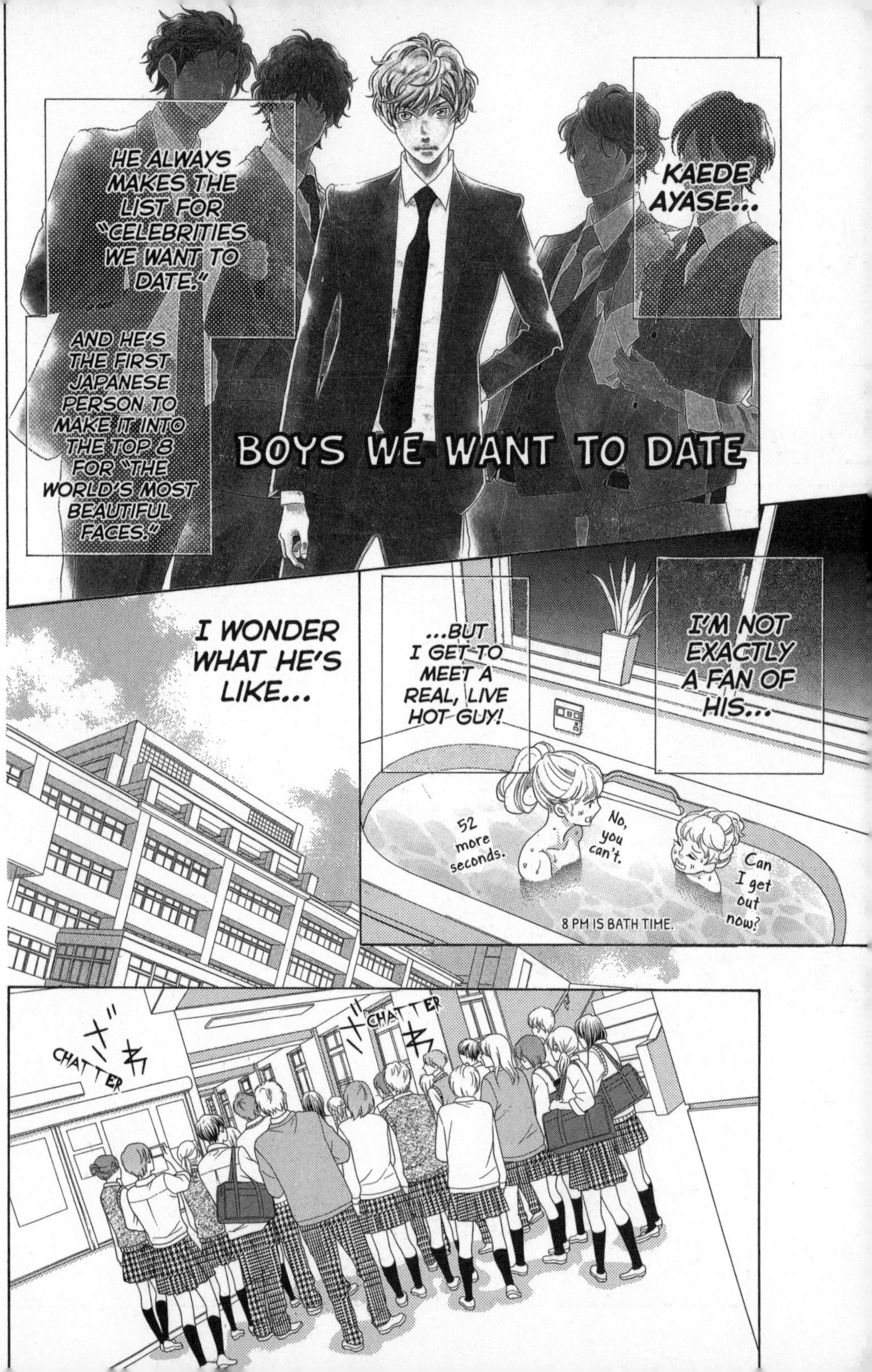
KAEDE AYASE...
HE ALWAYS MAKES THE LIST FOR "CELEBRITIES WE WANT TO DATE."
AND HE'S THE FIRST JAPANESE PERSON TO MAKE IT INTO THE TOP 8 FOR "THE WORLD'S MOST BEAUTIFUL FACES."
BOYS WE WANT TO DATE
I'M NOT EXACTLY A FAN OF HIS...
...BUT I GET TO MEET A REAL, LIVE HOT GUY!
Can I get out now?
No, you can't.
52 more seconds.
8 PM IS BATH TIME.
I WONDER WHAT HE'S LIKE...
CHATTER
CHATTER

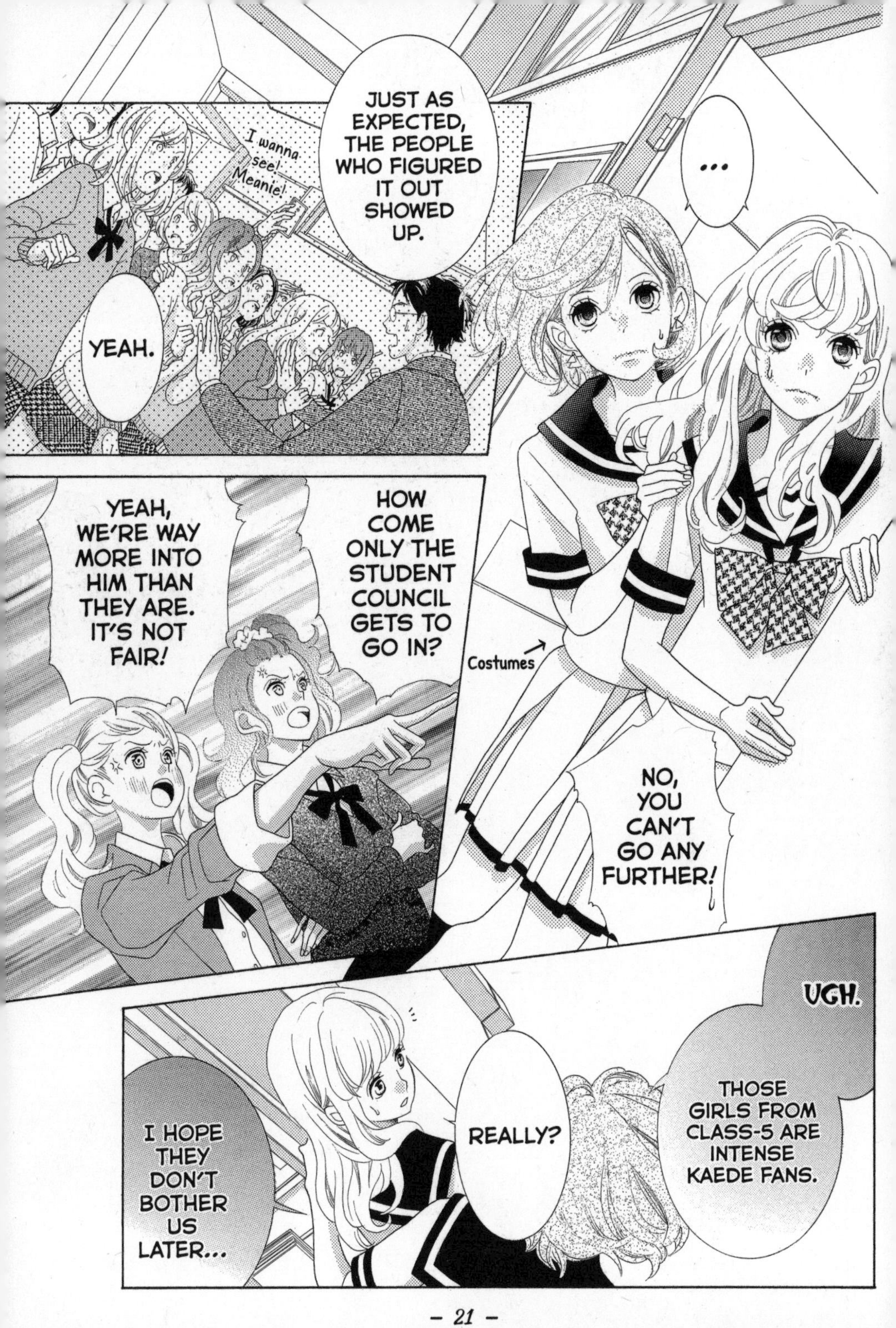
...
JUST AS EXPECTED, THE PEOPLE WHO FIGURED IT OUT SHOWED UP.
YEAH.
I wanna see! Meanie!
HOW COME ONLY THE STUDENT COUNCIL GETS TO GO IN?
YEAH, WE'RE WAY MORE INTO HIM THAN THEY ARE. IT'S NOT FAIR!
Costumes
NO, YOU CAN'T GO ANY FURTHER!
UGH.
THOSE GIRLS FROM CLASS-5 ARE INTENSE KAEDE FANS.
REALLY?
I HOPE THEY DON'T BOTHER US LATER...

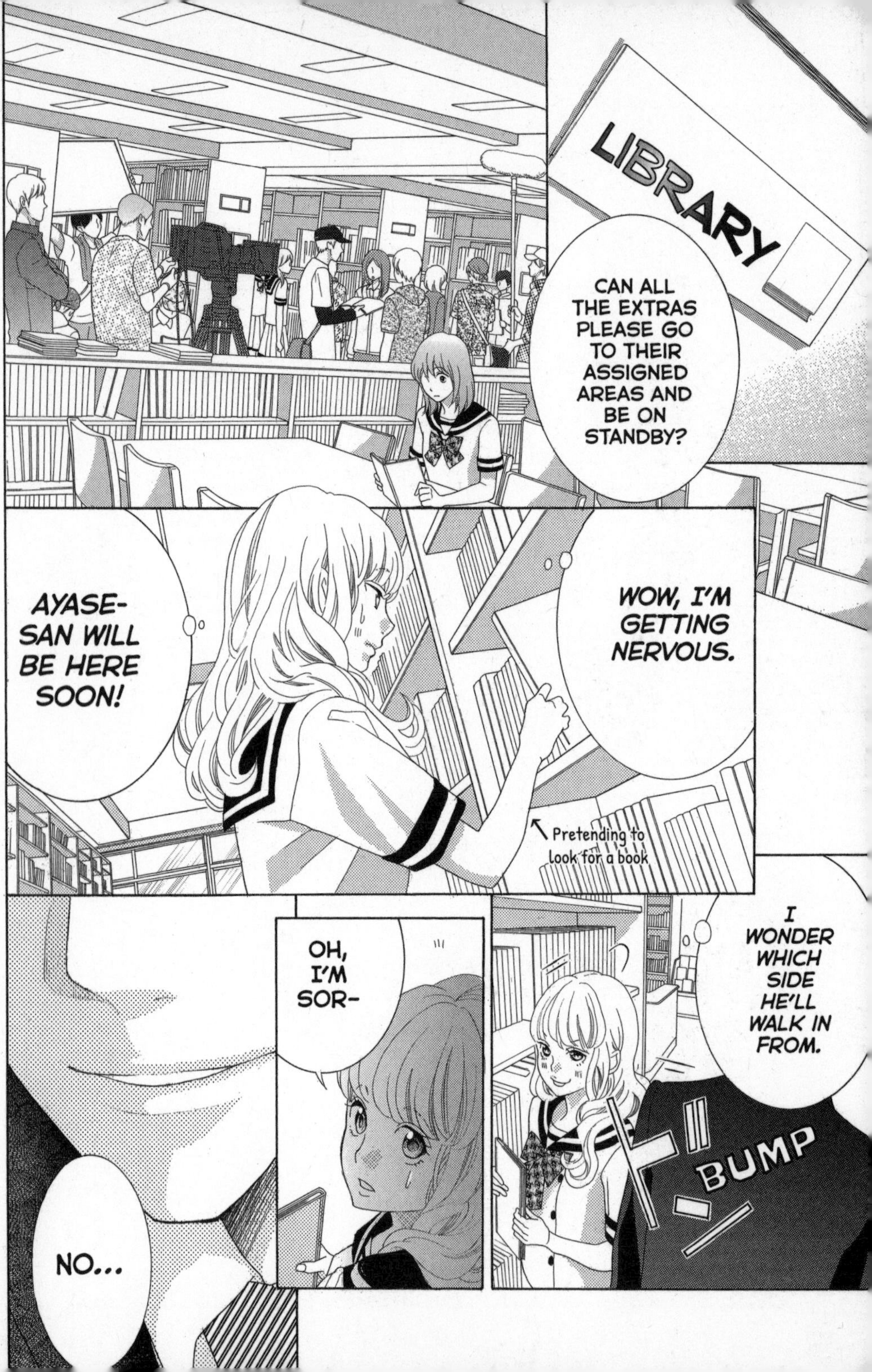
LIBRARY
CAN ALL THE EXTRAS PLEASE GO TO THEIR ASSIGNED AREAS AND BE ON STANDBY?
WOW, I'M GETTING NERVOUS.
AYASE-SAN WILL BE HERE SOON!
Pretending to look for a book
I WONDER WHICH SIDE HE'LL WALK IN FROM.
BUMP
OH, I'M SOR-
NO...

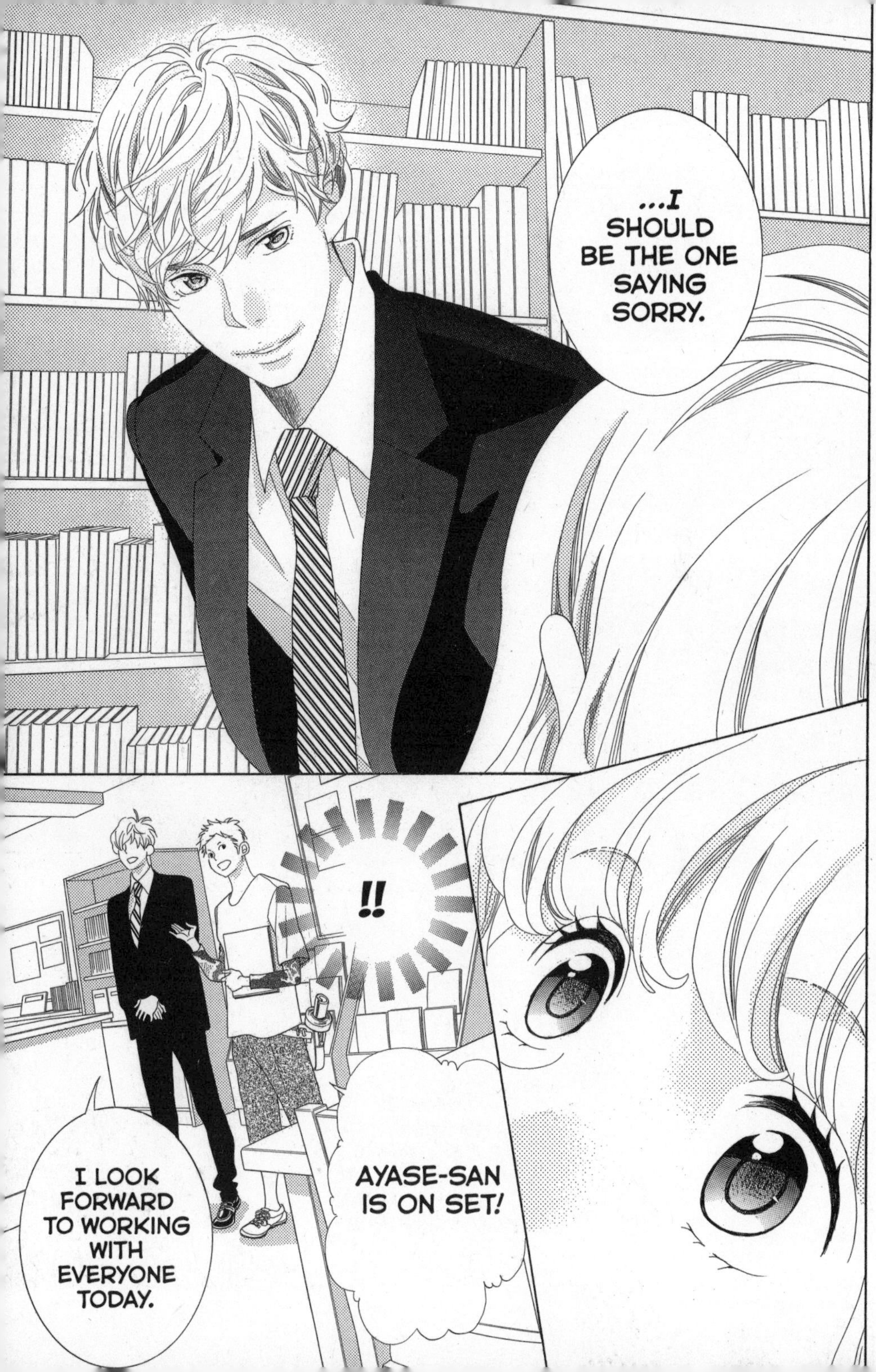
...I SHOULD BE THE ONE SAYING SORRY.
!!
AYASE-SAN IS ON SET!
I LOOK FORWARD TO WORKING WITH EVERYONE TODAY.

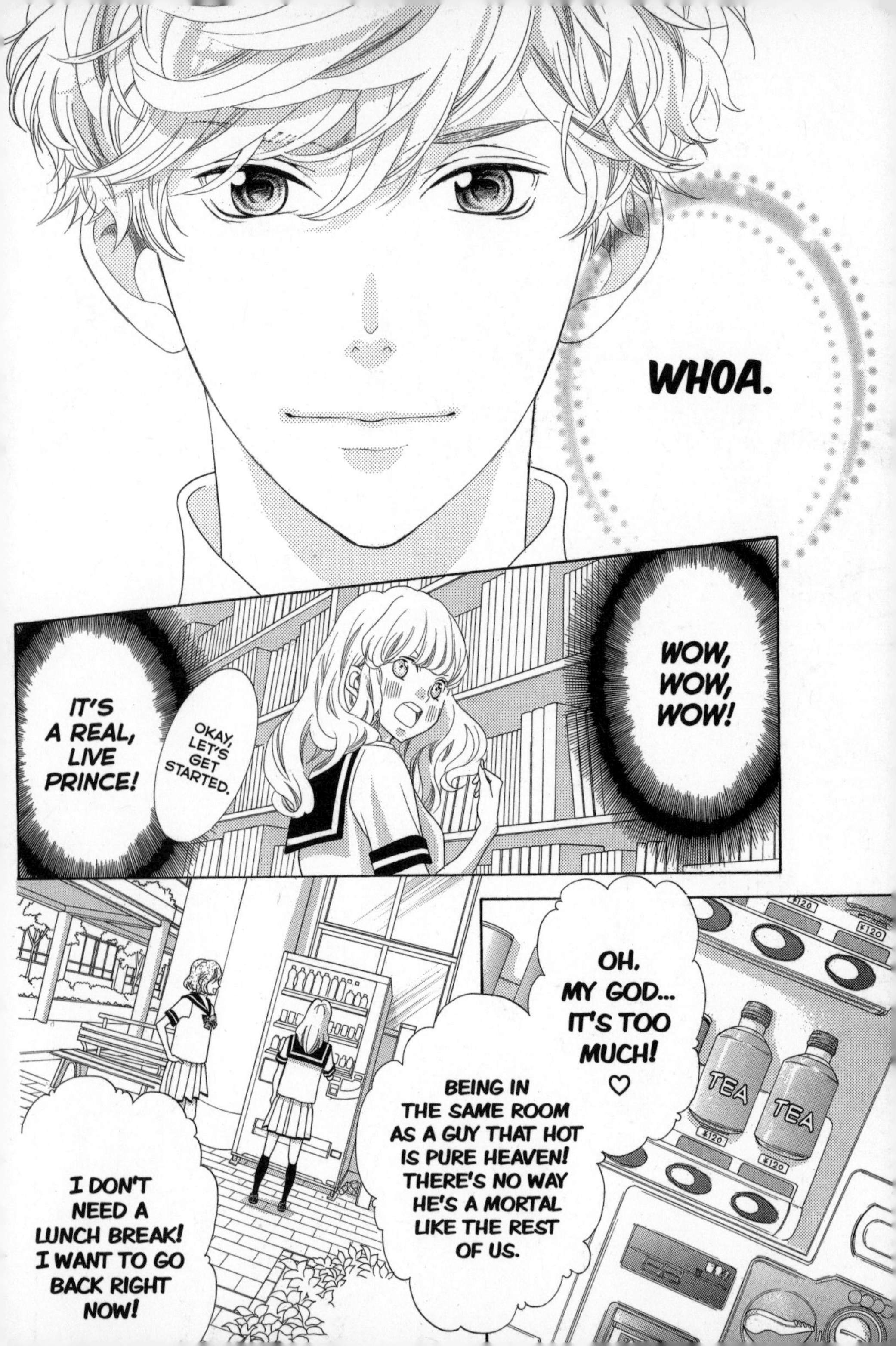
WHOA.
WOW, WOW, WOW!
OKAY, LET'S GET STARTED.
IT'S A REAL, LIVE PRINCE!
OH. MY GOD... IT'S TOO MUCH! ♡
BEING IN THE SAME ROOM AS A GUY THAT HOT IS PURE HEAVEN! THERE'S NO WAY HE'S A MORTAL LIKE THE REST OF US.
I DON'T NEED A LUNCH BREAK! I WANT TO GO BACK RIGHT NOW!
TEA
TEA

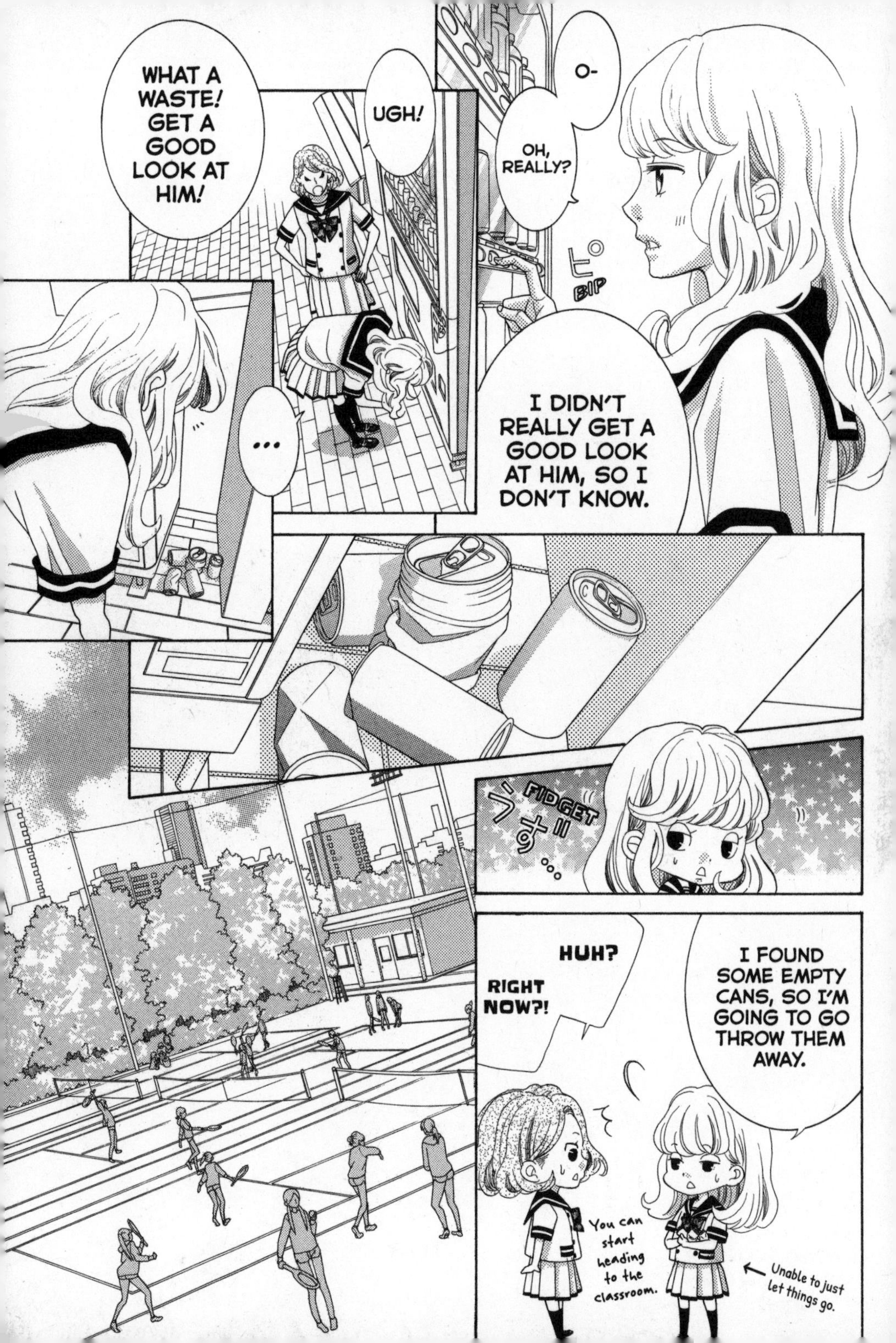
O-
OH, REALLY?
BIP
I DIDN'T REALLY GET A GOOD LOOK AT HIM, SO I DON'T KNOW.
UGH!
WHAT A WASTE! GET A GOOD LOOK AT HIM!
...
FIDGET
I FOUND SOME EMPTY CANS, SO I'M GOING TO GO THROW THEM AWAY.
HUH?
RIGHT NOW?!
Unable to just let things go.
You can start heading to the classroom.

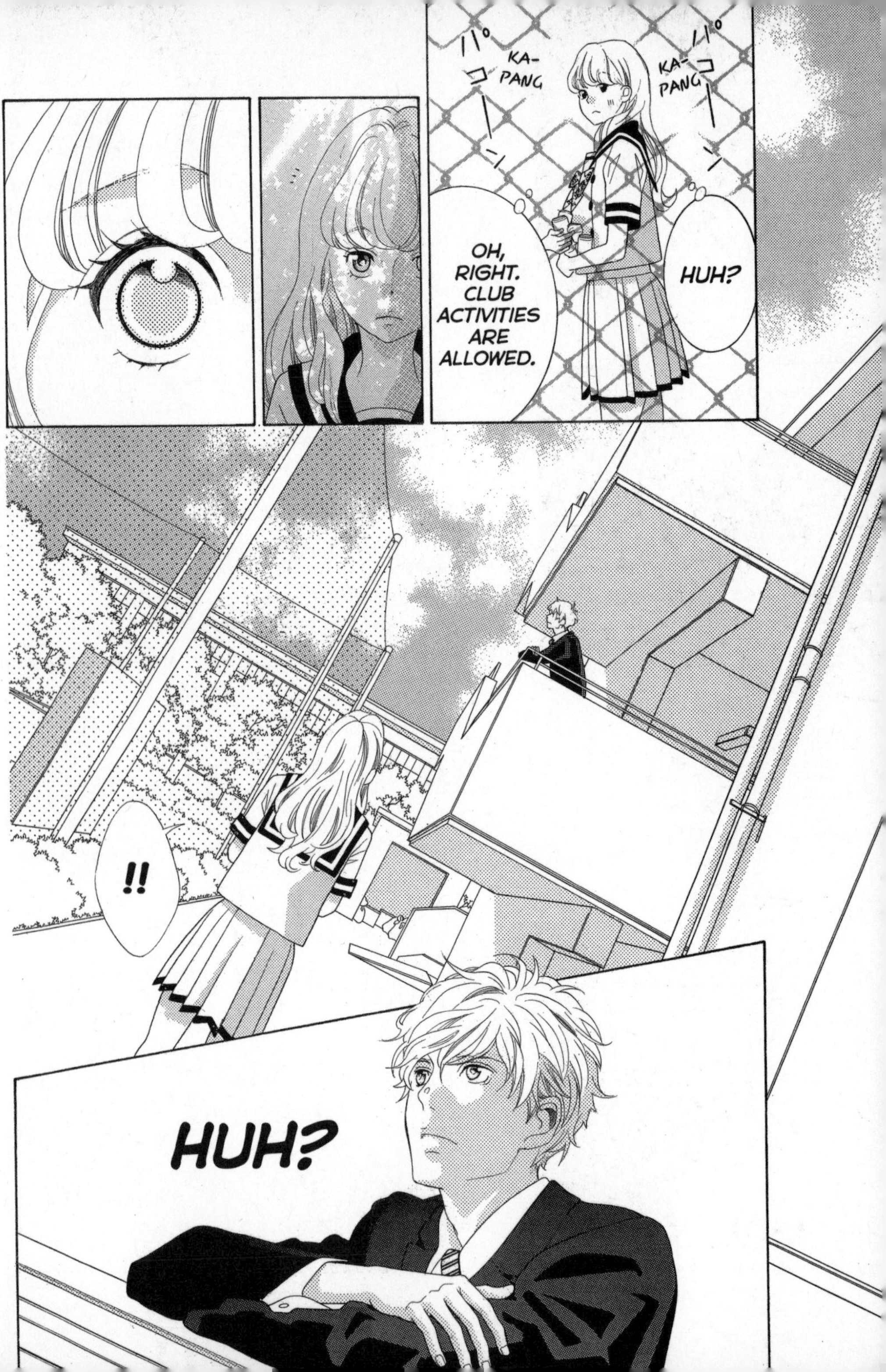
KA-PANG
KA-PANG
HUH?
OH, RIGHT. CLUB ACTIVITIES ARE ALLOWED.
!!
HUH?

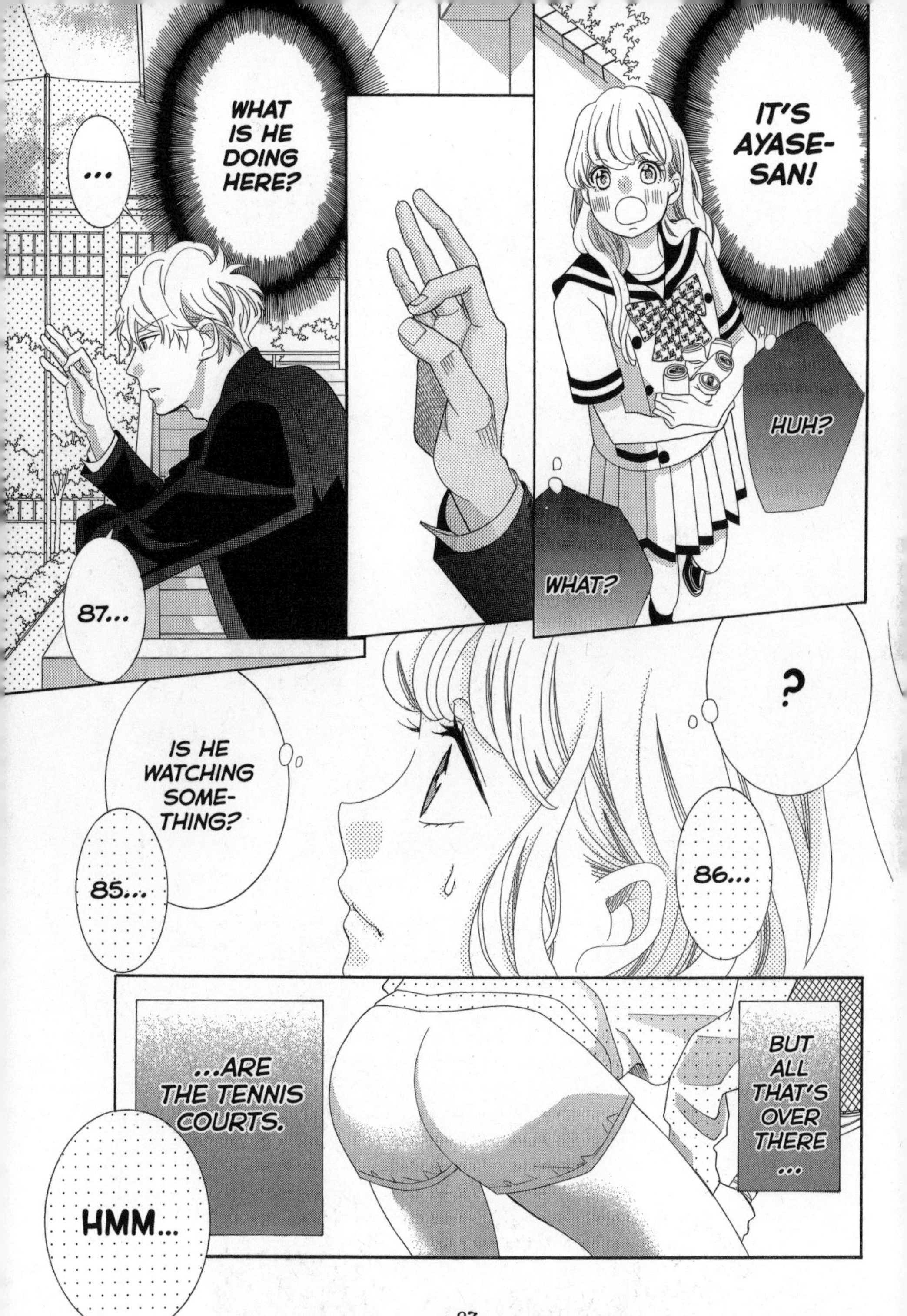
IT'S AYASE-SAN!
HUH?
WHAT?
WHAT IS HE DOING HERE?
...
87...
?
86...
IS HE WATCHING SOME-THING?
85...
BUT ALL THAT'S OVER THERE ...
...ARE THE TENNIS COURTS.
HMM...

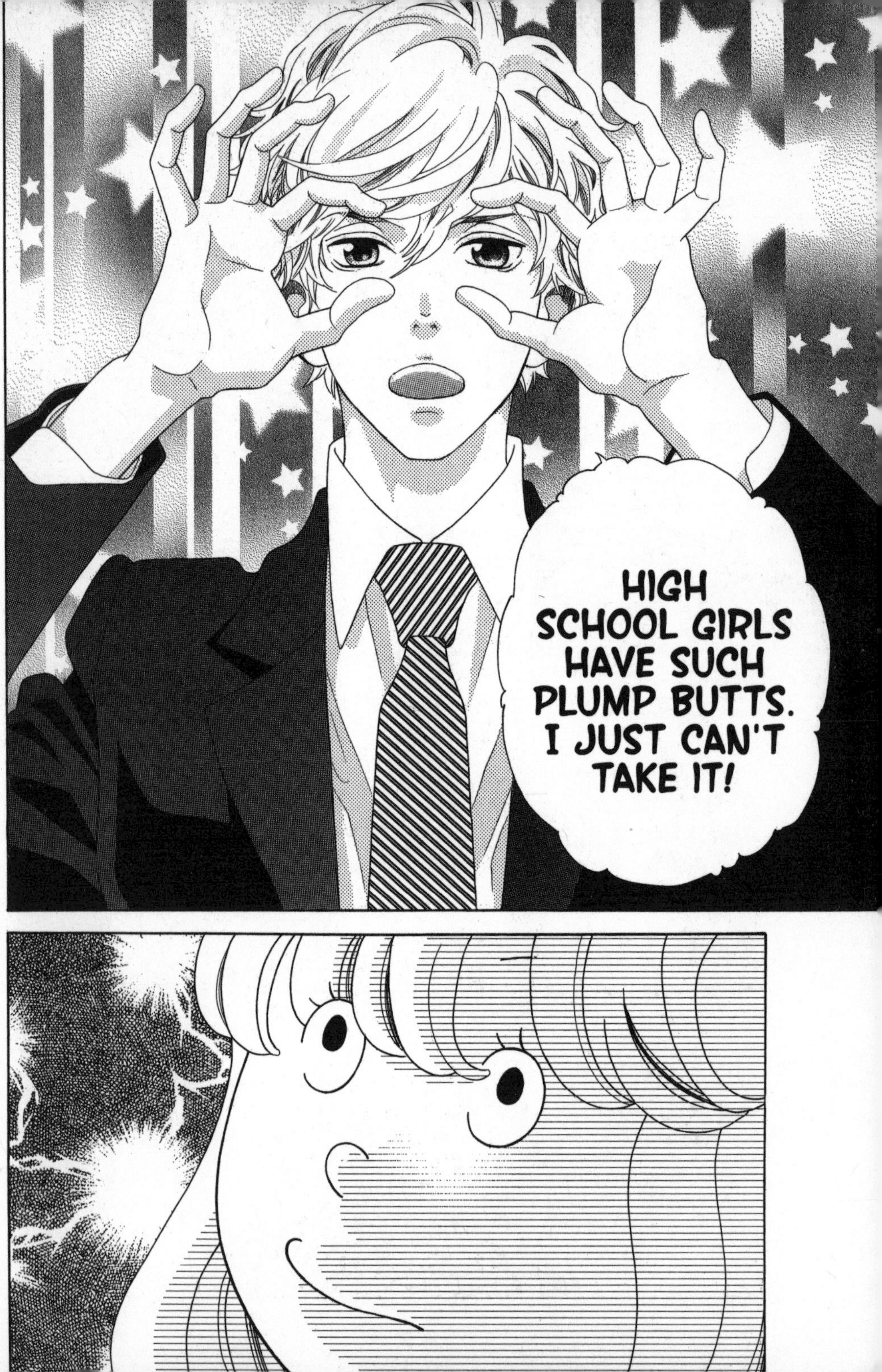
HIGH SCHOOL GIRLS HAVE SUCH PLUMP BUTTS. I JUST CAN'T TAKE IT!

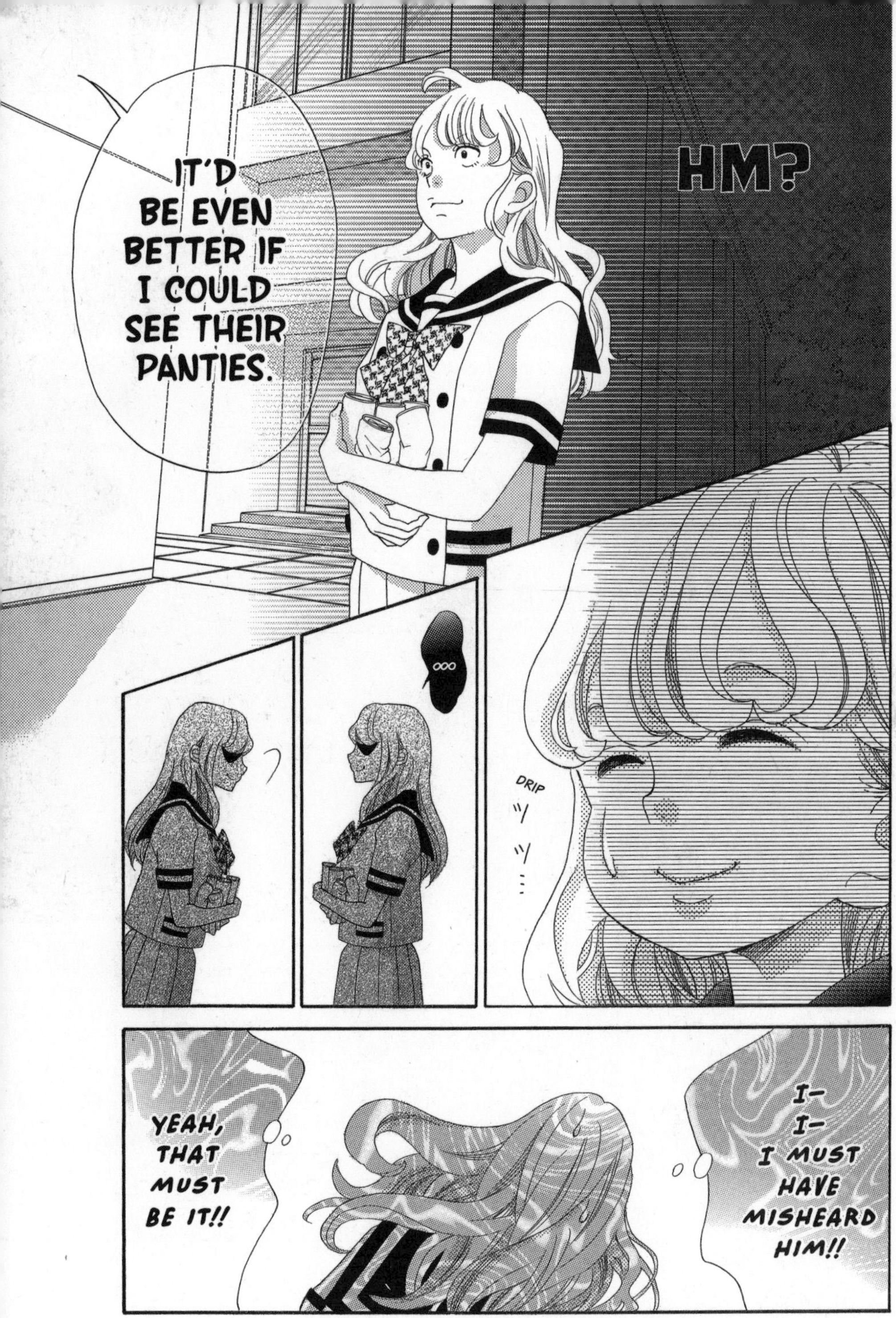
HM?
IT'D BE EVEN BETTER IF I COULD SEE THEIR PANTIES.
DRIP
I- I- I MUST HAVE MISHEARD HIM!!
YEAH, THAT MUST BE IT!!

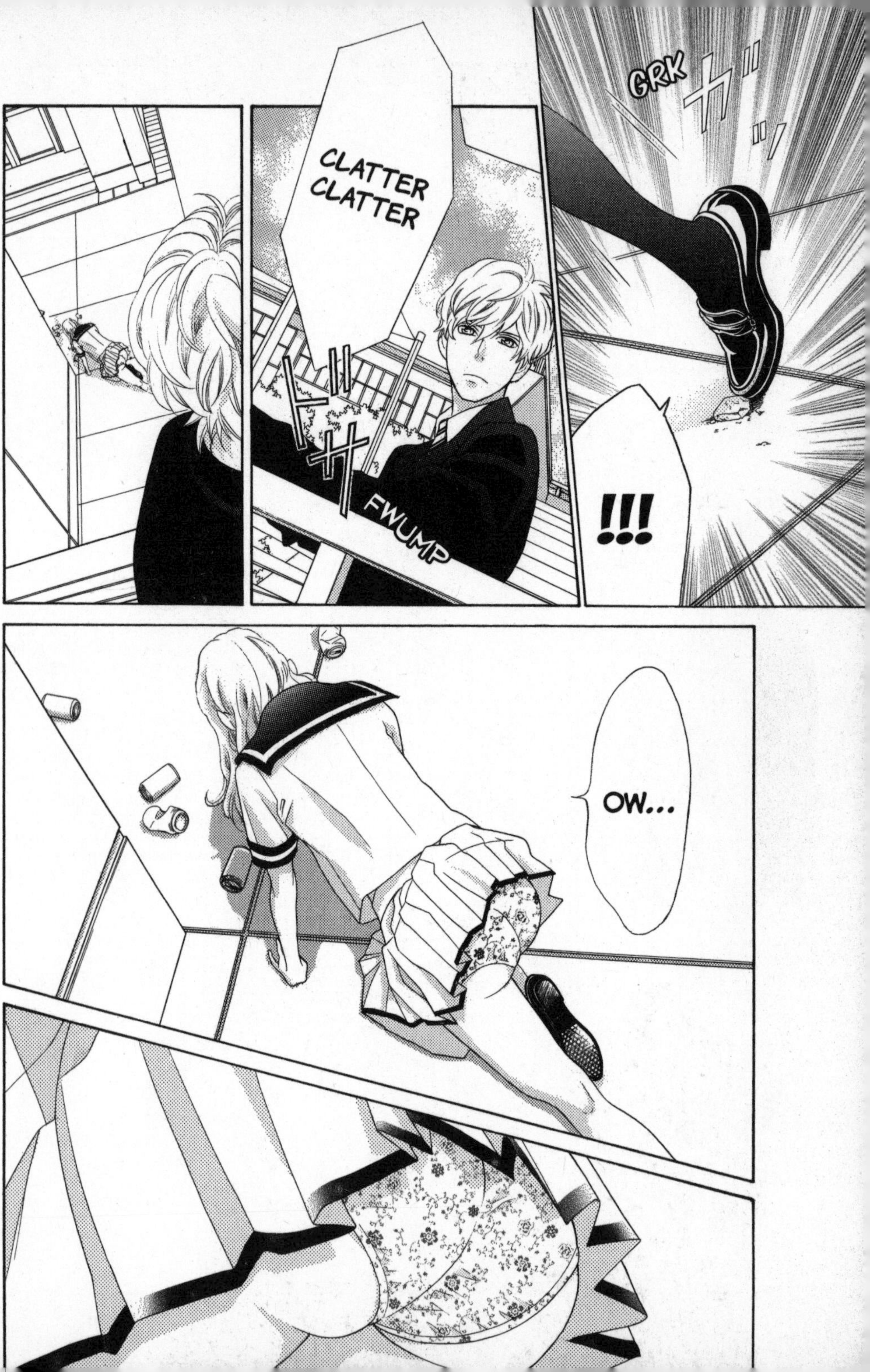
GRK
!!!
CLATTER CLATTER
FWUMP
OW...

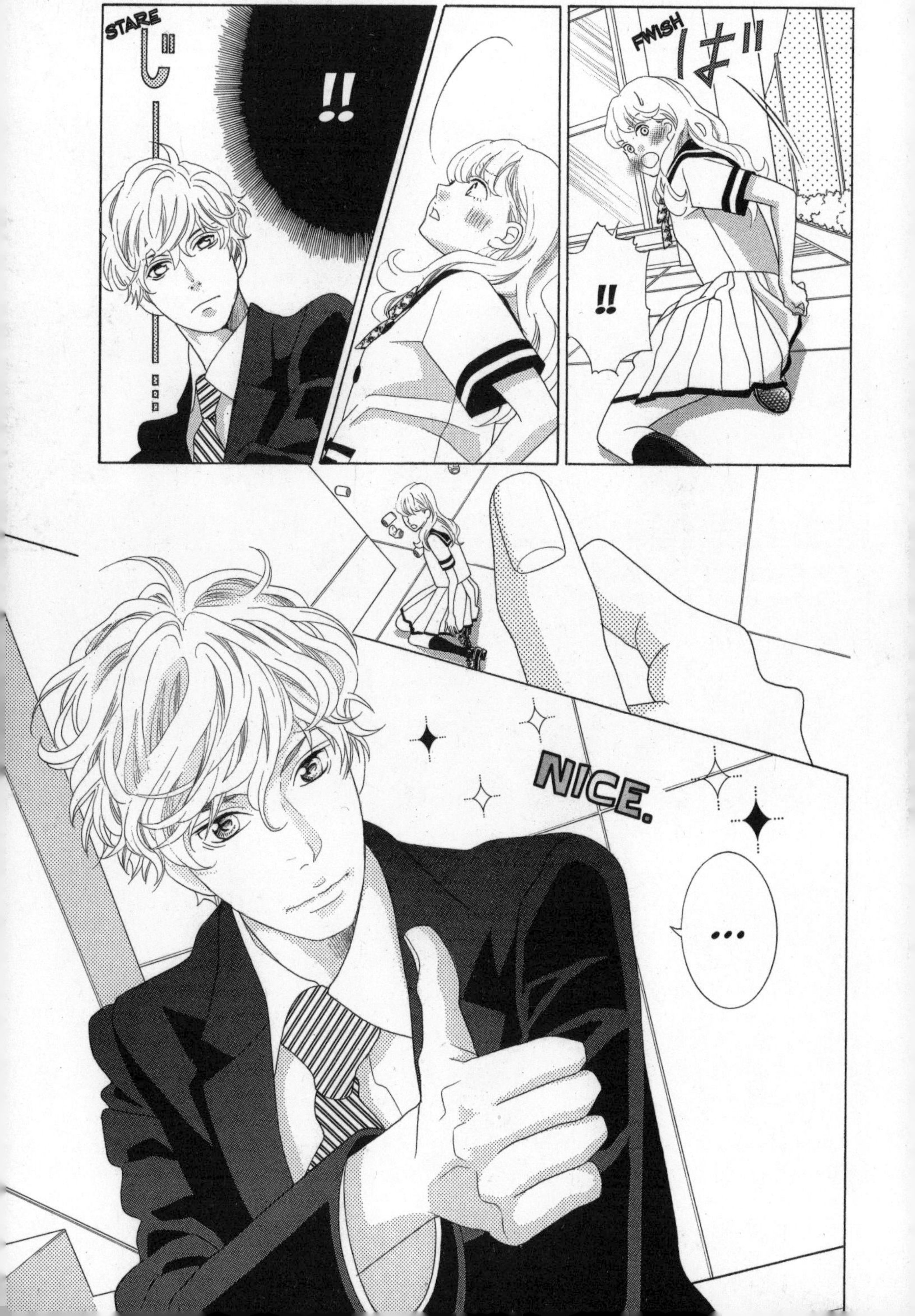
FWISH
はっ
!!
STARE
じー…
!!
NICE.
...

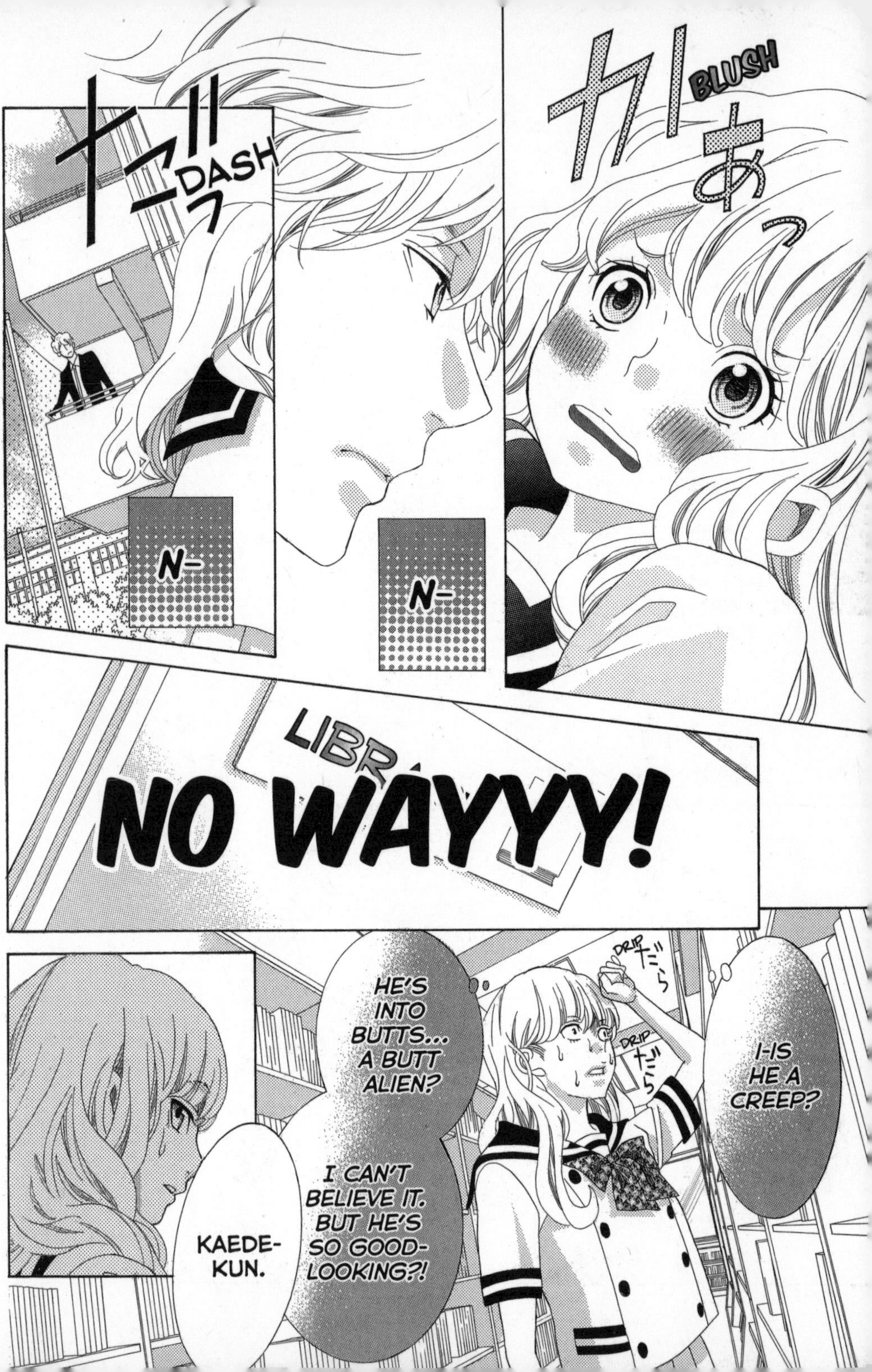
BLUSH
N-
DASH
N-
LIBR
NO WAYYY!
DRIP
DRIP
I-IS HE A CREEP?
HE'S INTO BUTTS... A BUTT ALIEN?
I CAN'T BELIEVE IT. BUT HE'S SO GOOD-LOOKING?!
KAEDE-KUN.

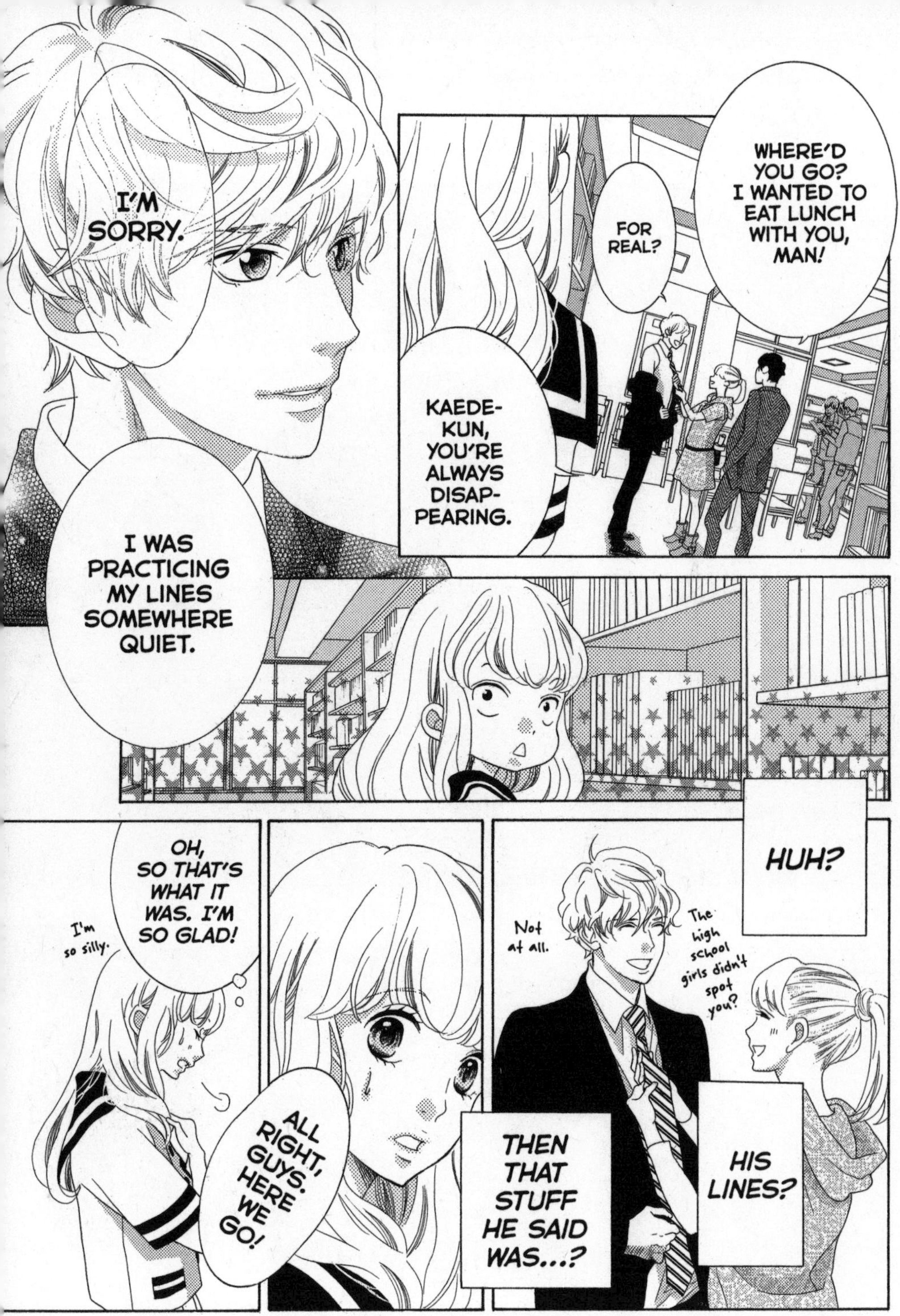
WHERE'D YOU GO? I WANTED TO EAT LUNCH WITH YOU, MAN!
FOR REAL?
KAEDE-KUN, YOU'RE ALWAYS DISAP-PEARING.
I'M SORRY.
I WAS PRACTICING MY LINES SOMEWHERE QUIET.
HUH?
The high school girls didn't spot you?
Not at all.
HIS LINES?
THEN THAT STUFF HE SAID WAS...?
ALL RIGHT, GUYS. HERE WE GO!
OH, SO THAT'S WHAT IT WAS. I'M SO GLAD!
I'm so silly.

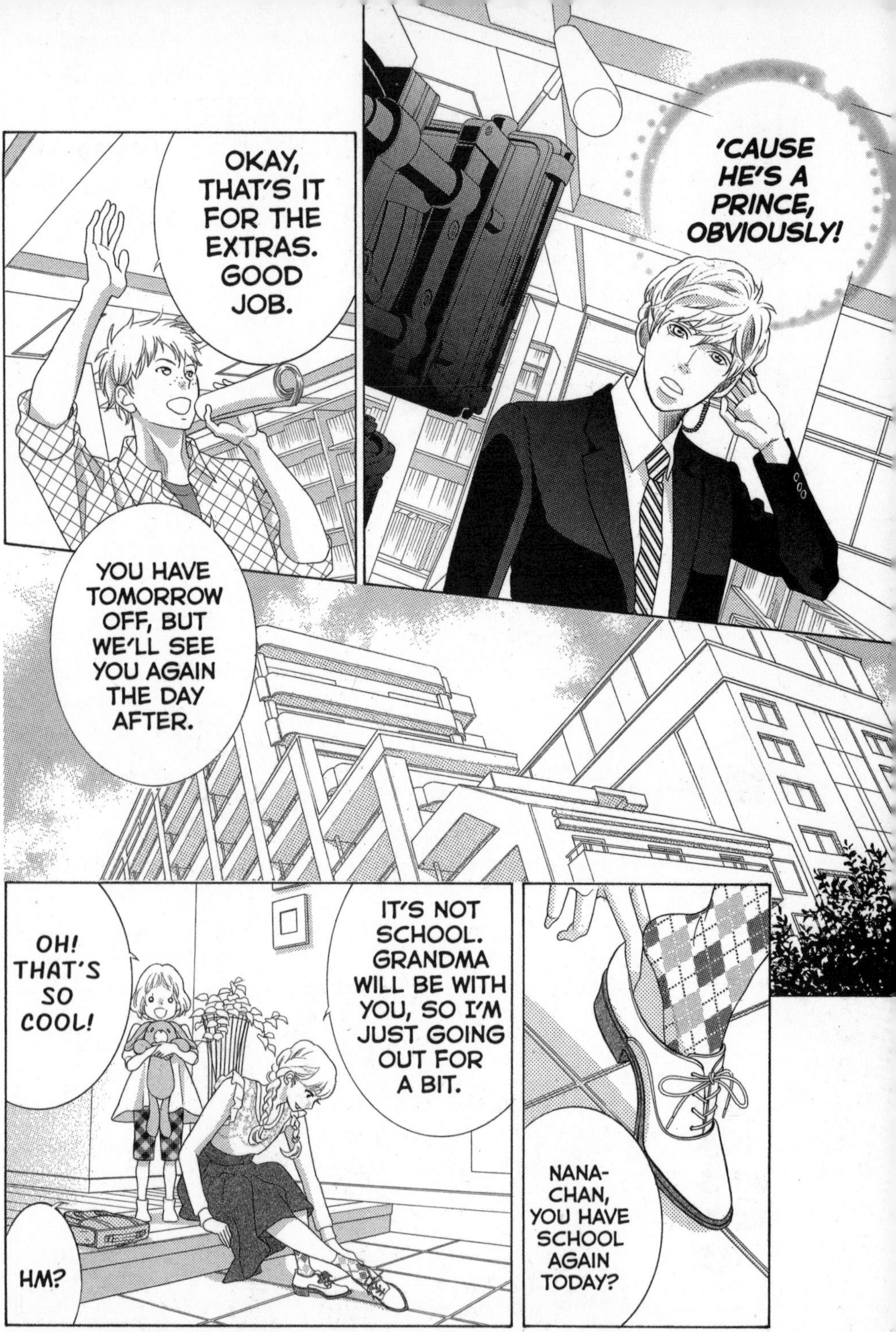
'CAUSE HE'S A PRINCE, OBVIOUSLY!
OKAY, THAT'S IT FOR THE EXTRAS. GOOD JOB.
YOU HAVE TOMORROW OFF, BUT WE'LL SEE YOU AGAIN THE DAY AFTER.
NANA-CHAN, YOU HAVE SCHOOL AGAIN TODAY?
IT'S NOT SCHOOL. GRANDMA WILL BE WITH YOU, SO I'M JUST GOING OUT FOR A BIT.
OH! THAT'S SO COOL!
HM?

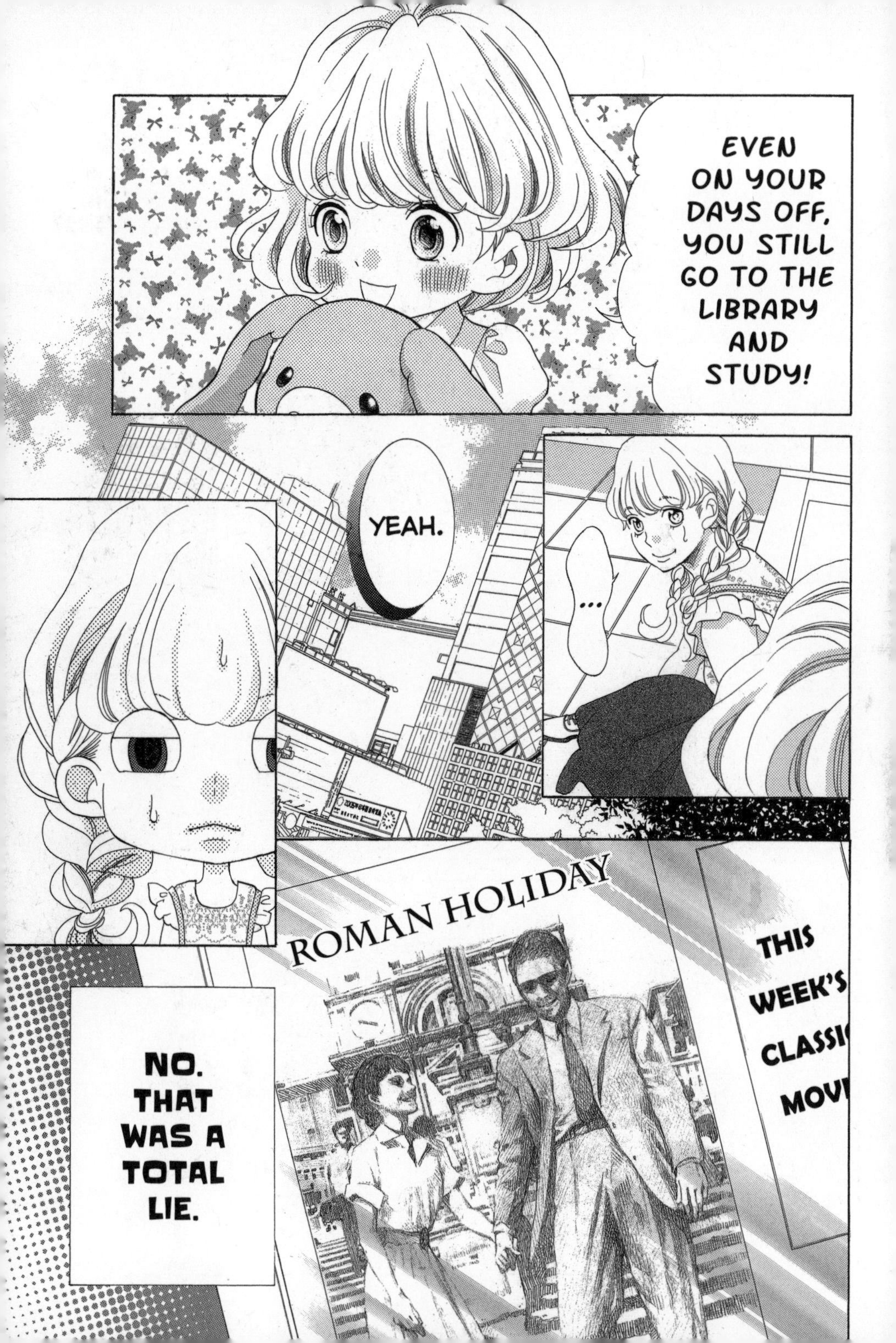
EVEN ON YOUR DAYS OFF, YOU STILL GO TO THE LIBRARY AND STUDY!
...
YEAH.
THIS WEEK'S CLASSI MOV
ROMAN HOLIDAY
NO. THAT WAS A TOTAL LIE.

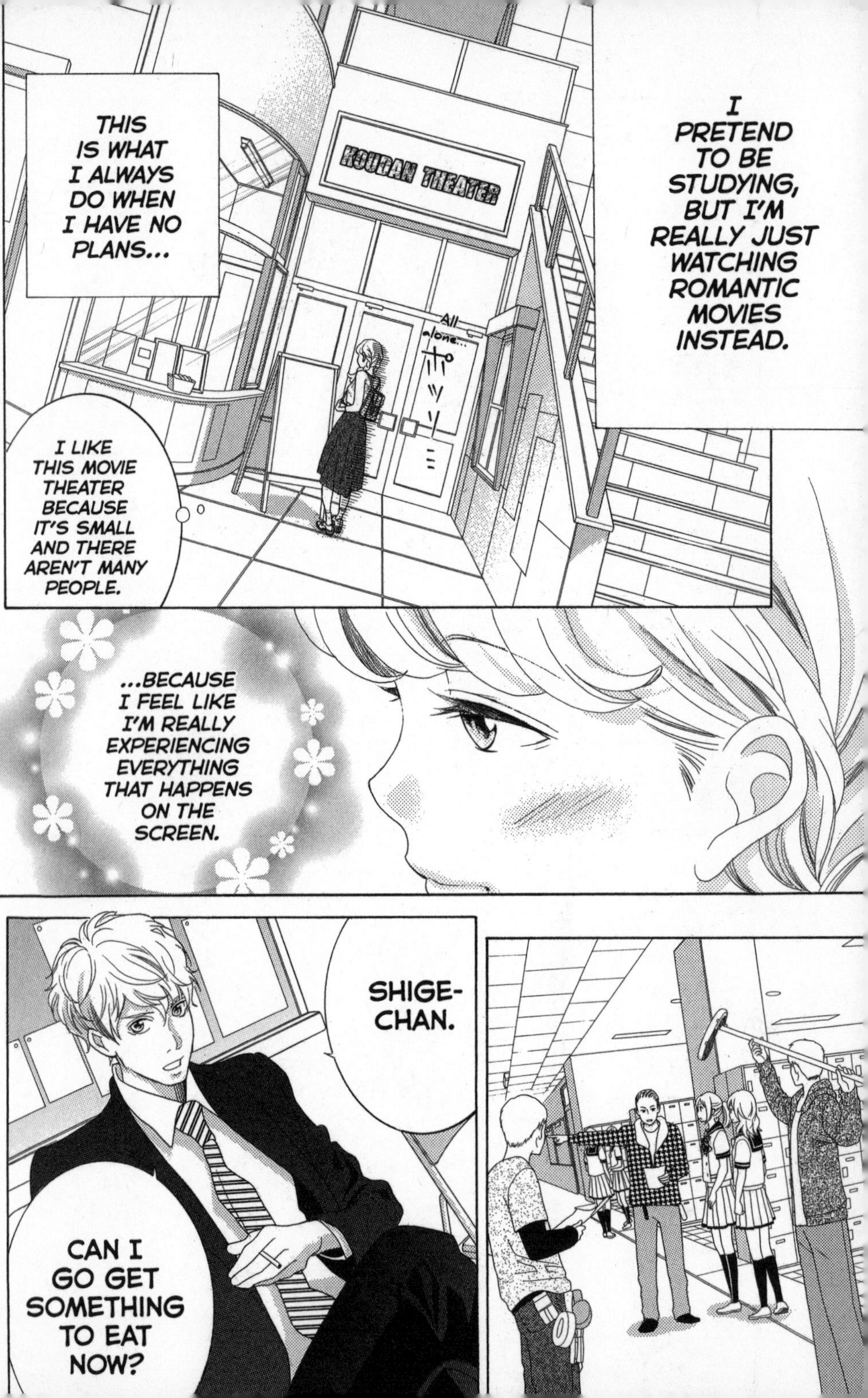
I PRETEND TO BE STUDYING, BUT I'M REALLY JUST WATCHING ROMANTIC MOVIES INSTEAD.
THIS IS WHAT I ALWAYS DO WHEN I HAVE NO PLANS...
KOUDAN THEATER
All alone...
I LIKE THIS MOVIE THEATER BECAUSE IT'S SMALL AND THERE AREN'T MANY PEOPLE.
...BECAUSE I FEEL LIKE I'M REALLY EXPERIENCING EVERYTHING THAT HAPPENS ON THE SCREEN.
SHIGE-CHAN.
CAN I GO GET SOMETHING TO EAT NOW?

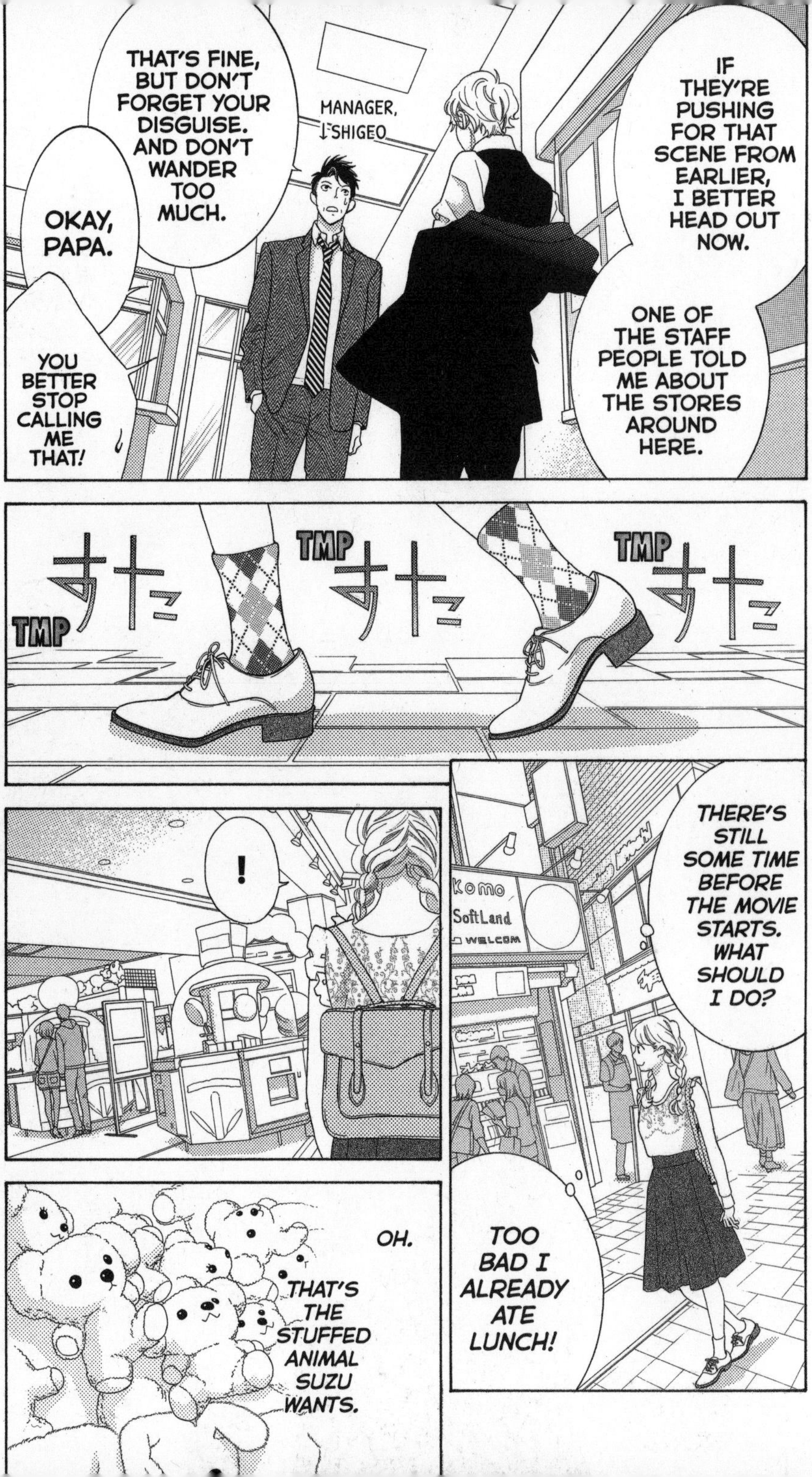

IF THEY'RE PUSHING FOR THAT SCENE FROM EARLIER, I BETTER HEAD OUT NOW.
ONE OF THE STAFF PEOPLE TOLD ME ABOUT THE STORES AROUND HERE.
THAT'S FINE, BUT DON'T FORGET YOUR DISGUISE. AND DON'T WANDER TOO MUCH.
MANAGER, SHIGEO
OKAY, PAPA.
YOU BETTER STOP CALLING ME THAT!
TMP
TMP
TMP
THERE'S STILL SOME TIME BEFORE THE MOVIE STARTS. WHAT SHOULD I DO?
komo
SoftLand
WELCOM
TOO BAD I ALREADY ATE LUNCH!
!
OH.
THAT'S THE STUFFED ANIMAL SUZU WANTS.

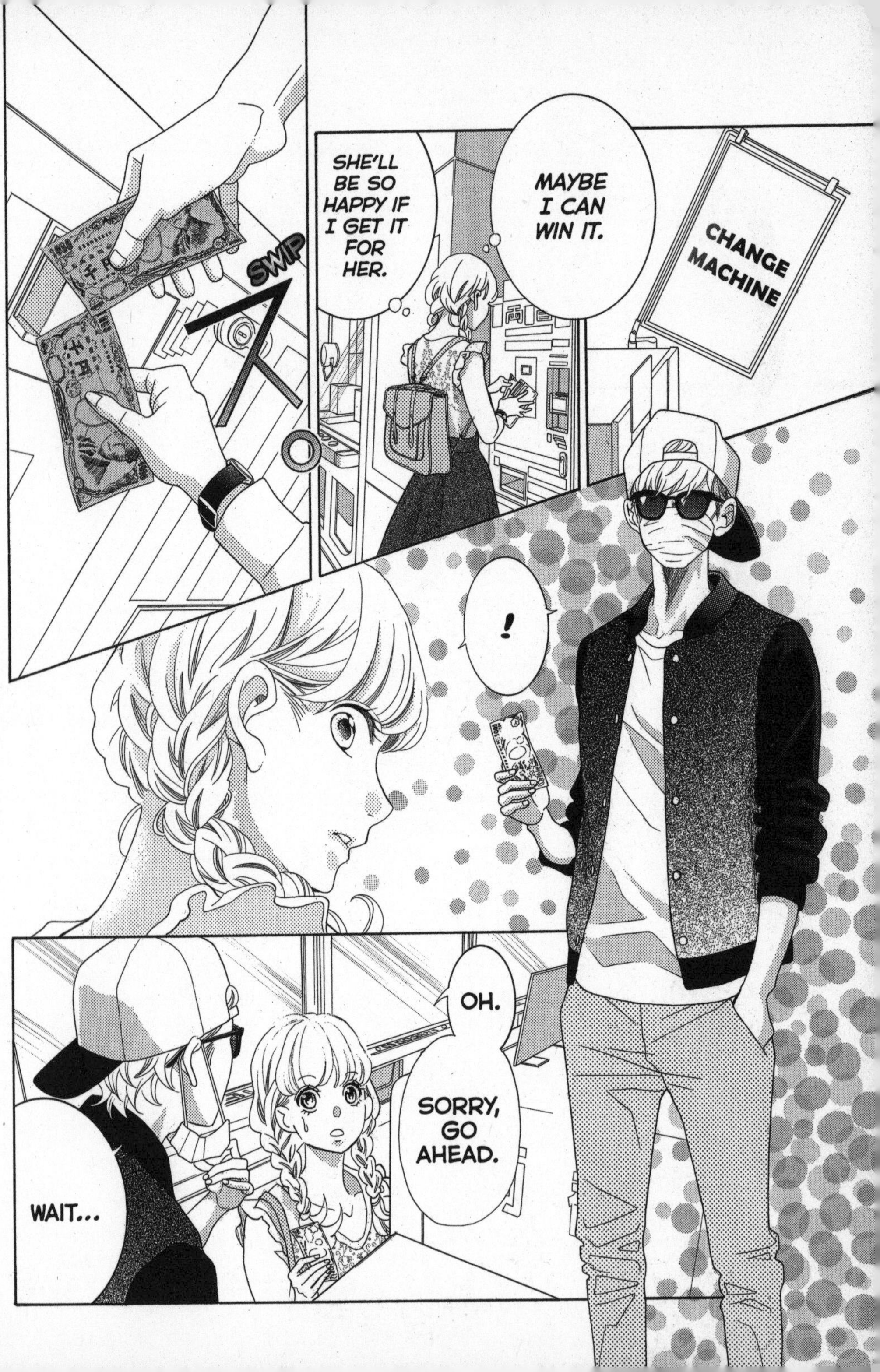
MAYBE I CAN WIN IT.
SHE'LL BE SO HAPPY IF I GET IT FOR HER.
CHANGE MACHINE
SWIP
!
OH.
SORRY, GO AHEAD.
WAIT...

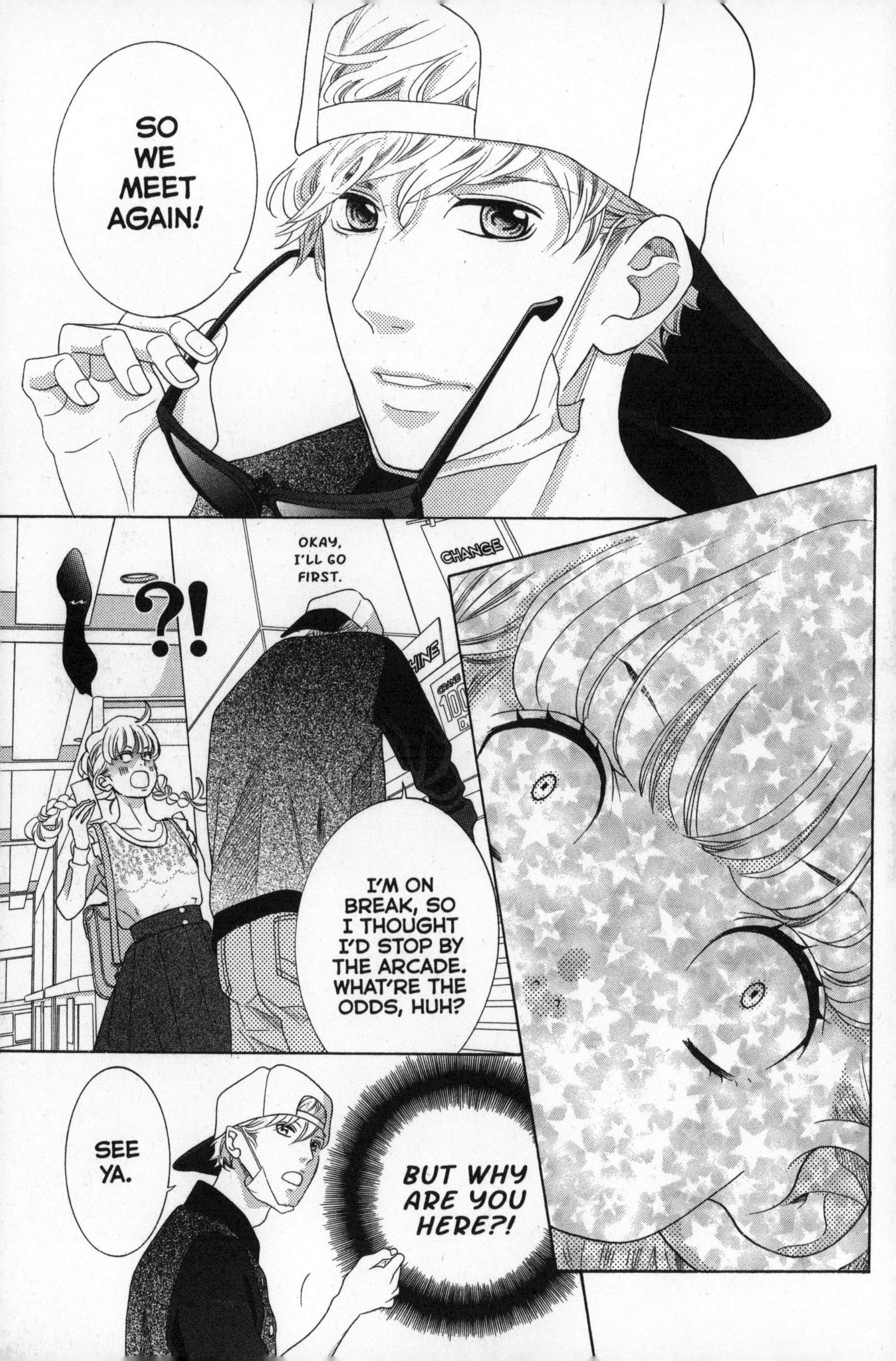
SO WE MEET AGAIN!
CHANGE
OKAY, I'LL GO FIRST.
?!
I'M ON BREAK, SO I THOUGHT I'D STOP BY THE ARCADE. WHAT'RE THE ODDS, HUH?
BUT WHY ARE YOU HERE?!
SEE YA.

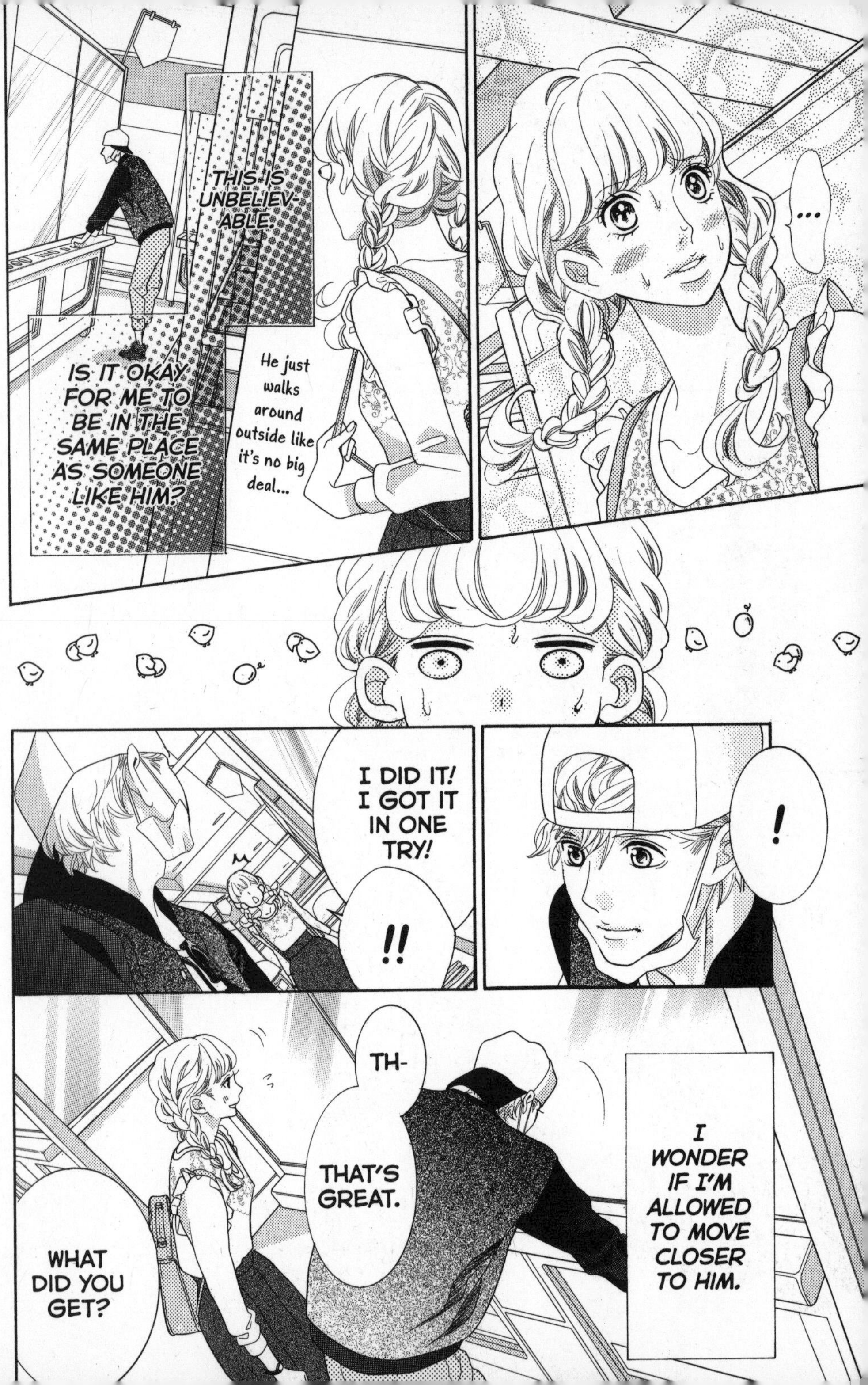
...
THIS IS UNBELIEVABLE.
He just walks around outside like it's no big deal...
IS IT OKAY FOR ME TO BE IN THE SAME PLACE AS SOMEONE LIKE HIM?
!
I DID IT! I GOT IT IN ONE TRY!
!!
I WONDER IF I'M ALLOWED TO MOVE CLOSER TO HIM.
TH-
THAT'S GREAT.
WHAT DID YOU GET?

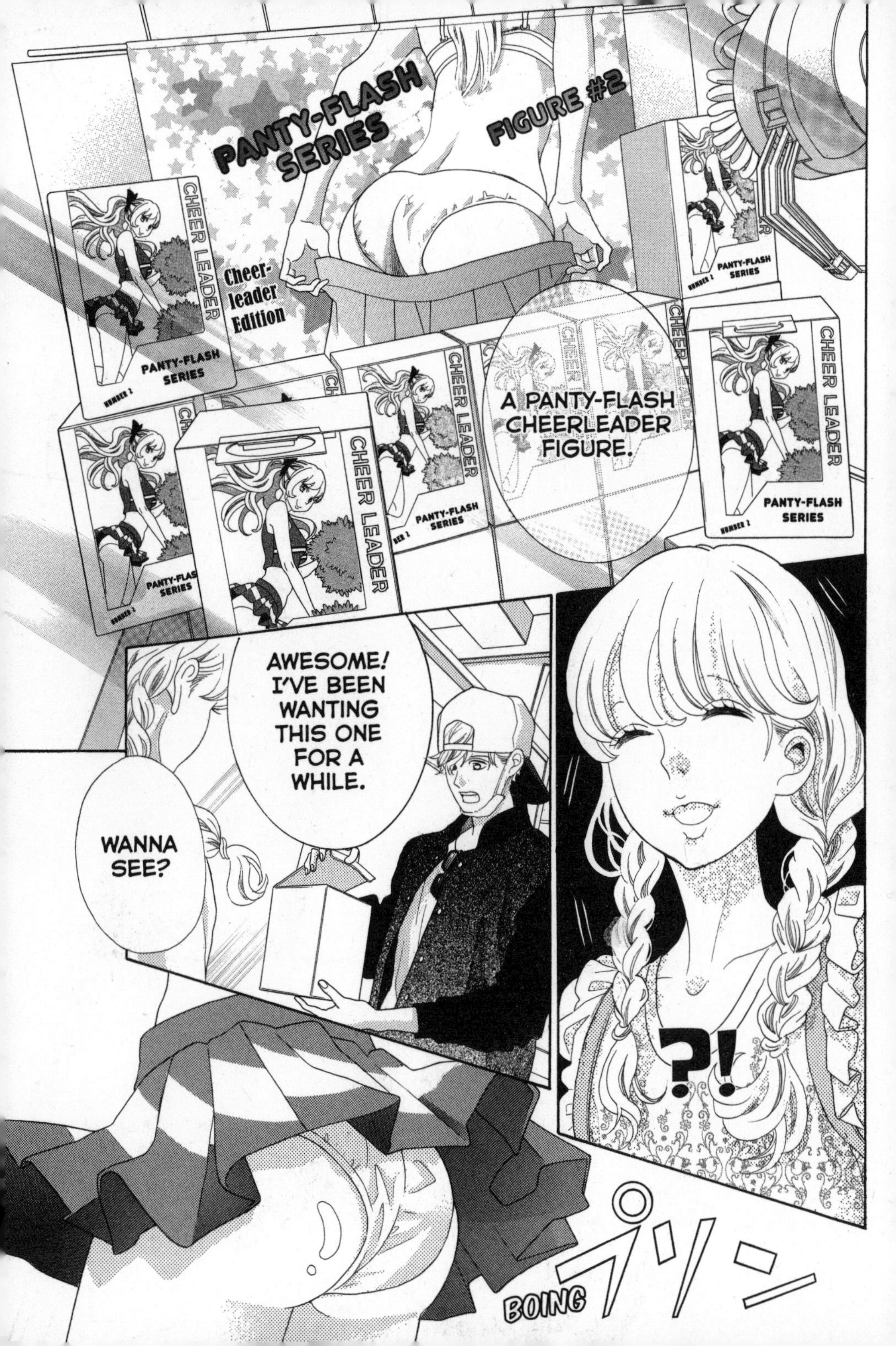

FIGURE #2
PANTY-FLASH SERIES
Cheer-leader Edition
CHEER LEADER
PANTY-FLASH SERIES
NUMBER 2
A PANTY-FLASH CHEERLEADER FIGURE.
?!
AWESOME! I'VE BEEN WANTING THIS ONE FOR A WHILE.
WANNA SEE?
BOING

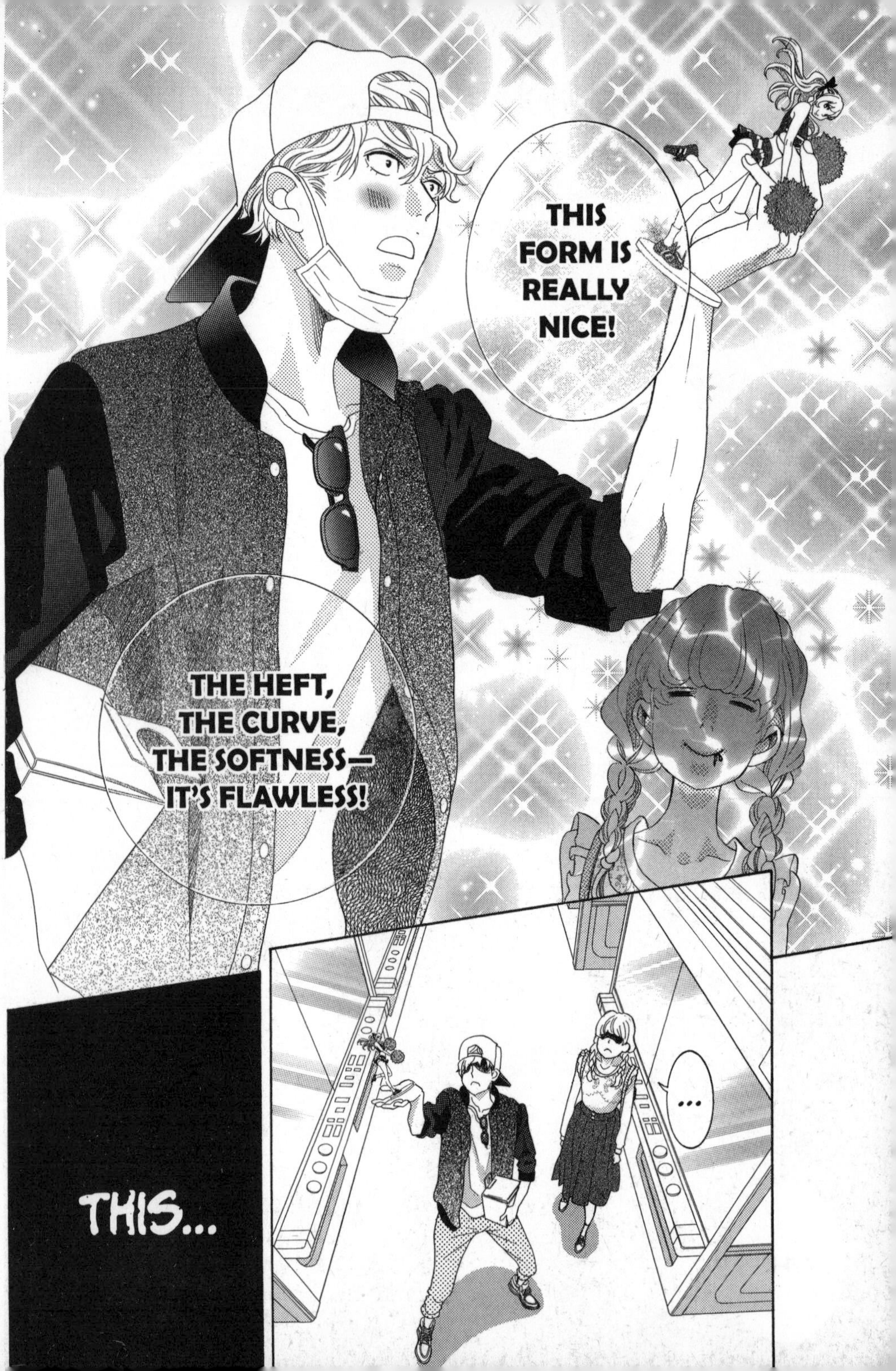
THIS FORM IS REALLY NICE!
THE HEFT, THE CURVE, THE SOFTNESS— IT'S FLAWLESS!
...
THIS...

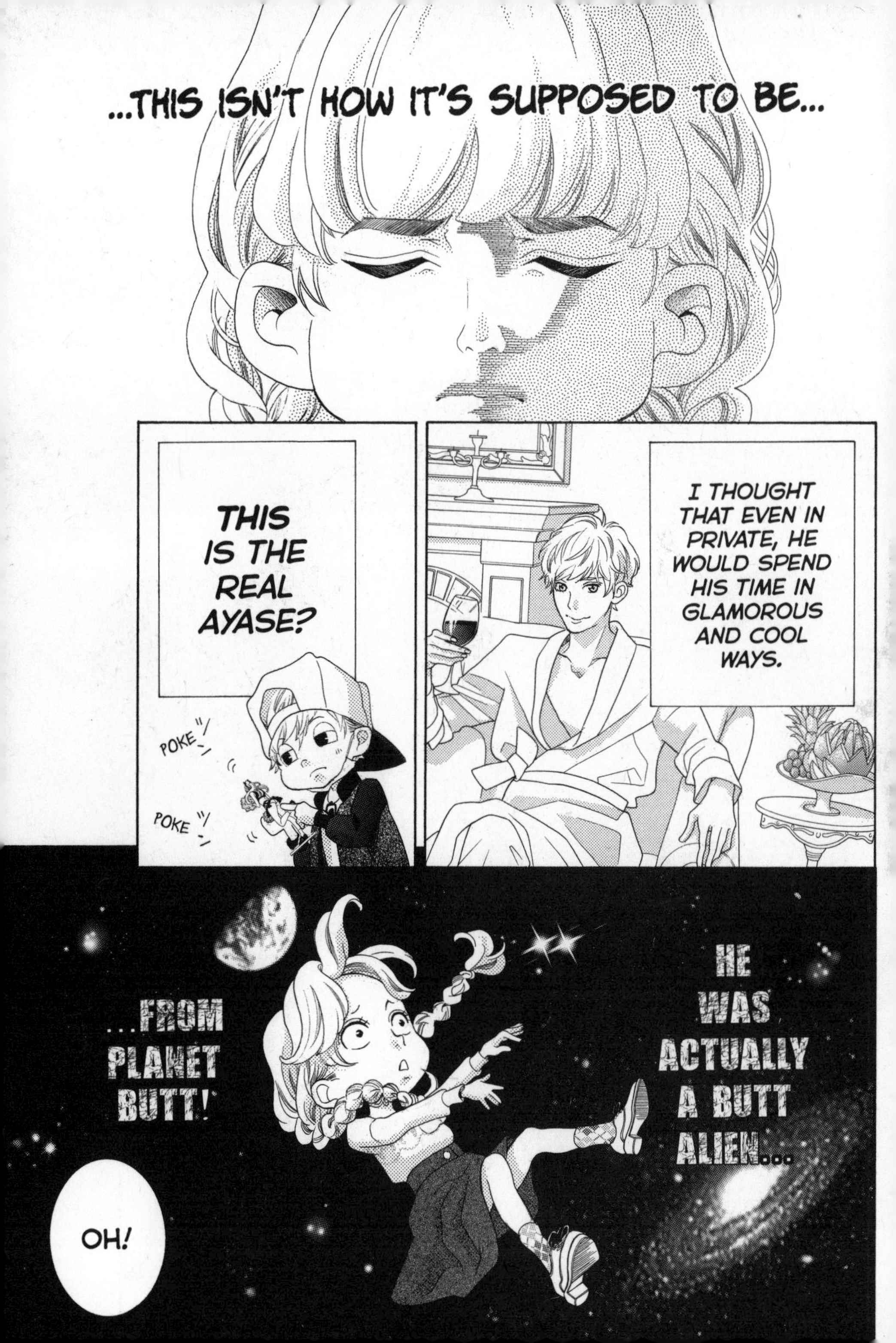
...THIS ISN'T HOW IT'S SUPPOSED TO BE...
I THOUGHT THAT EVEN IN PRIVATE, HE WOULD SPEND HIS TIME IN GLAMOROUS AND COOL WAYS.
THIS IS THE REAL AYASE?
POKE
POKE
HE WAS ACTUALLY A BUTT ALIEN...
...FROM PLANET BUTT!
OH!

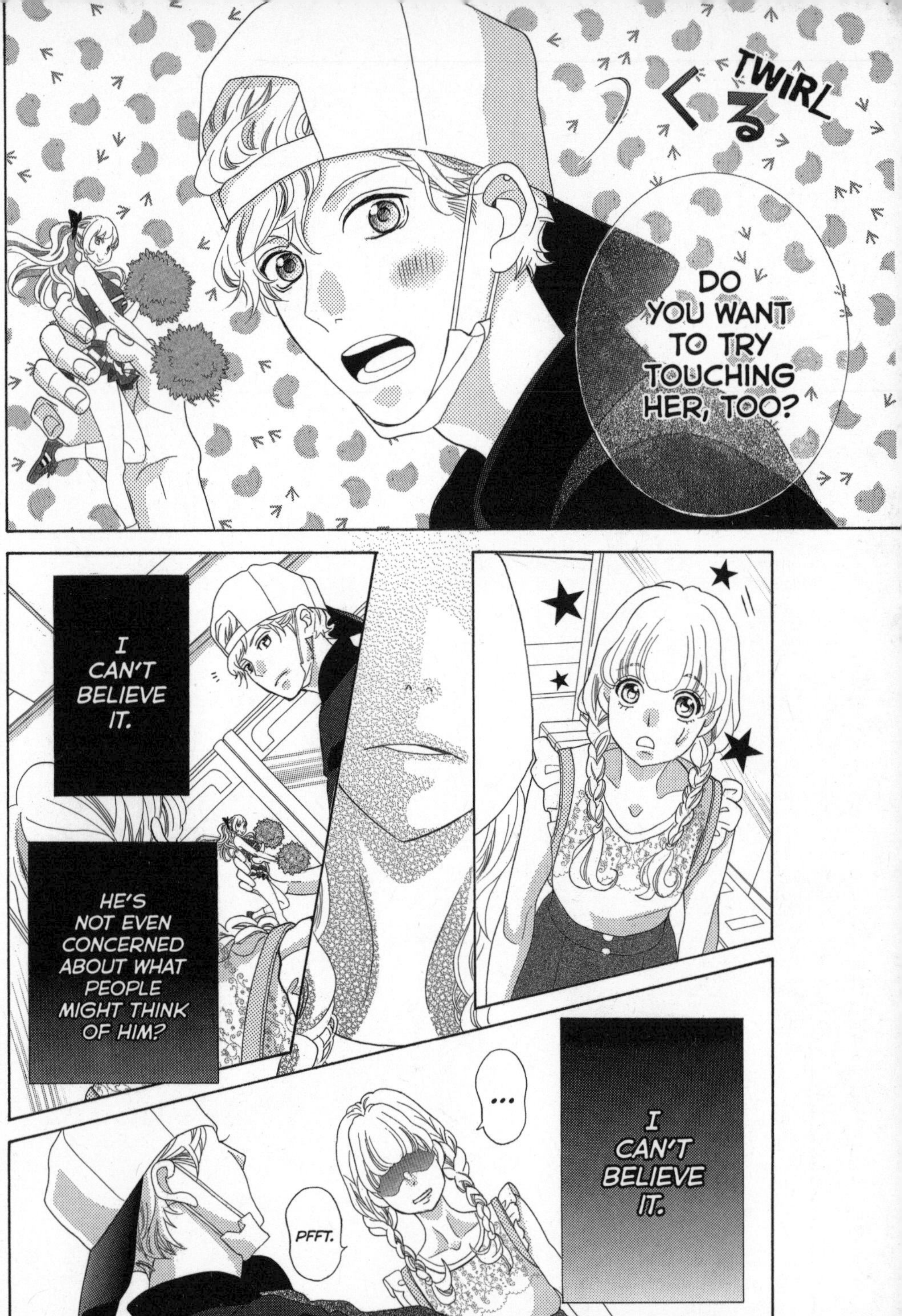
くる
TWIRL
DO YOU WANT TO TRY TOUCHING HER, TOO?
I CAN'T BELIEVE IT.
HE'S NOT EVEN CONCERNED ABOUT WHAT PEOPLE MIGHT THINK OF HIM?
I CAN'T BELIEVE IT.
...
PFFT.

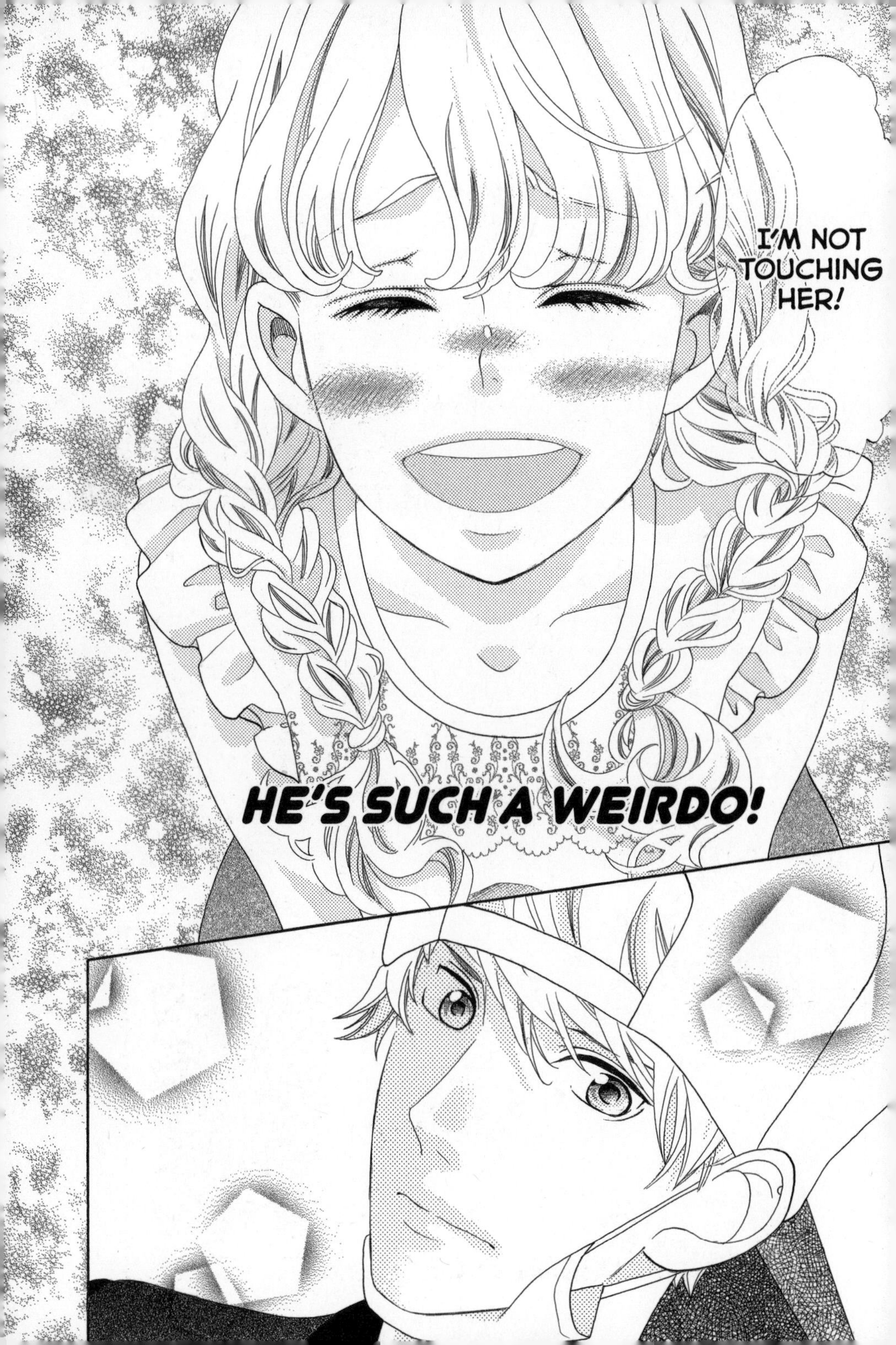
I'M NOT TOUCHING HER!
HE'S SUCH A WEIRDO!

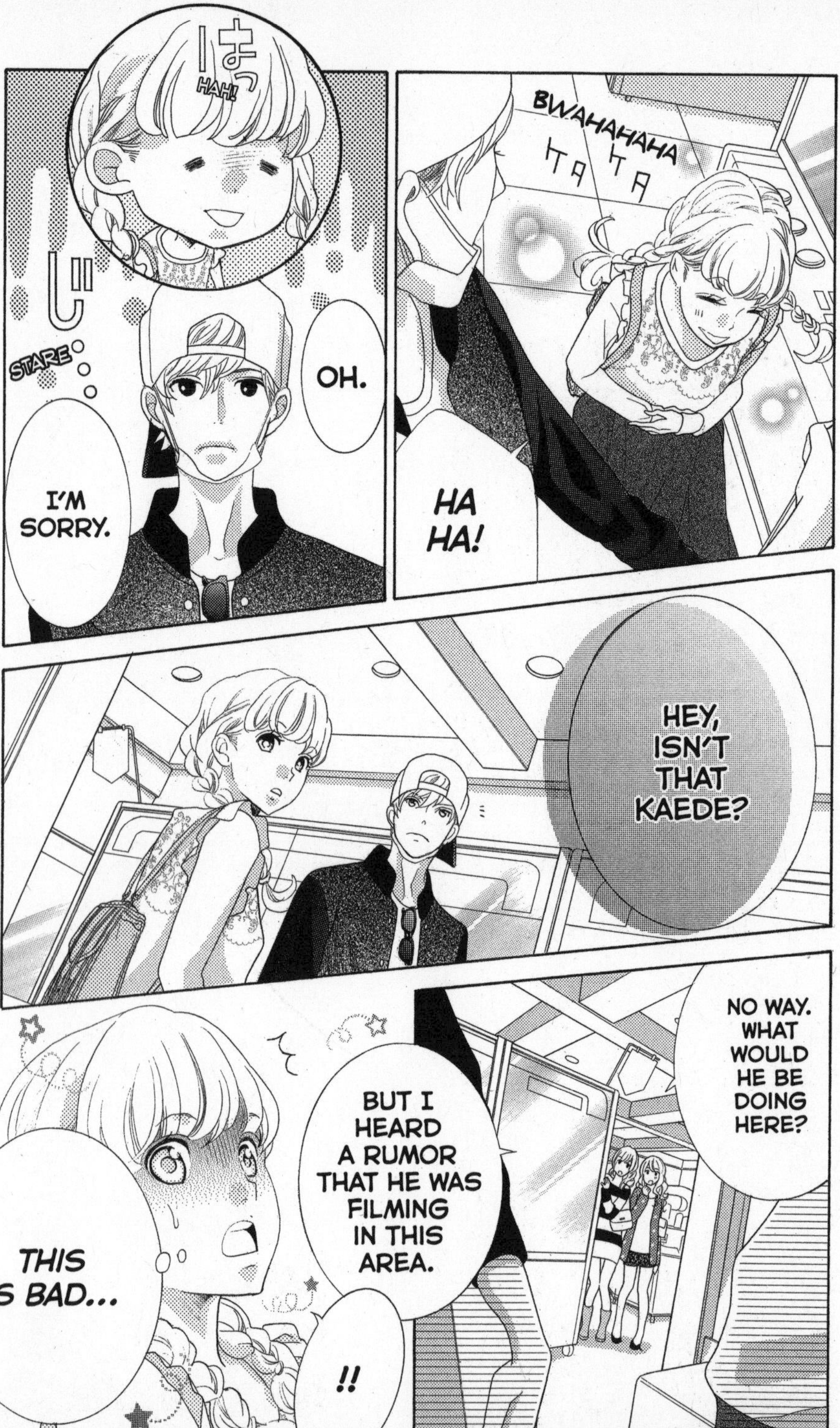
BWAHAHAHA
HA HA!
はっ
HAH!
じ
STARE
OH.
I'M SORRY.
HEY, ISN'T THAT KAEDE?
NO WAY. WHAT WOULD HE BE DOING HERE?
BUT I HEARD A RUMOR THAT HE WAS FILMING IN THIS AREA.
!!
THIS IS BAD...

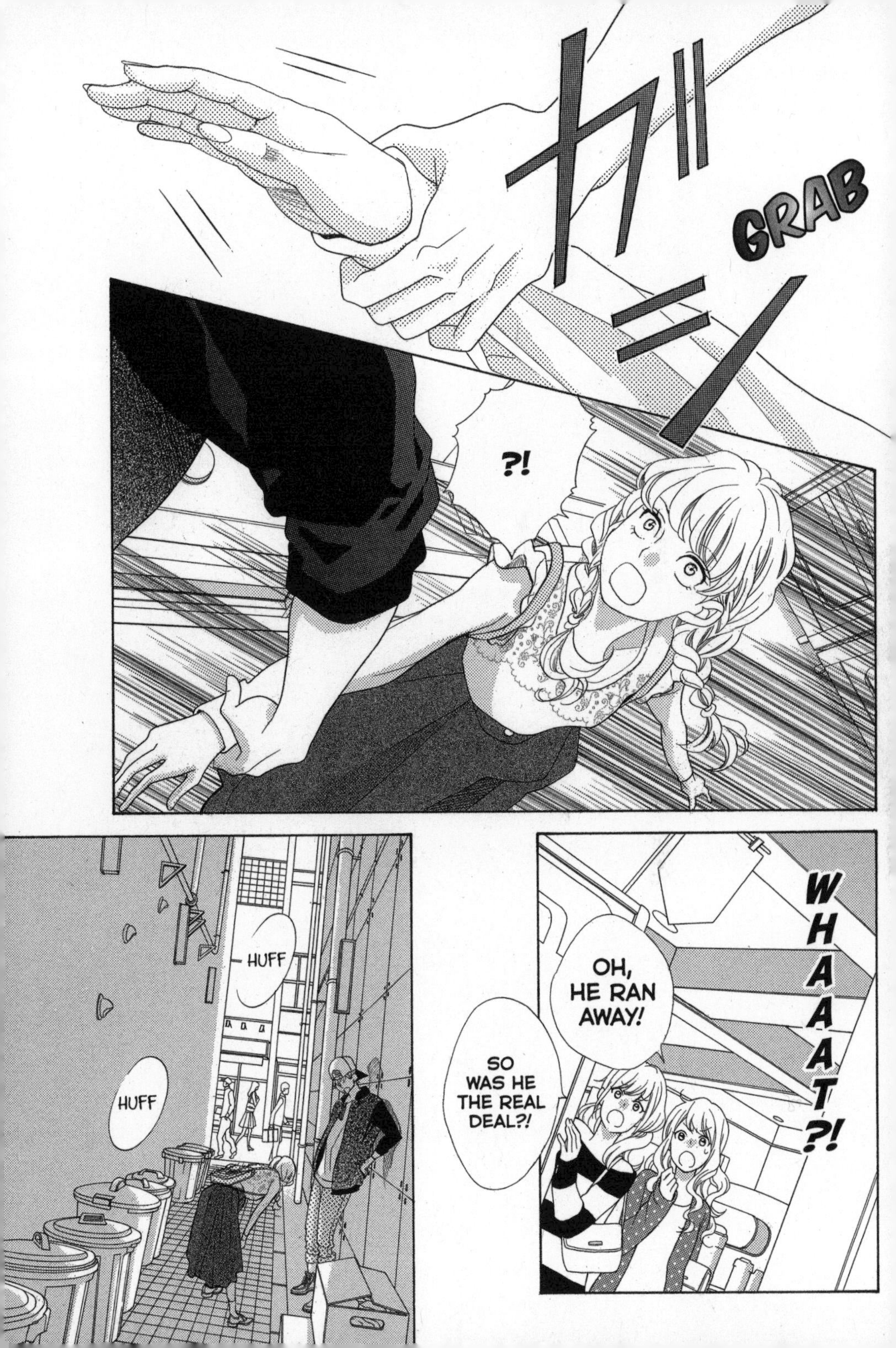
GRAB
?!
WHAAAAT?!
OH, HE RAN AWAY!
SO WAS HE THE REAL DEAL?!
HUFF
HUFF

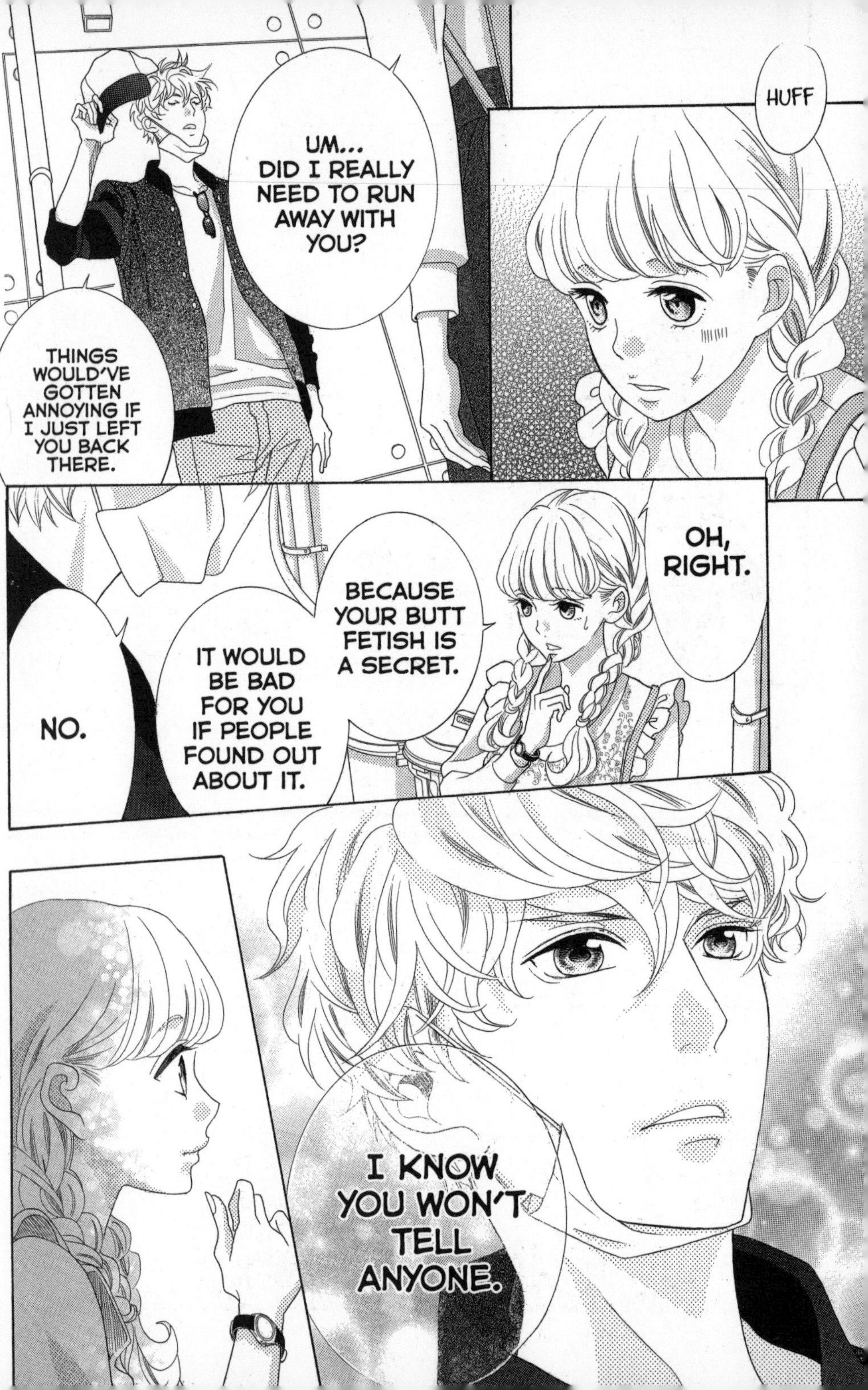
HUFF
UM... DID I REALLY NEED TO RUN AWAY WITH YOU?
THINGS WOULD'VE GOTTEN ANNOYING IF I JUST LEFT YOU BACK THERE.
OH, RIGHT.
BECAUSE YOUR BUTT FETISH IS A SECRET.
IT WOULD BE BAD FOR YOU IF PEOPLE FOUND OUT ABOUT IT.
NO.
I KNOW YOU WON'T TELL ANYONE.

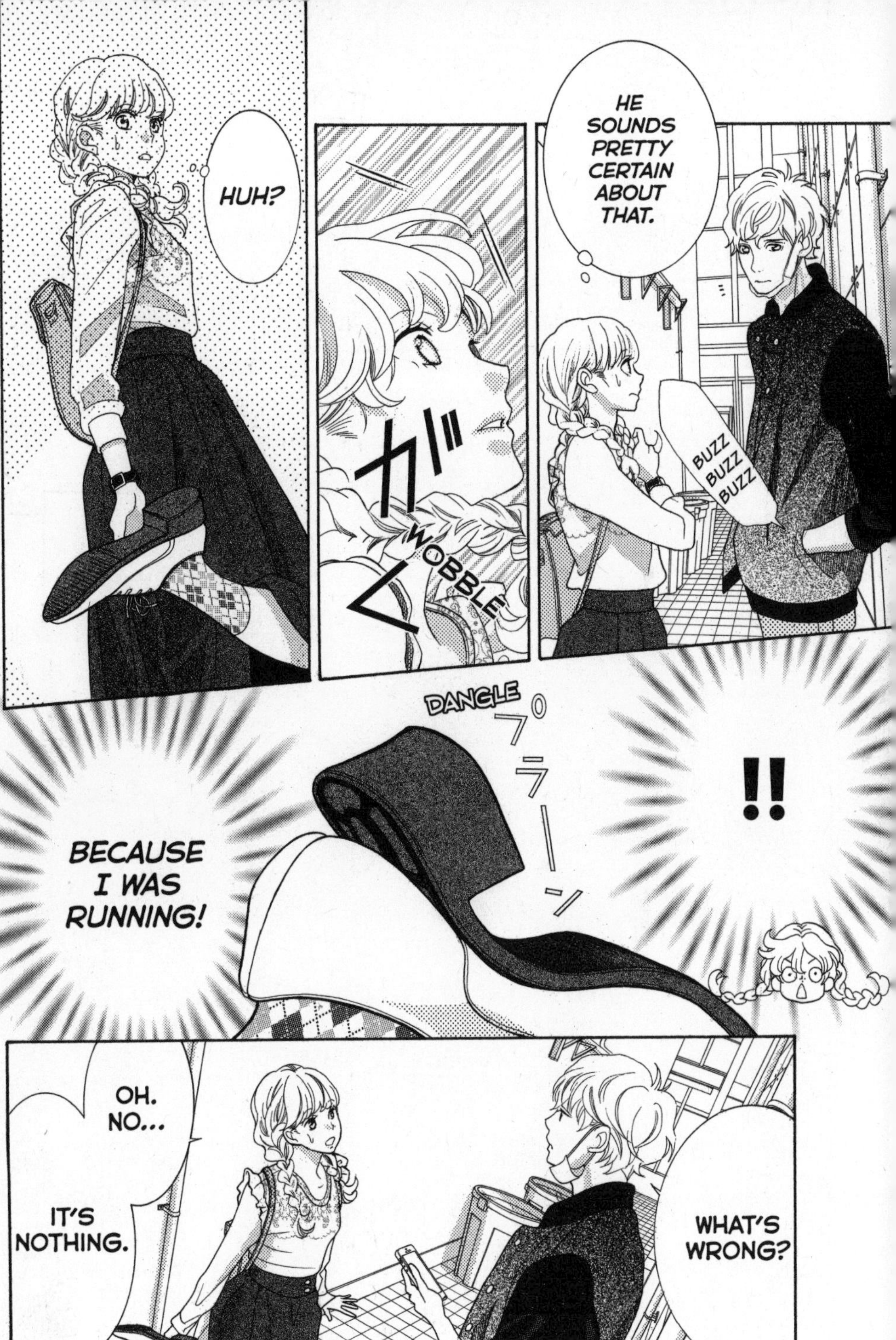
HE SOUNDS PRETTY CERTAIN ABOUT THAT.
BUZZ BUZZ BUZZ
WOBBLE
HUH?
!!
DANGLE
BECAUSE I WAS RUNNING!
WHAT'S WRONG?
OH. NO...
IT'S NOTHING.

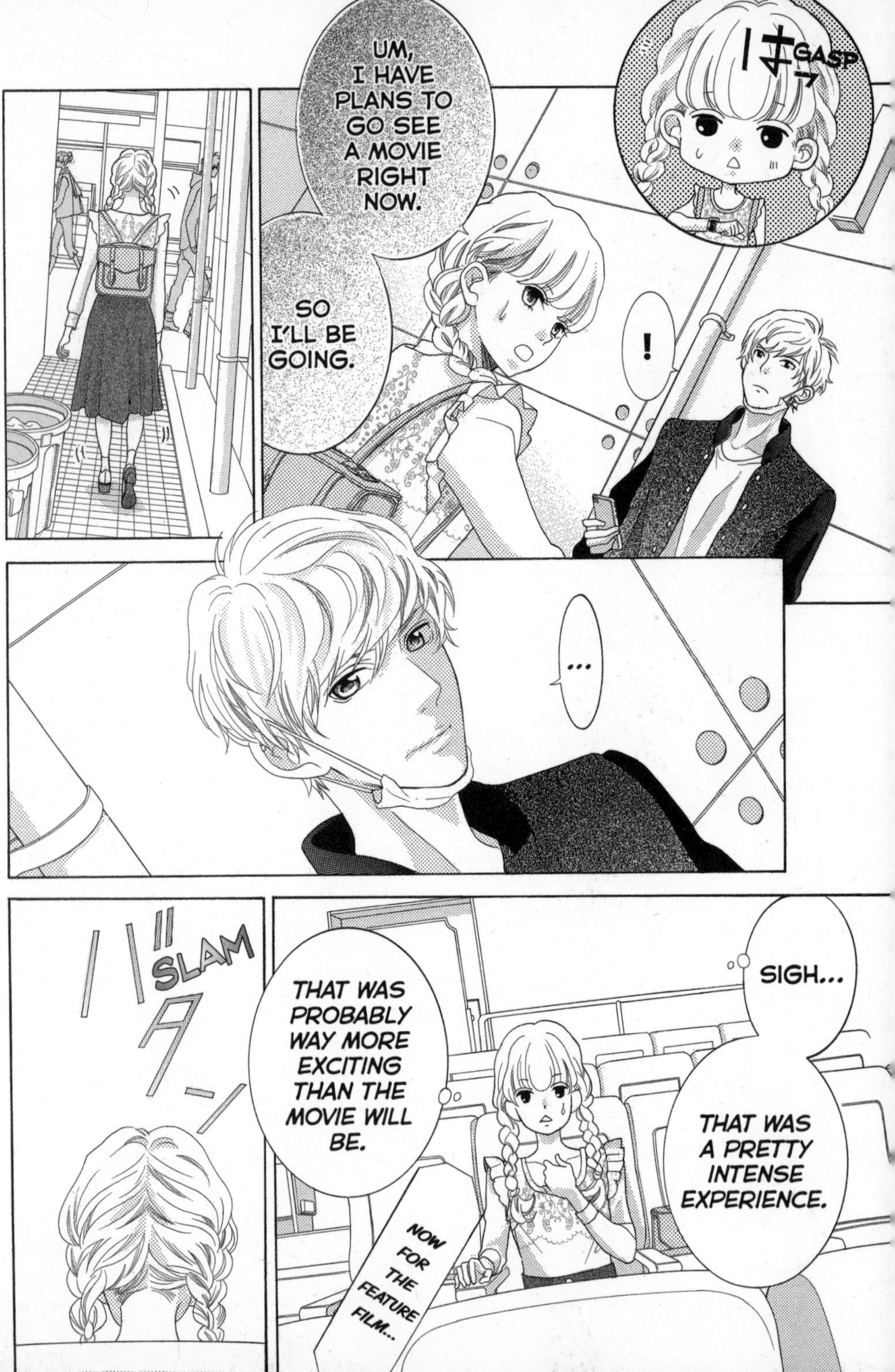
GASP
UM, I HAVE PLANS TO GO SEE A MOVIE RIGHT NOW.
SO I'LL BE GOING.
!
...
SIGH...
THAT WAS A PRETTY INTENSE EXPERIENCE.
THAT WAS PROBABLY WAY MORE EXCITING THAN THE MOVIE WILL BE.
NOW FOR THE FEATURE FILM...
SLAM

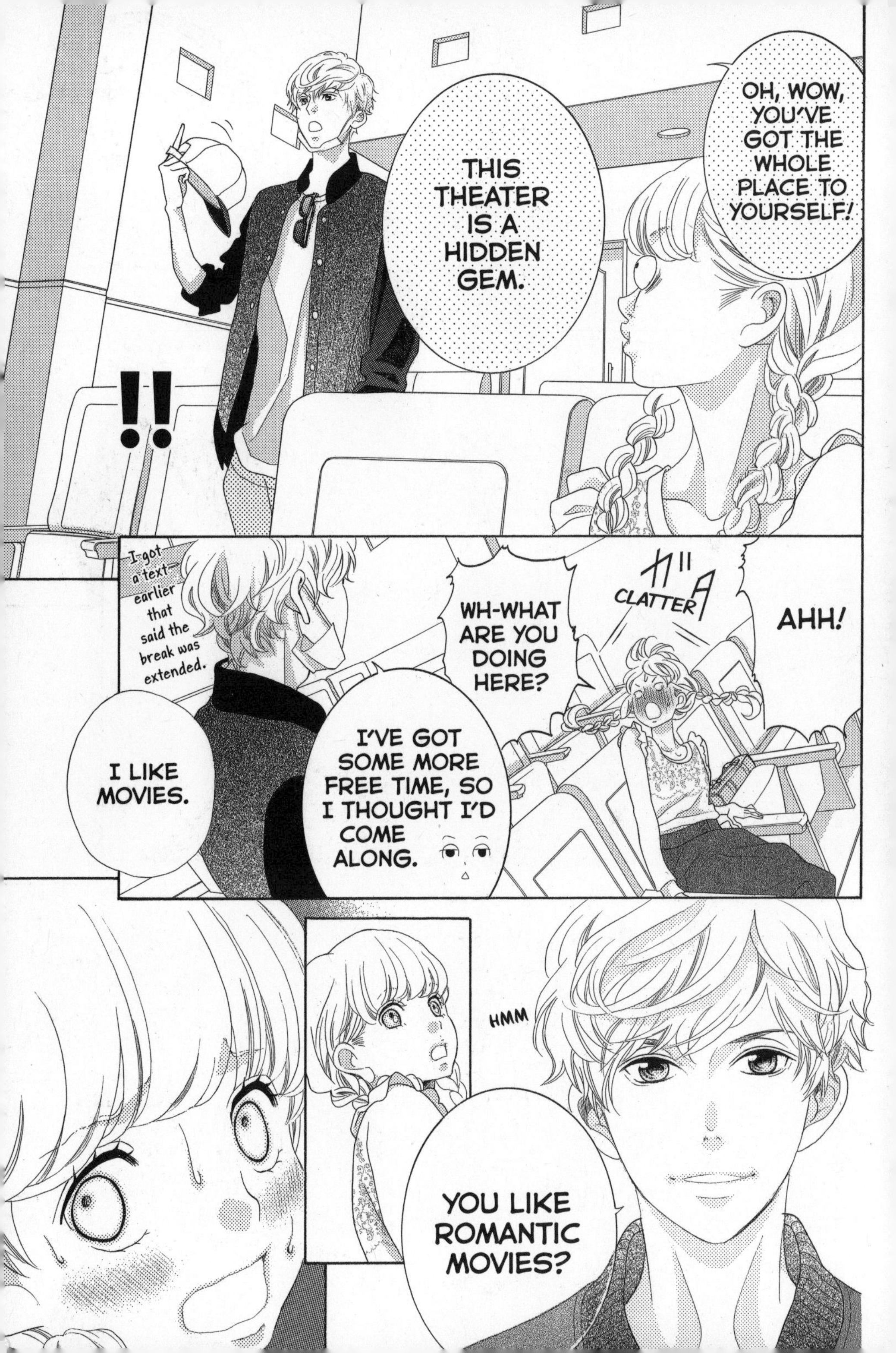
OH, WOW, YOU'VE GOT THE WHOLE PLACE TO YOURSELF!
THIS THEATER IS A HIDDEN GEM.
!!
AHH!
ガタ
CLATTER
WH-WHAT ARE YOU DOING HERE?
I'VE GOT SOME MORE FREE TIME, SO I THOUGHT I'D COME ALONG.
I LIKE MOVIES.
I got a text earlier that said the break was extended.
HMM
YOU LIKE ROMANTIC MOVIES?

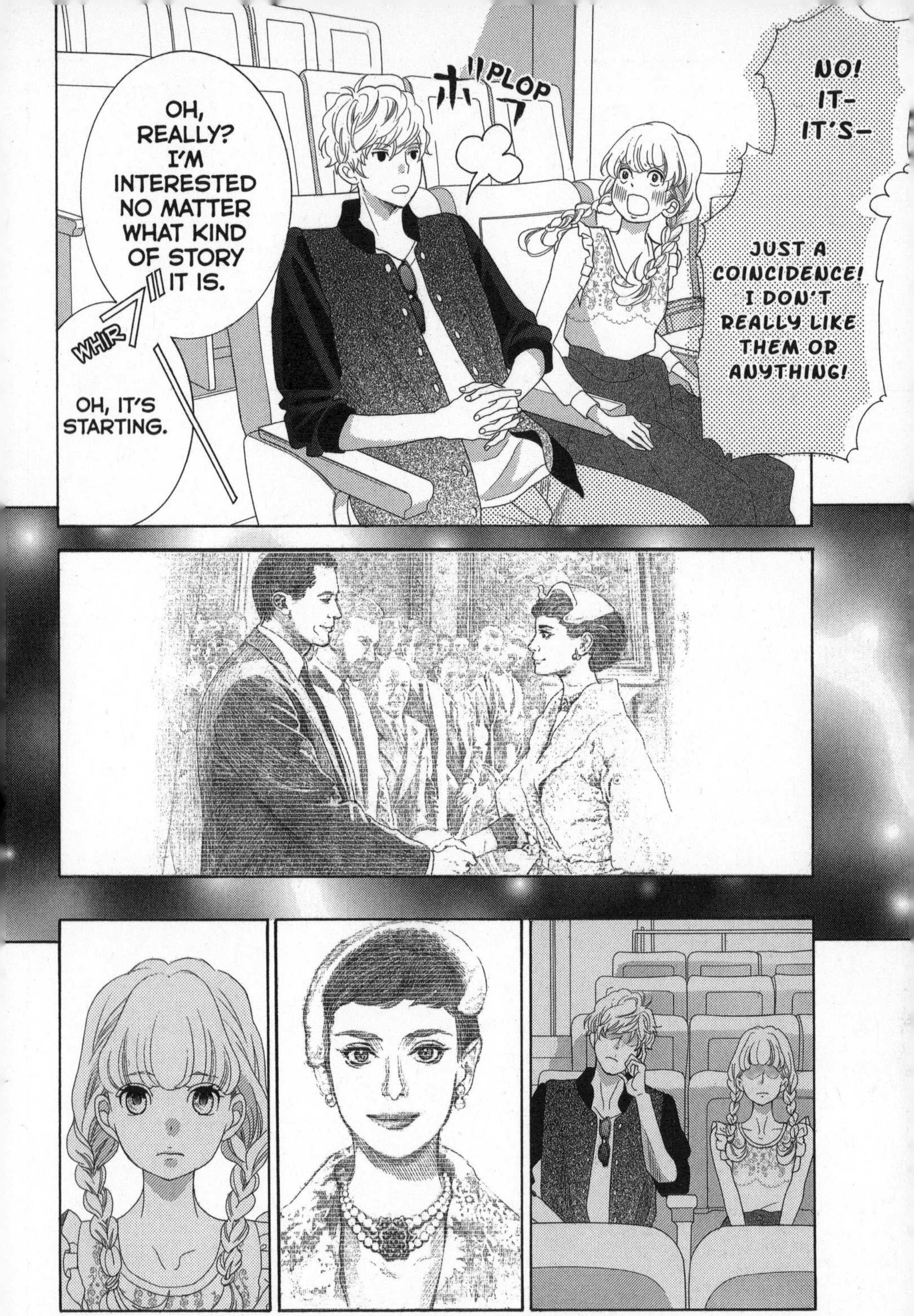
NO! IT- IT'S-
JUST A COINCIDENCE! I DON'T REALLY LIKE THEM OR ANYTHING!
PLOP
OH, REALLY? I'M INTERESTED NO MATTER WHAT KIND OF STORY IT IS.
WHIR
OH, IT'S STARTING.

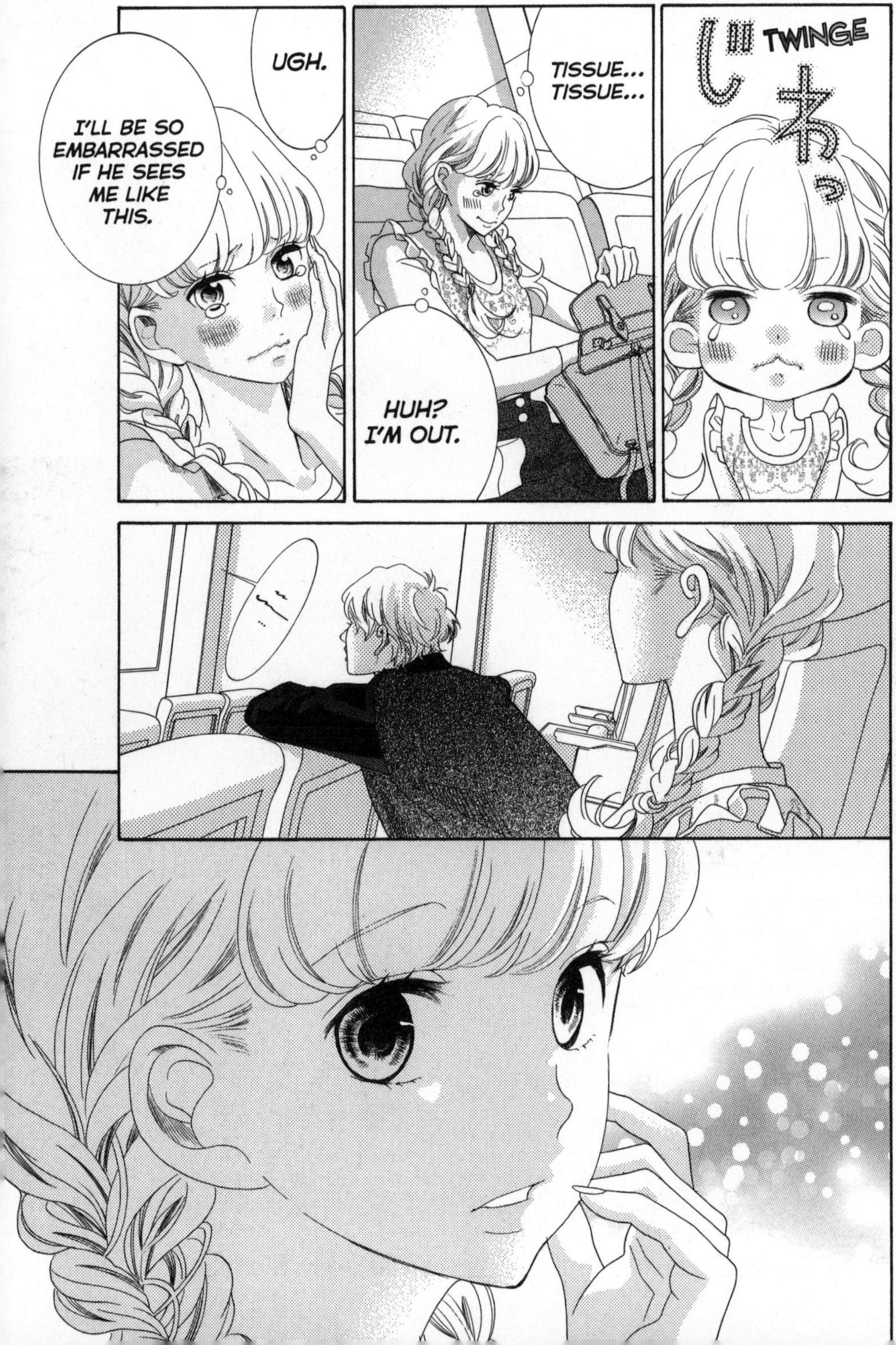
じわっ
TWINGE
TISSUE... TISSUE...
HUH? I'M OUT.
UGH.
I'LL BE SO EMBARRASSED IF HE SEES ME LIKE THIS.
...

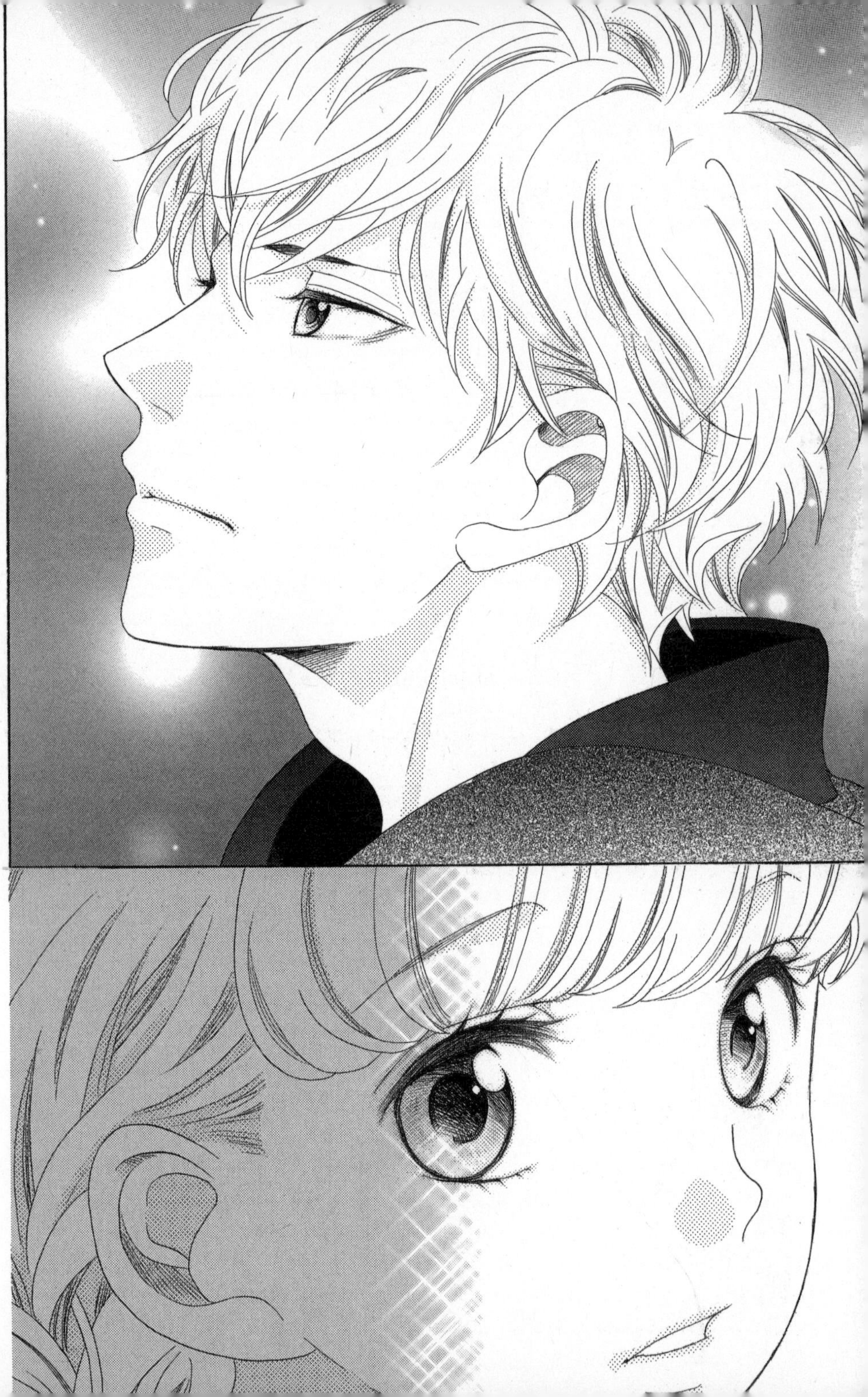

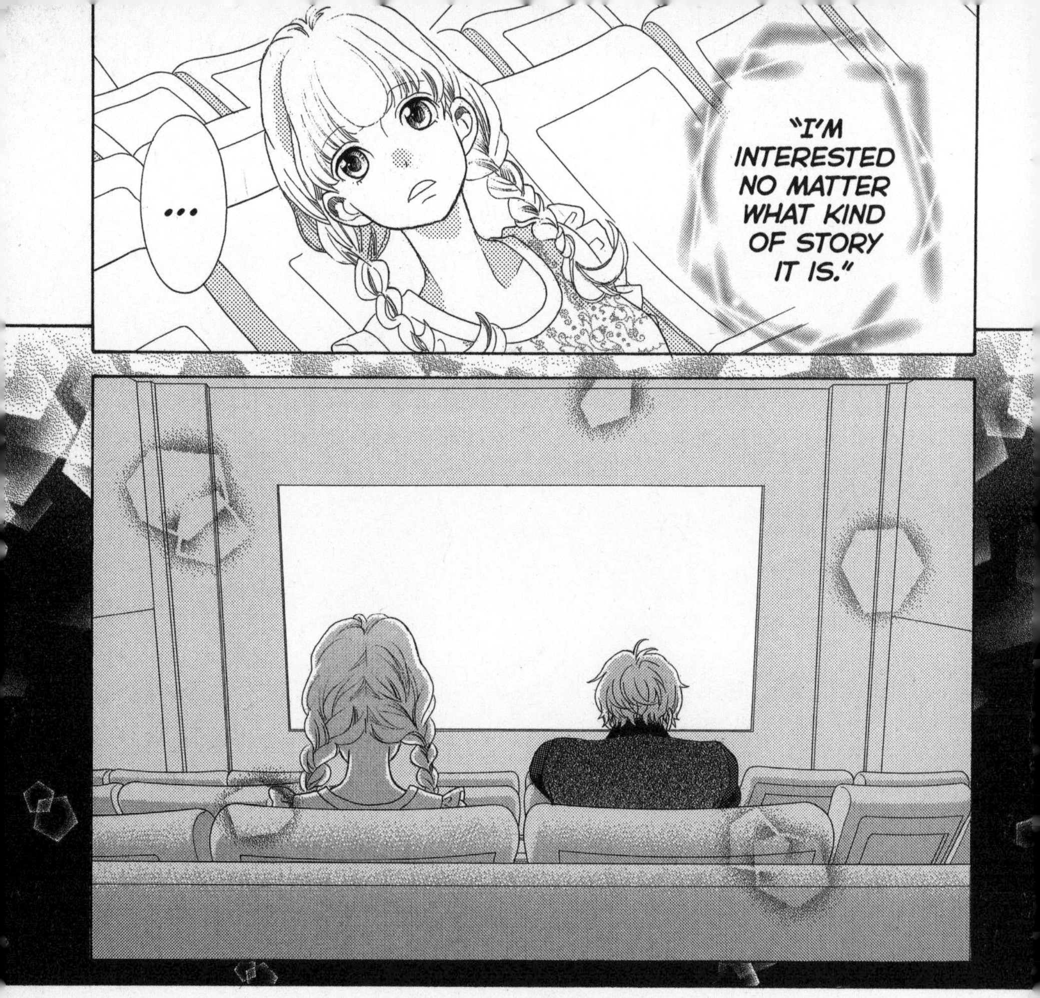
"I'M INTERESTED NO MATTER WHAT KIND OF STORY IT IS."
...

The End

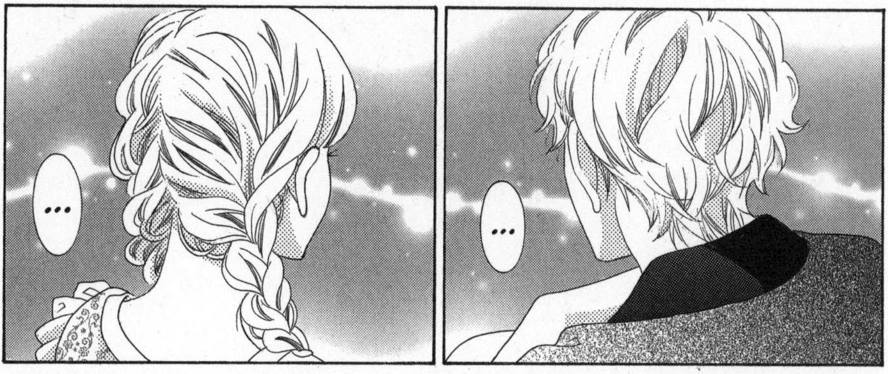
...
...

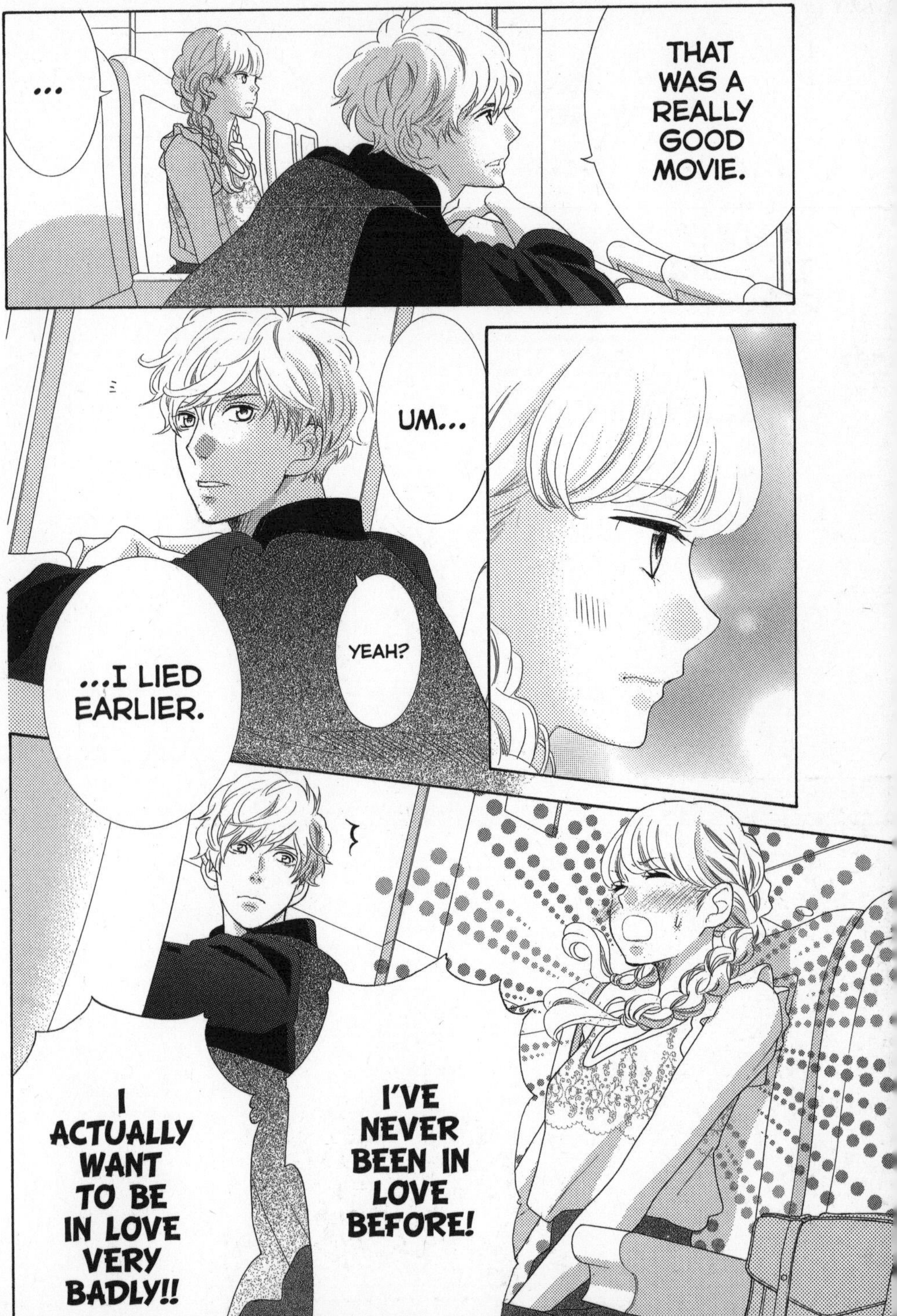
THAT WAS A REALLY GOOD MOVIE.
...
UM...
YEAH?
...I LIED EARLIER.
I'VE NEVER BEEN IN LOVE BEFORE!
I ACTUALLY WANT TO BE IN LOVE VERY BADLY!!

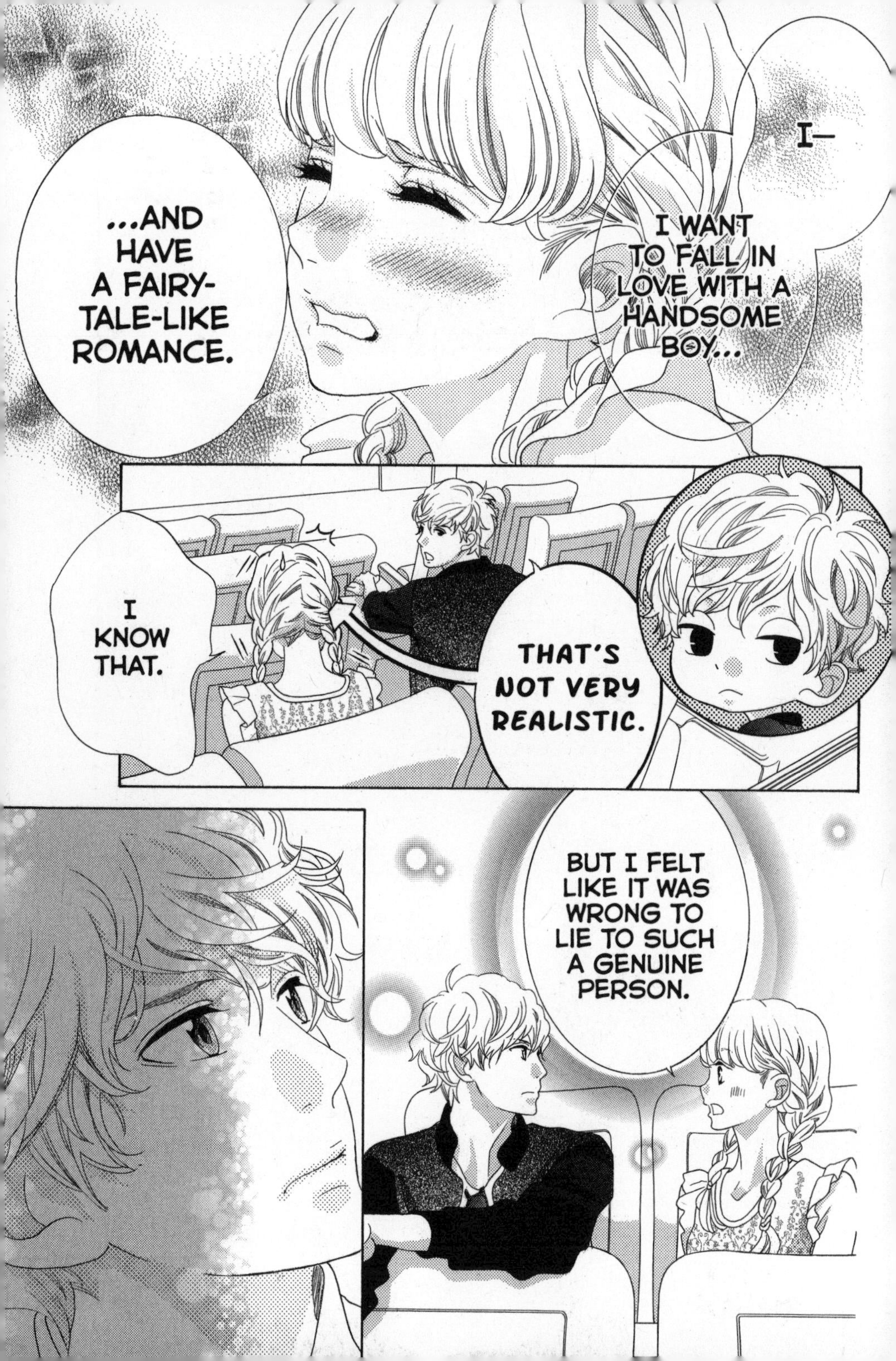
I—
I WANT TO FALL IN LOVE WITH A HANDSOME BOY...
...AND HAVE A FAIRY-TALE-LIKE ROMANCE.
THAT'S NOT VERY REALISTIC.
I KNOW THAT.
BUT I FELT LIKE IT WAS WRONG TO LIE TO SUCH A GENUINE PERSON.

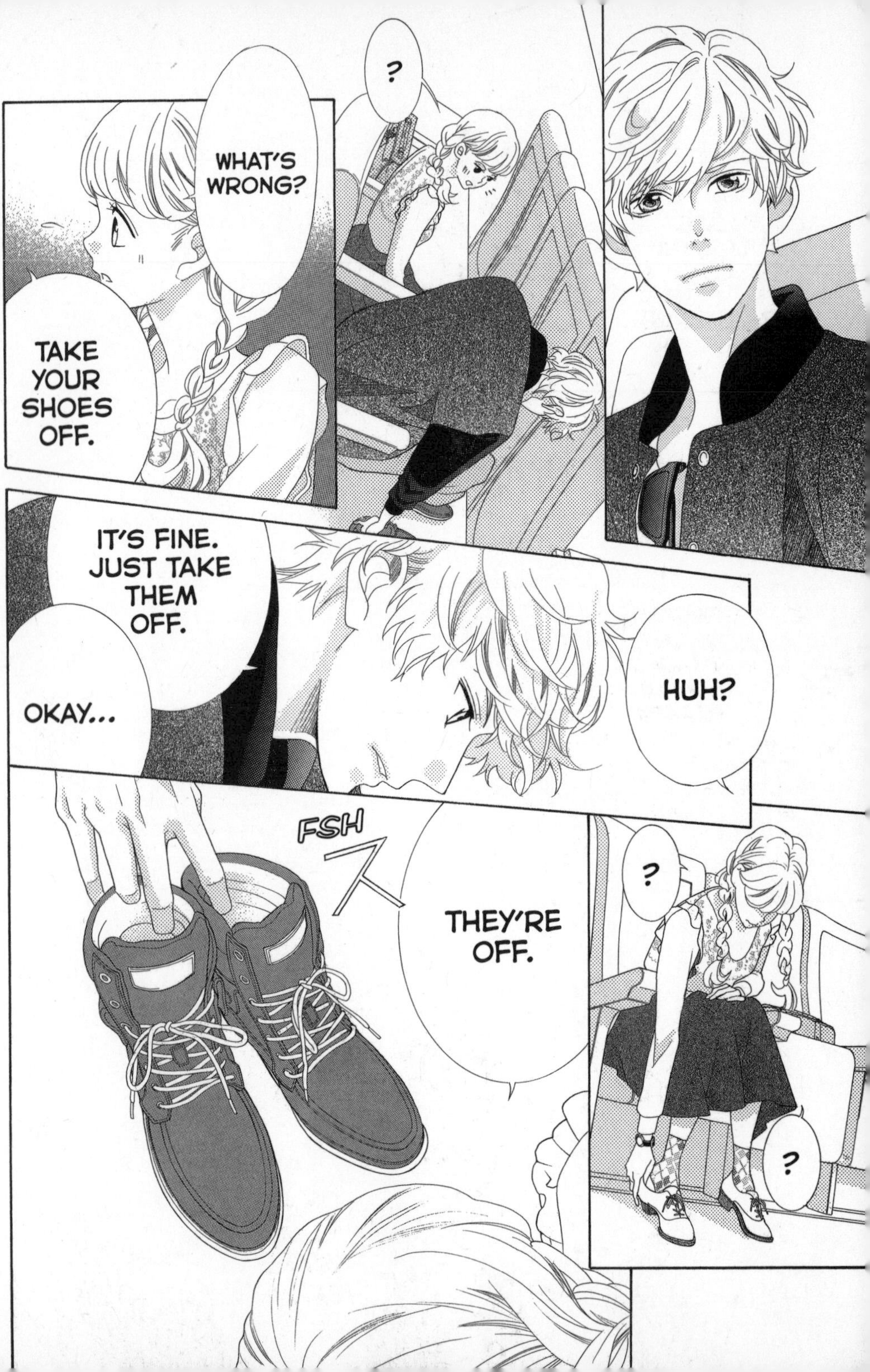
?
WHAT'S WRONG?
TAKE YOUR SHOES OFF.
HUH?
IT'S FINE. JUST TAKE THEM OFF.
OKAY...
?
?
THEY'RE OFF.
FSH

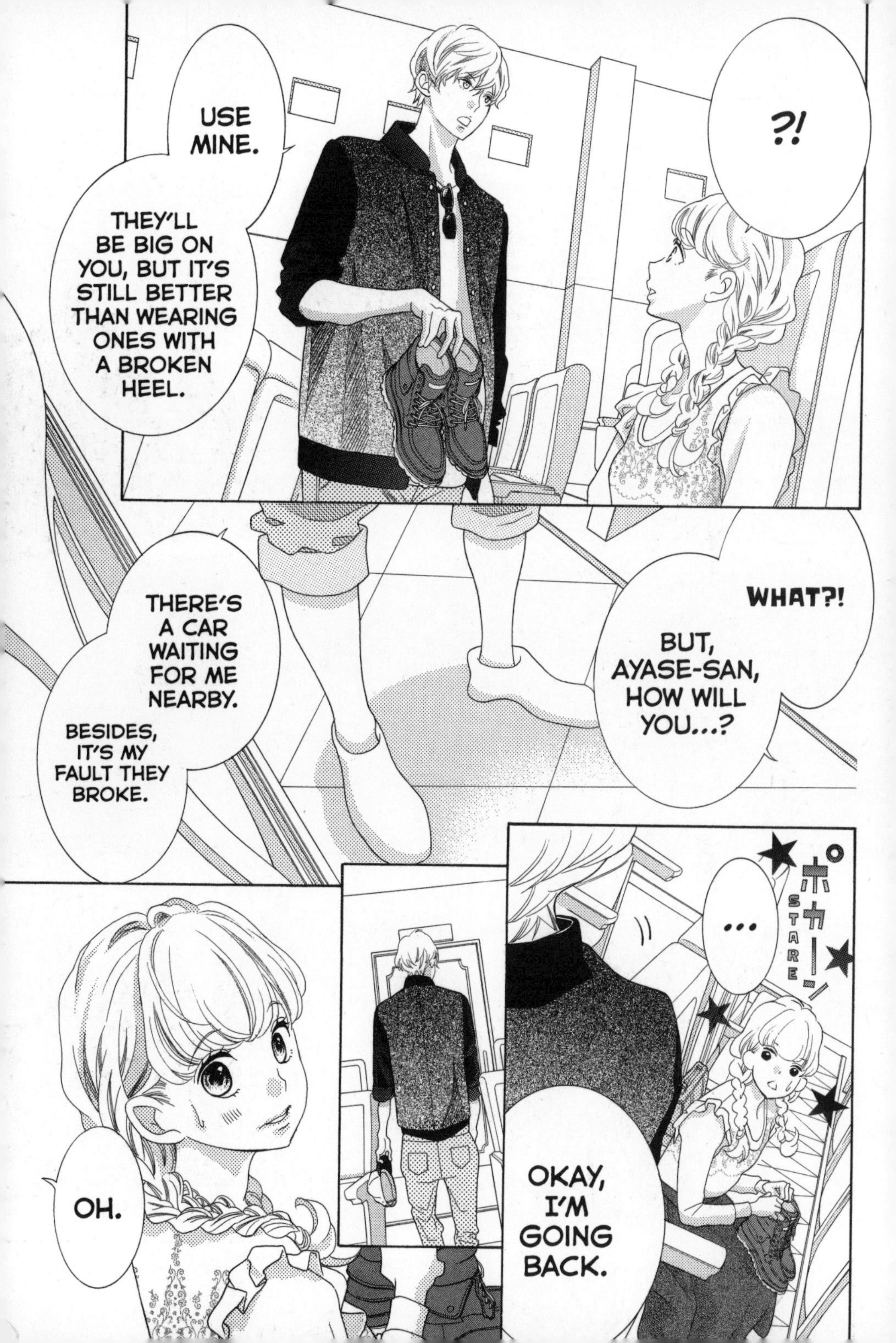
?!
USE MINE.
THEY'LL BE BIG ON YOU, BUT IT'S STILL BETTER THAN WEARING ONES WITH A BROKEN HEEL.
WHAT?!
BUT, AYASE-SAN, HOW WILL YOU...?
THERE'S A CAR WAITING FOR ME NEARBY.
BESIDES, IT'S MY FAULT THEY BROKE.
STARE
...
OKAY, I'M GOING BACK.
OH.

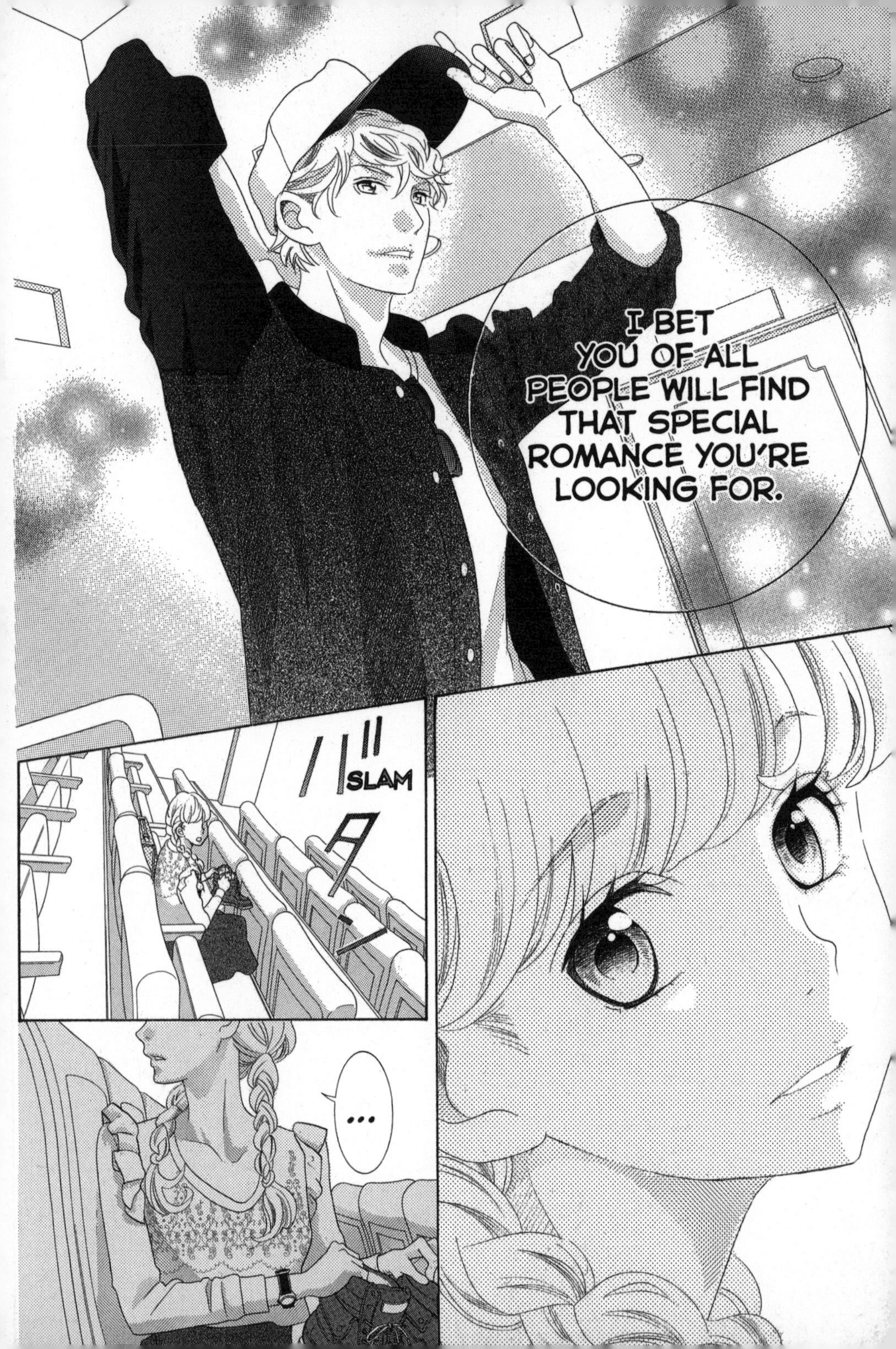
I BET YOU OF ALL PEOPLE WILL FIND THAT SPECIAL ROMANCE YOU'RE LOOKING FOR.
SLAM
...

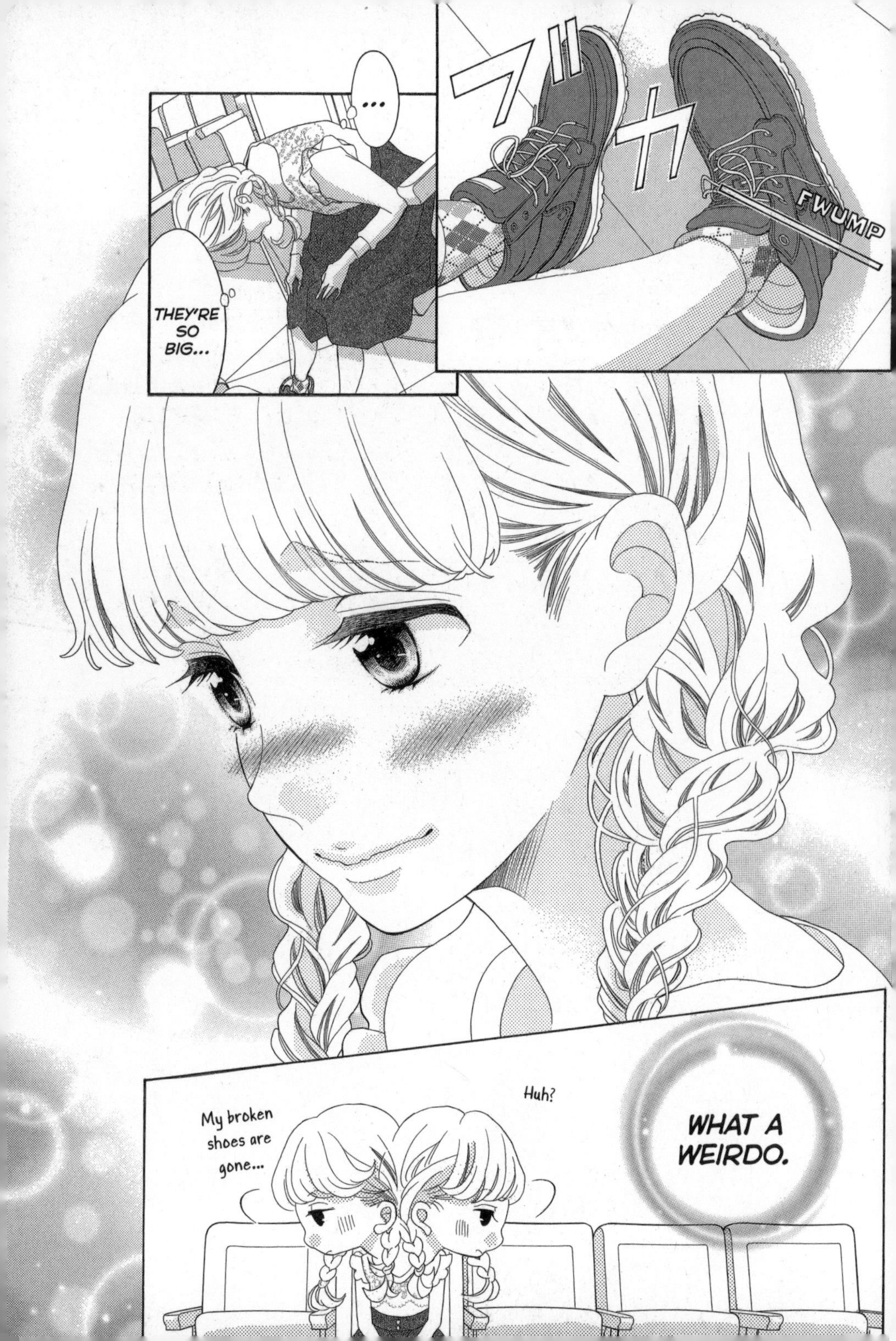
FWUMP
...
THEY'RE SO BIG...
WHAT A WEIRDO.
Huh?
My broken shoes are gone...

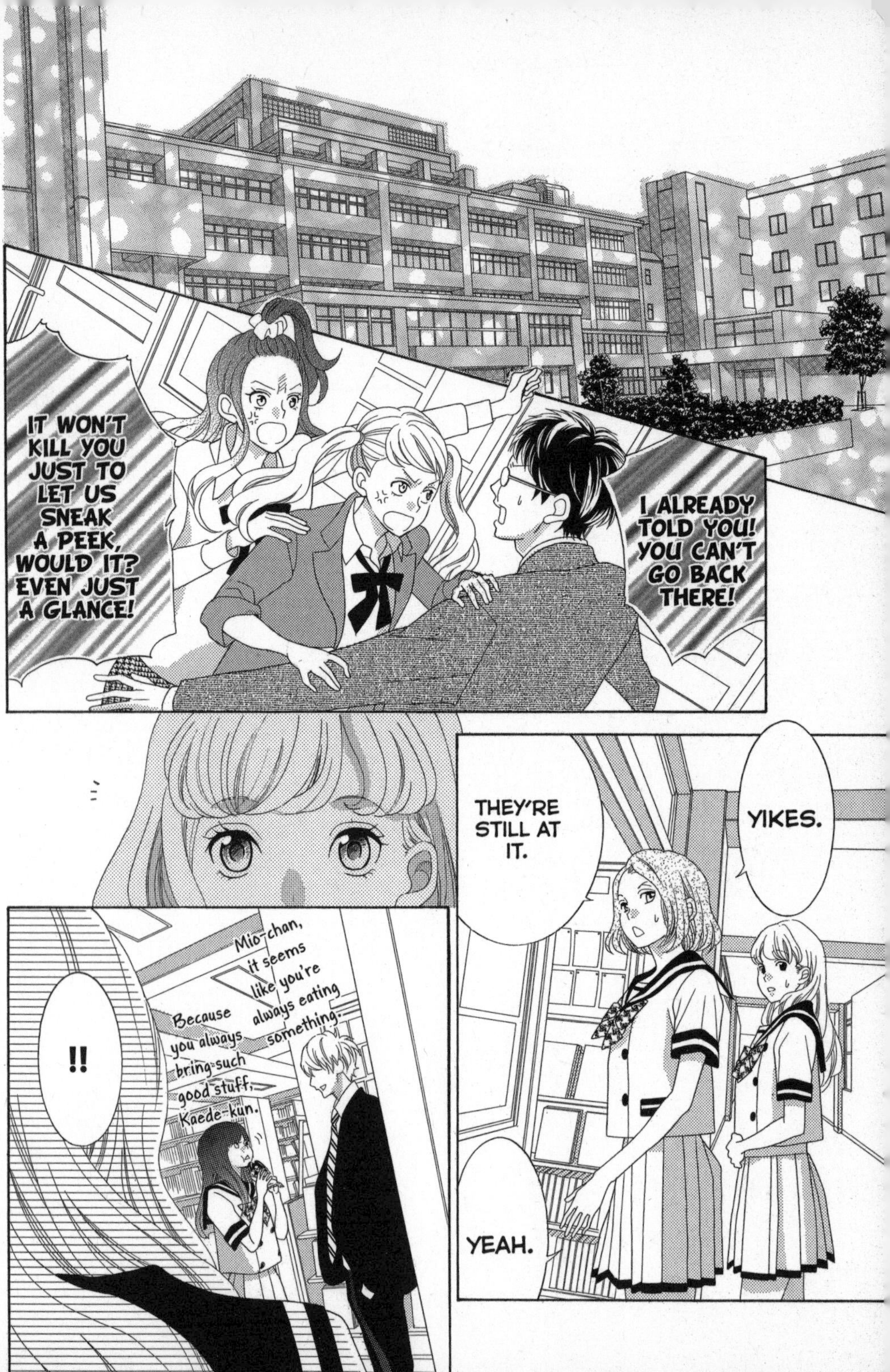
I ALREADY TOLD YOU! YOU CAN'T GO BACK THERE!
IT WON'T KILL YOU JUST TO LET US SNEAK A PEEK, WOULD IT? EVEN JUST A GLANCE!
YIKES.
THEY'RE STILL AT IT.
YEAH.
Mio-chan, it seems like you're always eating something.
Because you always bring such good stuff, Kaede-kun.
!!

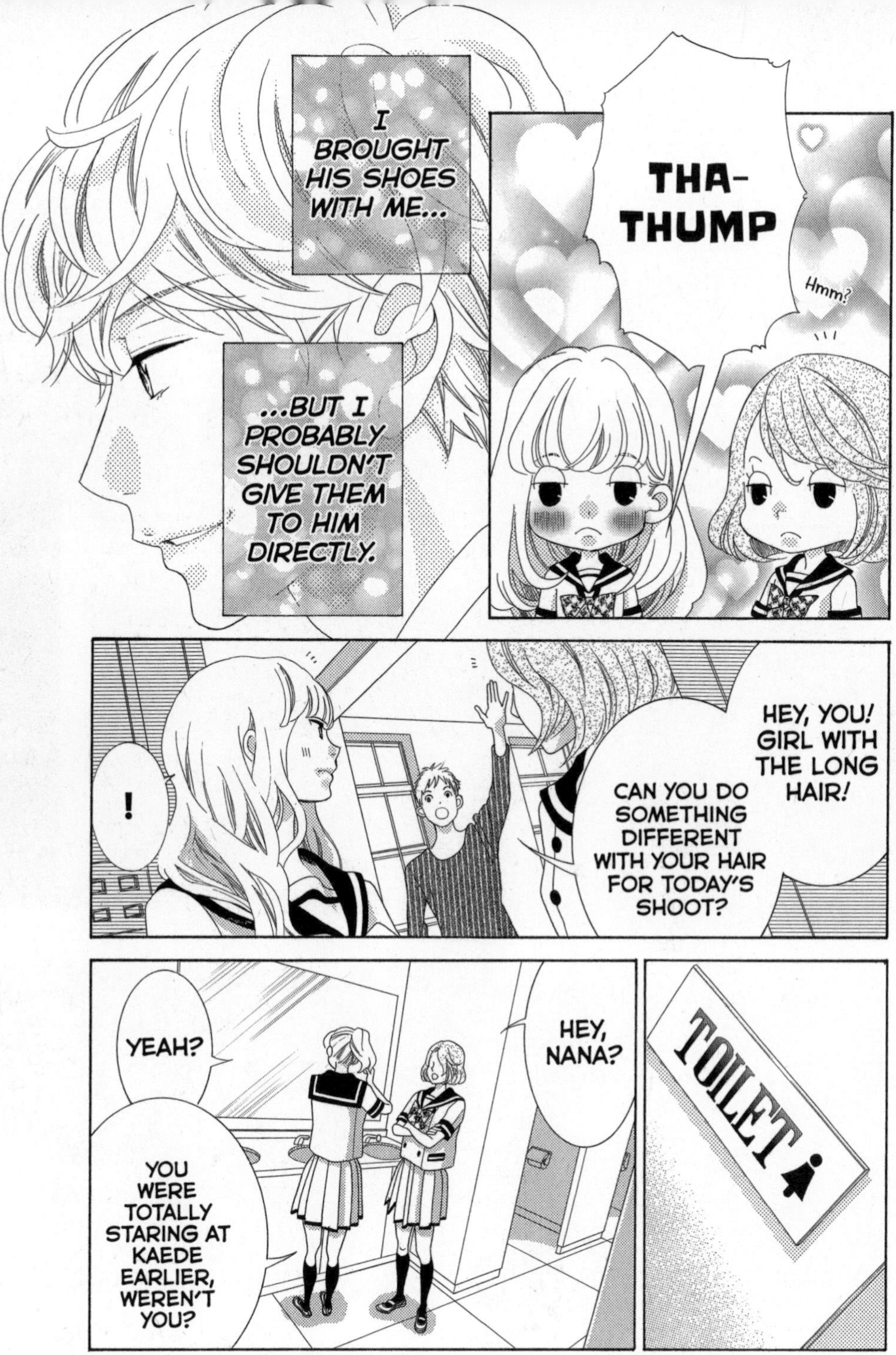
THA-THUMP
Hmm?
I BROUGHT HIS SHOES WITH ME...
...BUT I PROBABLY SHOULDN'T GIVE THEM TO HIM DIRECTLY.
HEY, YOU! GIRL WITH THE LONG HAIR!
CAN YOU DO SOMETHING DIFFERENT WITH YOUR HAIR FOR TODAY'S SHOOT?
!
TOILET
HEY, NANA?
YEAH?
YOU WERE TOTALLY STARING AT KAEDE EARLIER, WEREN'T YOU?

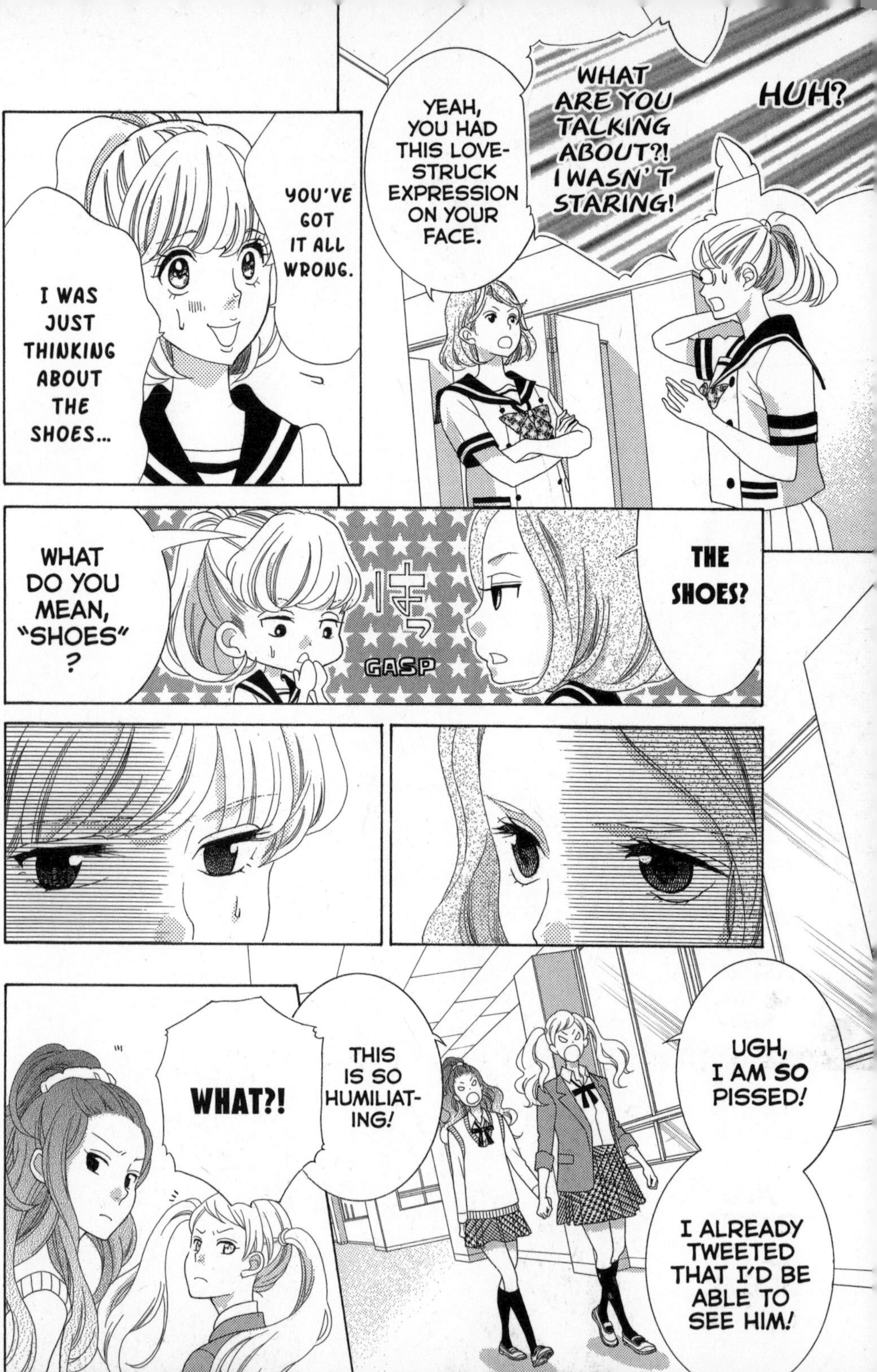
HUH?
WHAT ARE YOU TALKING ABOUT?! I WASN'T STARING!
YEAH, YOU HAD THIS LOVE-STRUCK EXPRESSION ON YOUR FACE.
YOU'VE GOT IT ALL WRONG.
I WAS JUST THINKING ABOUT THE SHOES...
THE SHOES?
はっ
GASP
WHAT DO YOU MEAN, "SHOES"?
UGH, I AM SO PISSED!
I ALREADY TWEETED THAT I'D BE ABLE TO SEE HIM!
THIS IS SO HUMILIATING!
WHAT?!

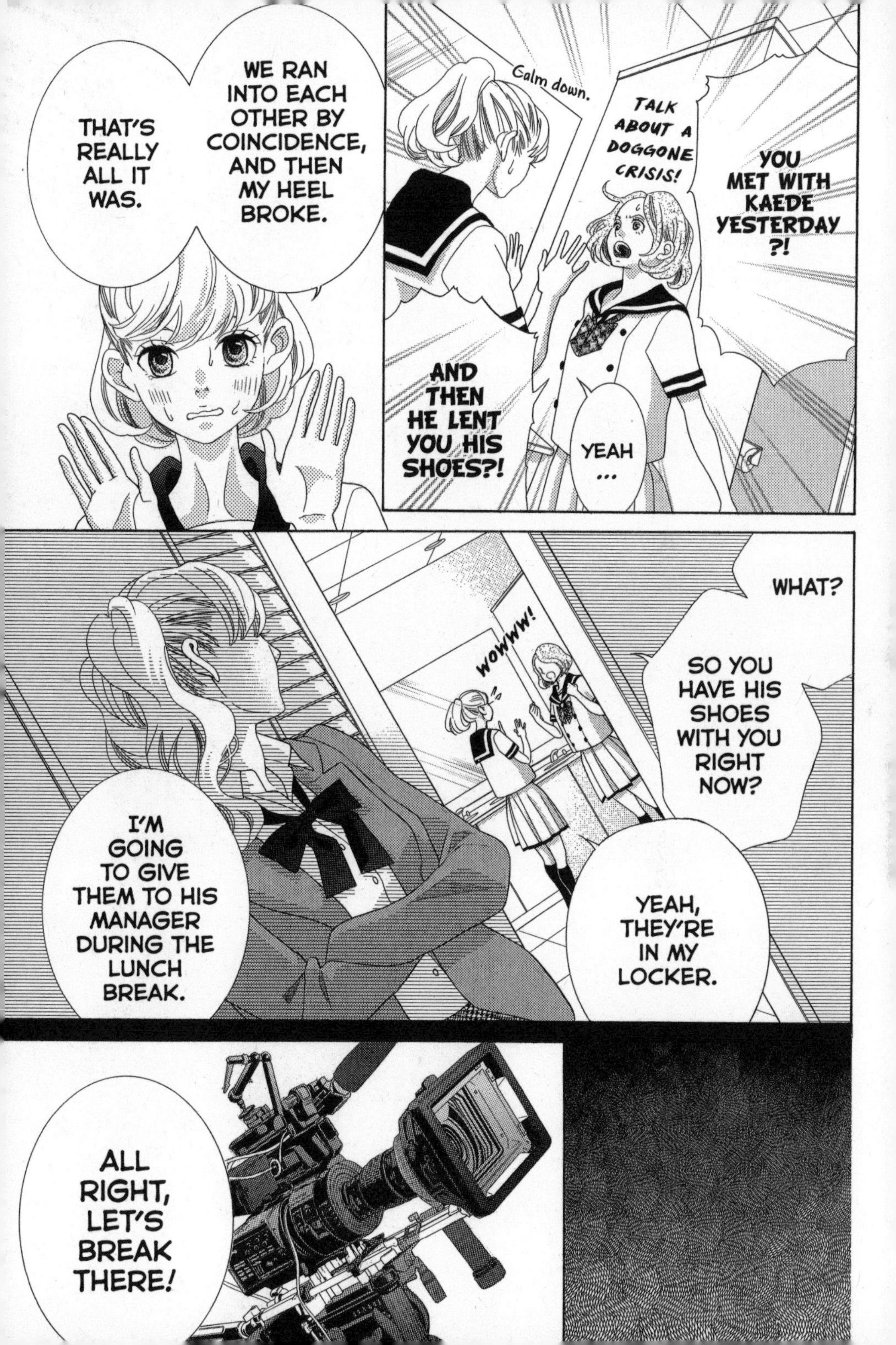
YOU MET WITH KAEDE YESTERDAY?!
TALK ABOUT A DOGGONE CRISIS!
Calm down.
YEAH...
AND THEN HE LENT YOU HIS SHOES?!
WE RAN INTO EACH OTHER BY COINCIDENCE, AND THEN MY HEEL BROKE.
THAT'S REALLY ALL IT WAS.
WHAT?
SO YOU HAVE HIS SHOES WITH YOU RIGHT NOW?
WOWWW!
YEAH, THEY'RE IN MY LOCKER.
I'M GOING TO GIVE THEM TO HIS MANAGER DURING THE LUNCH BREAK.
ALL RIGHT, LET'S BREAK THERE!

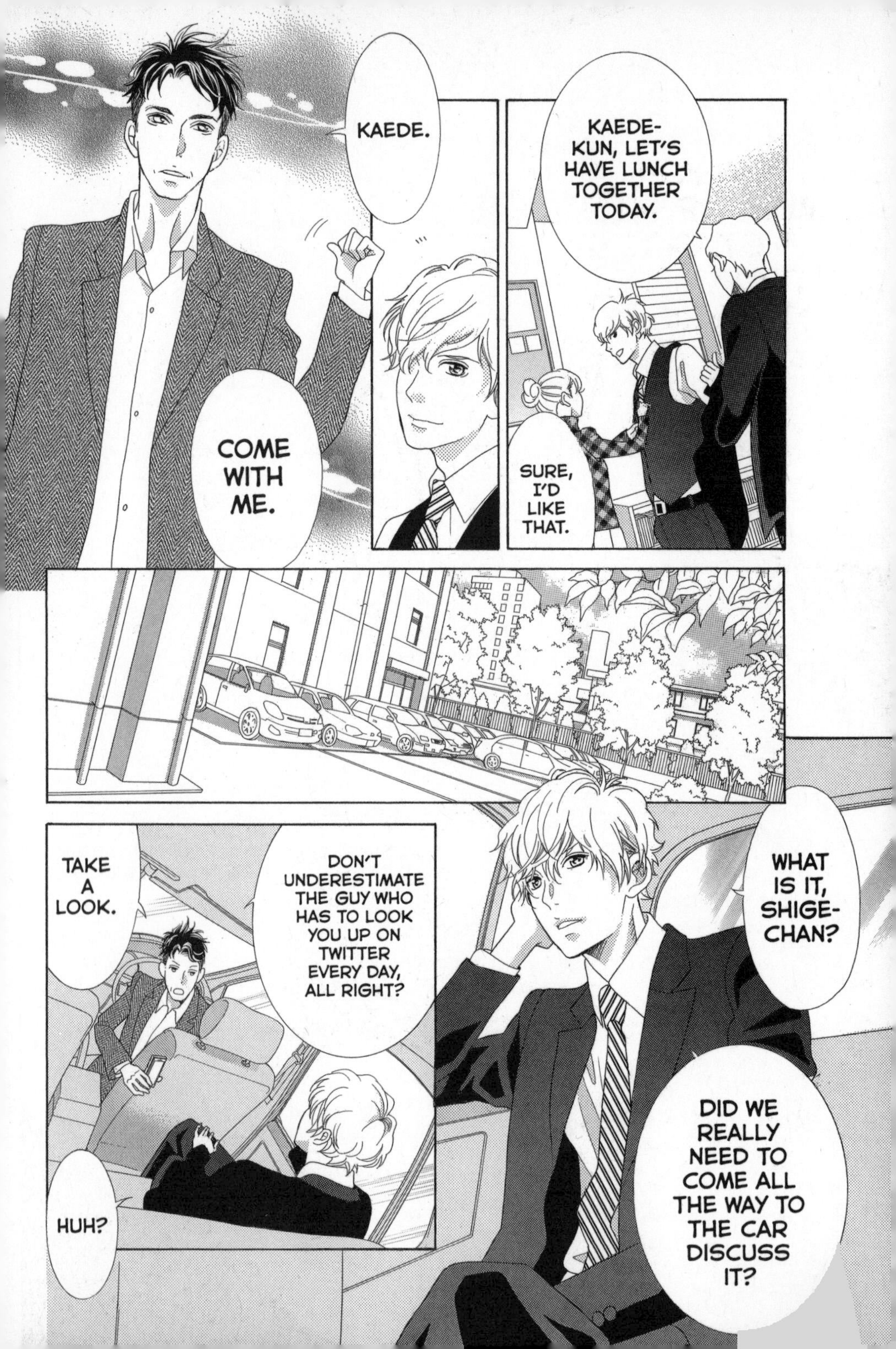
KAEDE-KUN, LET'S HAVE LUNCH TOGETHER TODAY.
SURE, I'D LIKE THAT.
KAEDE.
COME WITH ME.
WHAT IS IT, SHIGE-CHAN?
DID WE REALLY NEED TO COME ALL THE WAY TO THE CAR DISCUSS IT?
DON'T UNDERESTIMATE THE GUY WHO HAS TO LOOK YOU UP ON TWITTER EVERY DAY, ALL RIGHT?
TAKE A LOOK.
HUH?

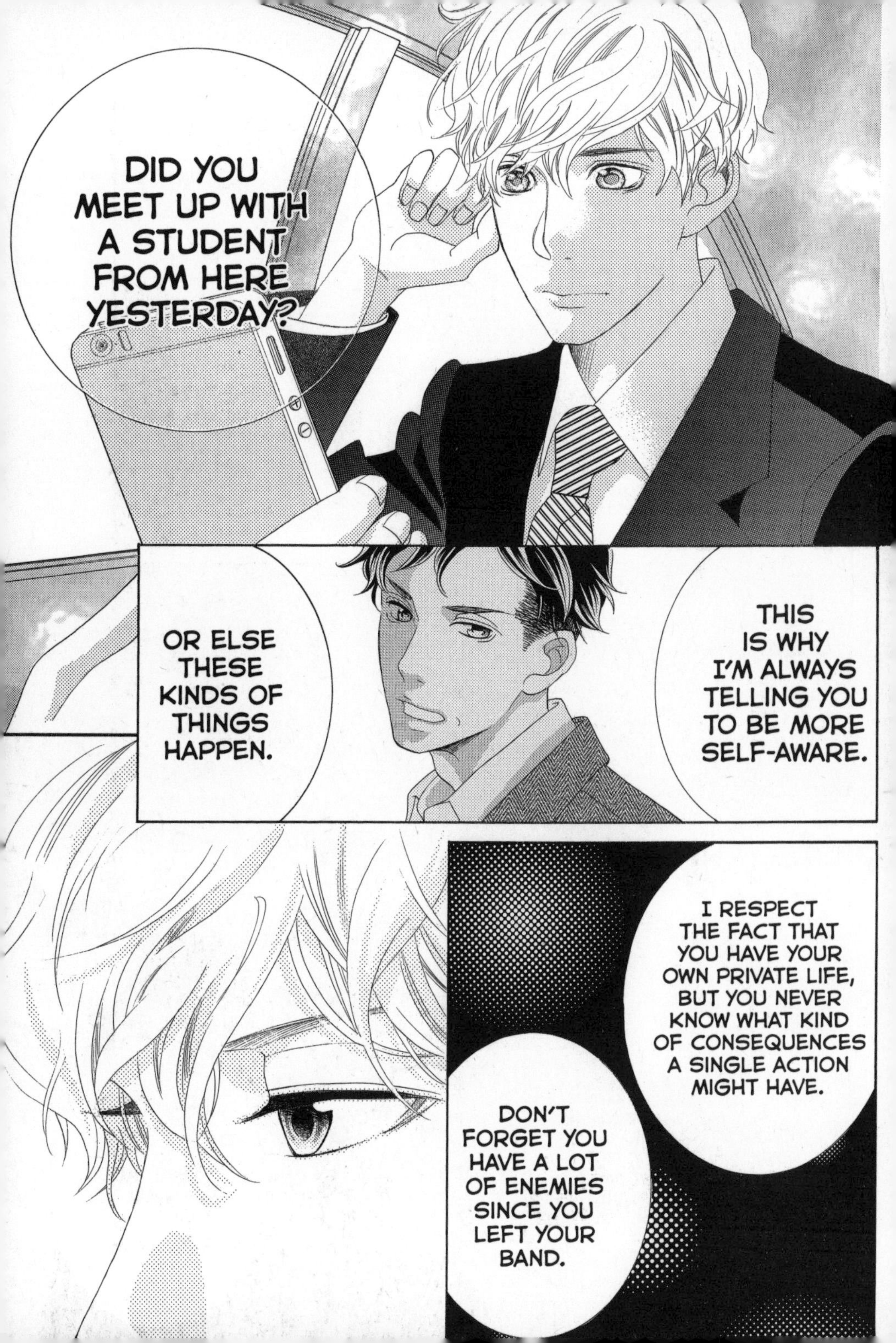
DID YOU MEET UP WITH A STUDENT FROM HERE YESTERDAY?
THIS IS WHY I'M ALWAYS TELLING YOU TO BE MORE SELF-AWARE.
OR ELSE THESE KINDS OF THINGS HAPPEN.
I RESPECT THE FACT THAT YOU HAVE YOUR OWN PRIVATE LIFE, BUT YOU NEVER KNOW WHAT KIND OF CONSEQUENCES A SINGLE ACTION MIGHT HAVE.
DON'T FORGET YOU HAVE A LOT OF ENEMIES SINCE YOU LEFT YOUR BAND.

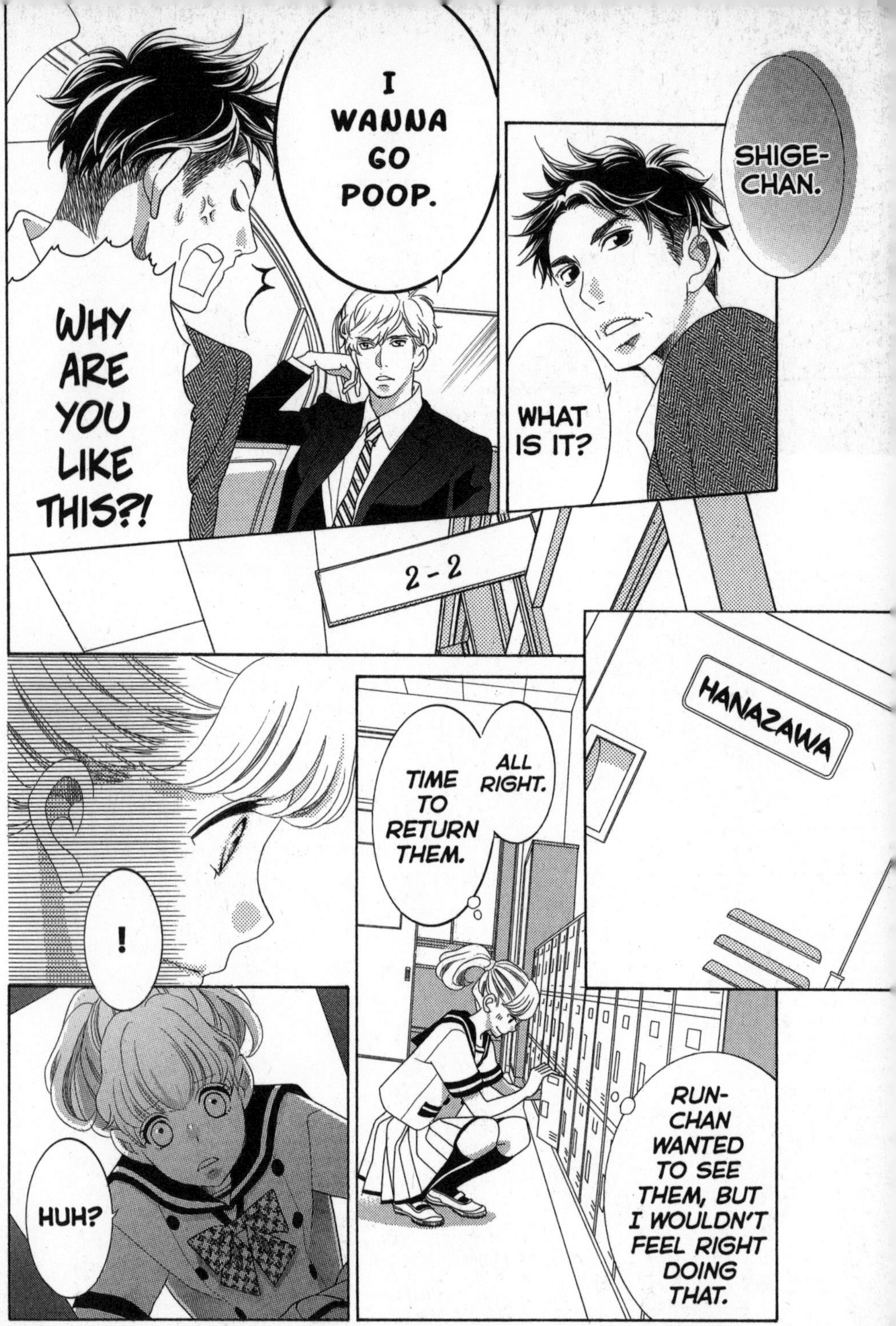
SHIGE-CHAN.
WHAT IS IT?
I WANNA GO POOP.
WHY ARE YOU LIKE THIS?!
2-2
HANAZAWA
ALL RIGHT.
TIME TO RETURN THEM.
RUN-CHAN WANTED TO SEE THEM, BUT I WOULDN'T FEEL RIGHT DOING THAT.
!
HUH?

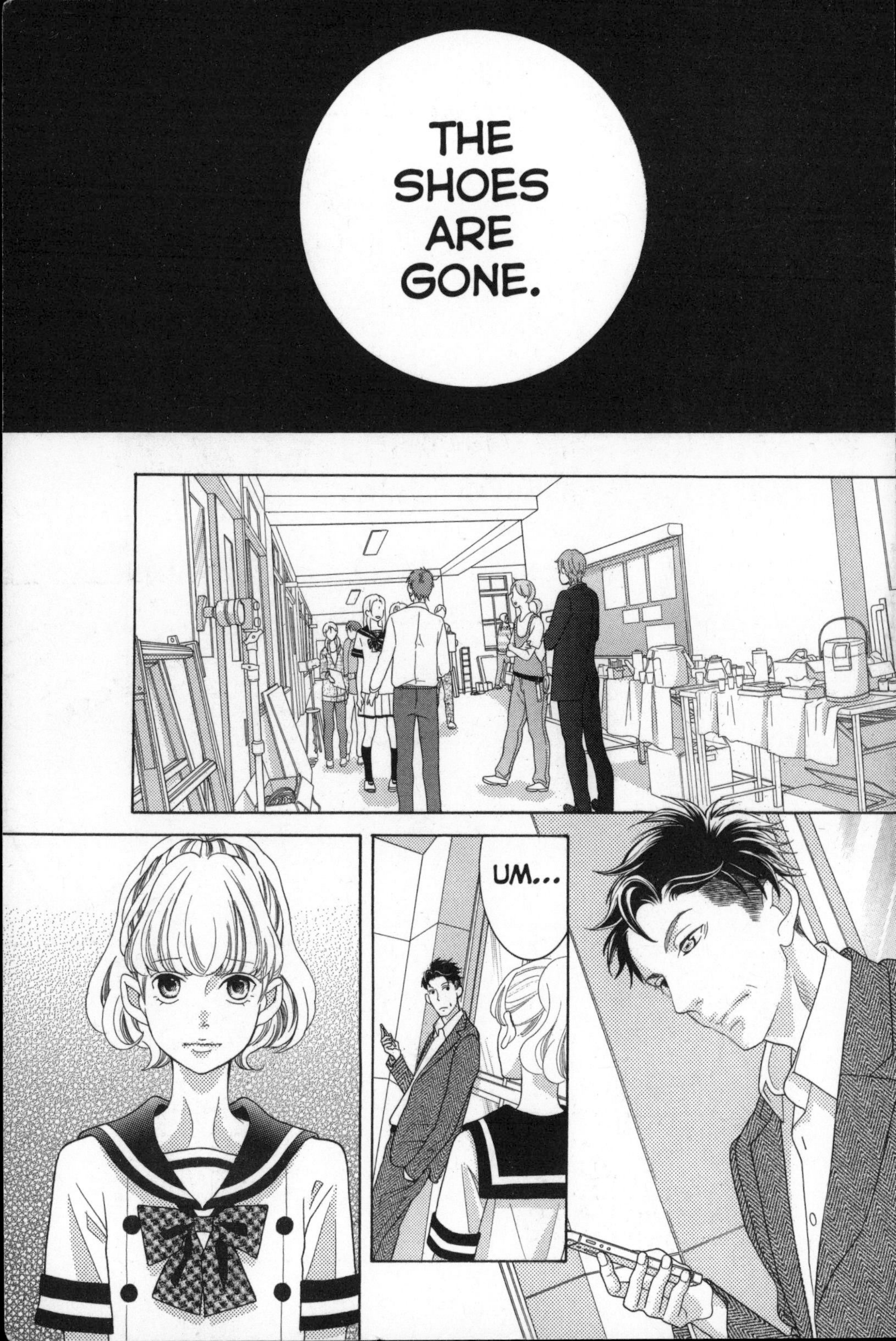
THE SHOES ARE GONE.
UM...

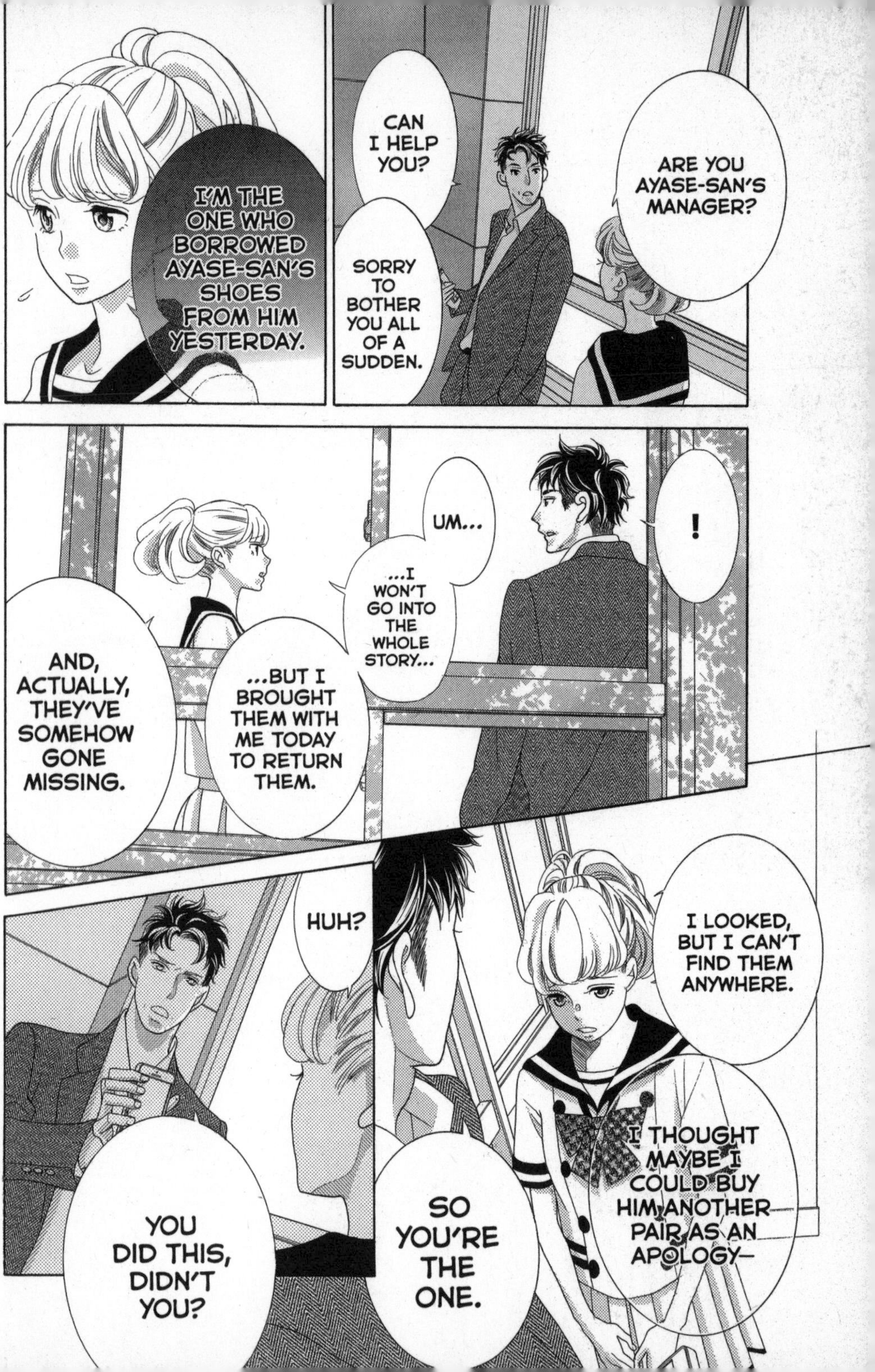
ARE YOU AYASE-SAN'S MANAGER?
CAN I HELP YOU?
SORRY TO BOTHER YOU ALL OF A SUDDEN.
I'M THE ONE WHO BORROWED AYASE-SAN'S SHOES FROM HIM YESTERDAY.
!
UM...
...I WON'T GO INTO THE WHOLE STORY...
...BUT I BROUGHT THEM WITH ME TODAY TO RETURN THEM.
AND, ACTUALLY, THEY'VE SOMEHOW GONE MISSING.
I LOOKED, BUT I CAN'T FIND THEM ANYWHERE.
I THOUGHT MAYBE I COULD BUY HIM ANOTHER PAIR AS AN APOLOGY—
SO YOU'RE THE ONE.
HUH?
YOU DID THIS, DIDN'T YOU?

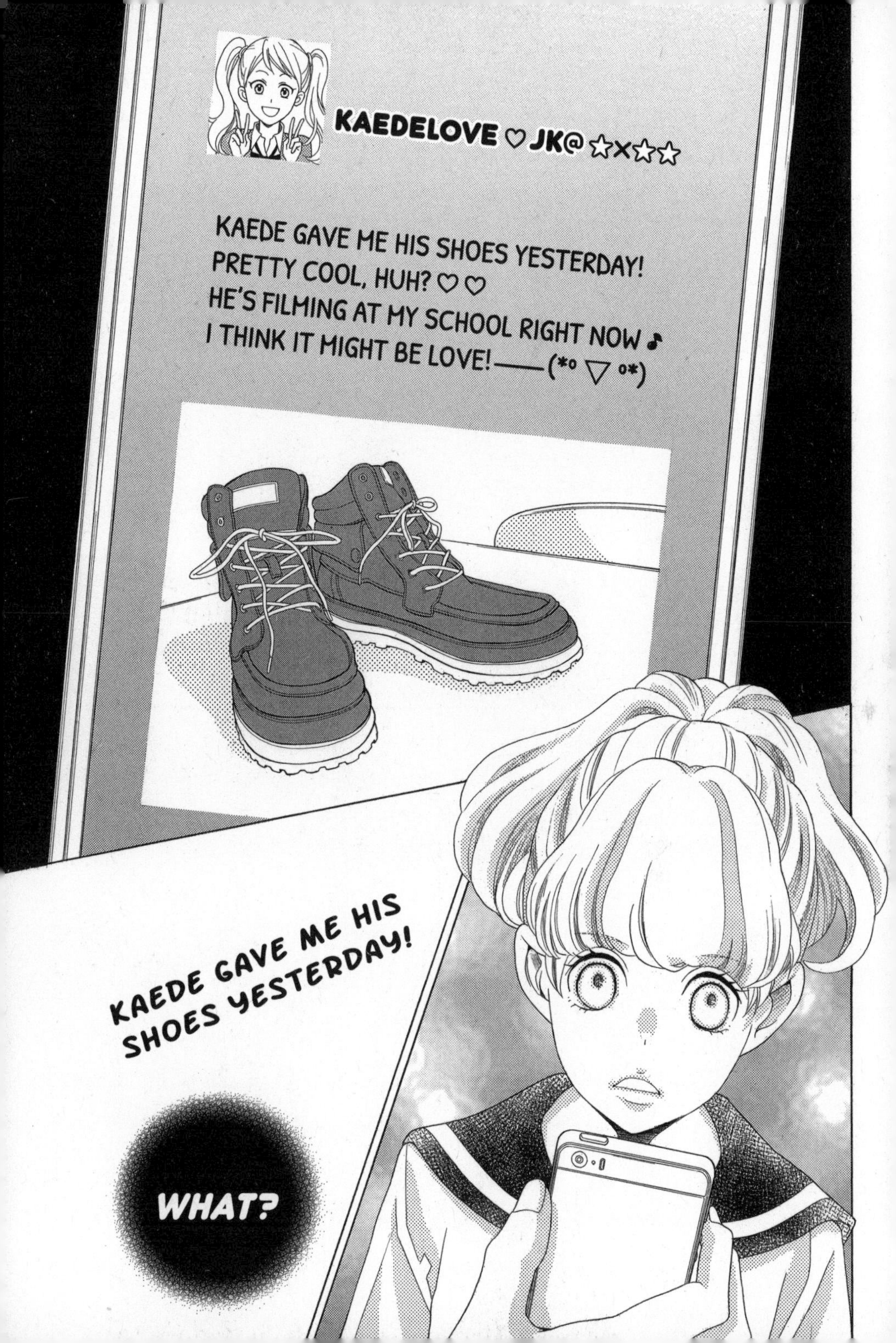
KAEDELOVE ♡ JK@ ☆×☆☆
KAEDE GAVE ME HIS SHOES YESTERDAY! PRETTY COOL, HUH? ♡♡ HE'S FILMING AT MY SCHOOL RIGHT NOW ♪ I THINK IT MIGHT BE LOVE!——(*o ▽ o*)
KAEDE GAVE ME HIS SHOES YESTERDAY!
WHAT?

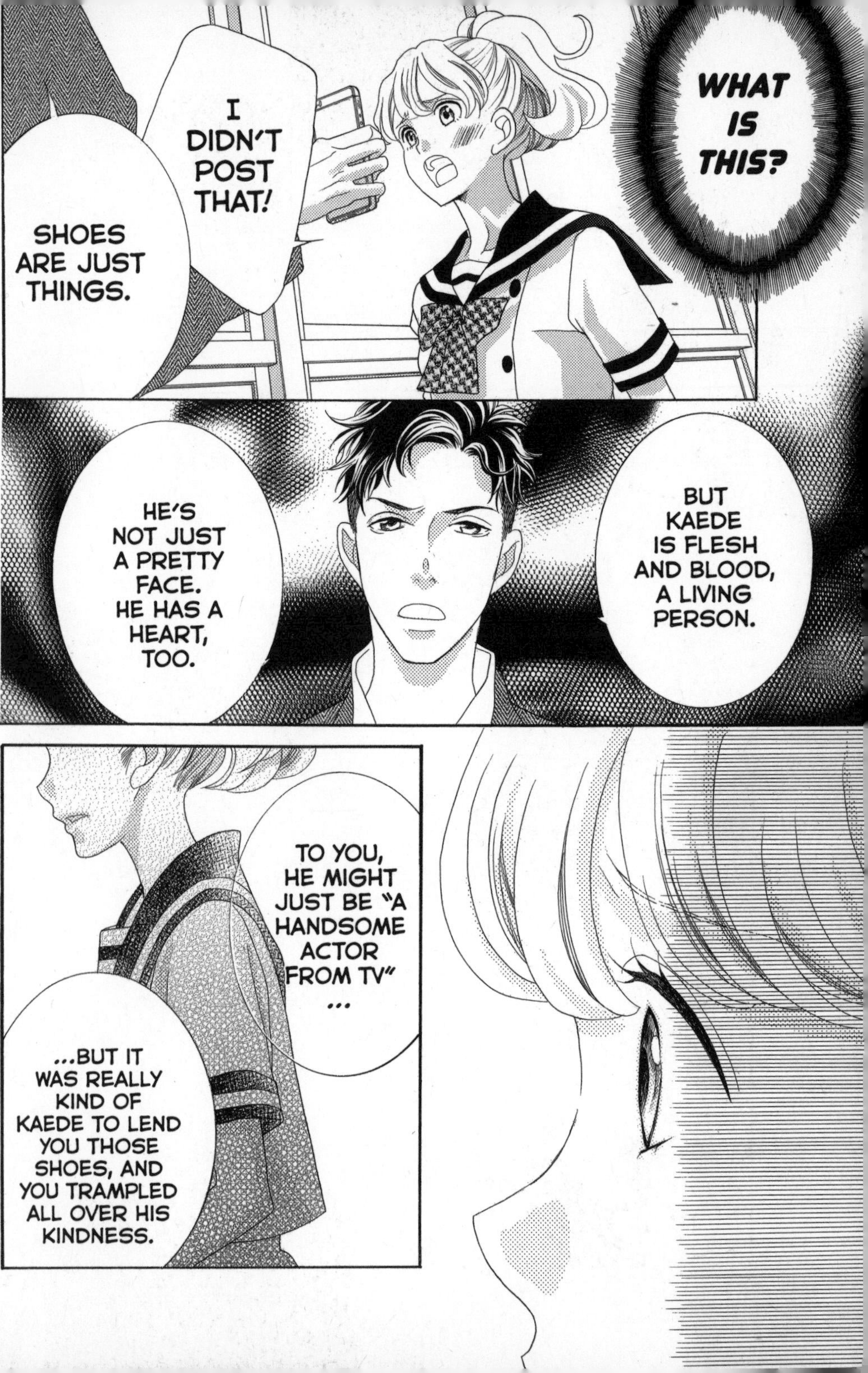
WHAT IS THIS?
I DIDN'T POST THAT!
SHOES ARE JUST THINGS.
BUT KAEDE IS FLESH AND BLOOD, A LIVING PERSON.
HE'S NOT JUST A PRETTY FACE. HE HAS A HEART, TOO.
TO YOU, HE MIGHT JUST BE "A HANDSOME ACTOR FROM TV"...
...BUT IT WAS REALLY KIND OF KAEDE TO LEND YOU THOSE SHOES, AND YOU TRAMPLED ALL OVER HIS KINDNESS.

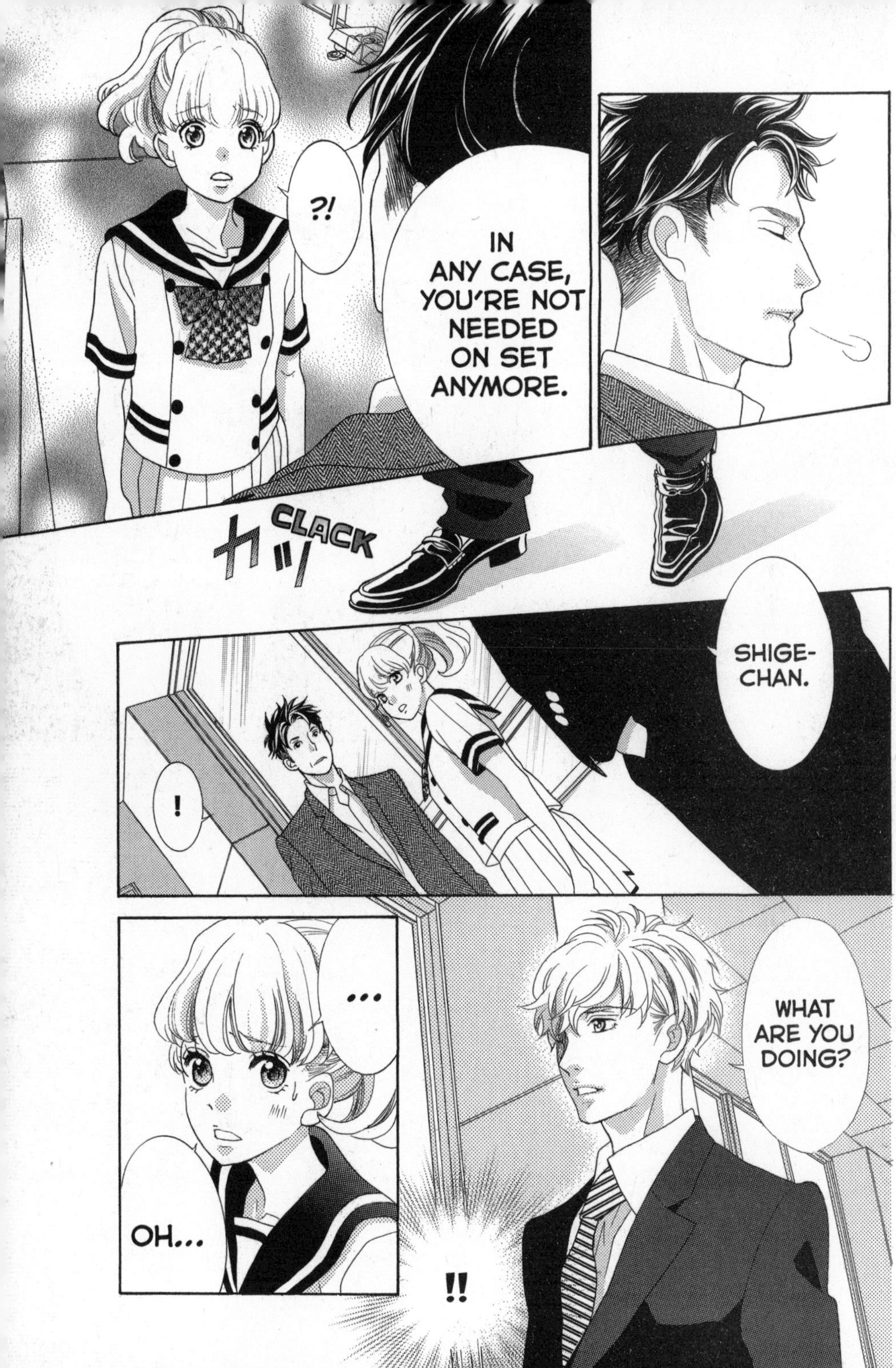
IN ANY CASE, YOU'RE NOT NEEDED ON SET ANYMORE.
?!
カッ CLACK
SHIGE-CHAN.
!
WHAT ARE YOU DOING?
!!
...
OH...

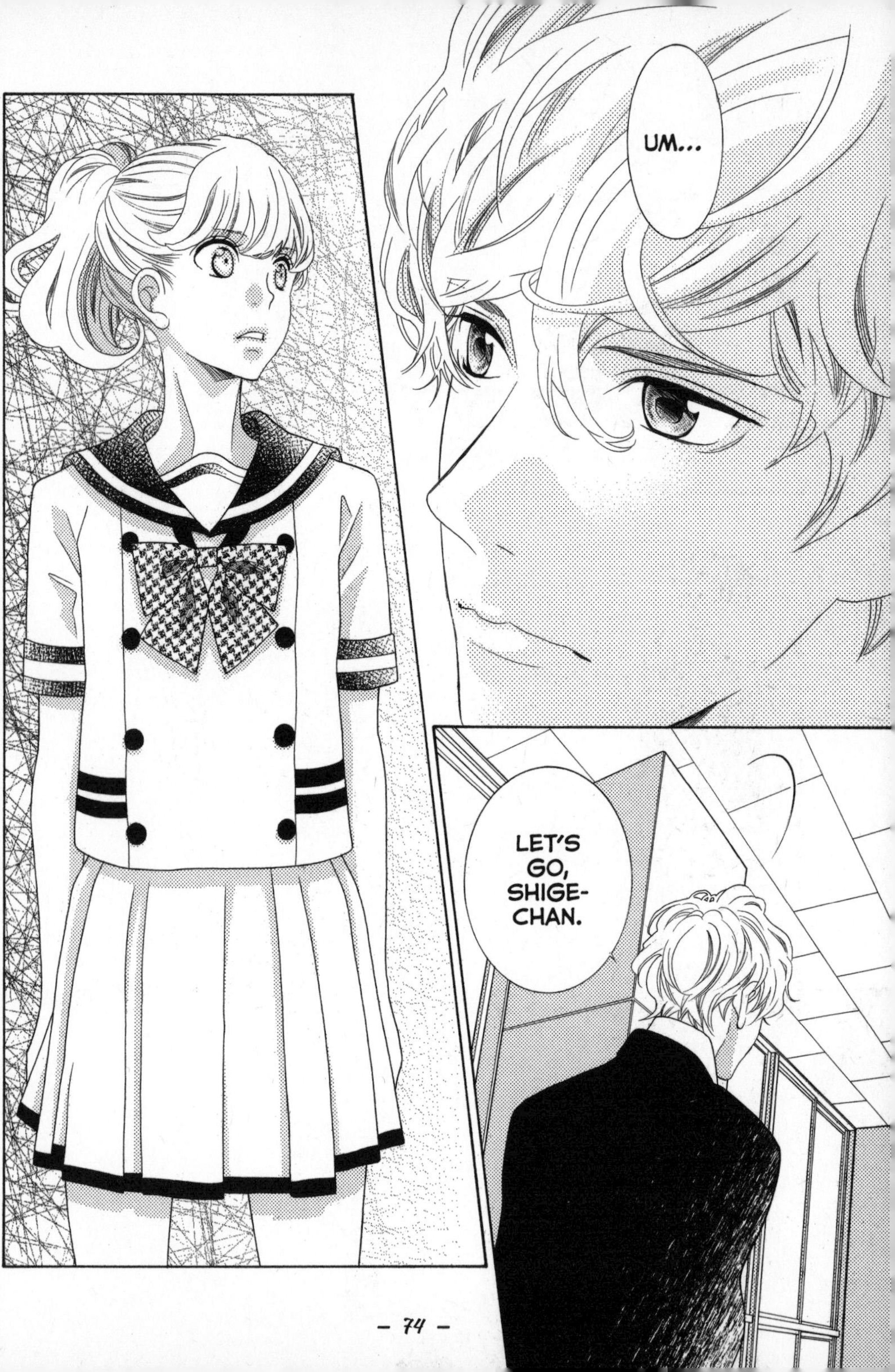
UM...
LET'S GO, SHIGE-CHAN.

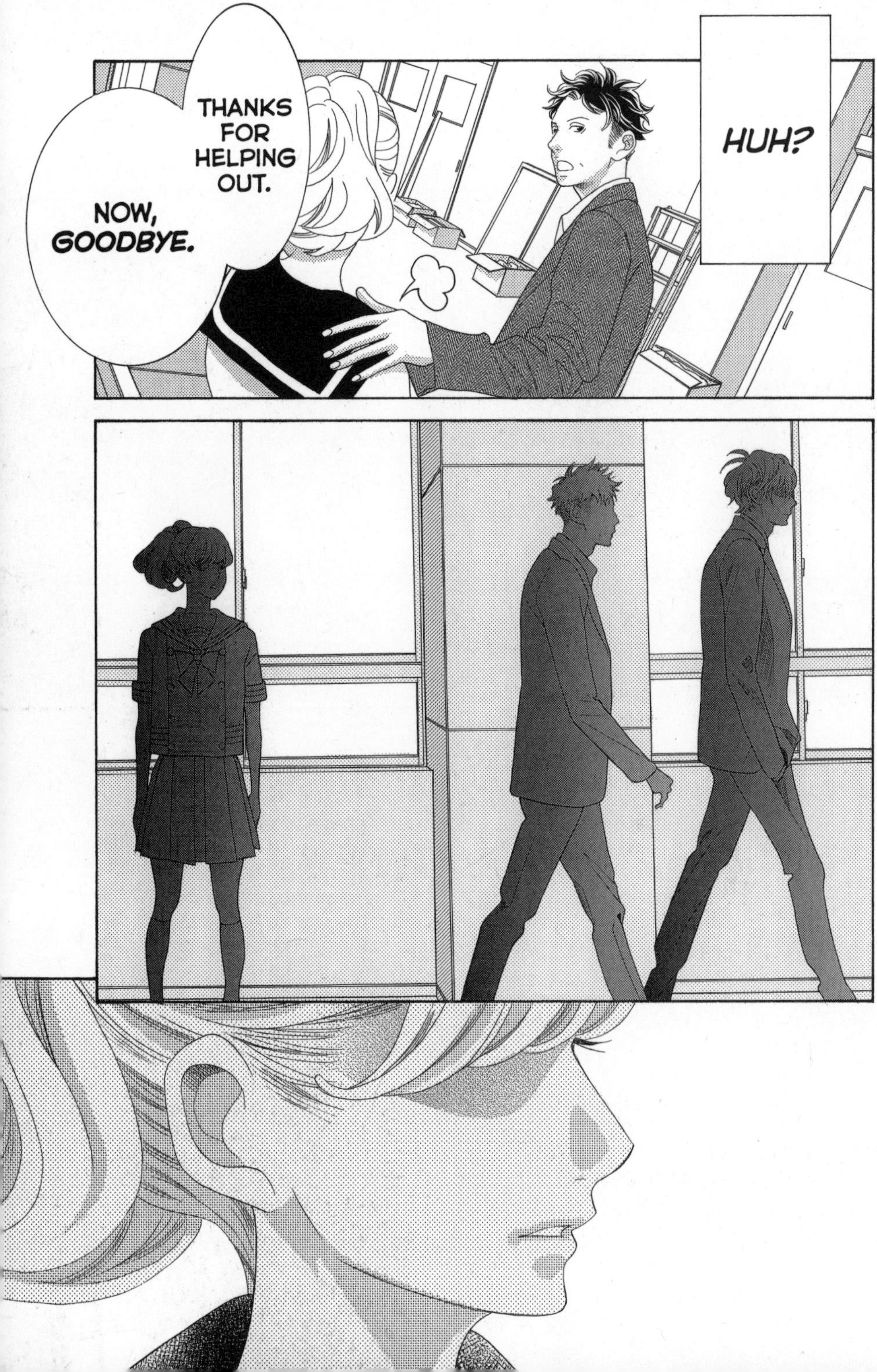
HUH?
THANKS FOR HELPING OUT.
NOW, GOODBYE.

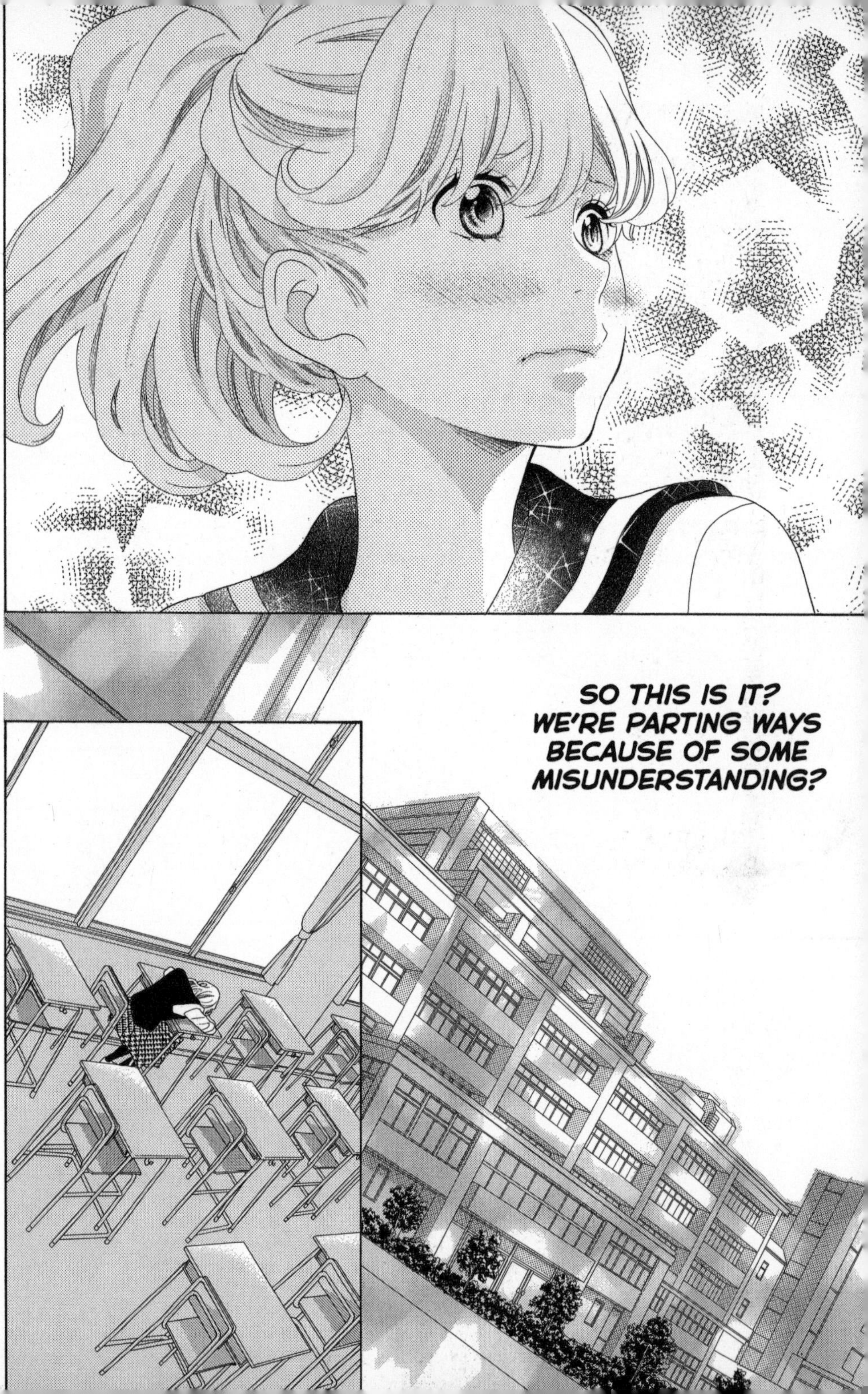
SO THIS IS IT?
WE'RE PARTING WAYS
BECAUSE OF SOME
MISUNDERSTANDING?

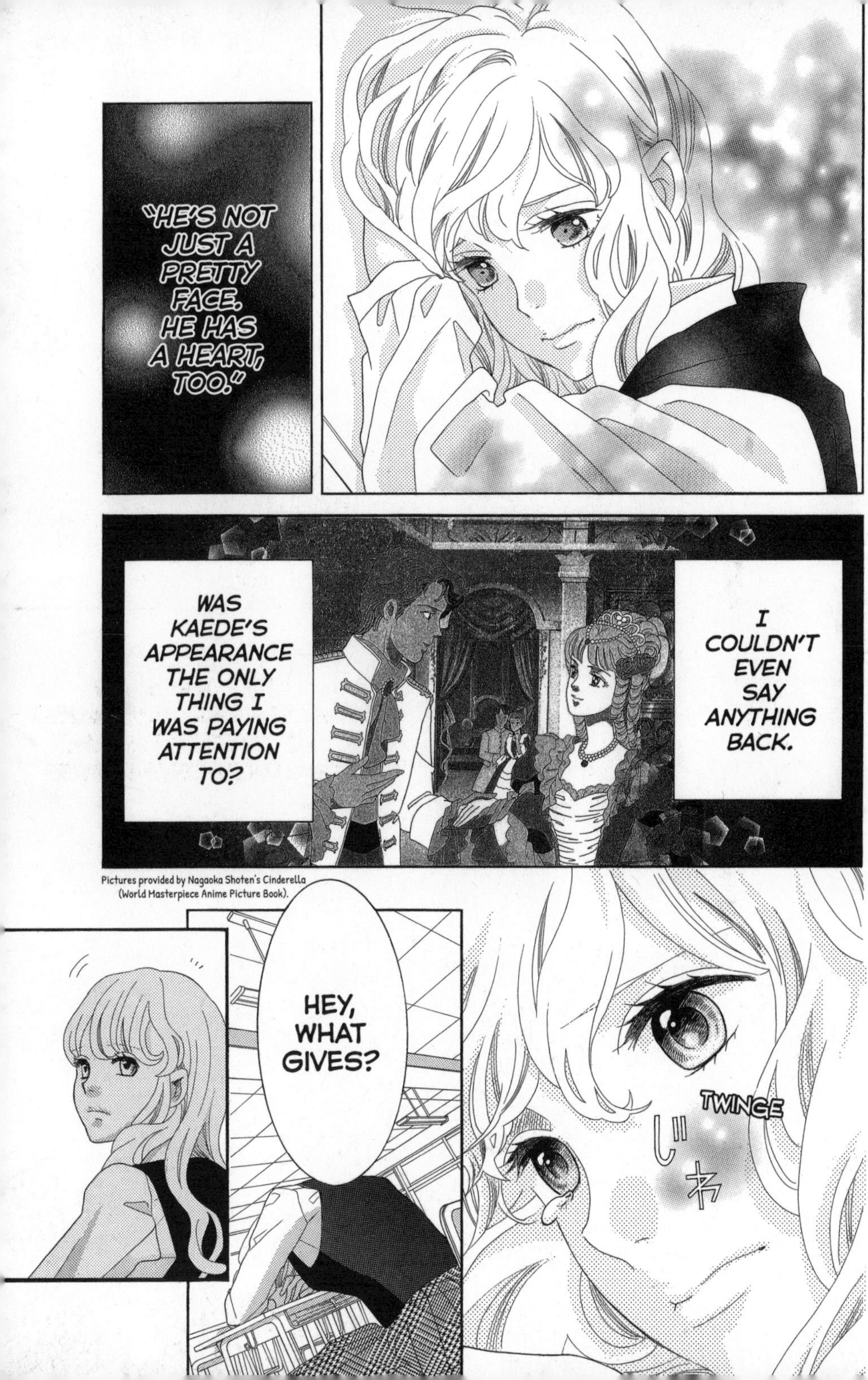
"HE'S NOT JUST A PRETTY FACE. HE HAS A HEART, TOO."
I COULDN'T EVEN SAY ANYTHING BACK.
WAS KAEDE'S APPEARANCE THE ONLY THING I WAS PAYING ATTENTION TO?
TWINGE
じわ
HEY, WHAT GIVES?

Pictures provided by Nagaoka Shoten's Cinderella (World Masterpiece Anime Picture Book).

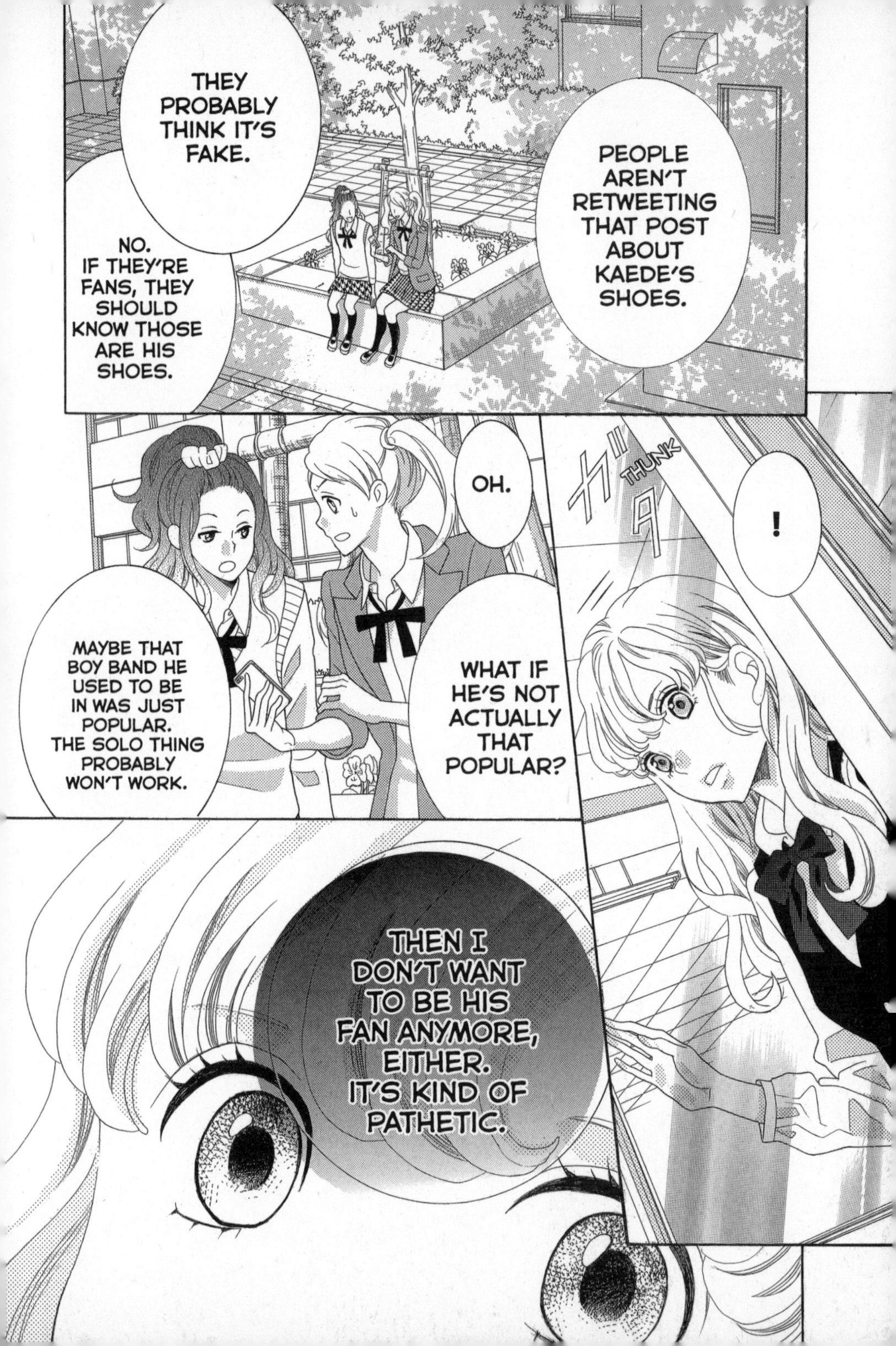
PEOPLE AREN'T RETWEETING THAT POST ABOUT KAEDE'S SHOES.
THEY PROBABLY THINK IT'S FAKE.
NO. IF THEY'RE FANS, THEY SHOULD KNOW THOSE ARE HIS SHOES.
THUNK
!
OH.
WHAT IF HE'S NOT ACTUALLY THAT POPULAR?
MAYBE THAT BOY BAND HE USED TO BE IN WAS JUST POPULAR. THE SOLO THING PROBABLY WON'T WORK.
THEN I DON'T WANT TO BE HIS FAN ANYMORE, EITHER. IT'S KIND OF PATHETIC.

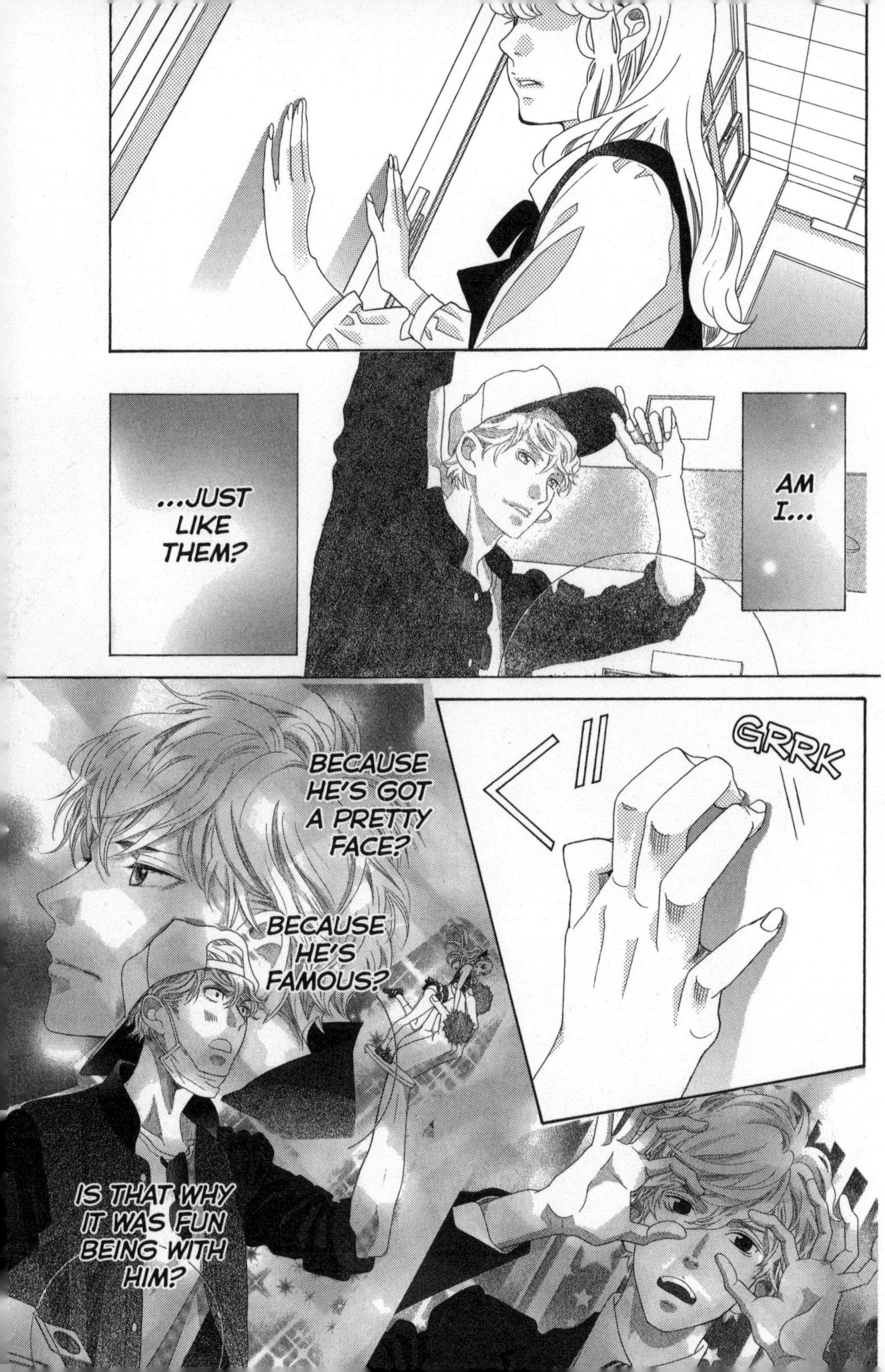
AM I...
...JUST LIKE THEM?
GRRK
BECAUSE HE'S GOT A PRETTY FACE?
BECAUSE HE'S FAMOUS?
IS THAT WHY IT WAS FUN BEING WITH HIM?

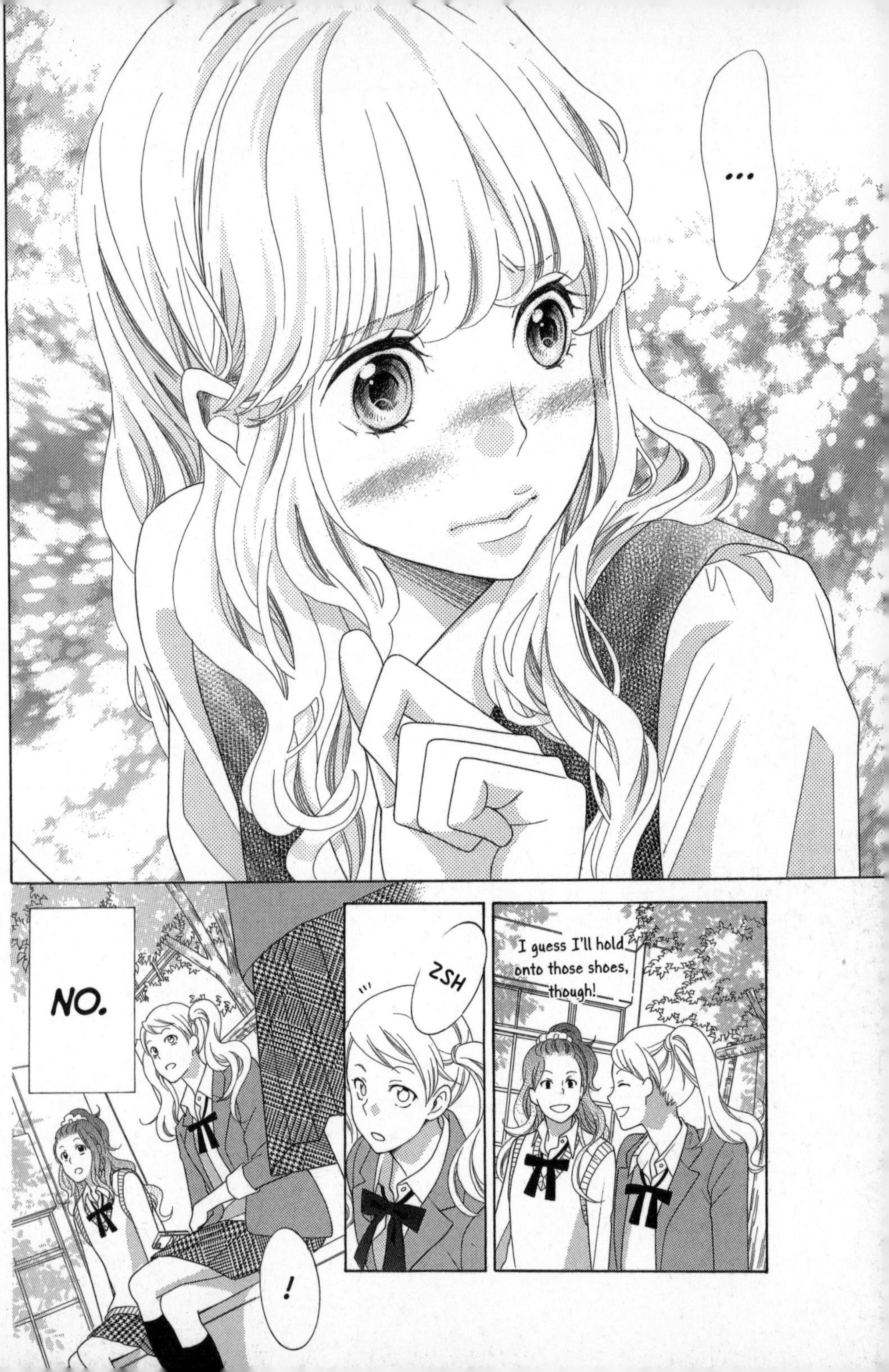
...
I guess I'll hold onto those shoes, though!
ZSH
NO.
!

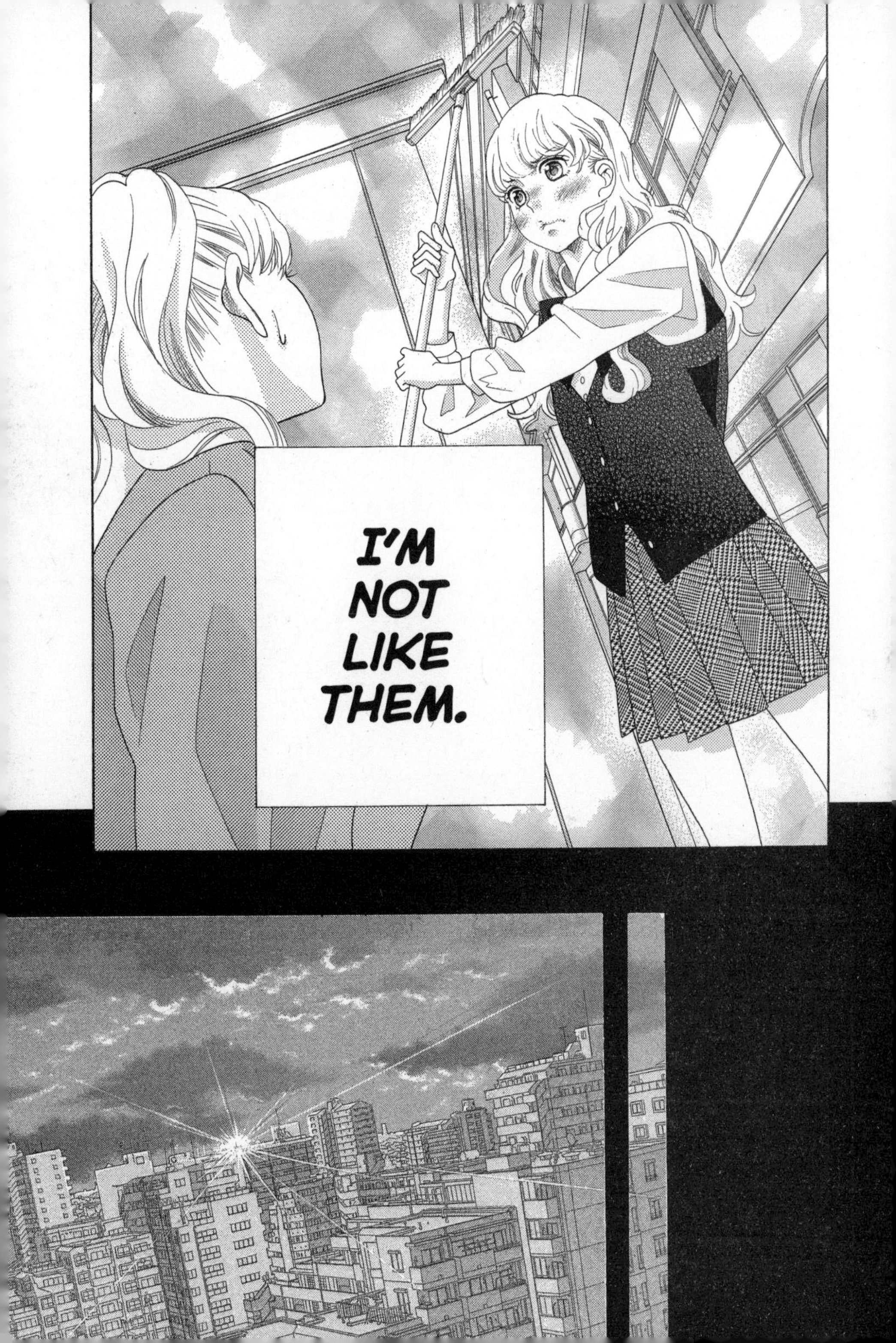
I'M NOT LIKE THEM.

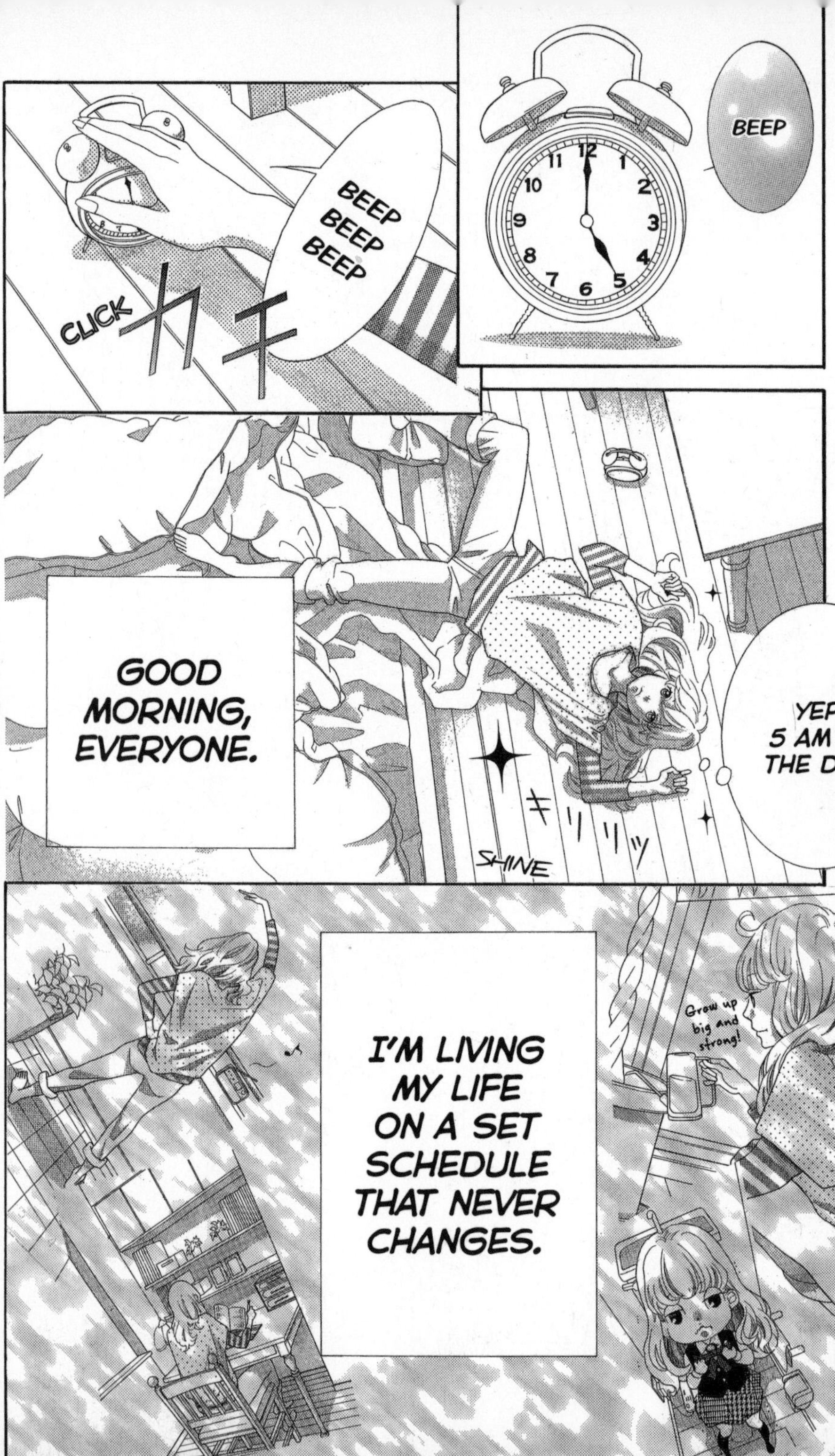
BEEP
BEEP BEEP BEEP
CLICK カチ
YEP, 5 AM ON THE DOT.
GOOD MORNING, EVERYONE.
SHINE キリリッ
Grow up big and strong!
I'M LIVING MY LIFE ON A SET SCHEDULE THAT NEVER CHANGES.

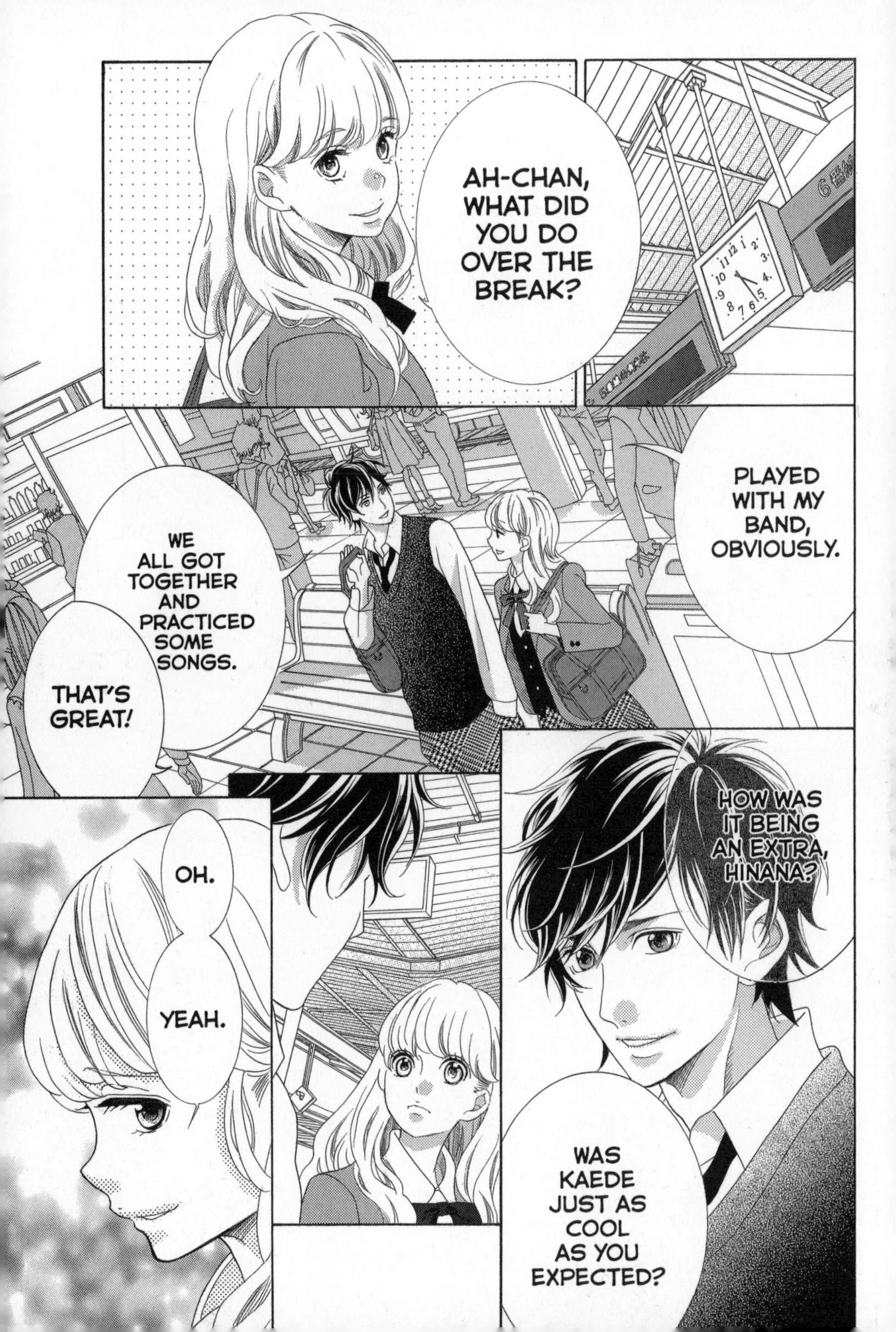
AH-CHAN, WHAT DID YOU DO OVER THE BREAK?
PLAYED WITH MY BAND, OBVIOUSLY.
WE ALL GOT TOGETHER AND PRACTICED SOME SONGS.
THAT'S GREAT!
HOW WAS IT BEING AN EXTRA, HINANA?
WAS KAEDE JUST AS COOL AS YOU EXPECTED?
OH.
YEAH.

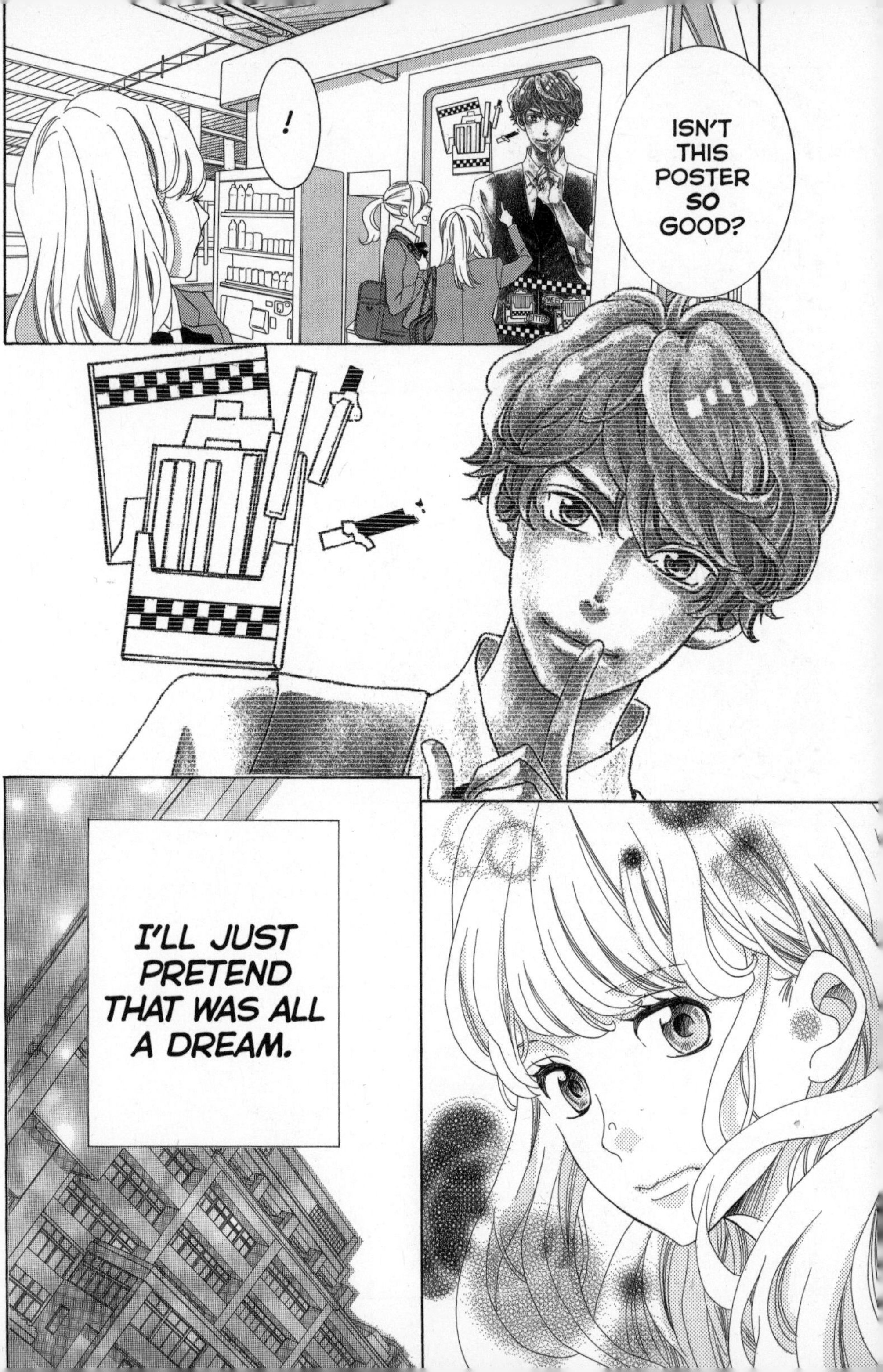
ISN'T THIS POSTER SO GOOD?
!
I'LL JUST PRETEND THAT WAS ALL A DREAM.

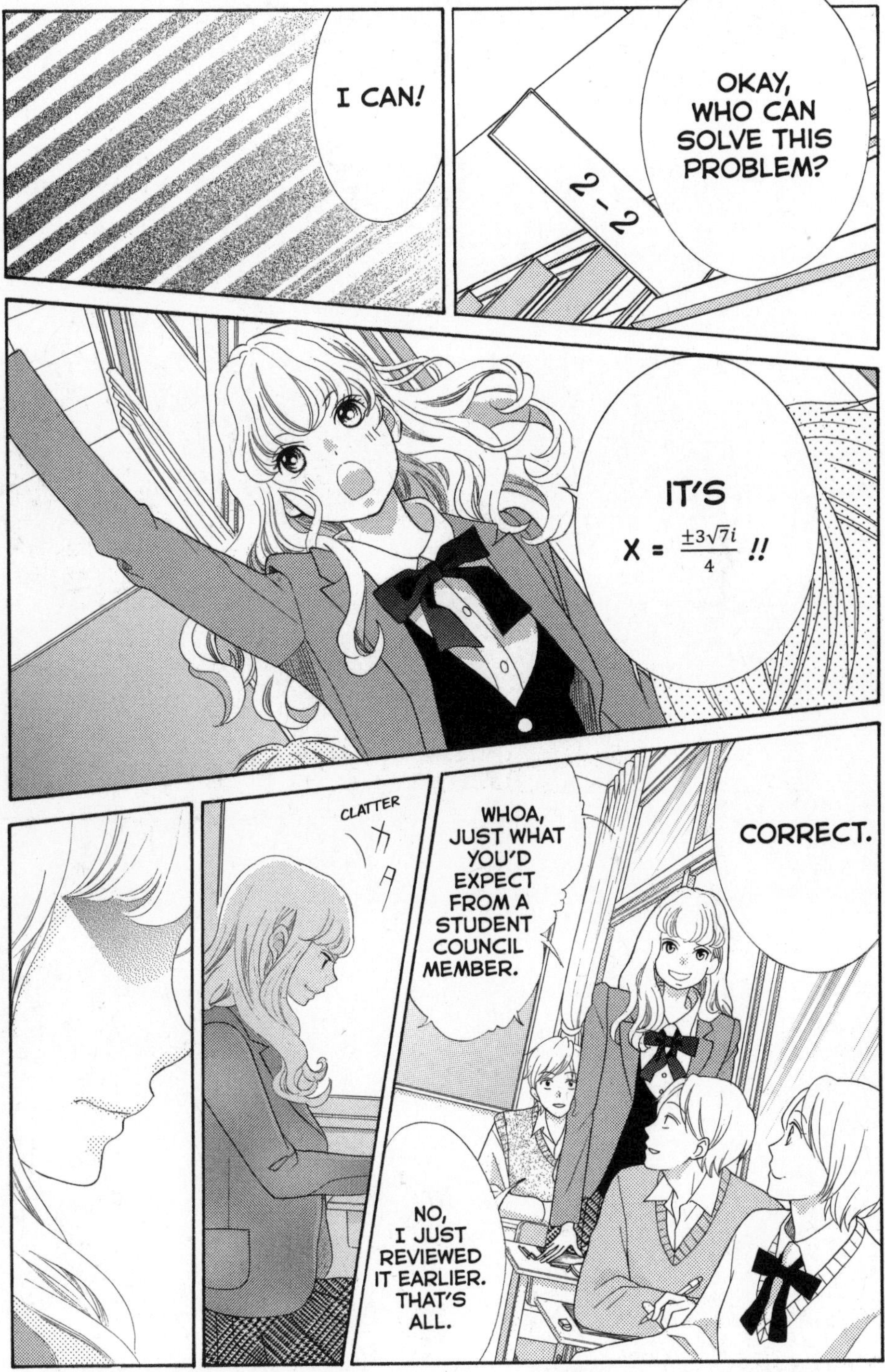
OKAY, WHO CAN SOLVE THIS PROBLEM?
2-2
I CAN!
IT'S
X = $\frac{\pm 3\sqrt{7}i}{4}$!!
CORRECT.
WHOA, JUST WHAT YOU'D EXPECT FROM A STUDENT COUNCIL MEMBER.
NO, I JUST REVIEWED IT EARLIER. THAT'S ALL.
CLATTER

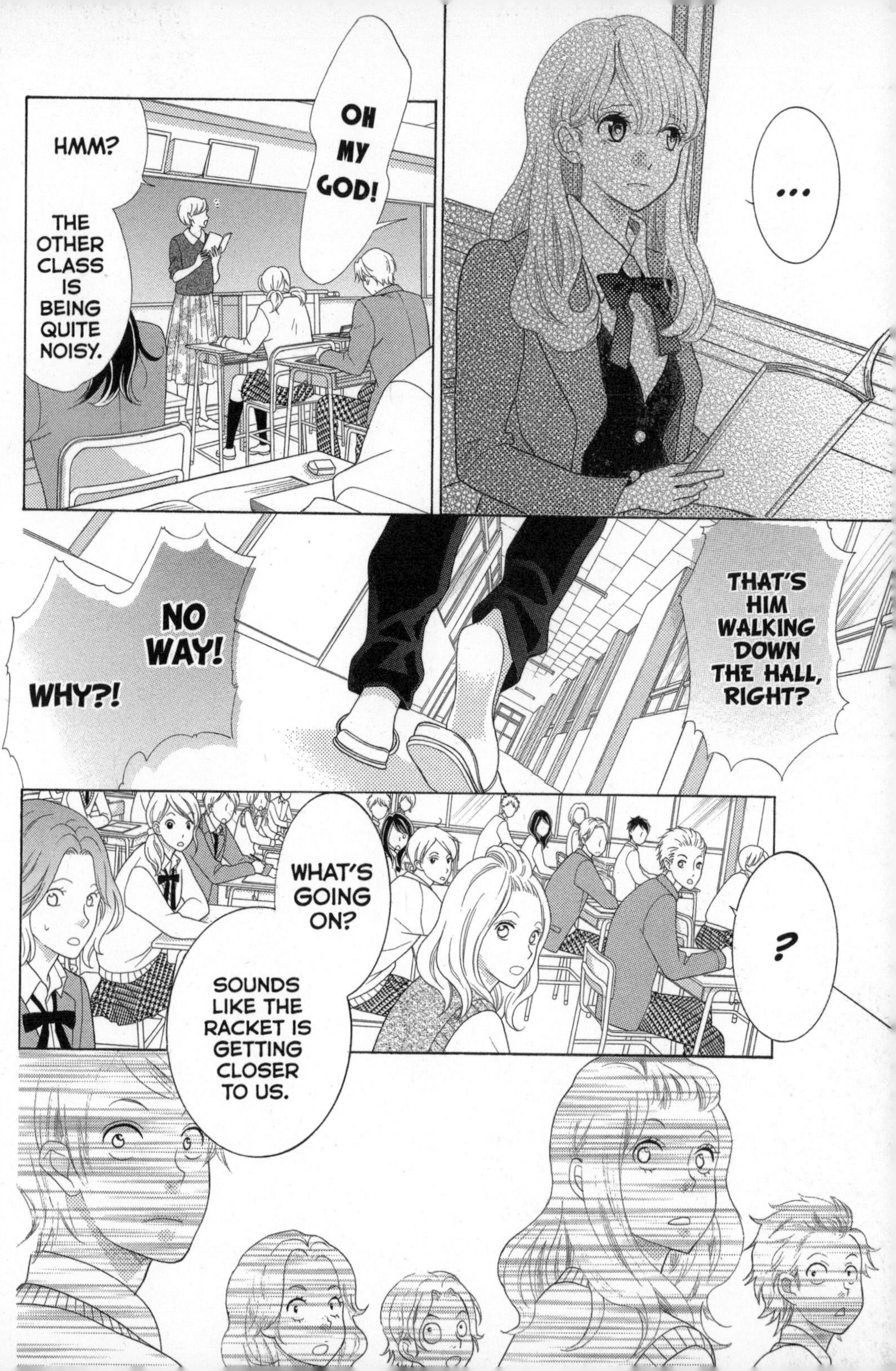
...
OH MY GOD!
HMM?
THE OTHER CLASS IS BEING QUITE NOISY.
THAT'S HIM WALKING DOWN THE HALL, RIGHT?
NO WAY!
WHY?!
?
WHAT'S GOING ON?
SOUNDS LIKE THE RACKET IS GETTING CLOSER TO US.

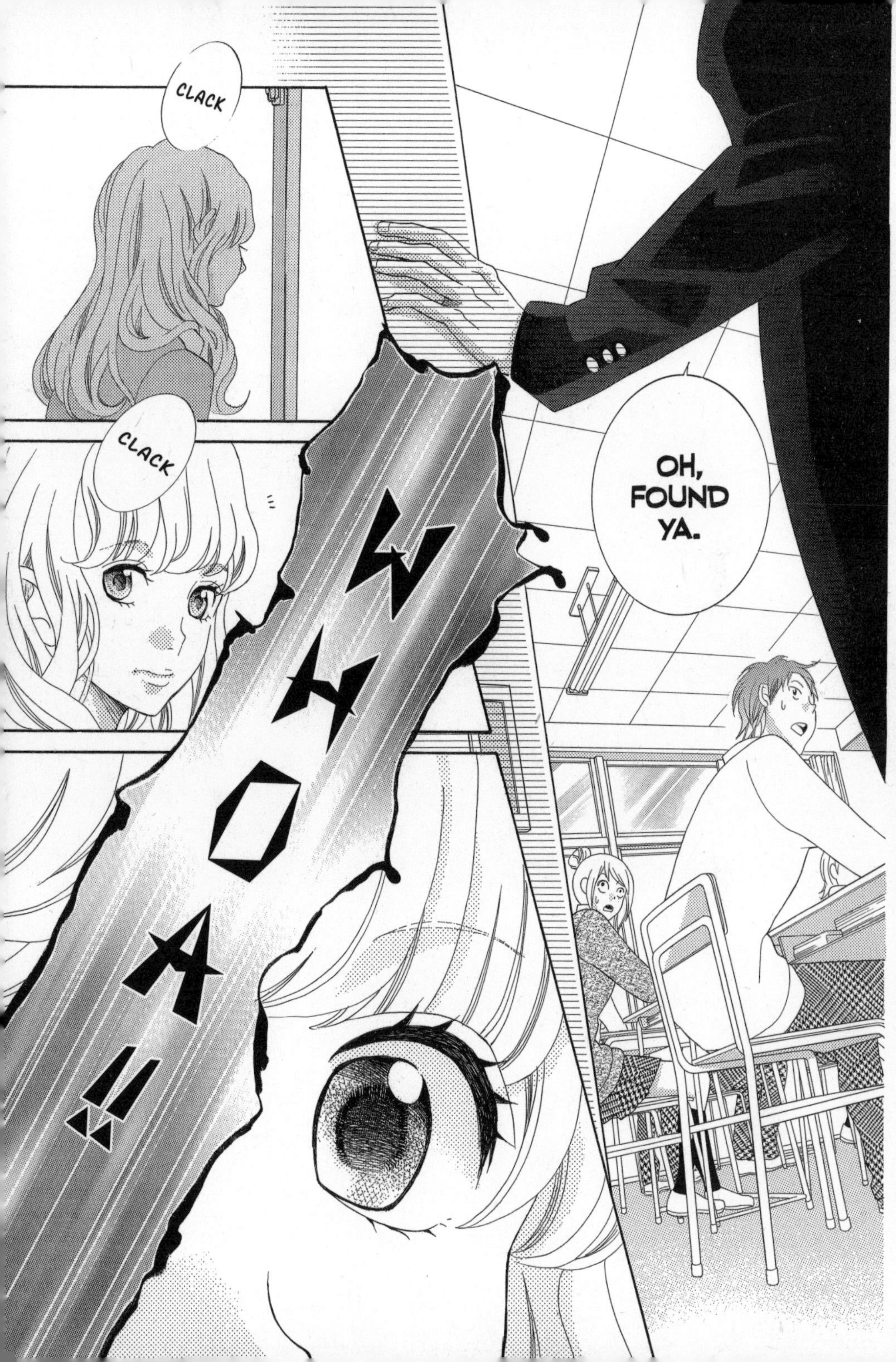
OH, FOUND YA.
CLACK
CLACK
WHOA!!

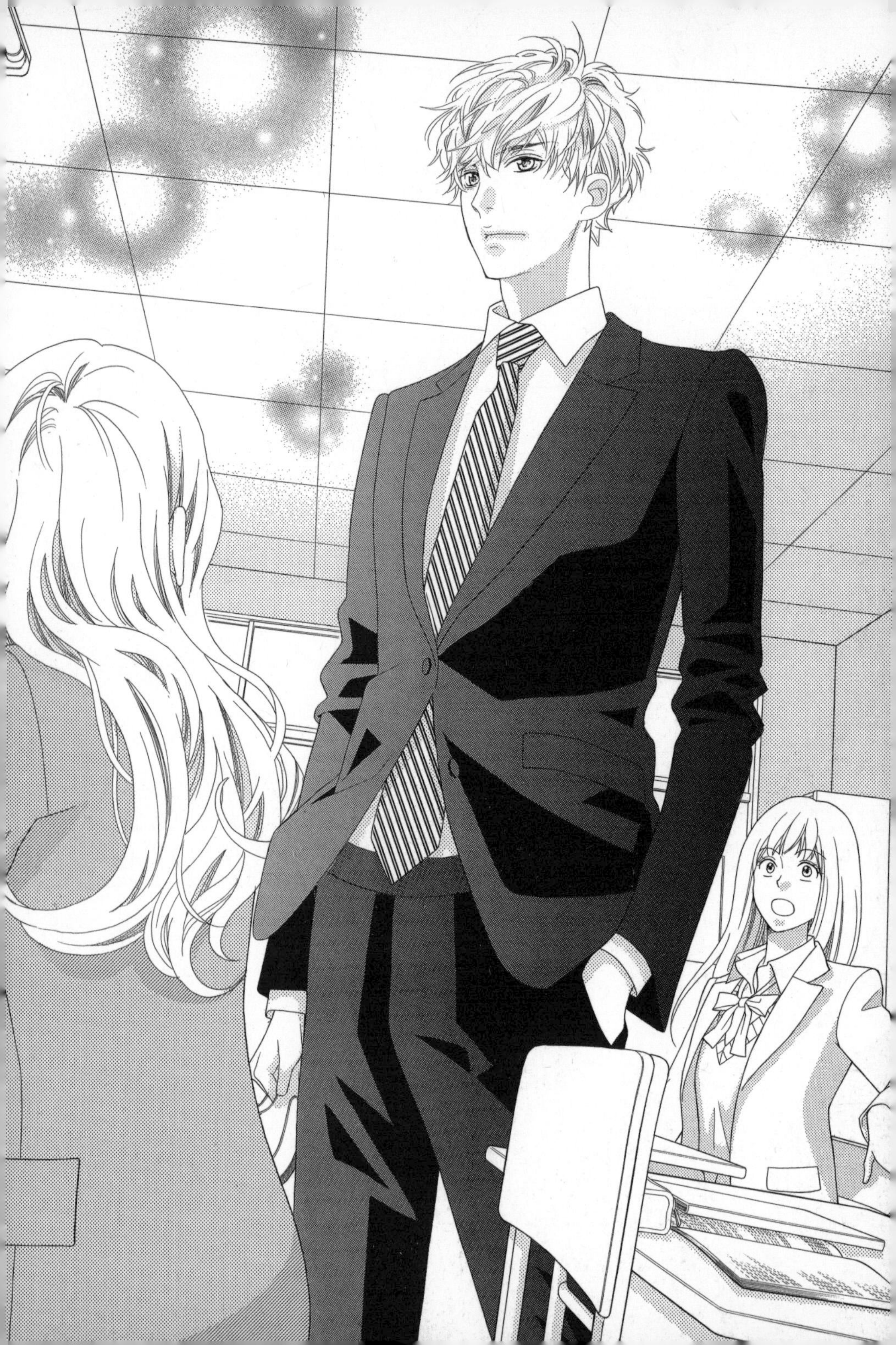

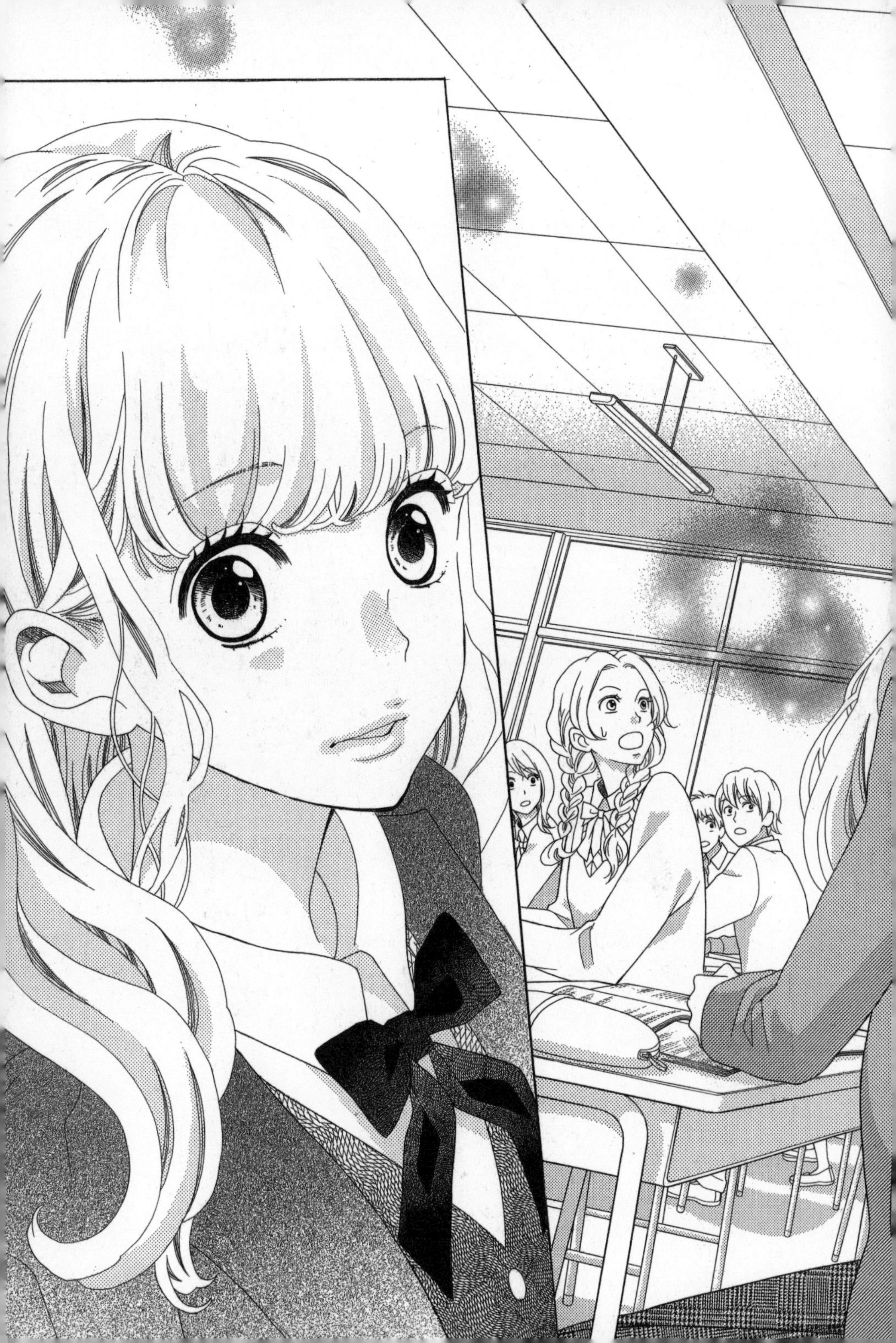

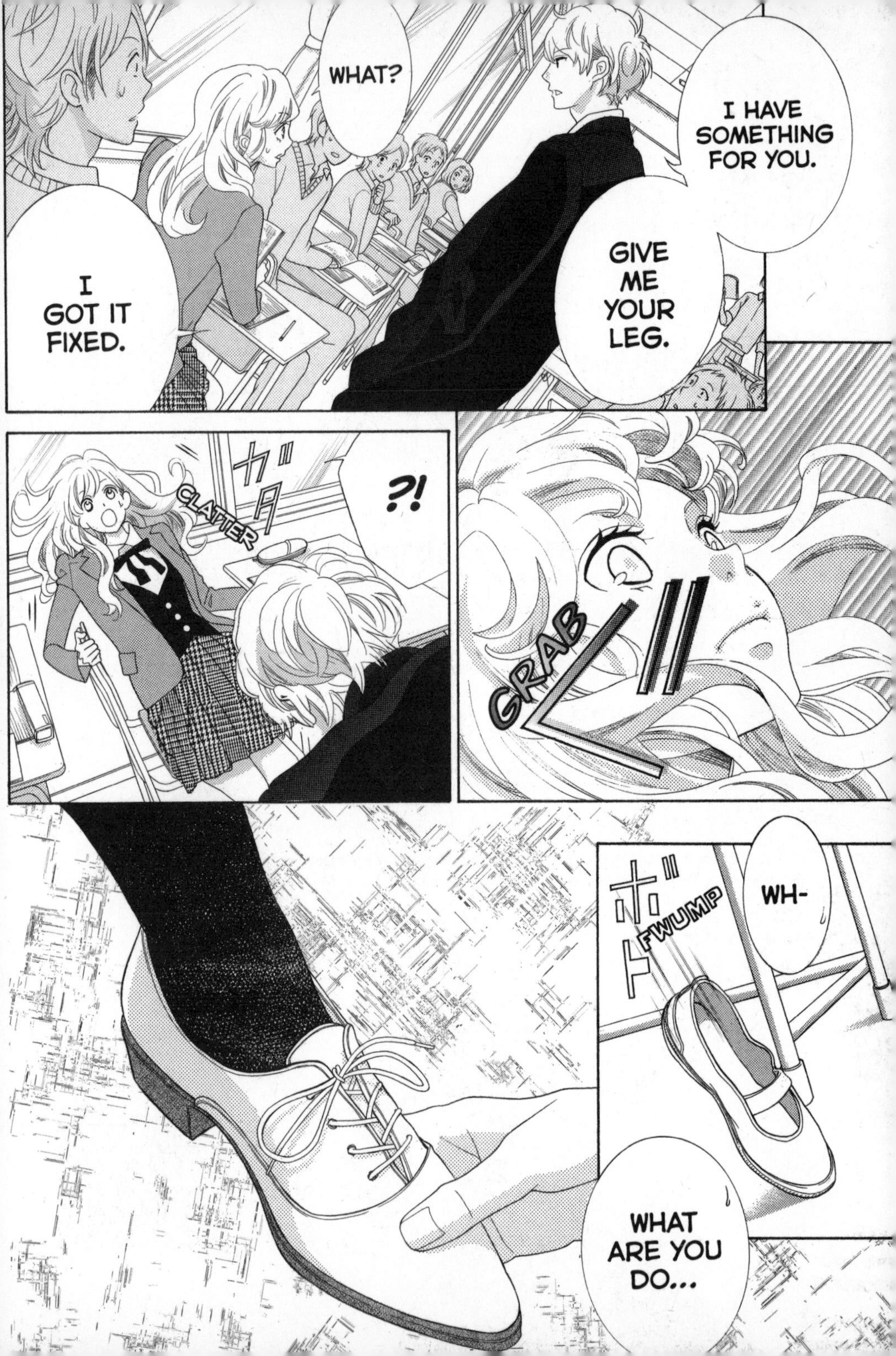
I HAVE SOMETHING FOR YOU.
WHAT?
GIVE ME YOUR LEG.
I GOT IT FIXED.
GRAB
?!
CLATTER
FWUMP
WH-
WHAT ARE YOU DO...

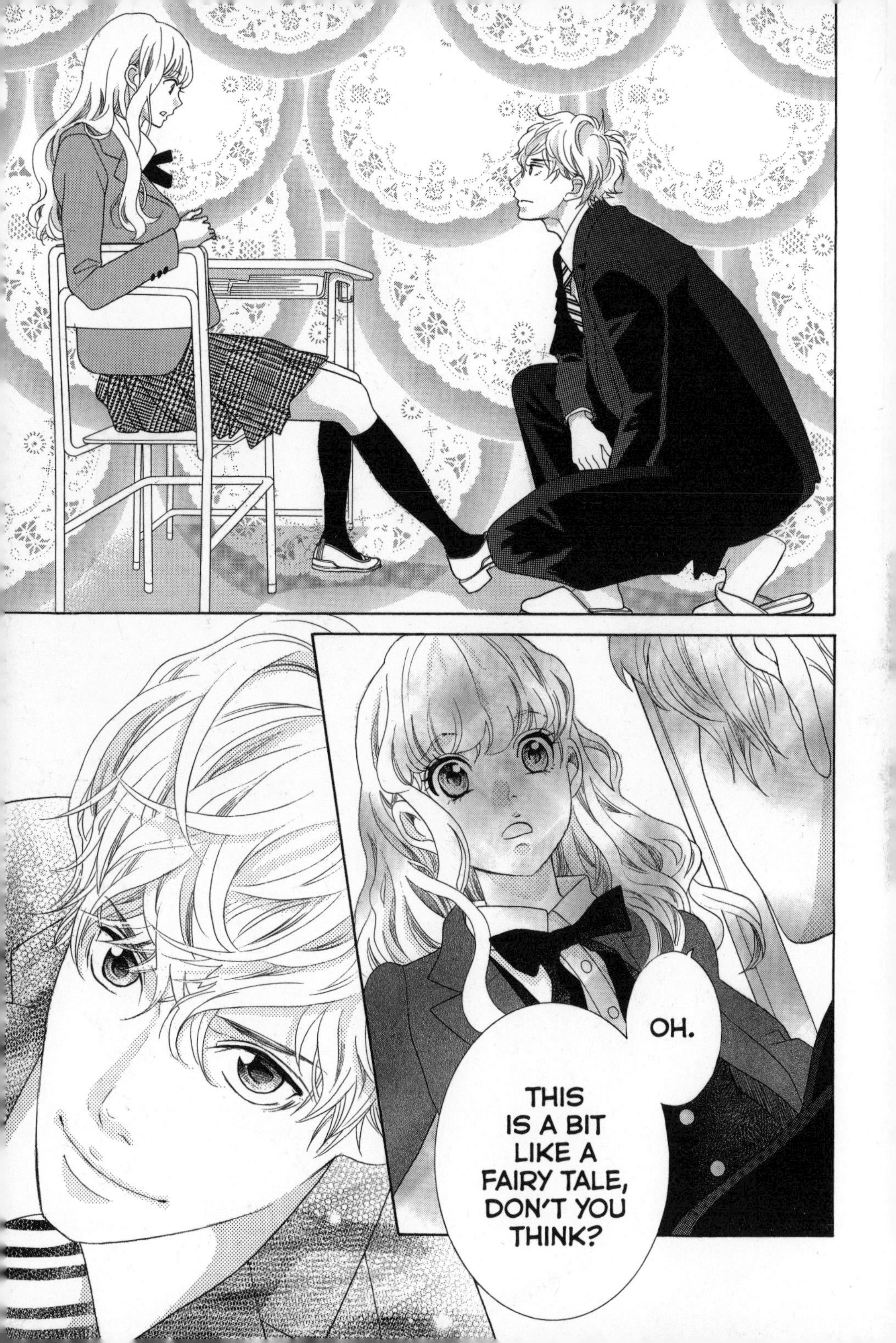
OH.
THIS IS A BIT LIKE A FAIRY TALE, DON'T YOU THINK?

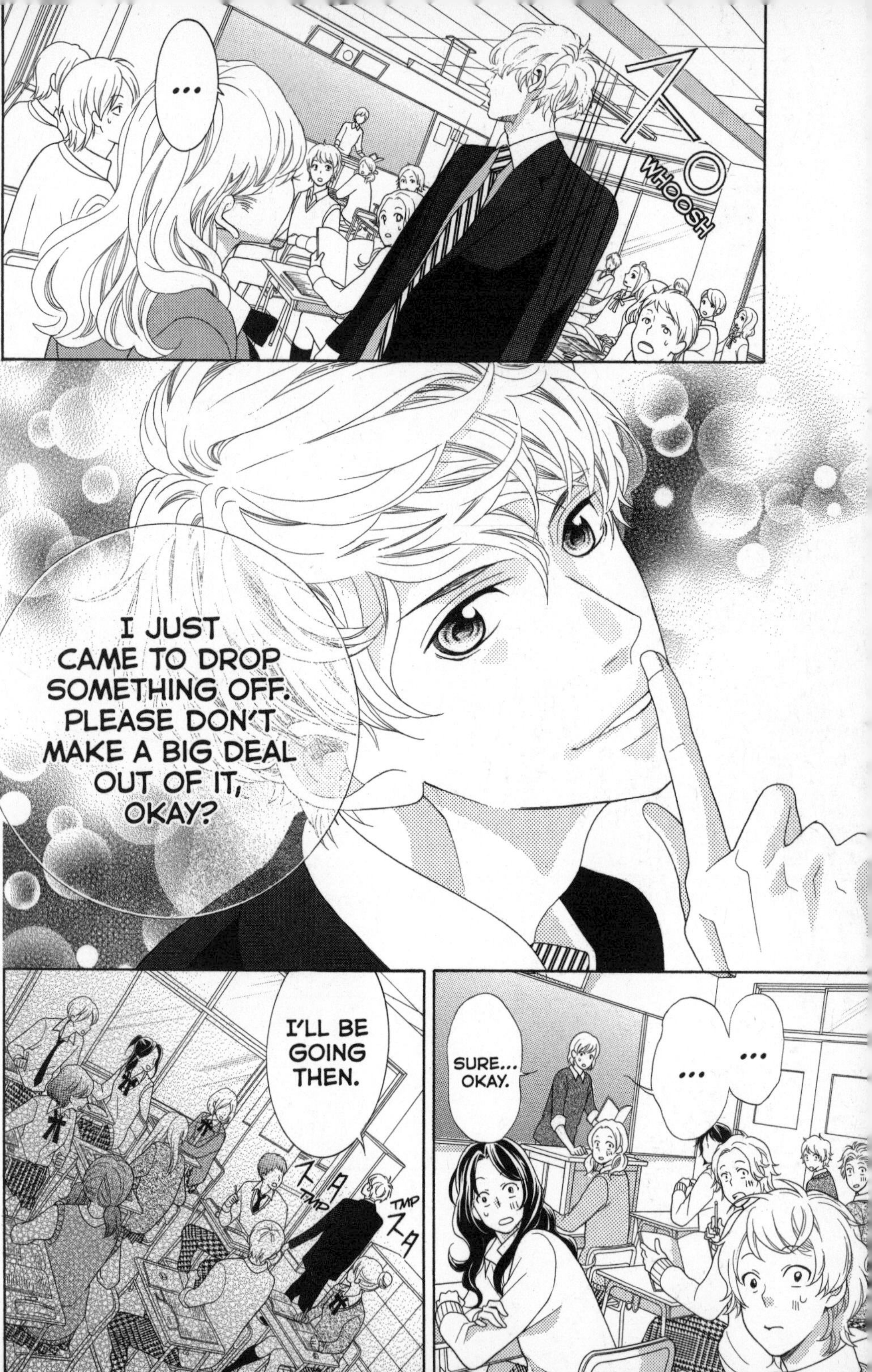
WHOOSH
...
I JUST CAME TO DROP SOMETHING OFF. PLEASE DON'T MAKE A BIG DEAL OUT OF IT, OKAY?
...
...
SURE... OKAY.
I'LL BE GOING THEN.
TMP
TMP

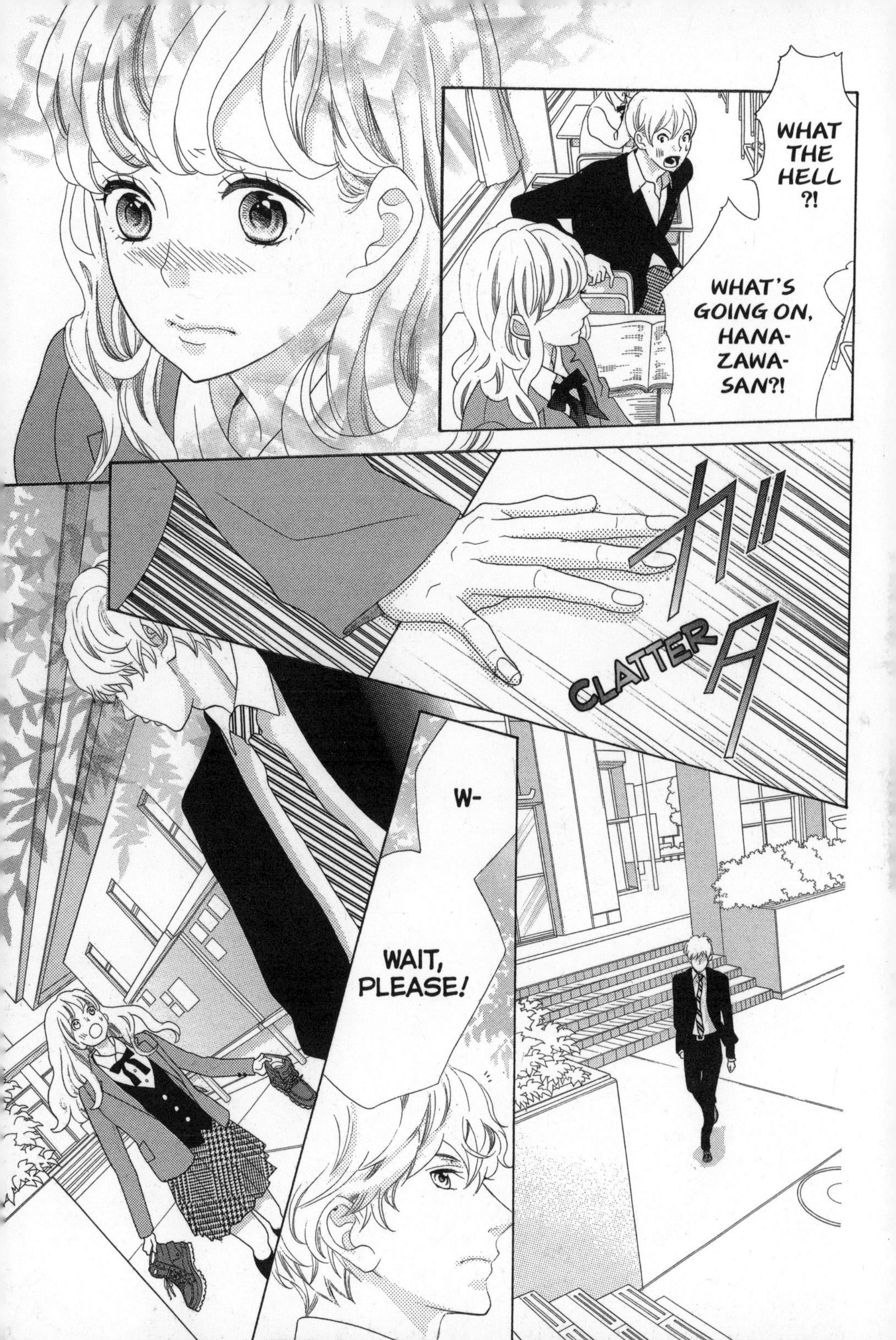
WHAT THE HELL ?!
WHAT'S GOING ON, HANA-ZAWA-SAN?!
CLATTER
W-
WAIT, PLEASE!

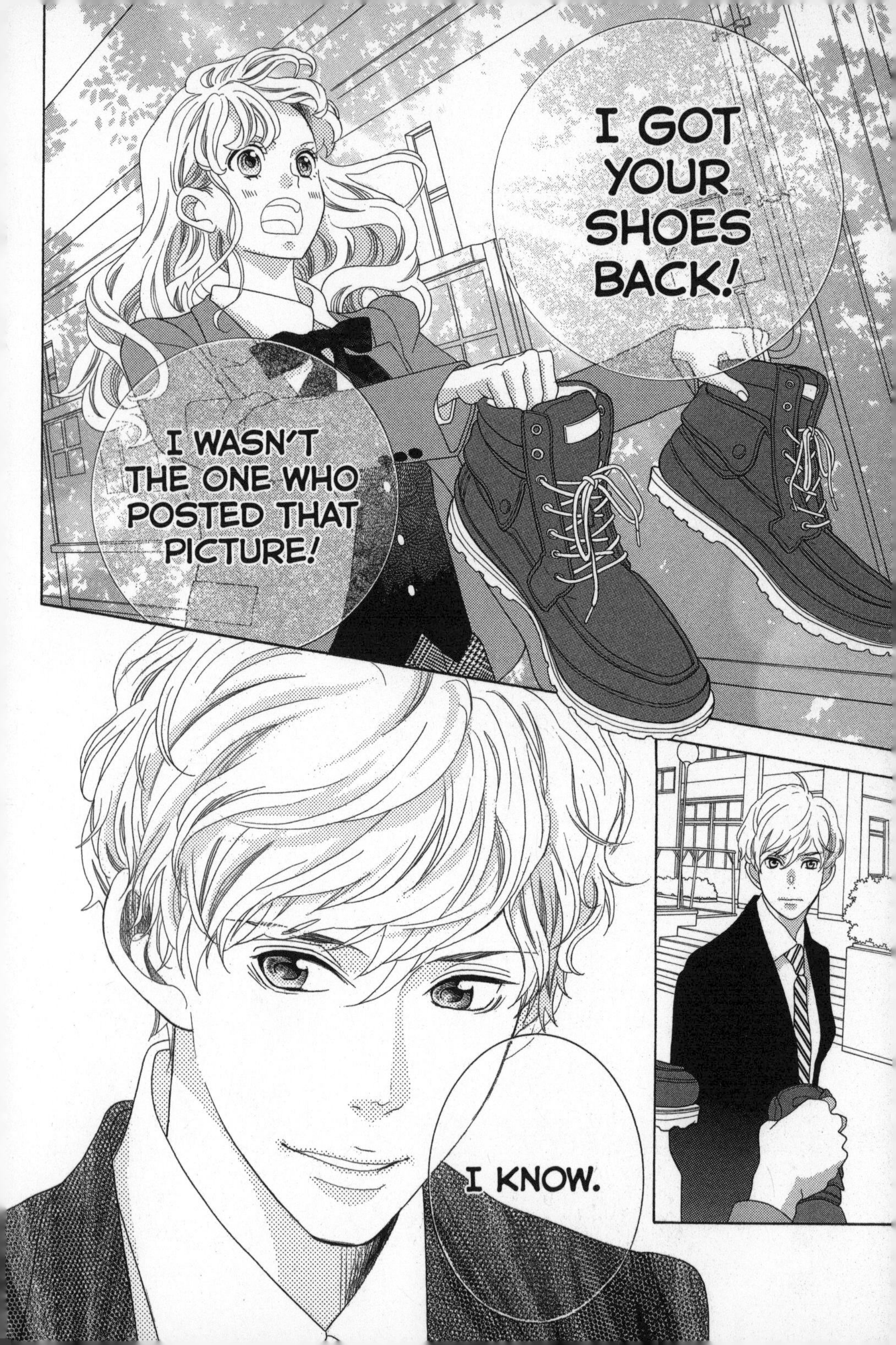
I GOT YOUR SHOES BACK!
I WASN'T THE ONE WHO POSTED THAT PICTURE!
I KNOW.

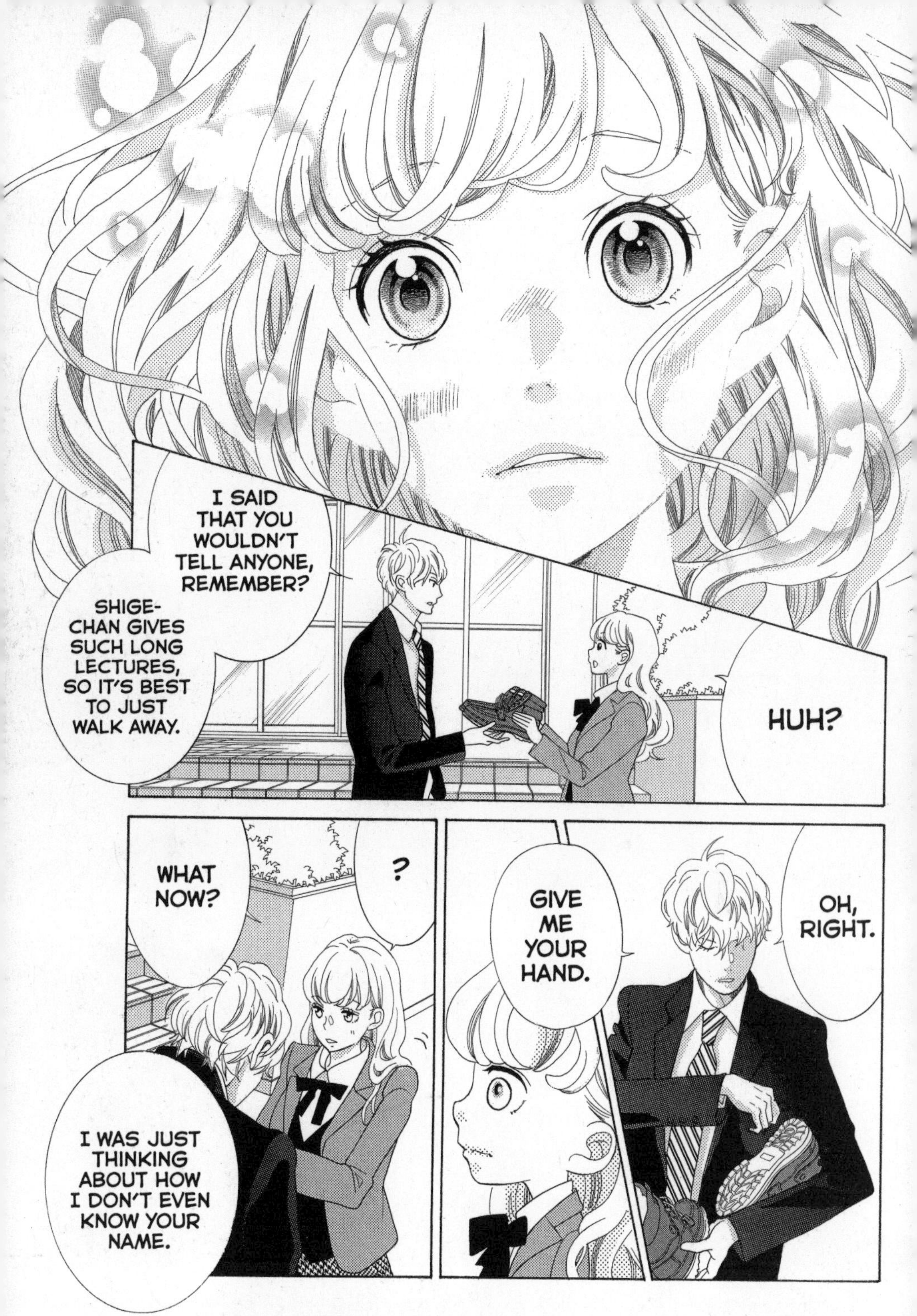
HUH?
I SAID THAT YOU WOULDN'T TELL ANYONE, REMEMBER?
SHIGE-CHAN GIVES SUCH LONG LECTURES, SO IT'S BEST TO JUST WALK AWAY.
OH, RIGHT.
GIVE ME YOUR HAND.
?
WHAT NOW?
I WAS JUST THINKING ABOUT HOW I DON'T EVEN KNOW YOUR NAME.

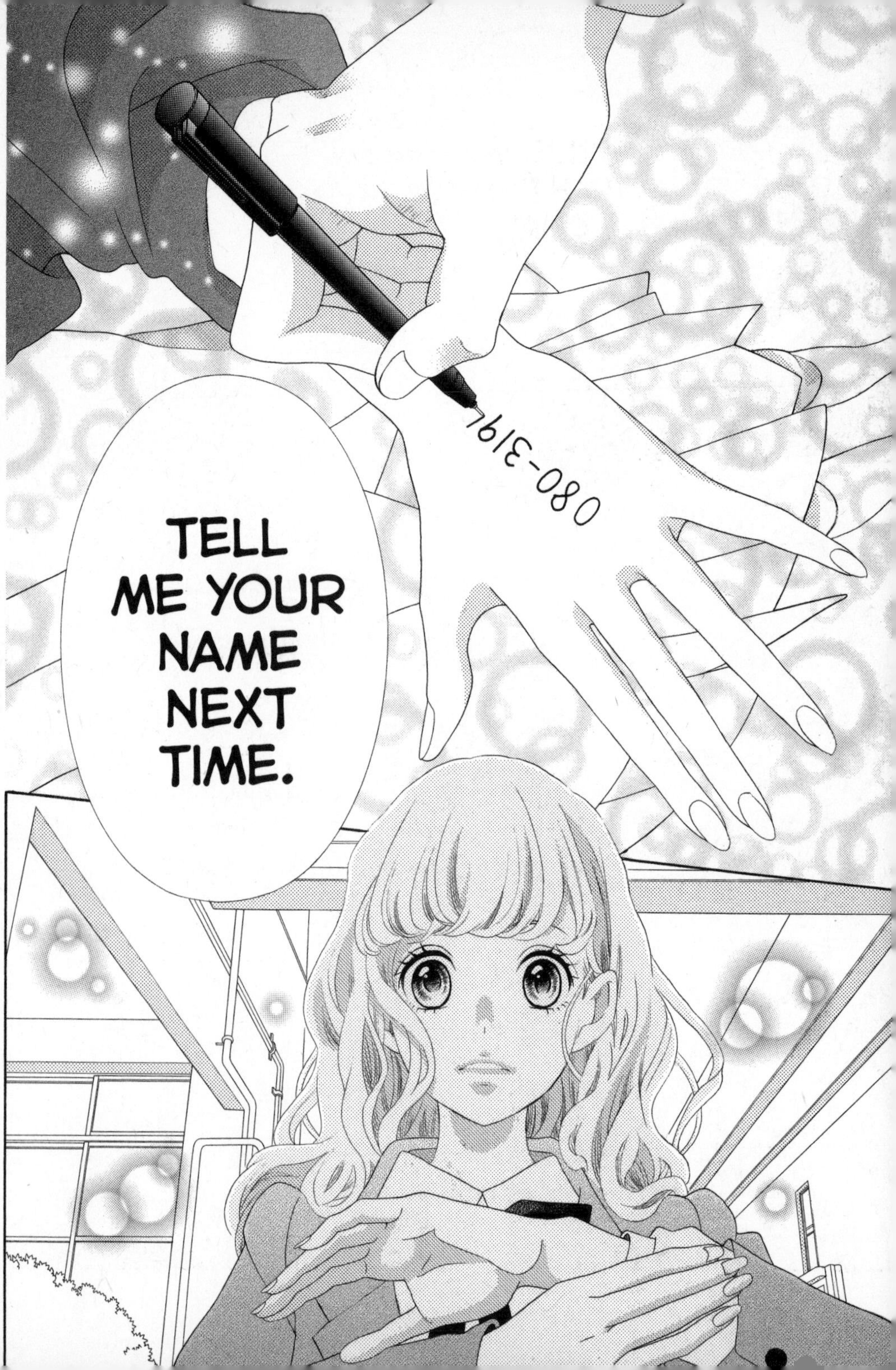
080-3191
TELL ME YOUR NAME NEXT TIME.

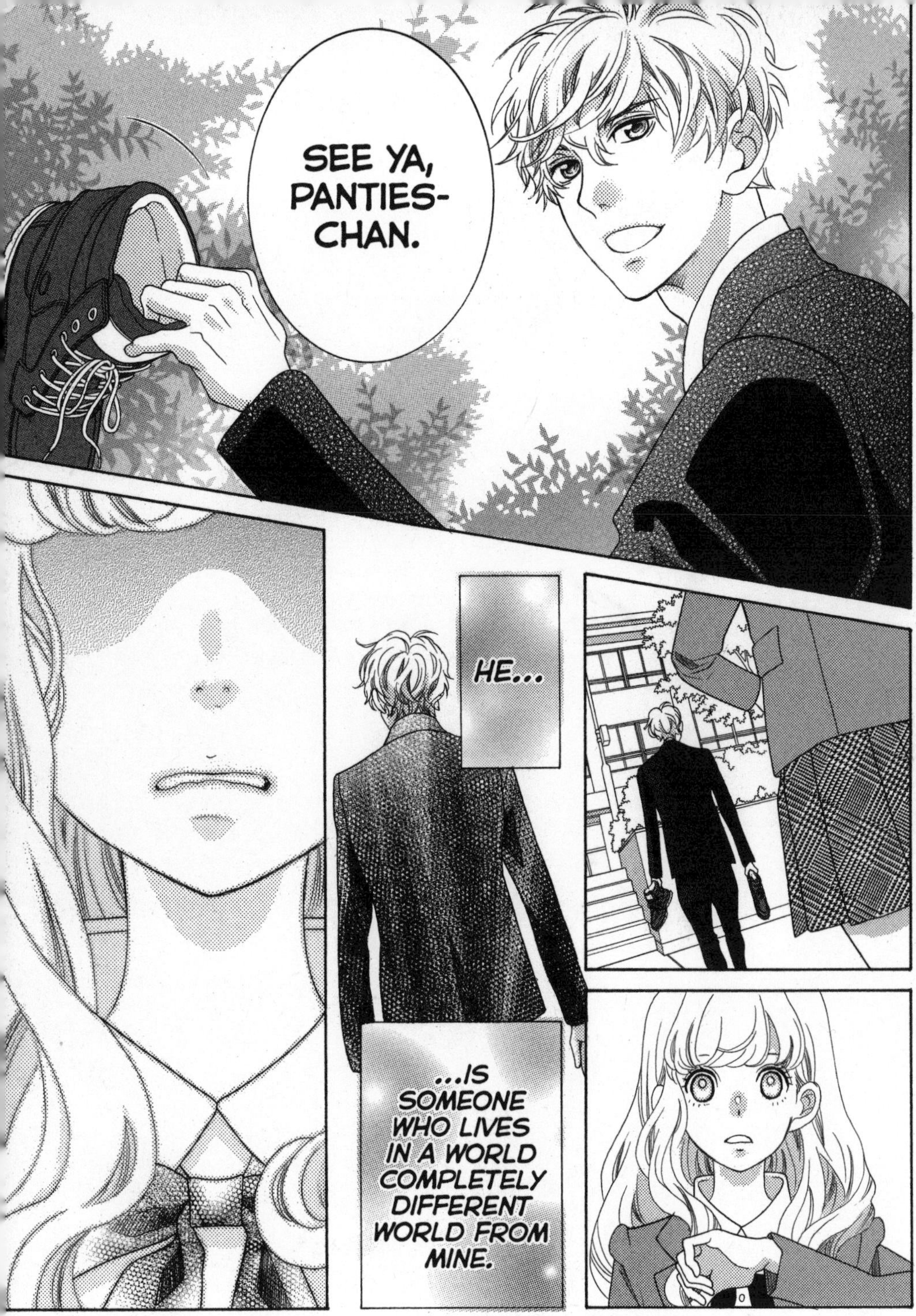
SEE YA, PANTIES-CHAN.
HE...
...IS SOMEONE WHO LIVES IN A WORLD COMPLETELY DIFFERENT WORLD FROM MINE.

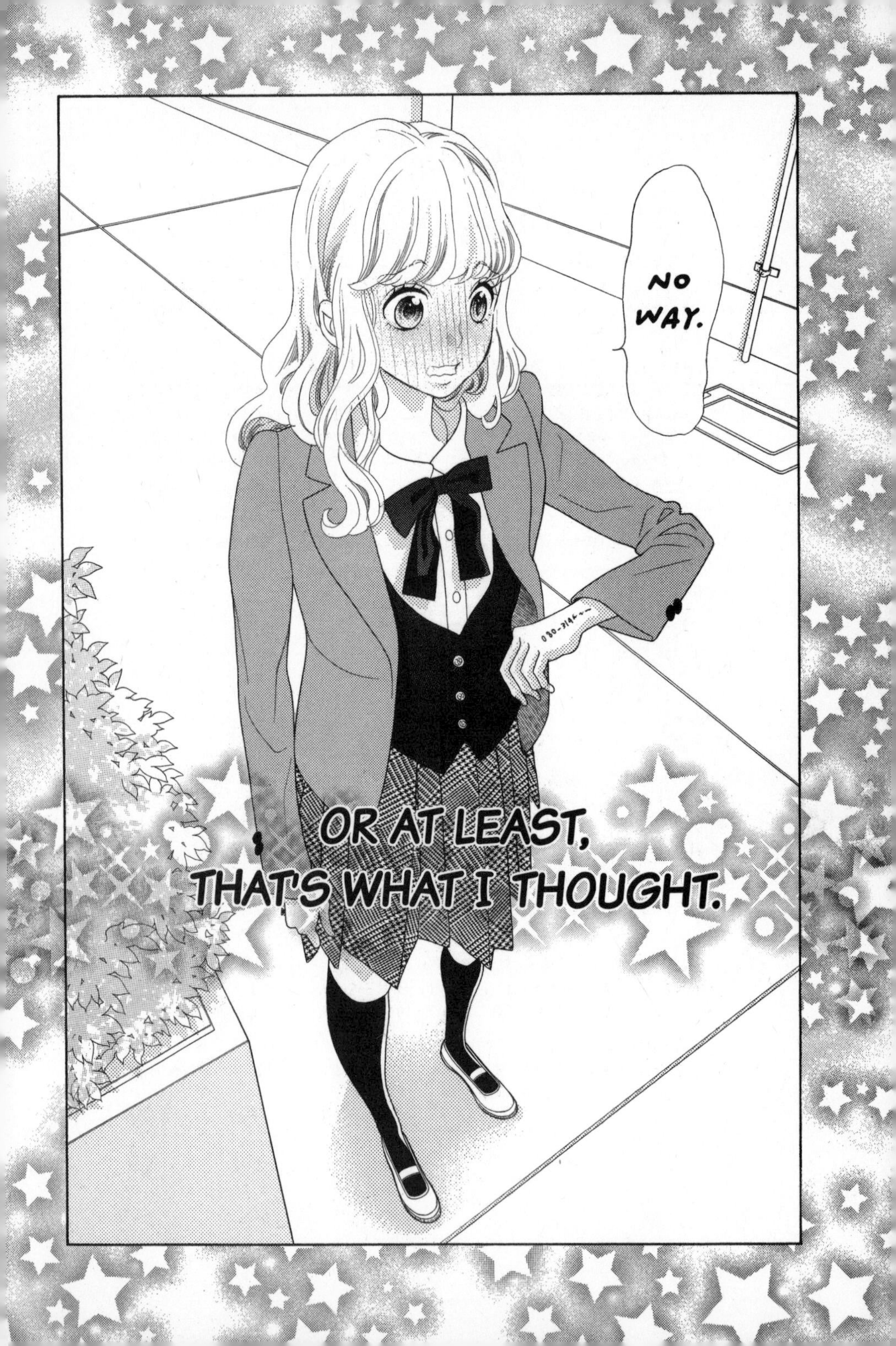
NO WAY.
OR AT LEAST, THAT'S WHAT I THOUGHT.

GREETINGS ②

EVERY MONTH, THE MAGAZINE THIS STORY IS IN PUTS THE TAG LINE "A REAL CINDERELLA STORY" ON THIS MANGA. IN OTHER WORDS, IT'S A FUN, FANTASY-LIKE STORY THAT CAME FROM ME WANTING TO SHARE MY EXPERIENCES.

IN ANY CASE, THE REASON I DECIDED TO WRITE A STORY WITH AN ACTOR IN IT IS BECAUSE MY PREVIOUS WORK, *LOVE'S REACH (KINKYORI RENAI)*, WAS MADE INTO A MOVIE. MEETING ALL OF THE PROFESSIONALS (THE ACTORS, THE DIRECTOR, THE STAFF, THE SCREENWRITER, THE PRODUCERS) WHO WERE ABLE TO CONVEY THAT FANTASY STORY, TO THE FANS AND TO THE AUDIENCE, REALLY INSPIRED ME.

I THINK IT'S REALLY COOL HOW THEY ALL WORKED TOGETHER TO TRANSPORT THE AUDIENCE INTO A FICTIONAL WORLD.

THAT'S WHY I WANTED TO MAKE A STORY FOR THOSE OF YOU WHO ARE ALSO FANS OF SOMEONE FAMOUS. ALL I WANT IS FOR YOU TO BE ABLE TO DREAM ABOUT THINGS LIKE, "MAYBE I COULD MEET MY CELEBRITY CRUSH! AND THEN I COULD TALK TO THEM! AND WHAT IF THINGS JUST KEPT PROGRESSING FROM THERE?!"

BESIDES, WHILE CELEBRITIES ARE EXTRAORDINARY, THEY'RE STILL JUST PEOPLE. THEY GO TO THE BATHROOM JUST LIKE EVERYONE ELSE, AND THEY SPACE OUT AND DAYDREAM JUST LIKE EVERYONE ELSE. WE'RE REALLY ALL THE SAME, Y'KNOW?

I WANTED TO CAPTURE THINGS LIKE THAT IN MY STORY, TOO.

OH, BUT OF COURSE, THEY'RE STILL CELEBRITIES, SO THEY HAVE A SPARKLING AURA THAT'S ON ANOTHER LEVEL! (THESE ARE ALL JUST MY OWN PERSONAL THOUGHTS.)

BASICALLY, WHAT I'M TRYING TO SAY IS THAT I'M REALLY GRATEFUL THAT I GOT TO MEET EVERYONE WHO WORKED ON THE *LOVE'S REACH* MOVIE.

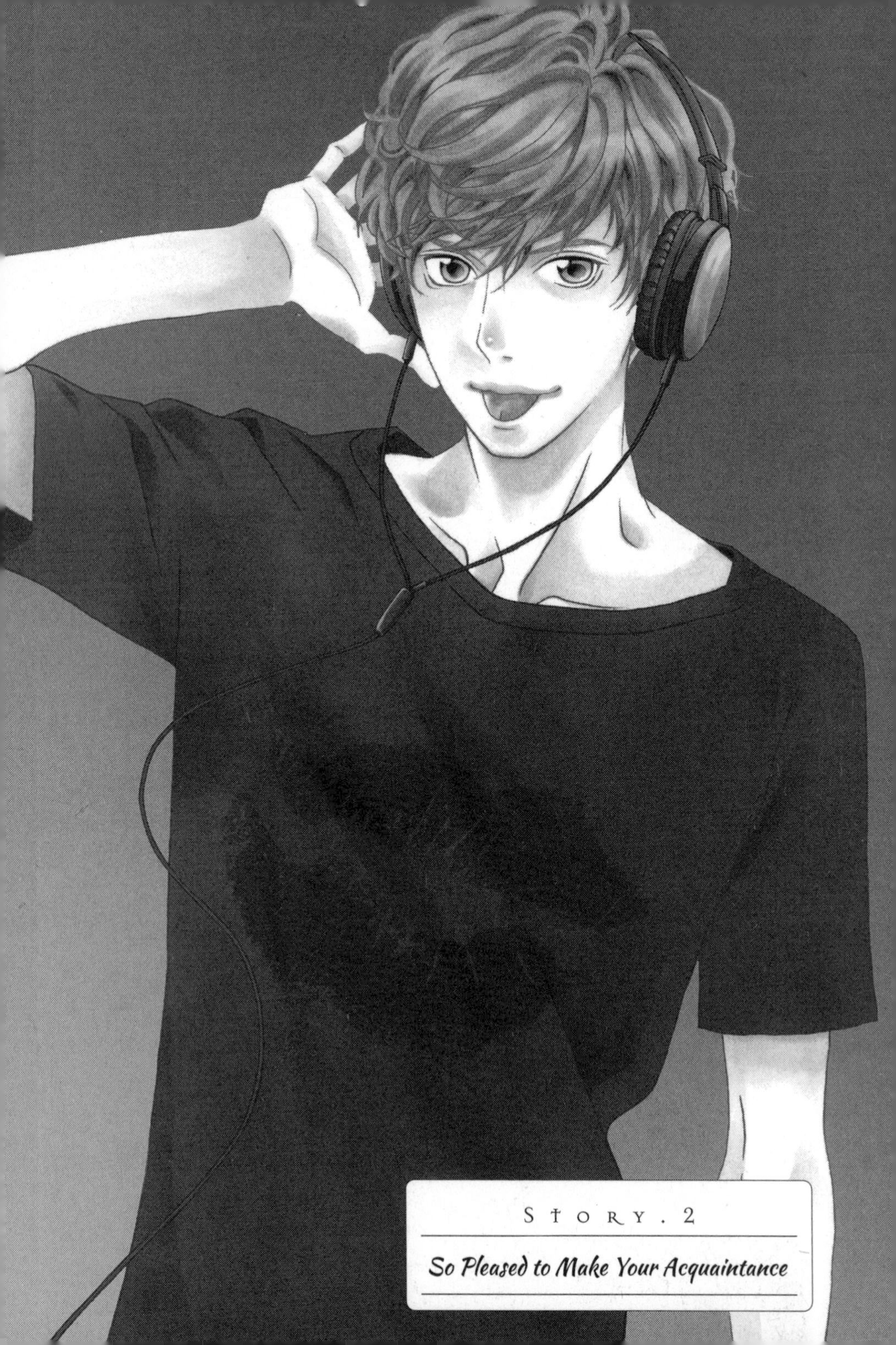

Story. 2

So Pleased to Make Your Acquaintance

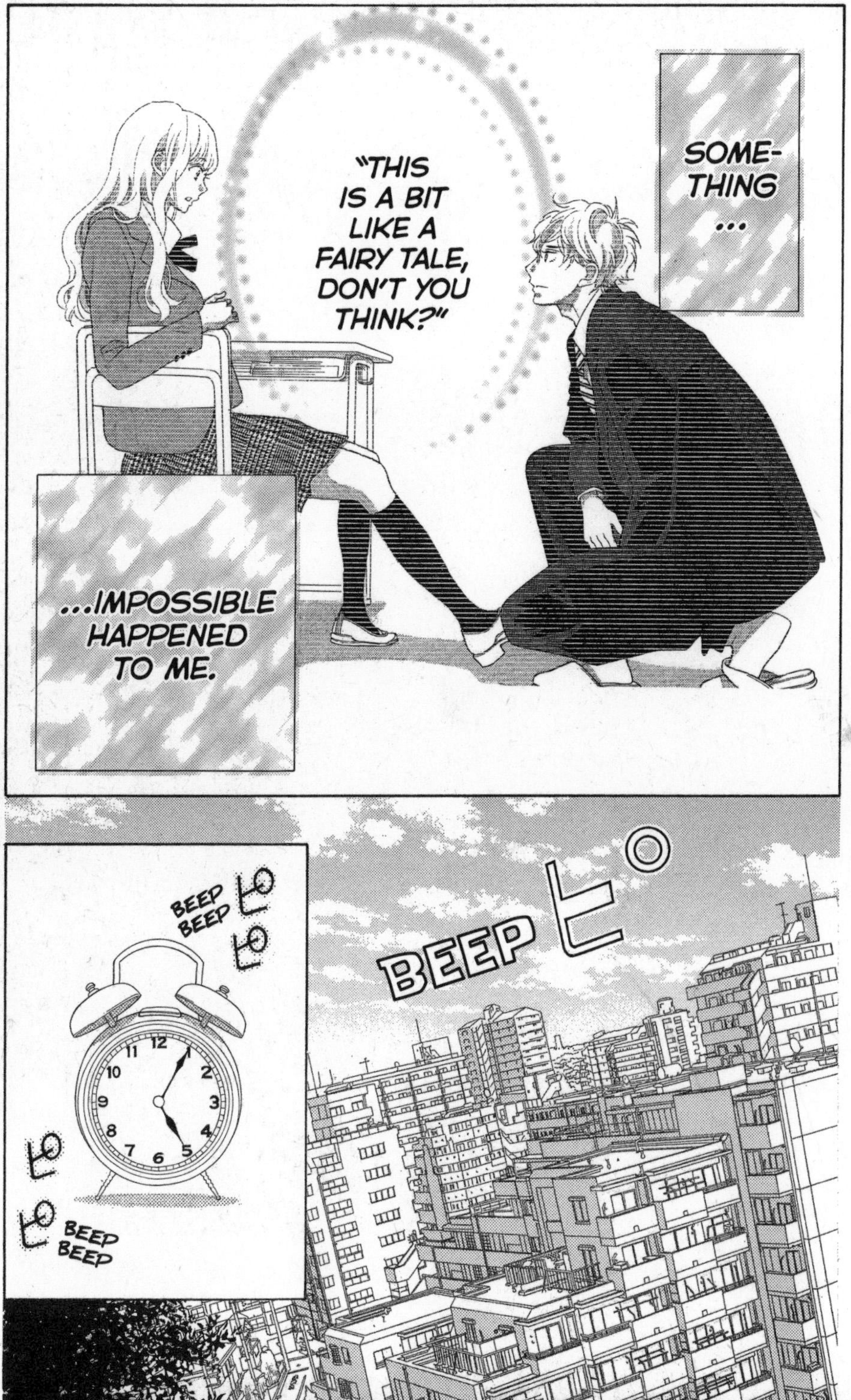
SOME-THING...
"THIS IS A BIT LIKE A FAIRY TALE, DON'T YOU THINK?"
...IMPOSSIBLE HAPPENED TO ME.
BEEP ピ
BEEP BEEP ピピ
ピピ BEEP BEEP

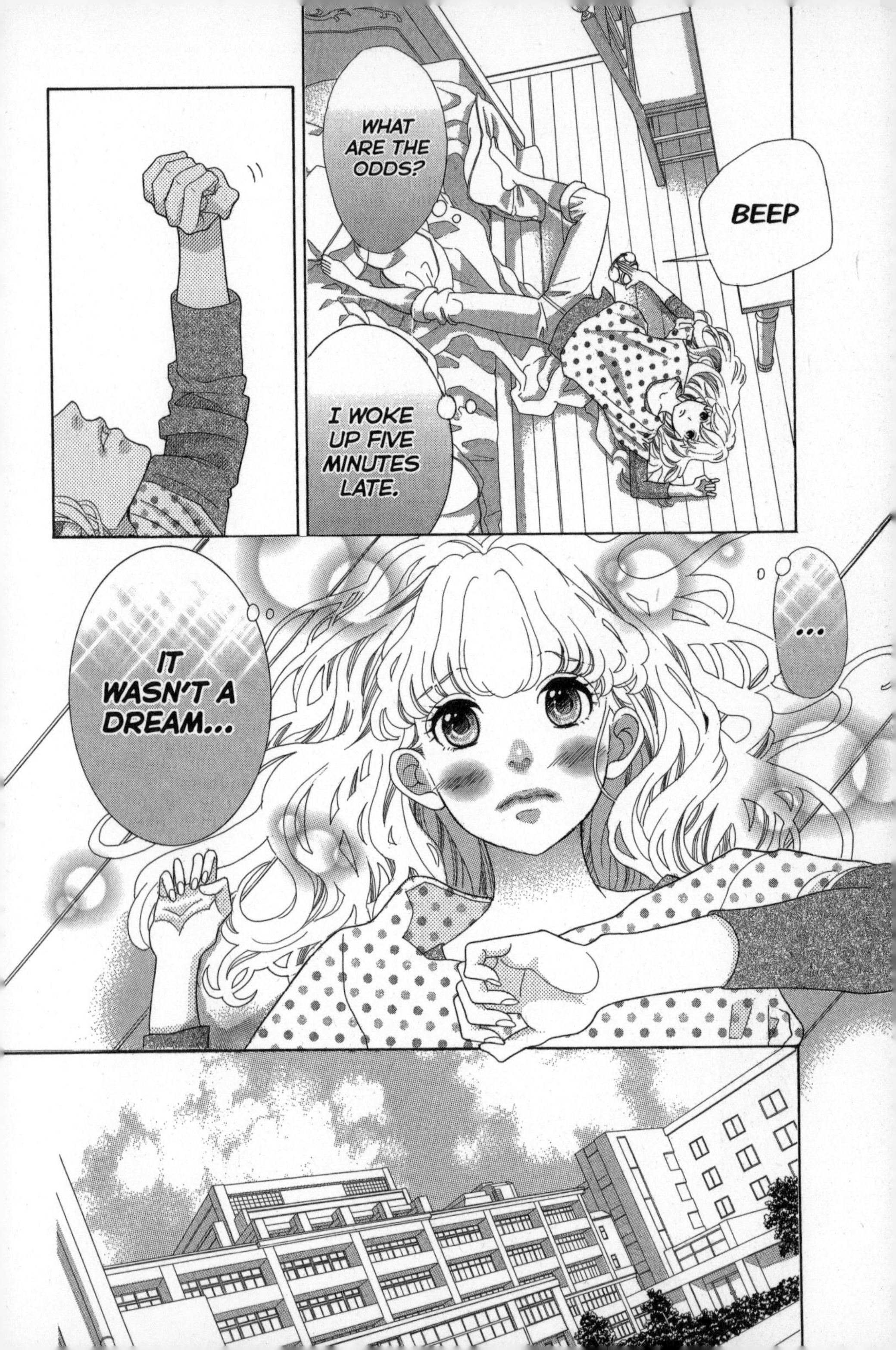
BEEP
WHAT ARE THE ODDS?
I WOKE UP FIVE MINUTES LATE.
...
IT WASN'T A DREAM...

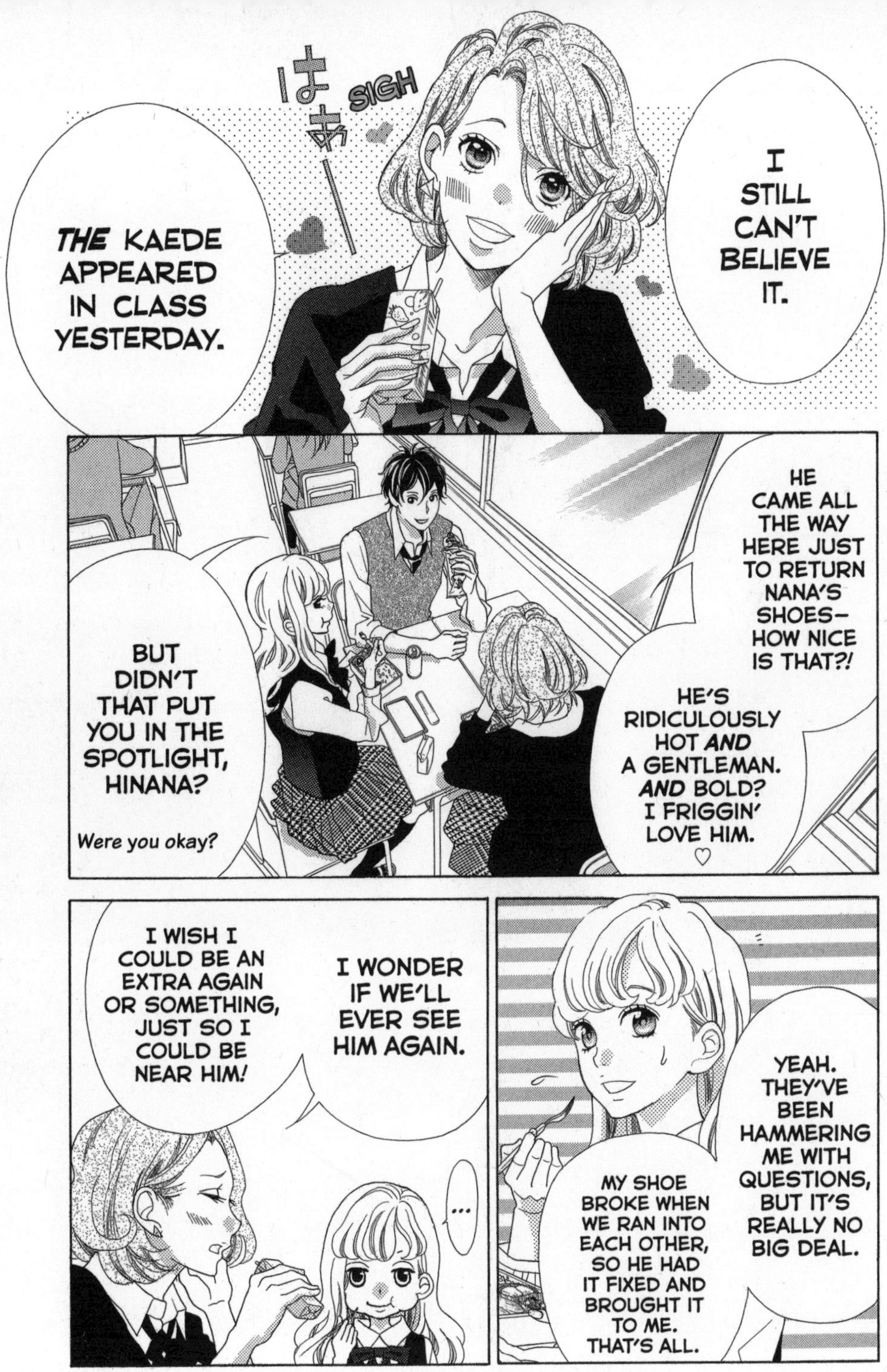
I STILL CAN'T BELIEVE IT.
はぁ
SIGH
THE KAEDE APPEARED IN CLASS YESTERDAY.
HE CAME ALL THE WAY HERE JUST TO RETURN NANA'S SHOES—HOW NICE IS THAT?!
HE'S RIDICULOUSLY HOT *AND* A GENTLEMAN. *AND* BOLD? I FRIGGIN' LOVE HIM. ♡
BUT DIDN'T THAT PUT YOU IN THE SPOTLIGHT, HINANA?
Were you okay?
YEAH. THEY'VE BEEN HAMMERING ME WITH QUESTIONS, BUT IT'S REALLY NO BIG DEAL.
MY SHOE BROKE WHEN WE RAN INTO EACH OTHER, SO HE HAD IT FIXED AND BROUGHT IT TO ME. THAT'S ALL.
I WONDER IF WE'LL EVER SEE HIM AGAIN.
I WISH I COULD BE AN EXTRA AGAIN OR SOMETHING, JUST SO I COULD BE NEAR HIM!
...

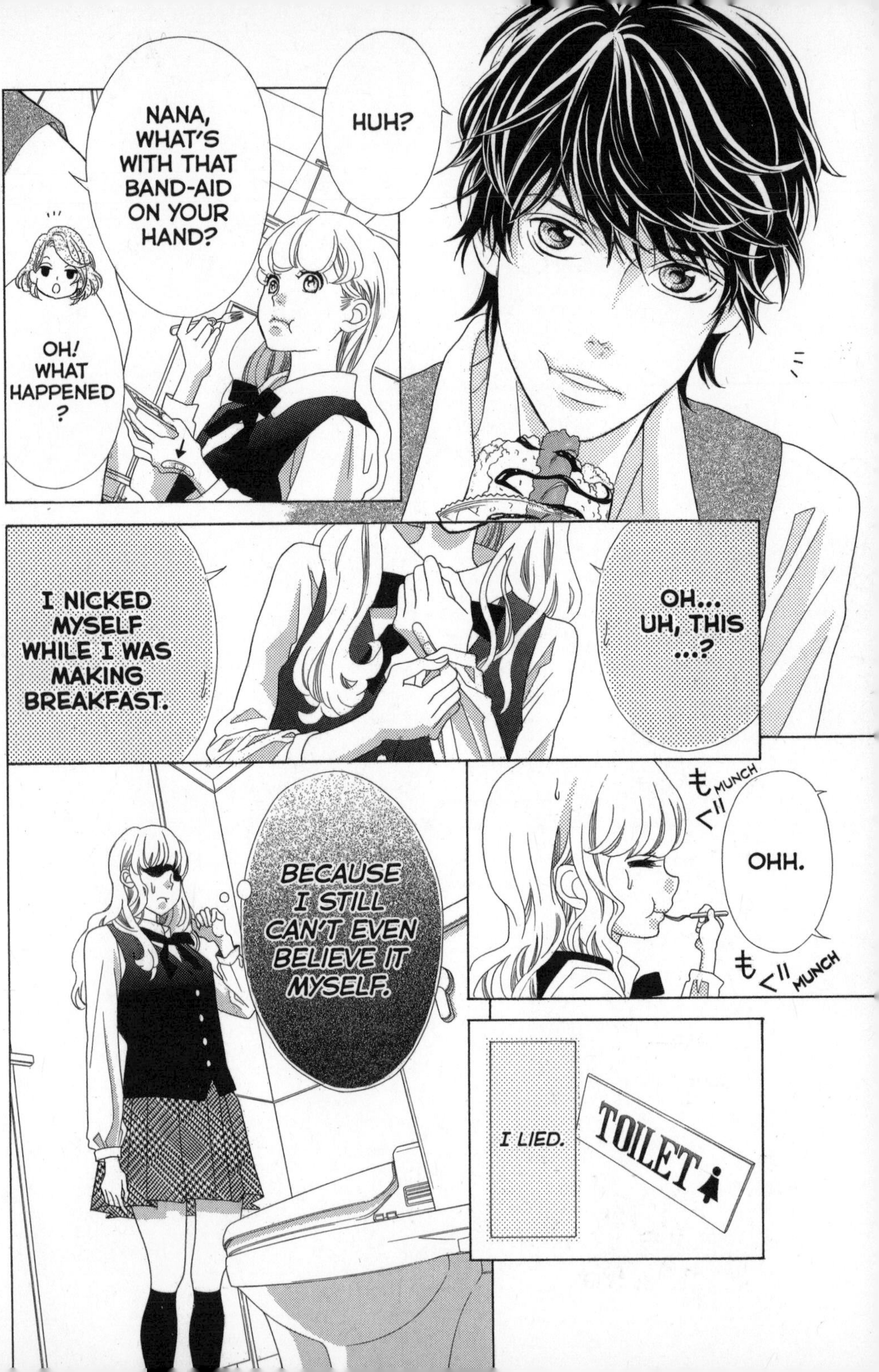
HUH?
NANA, WHAT'S WITH THAT BAND-AID ON YOUR HAND?
OH! WHAT HAPPENED?
OH... UH, THIS ...?
I NICKED MYSELF WHILE I WAS MAKING BREAKFAST.
もぐ MUNCH
OHH.
もぐ MUNCH
I LIED.
TOILET
BECAUSE I STILL CAN'T EVEN BELIEVE IT MYSELF.

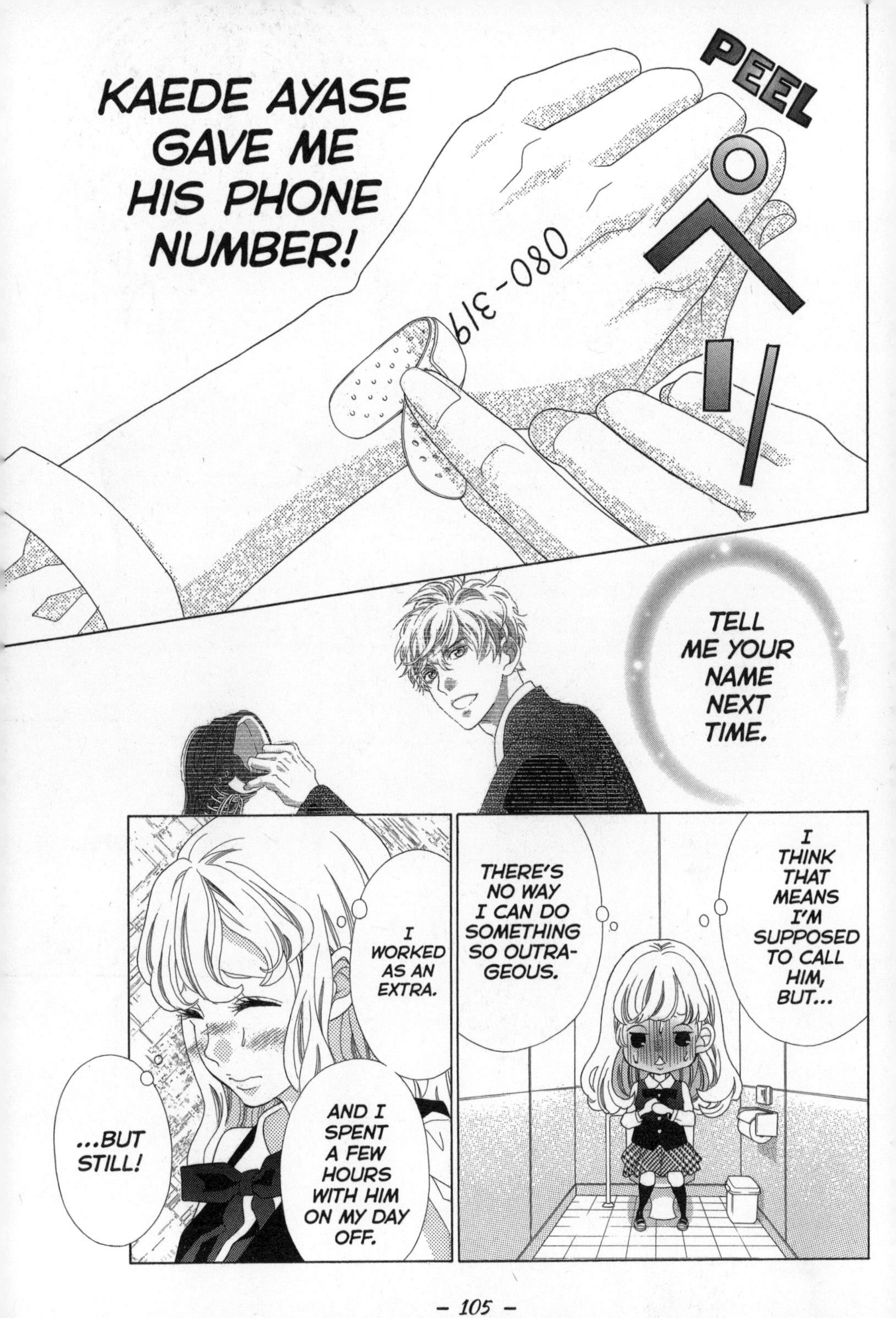
PEEL
080-319
KAEDE AYASE GAVE ME HIS PHONE NUMBER!
TELL ME YOUR NAME NEXT TIME.
I THINK THAT MEANS I'M SUPPOSED TO CALL HIM, BUT...
THERE'S NO WAY I CAN DO SOMETHING SO OUTRAGEOUS.
I WORKED AS AN EXTRA.
AND I SPENT A FEW HOURS WITH HIM ON MY DAY OFF.
...BUT STILL!

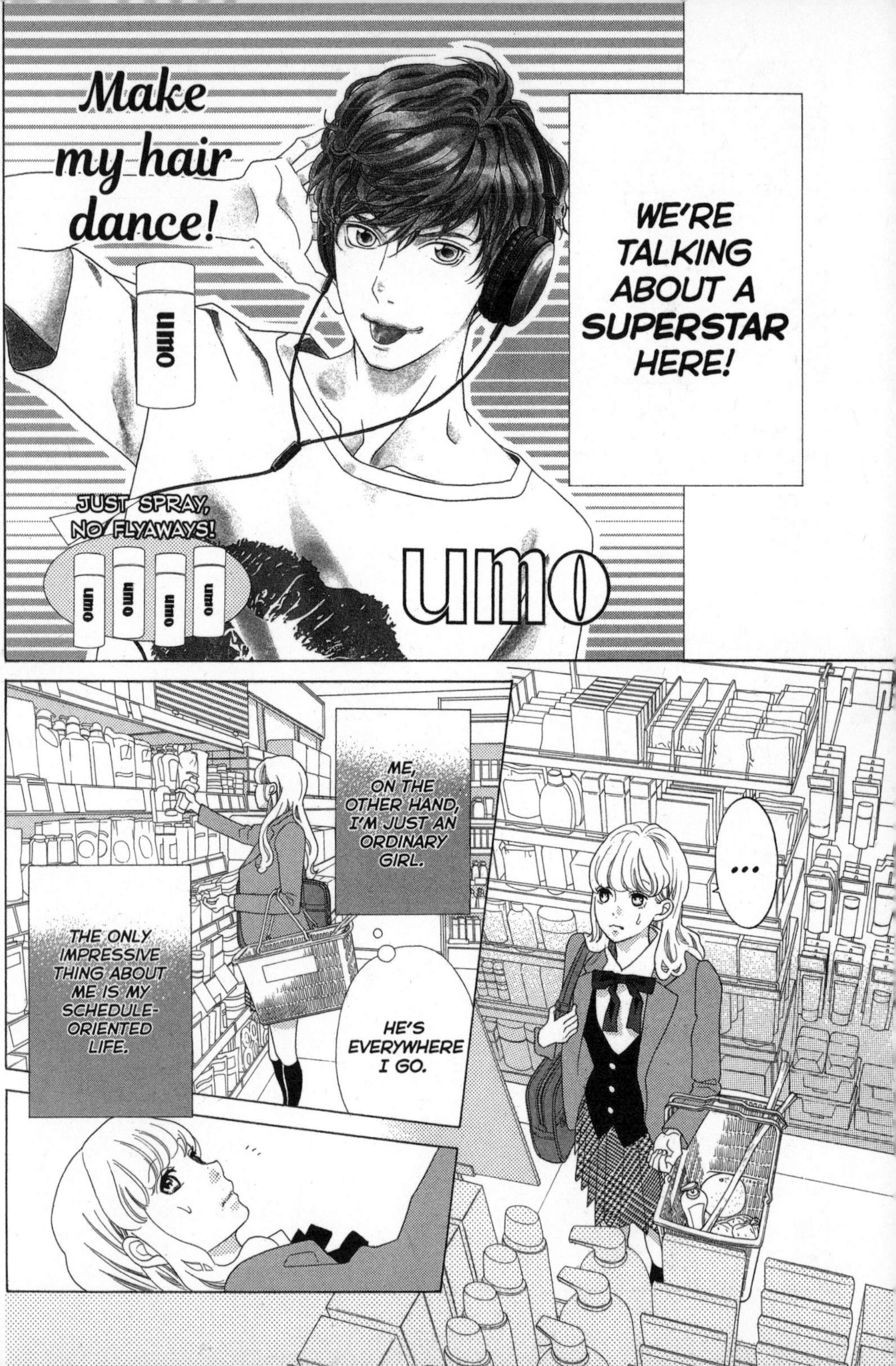
WE'RE TALKING ABOUT A SUPERSTAR HERE!
Make my hair dance!
umo
JUST SPRAY, NO FLYAWAYS!
umo
umo
umo
umo
umo
...
ME, ON THE OTHER HAND, I'M JUST AN ORDINARY GIRL.
HE'S EVERYWHERE I GO.
THE ONLY IMPRESSIVE THING ABOUT ME IS MY SCHEDULE-ORIENTED LIFE.

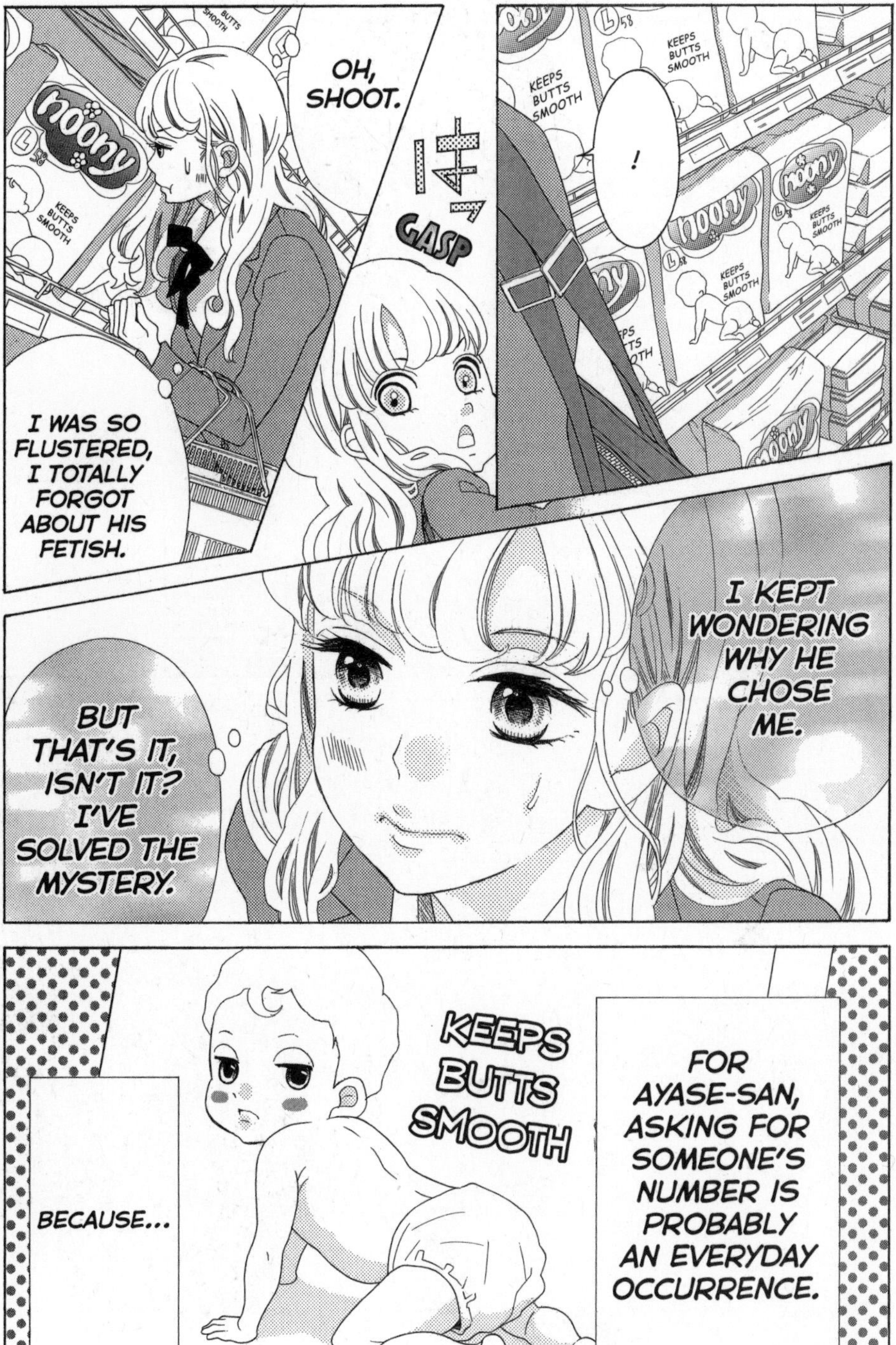

KEEPS BUTTS SMOOTH
!
OH, SHOOT.
GASP
I WAS SO FLUSTERED, I TOTALLY FORGOT ABOUT HIS FETISH.
I KEPT WONDERING WHY HE CHOSE ME.
BUT THAT'S IT, ISN'T IT? I'VE SOLVED THE MYSTERY.
FOR AYASE-SAN, ASKING FOR SOMEONE'S NUMBER IS PROBABLY AN EVERYDAY OCCURRENCE.
KEEPS BUTTS SMOOTH
BECAUSE...

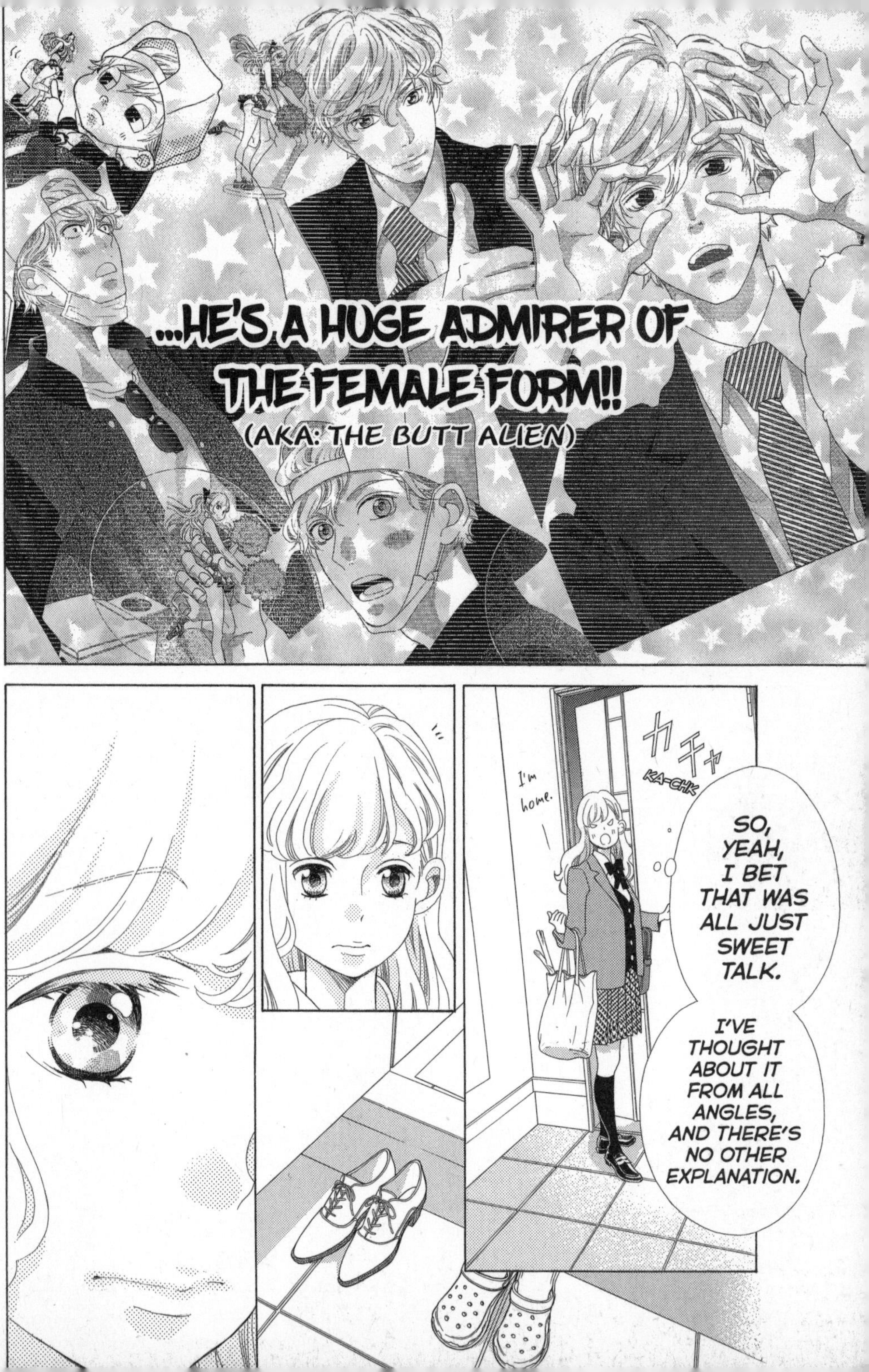
...HE'S A HUGE ADMIRER OF THE FEMALE FORM!!
(AKA: THE BUTT ALIEN)
カチャ
KA-CHK
I'm home.
SO, YEAH, I BET THAT WAS ALL JUST SWEET TALK.
I'VE THOUGHT ABOUT IT FROM ALL ANGLES, AND THERE'S NO OTHER EXPLANATION.

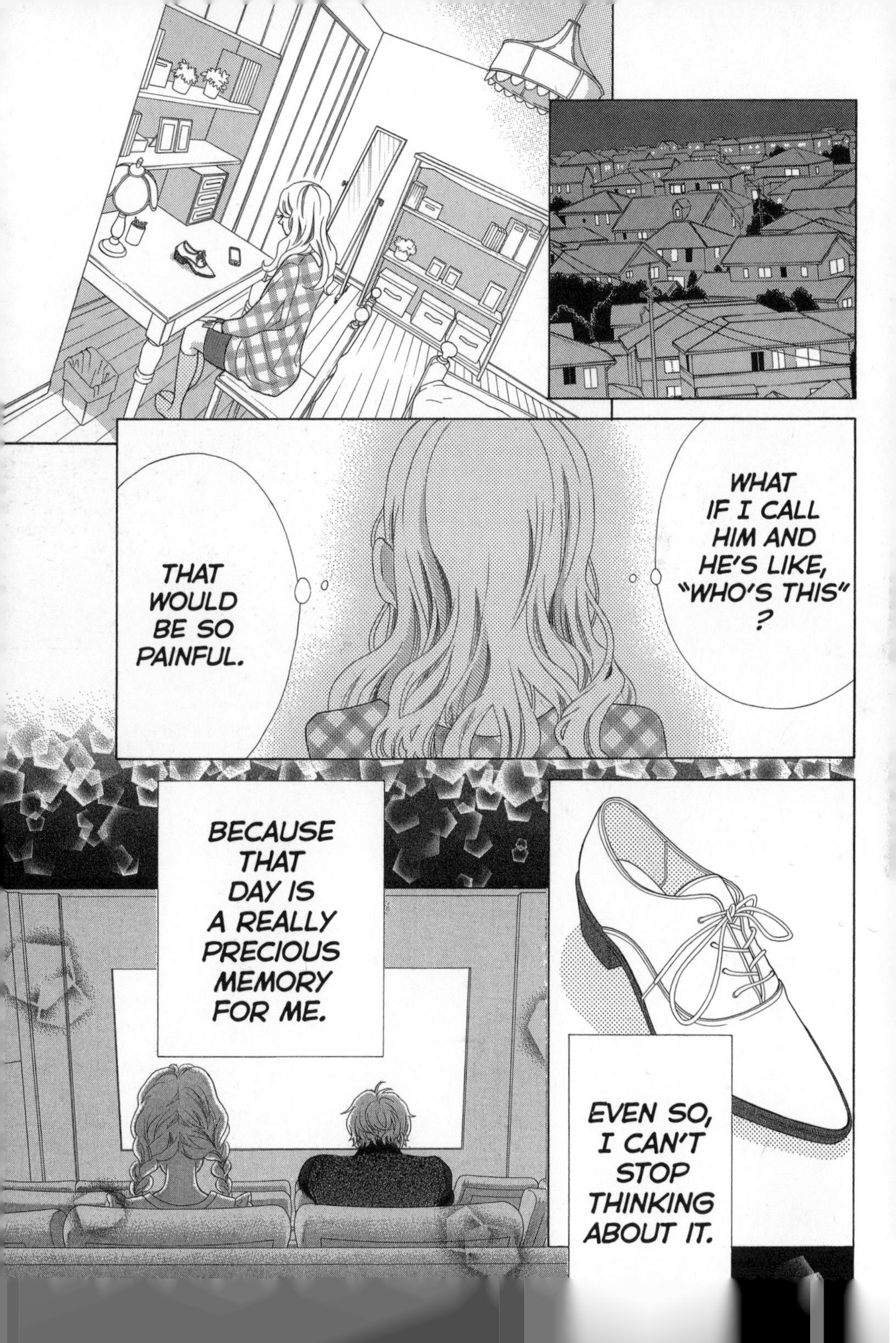
WHAT IF I CALL HIM AND HE'S LIKE, "WHO'S THIS" ?
THAT WOULD BE SO PAINFUL.
EVEN SO, I CAN'T STOP THINKING ABOUT IT.
BECAUSE THAT DAY IS A REALLY PRECIOUS MEMORY FOR ME.

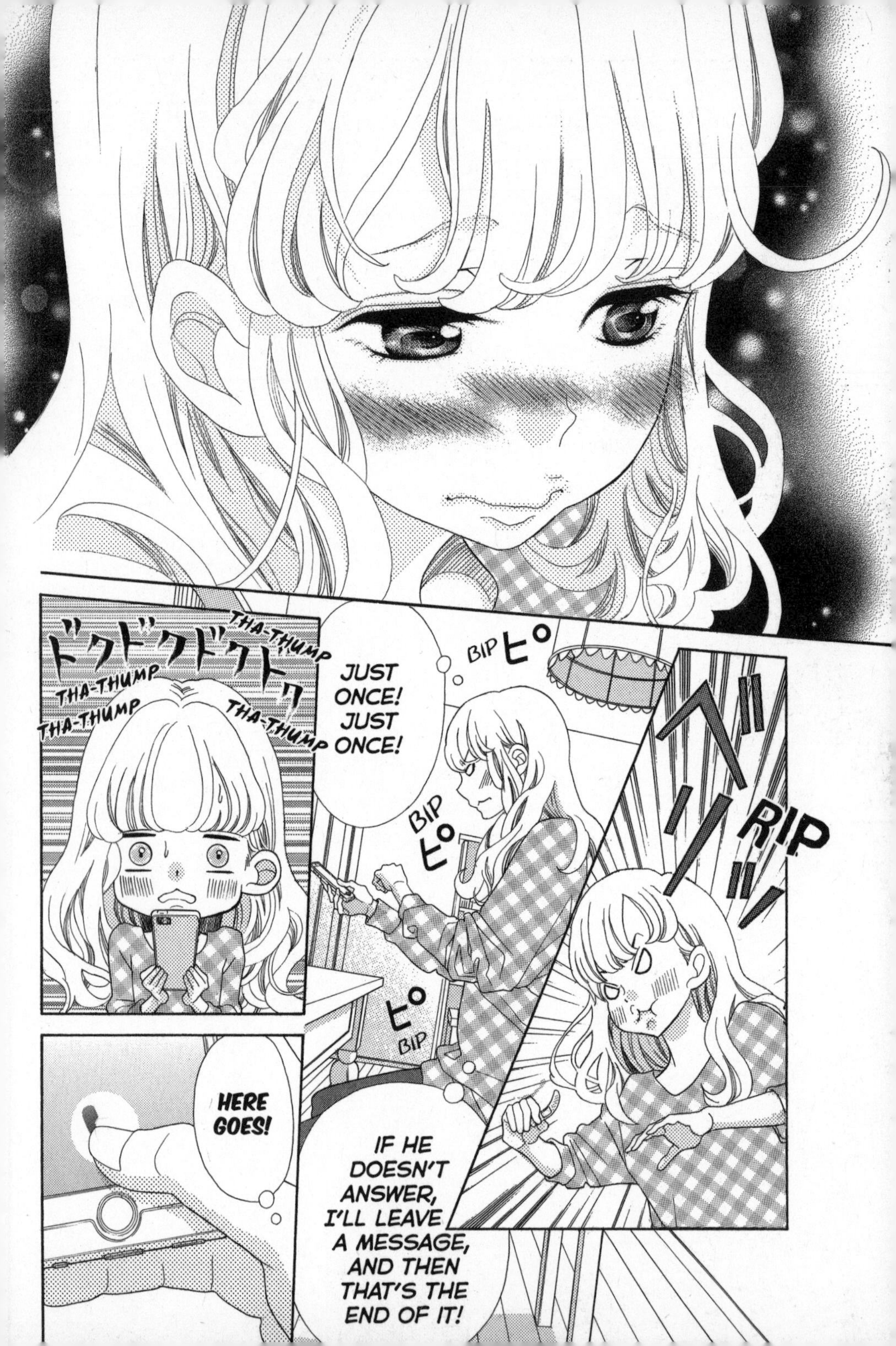

RIP
JUST ONCE! JUST ONCE!
BIP ピ
BIP ピ
ピ BIP
IF HE DOESN'T ANSWER, I'LL LEAVE A MESSAGE, AND THEN THAT'S THE END OF IT!
ドクドクドクドク
THA-THUMP
THA-THUMP
THA-THUMP
THA-THUMP
HERE GOES!

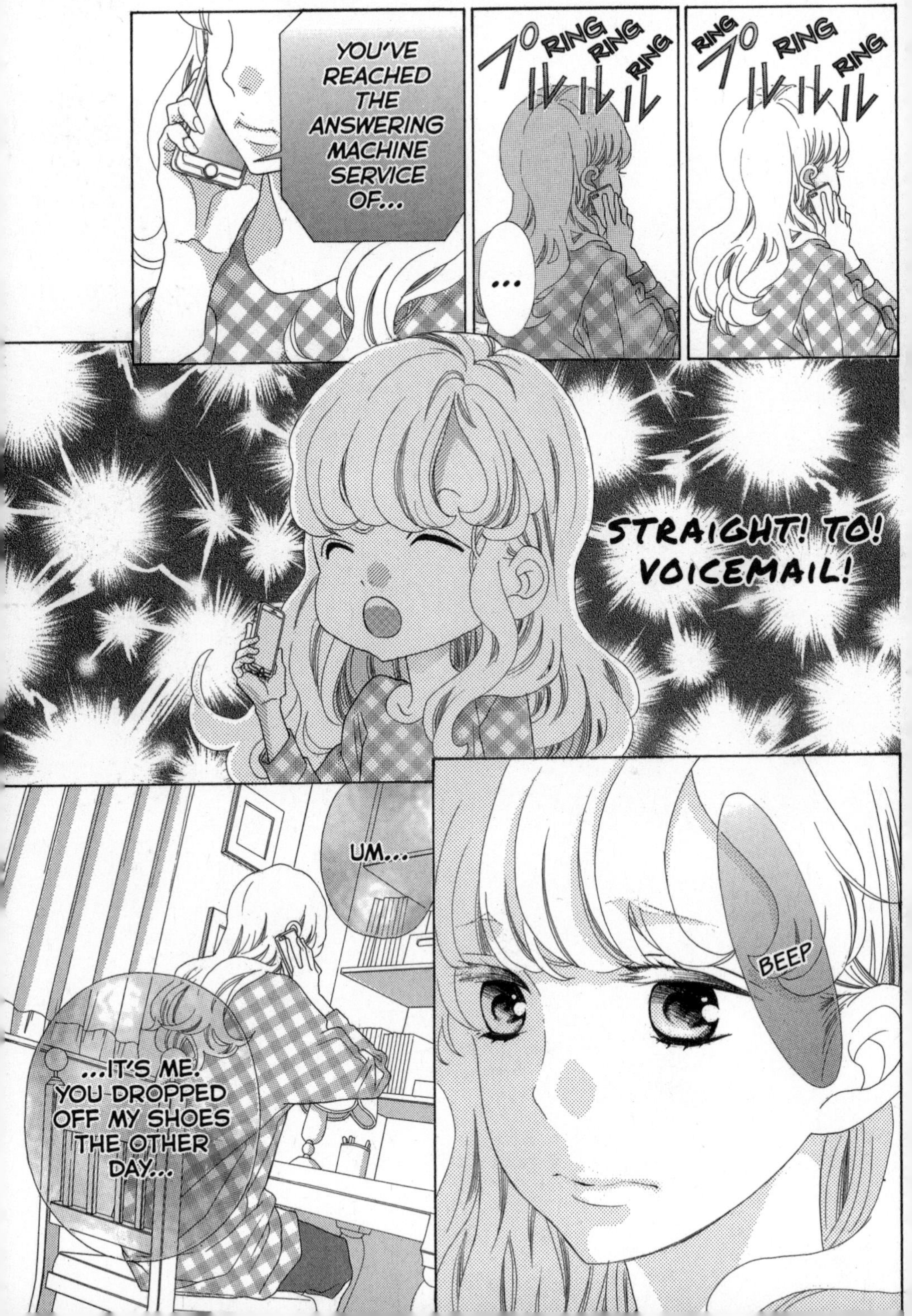
RING
RING
RING
RING
RING
RING
...
YOU'VE REACHED THE ANSWERING MACHINE SERVICE OF...
STRAIGHT! TO! VOICEMAIL!
BEEP
UM...
...IT'S ME. YOU DROPPED OFF MY SHOES THE OTHER DAY...

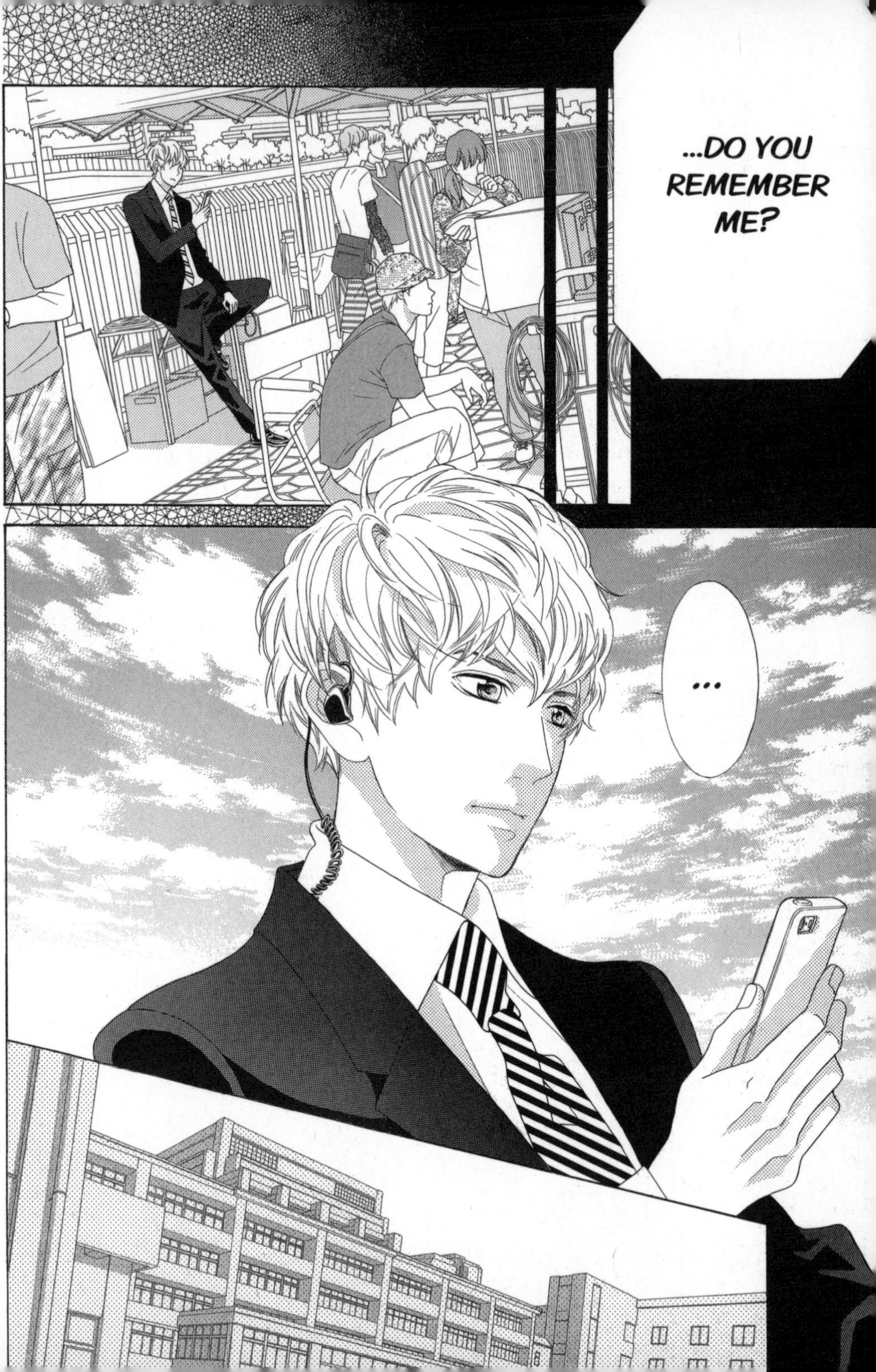
...DO YOU REMEMBER ME?
...

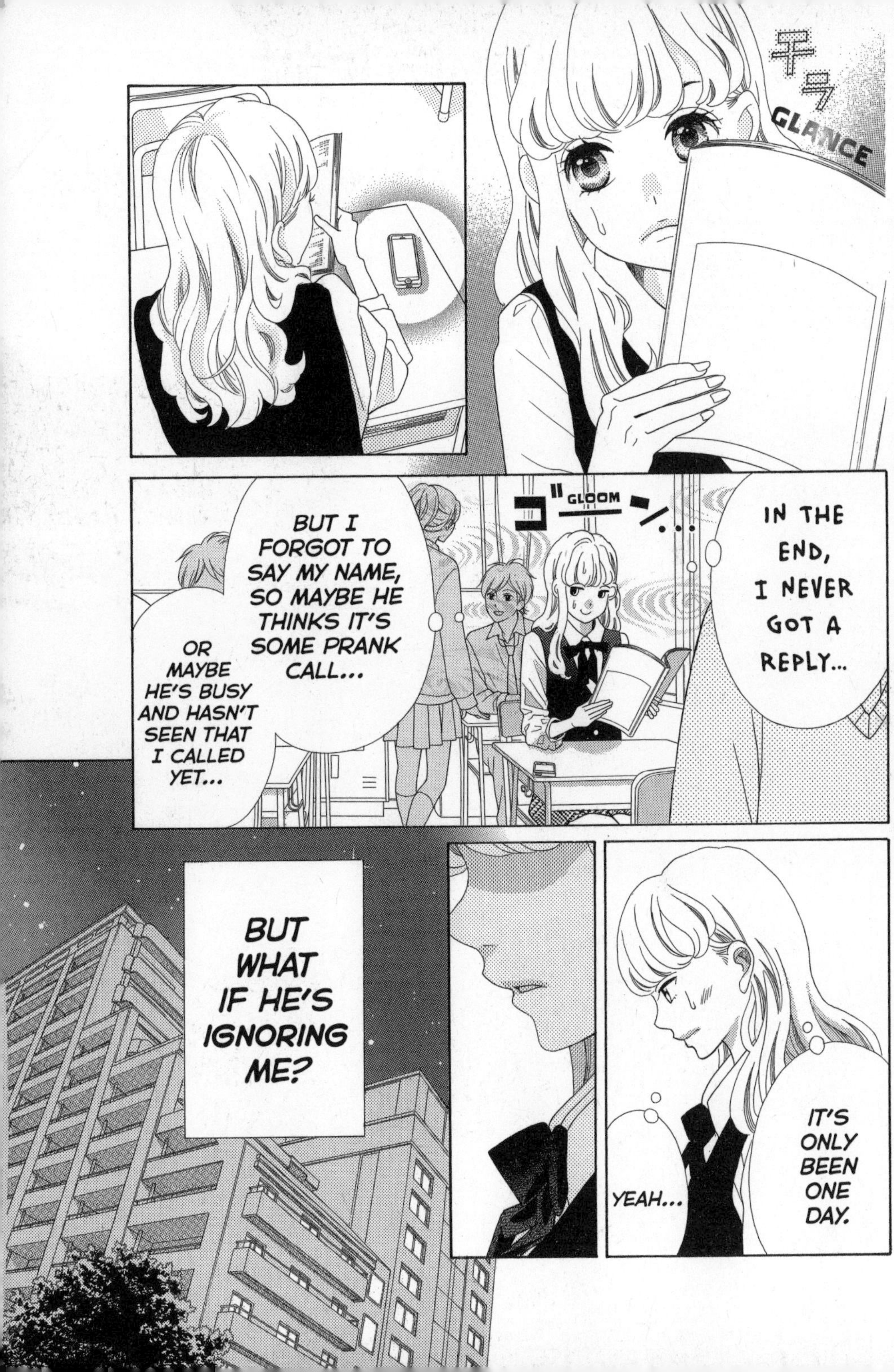
チラ
GLANCE
IN THE END, I NEVER GOT A REPLY...
GLOOM
BUT I FORGOT TO SAY MY NAME, SO MAYBE HE THINKS IT'S SOME PRANK CALL...
OR MAYBE HE'S BUSY AND HASN'T SEEN THAT I CALLED YET...
IT'S ONLY BEEN ONE DAY.
YEAH...
BUT WHAT IF HE'S IGNORING ME?

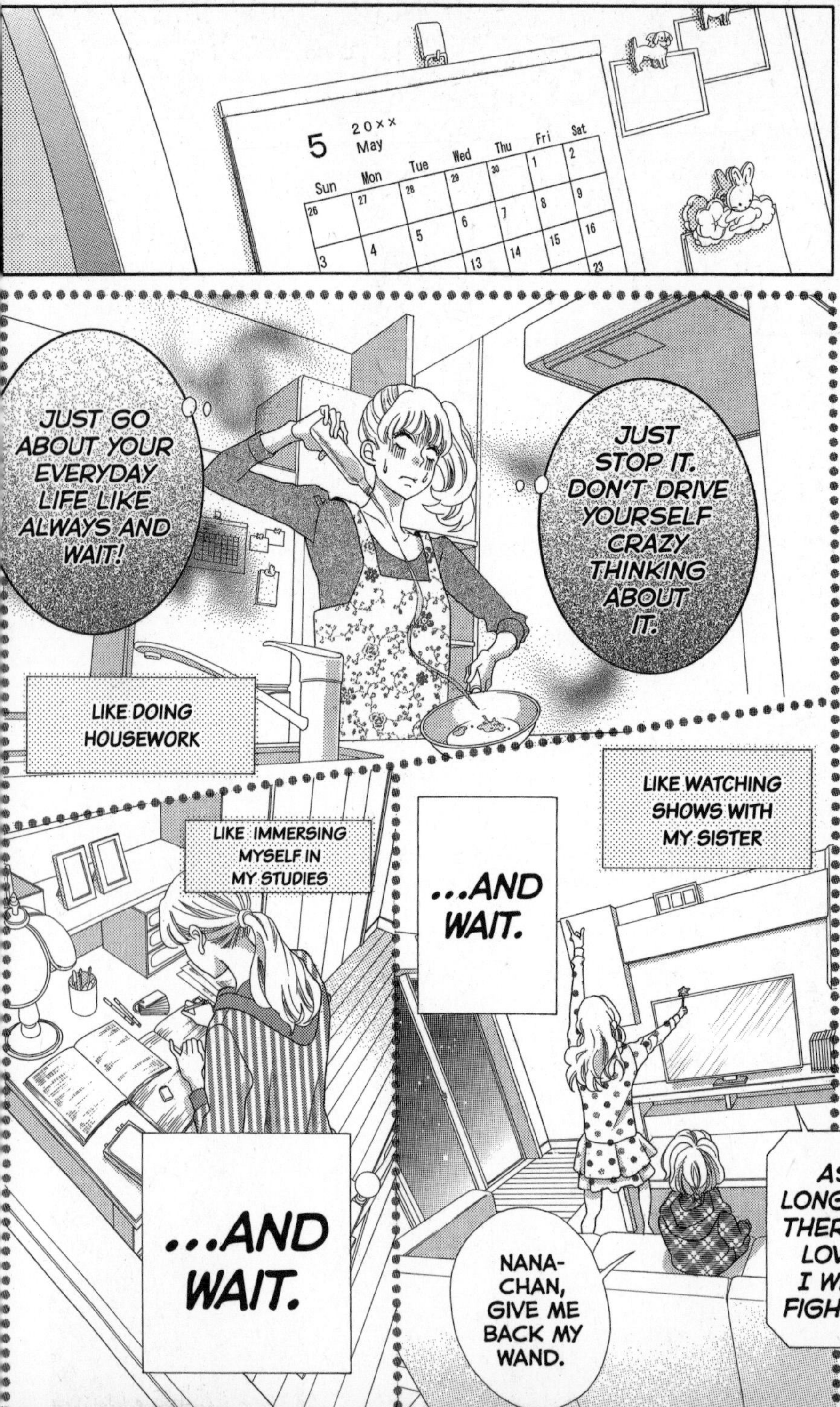
5
20××
May
Sun Mon Tue Wed Thu Fri Sat
JUST STOP IT. DON'T DRIVE YOURSELF CRAZY THINKING ABOUT IT.
JUST GO ABOUT YOUR EVERYDAY LIFE LIKE ALWAYS AND WAIT!
LIKE DOING HOUSEWORK
LIKE WATCHING SHOWS WITH MY SISTER
...AND WAIT.
AS LONG AS THERE'S LOVE, I WILL FIGHT!★
NANA-CHAN, GIVE ME BACK MY WAND.
LIKE IMMERSING MYSELF IN MY STUDIES
...AND WAIT.

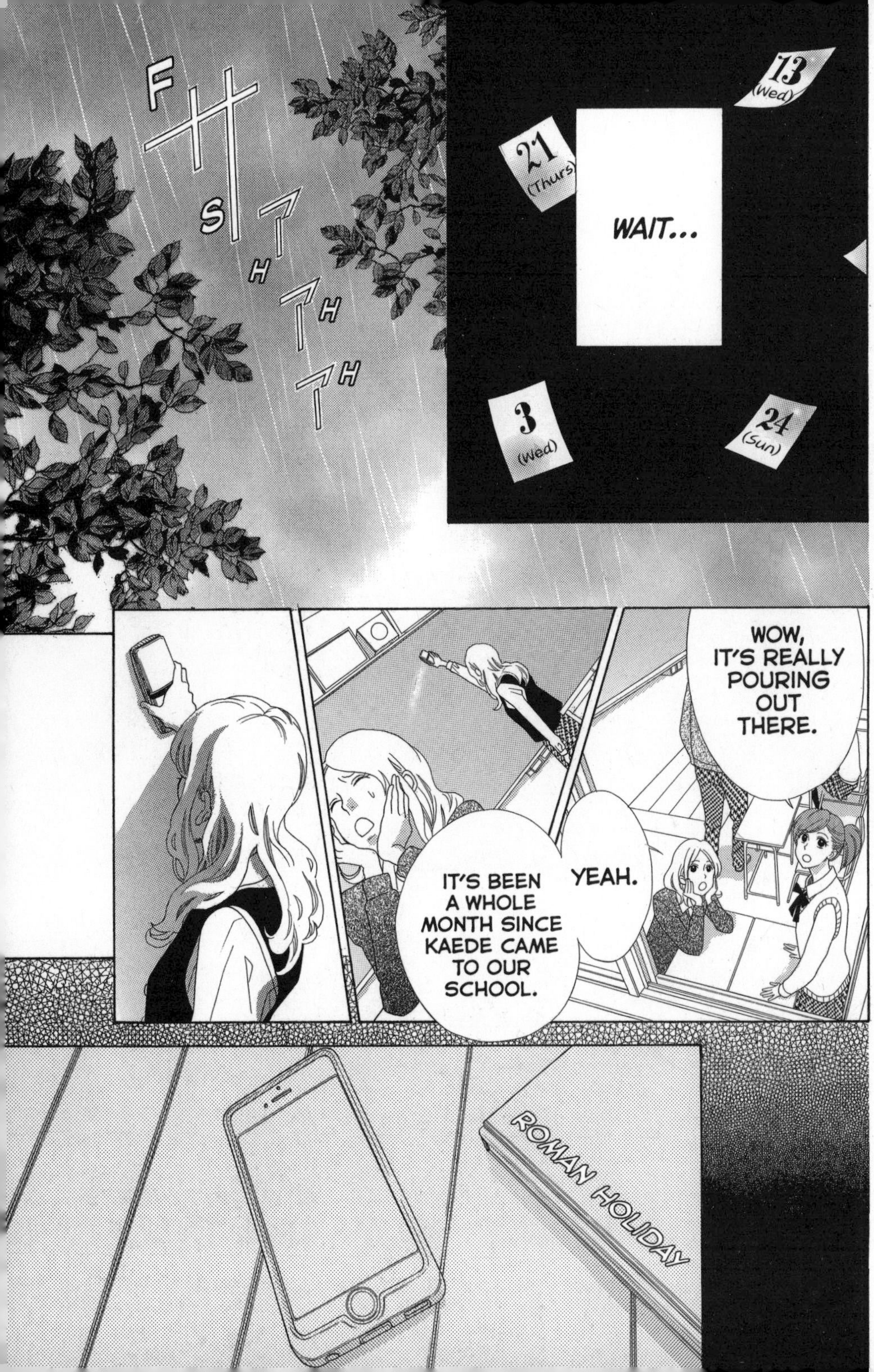

13 (Wed)
21 (Thurs)
WAIT...
3 (Wed)
24 (Sun)
FSHHH
WOW, IT'S REALLY POURING OUT THERE.
YEAH.
IT'S BEEN A WHOLE MONTH SINCE KAEDE CAME TO OUR SCHOOL.
ROMAN HOLIDAY

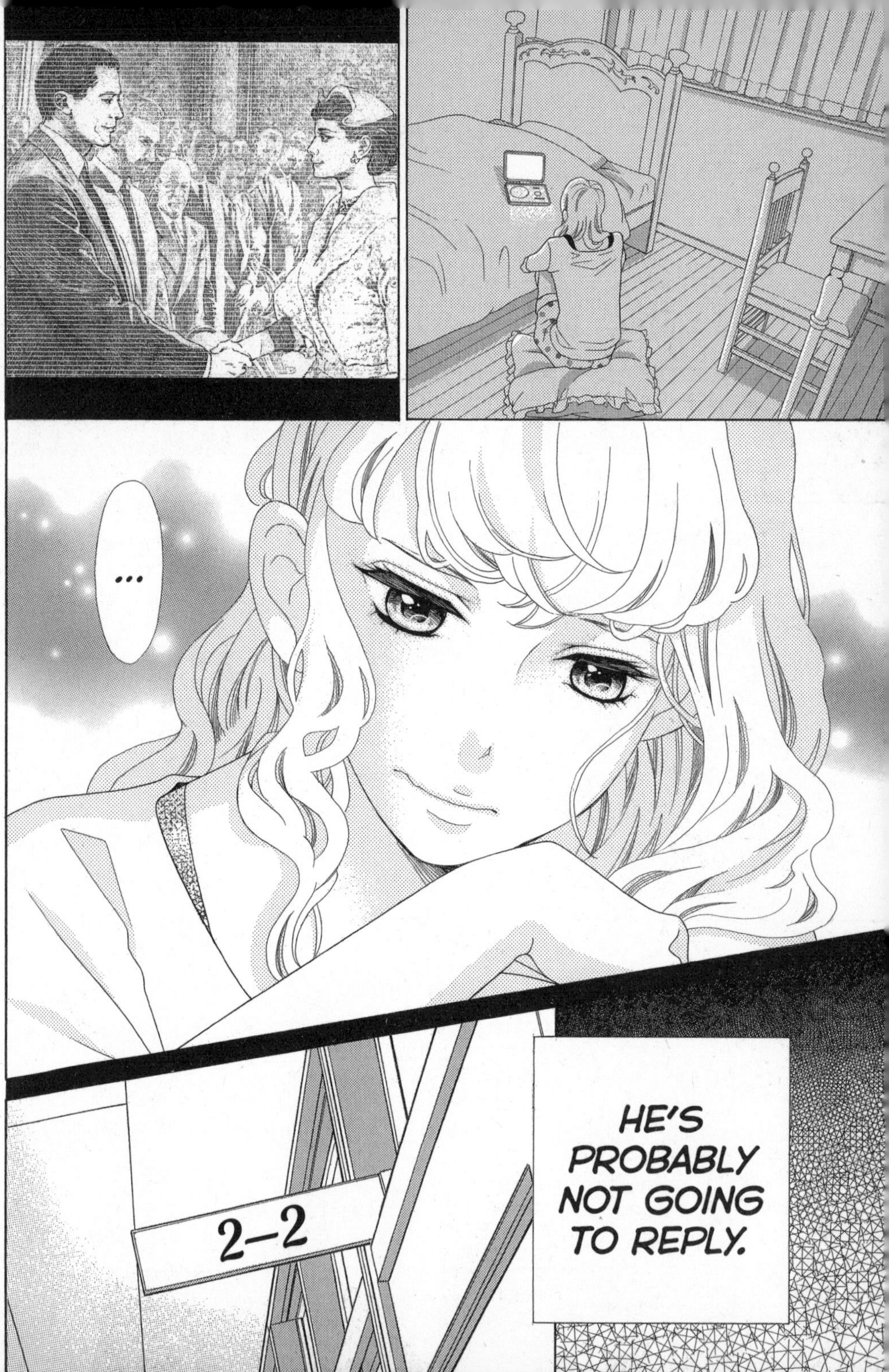
...
2-2
HE'S PROBABLY NOT GOING TO REPLY.

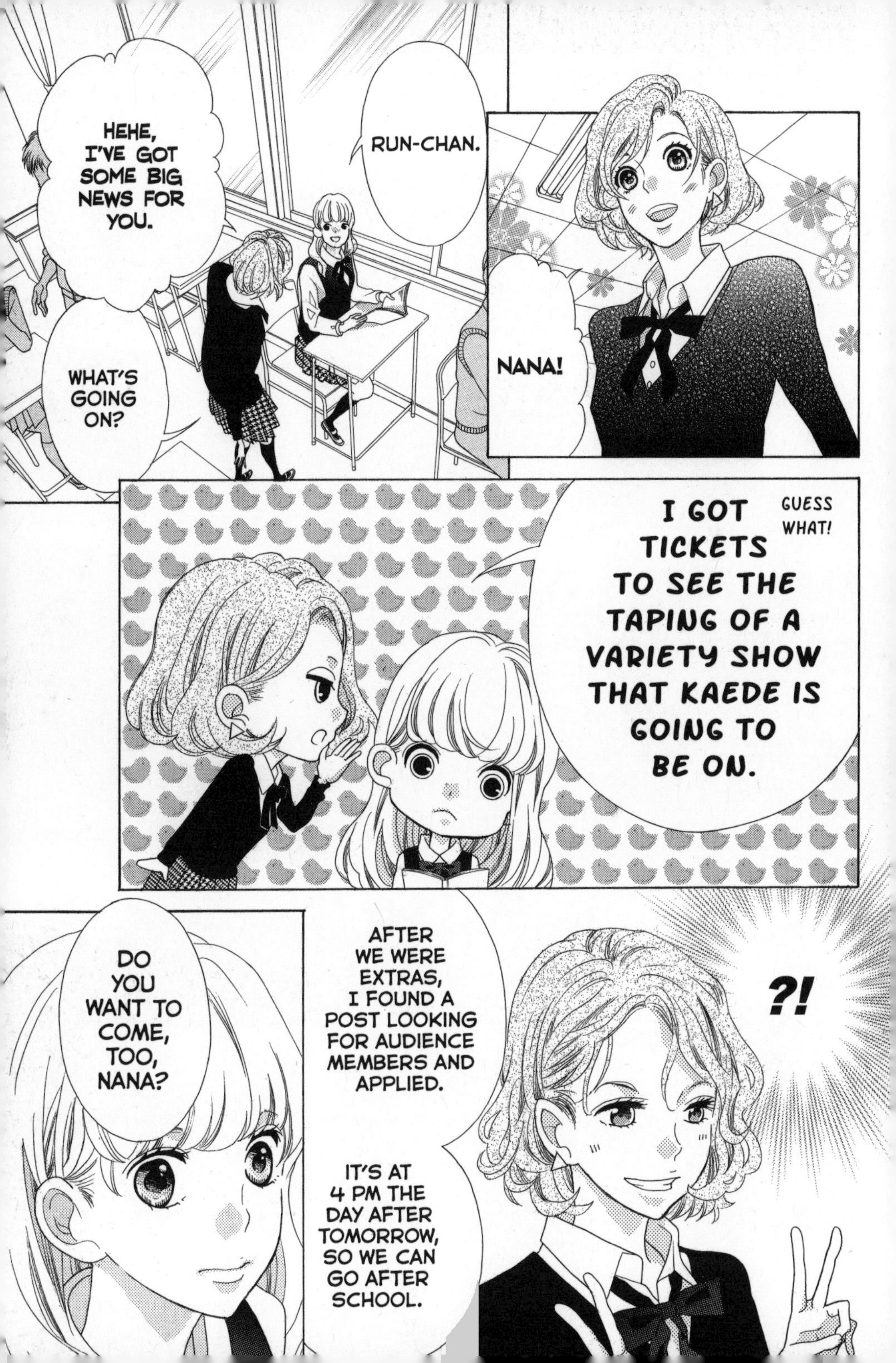
NANA!
RUN-CHAN.
HEHE, I'VE GOT SOME BIG NEWS FOR YOU.
WHAT'S GOING ON?
GUESS WHAT!
I GOT TICKETS TO SEE THE TAPING OF A VARIETY SHOW THAT KAEDE IS GOING TO BE ON.
?!
AFTER WE WERE EXTRAS, I FOUND A POST LOOKING FOR AUDIENCE MEMBERS AND APPLIED.
IT'S AT 4 PM THE DAY AFTER TOMORROW, SO WE CAN GO AFTER SCHOOL.
DO YOU WANT TO COME, TOO, NANA?

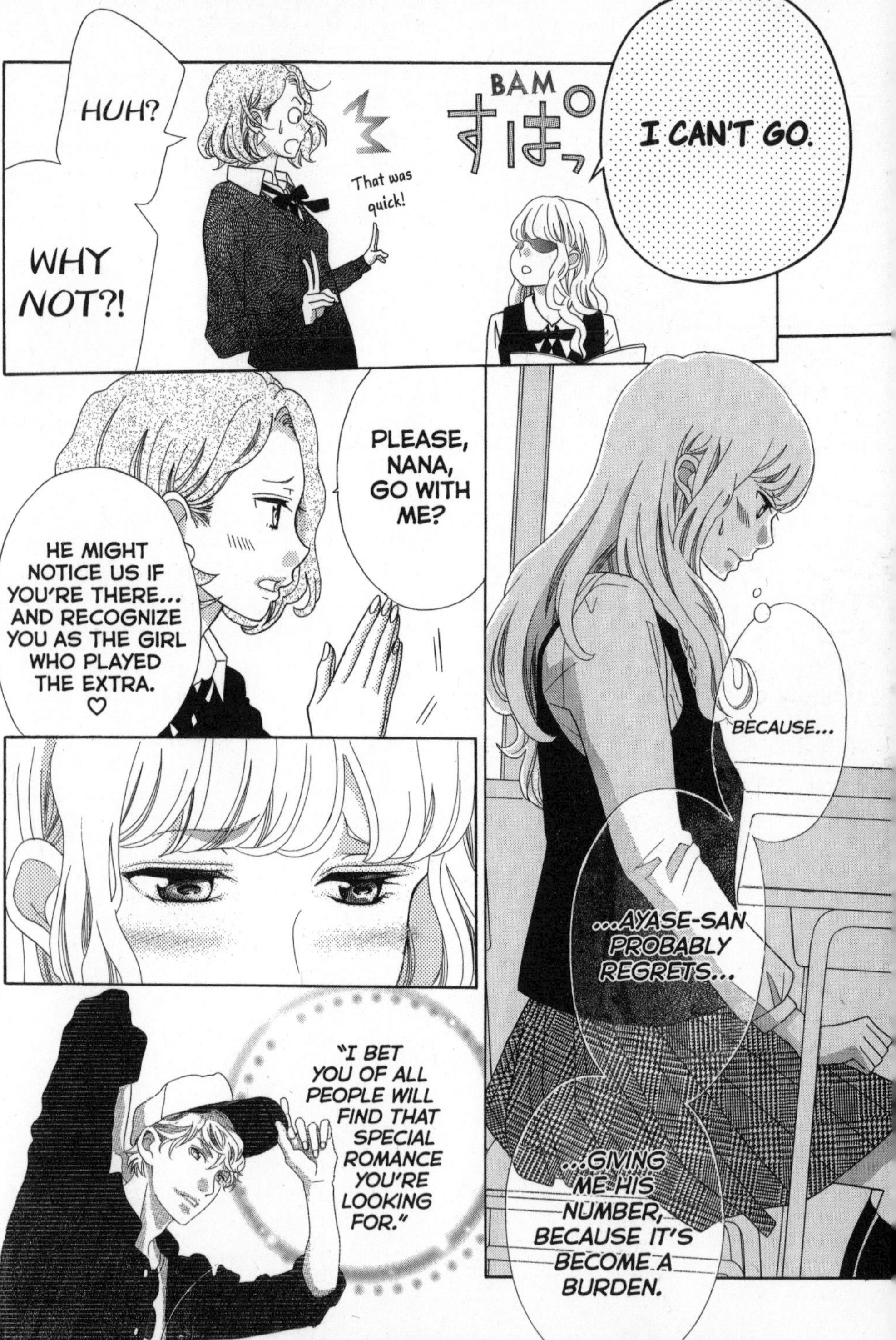
I CAN'T GO.
BAM
すぽっ
That was quick!
HUH?
WHY NOT?!
BECAUSE...
...AYASE-SAN PROBABLY REGRETS...
...GIVING ME HIS NUMBER, BECAUSE IT'S BECOME A BURDEN.
PLEASE, NANA, GO WITH ME?
HE MIGHT NOTICE US IF YOU'RE THERE... AND RECOGNIZE YOU AS THE GIRL WHO PLAYED THE EXTRA. ♡
"I BET YOU OF ALL PEOPLE WILL FIND THAT SPECIAL ROMANCE YOU'RE LOOKING FOR."

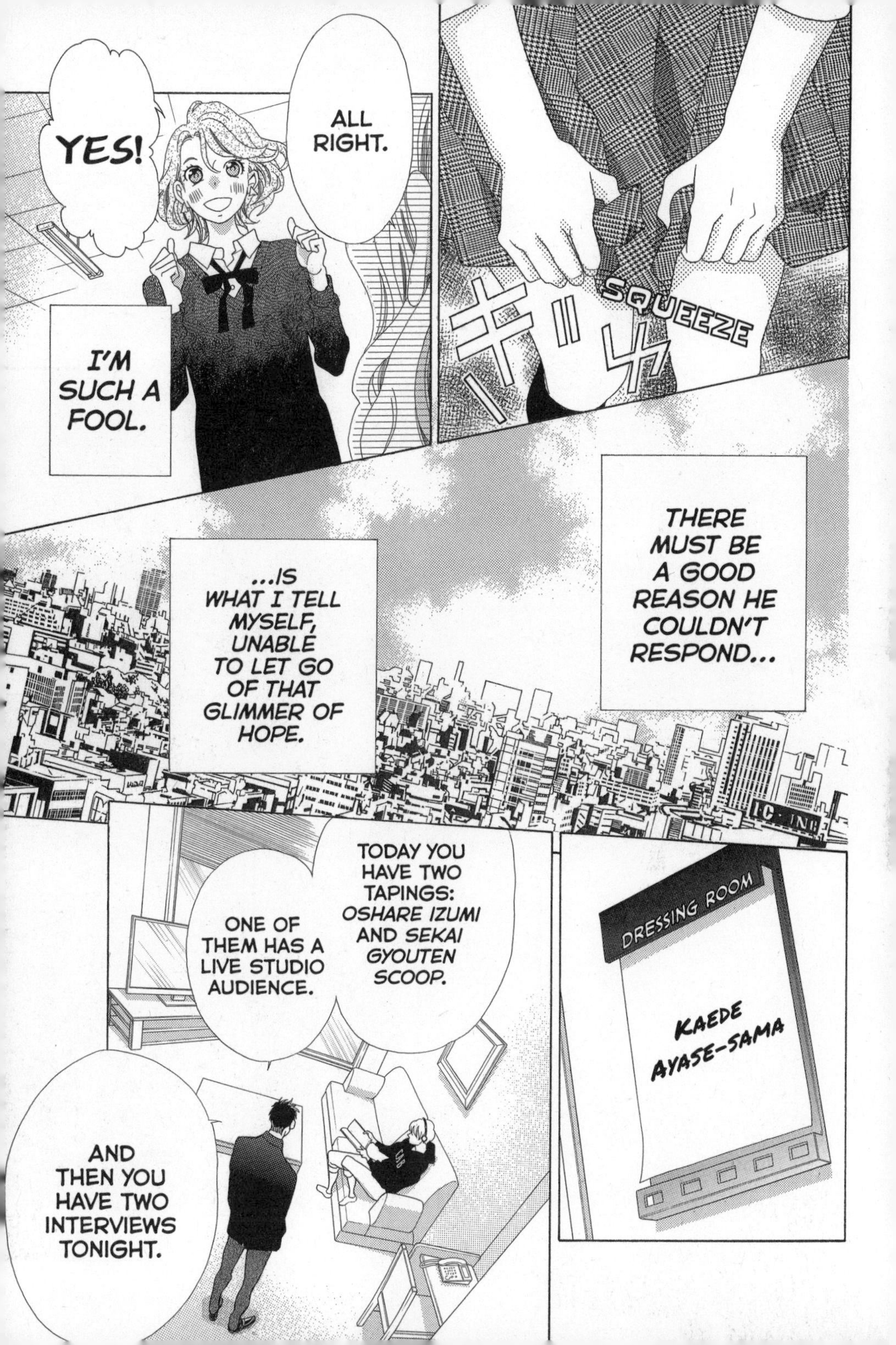
SQUEEZE
ALL RIGHT.
YES!
I'M SUCH A FOOL.
THERE MUST BE A GOOD REASON HE COULDN'T RESPOND...
...IS WHAT I TELL MYSELF, UNABLE TO LET GO OF THAT GLIMMER OF HOPE.
DRESSING ROOM
KAEDE AYASE-SAMA
TODAY YOU HAVE TWO TAPINGS: OSHARE IZUMI AND SEKAI GYOUTEN SCOOP.
ONE OF THEM HAS A LIVE STUDIO AUDIENCE.
AND THEN YOU HAVE TWO INTERVIEWS TONIGHT.

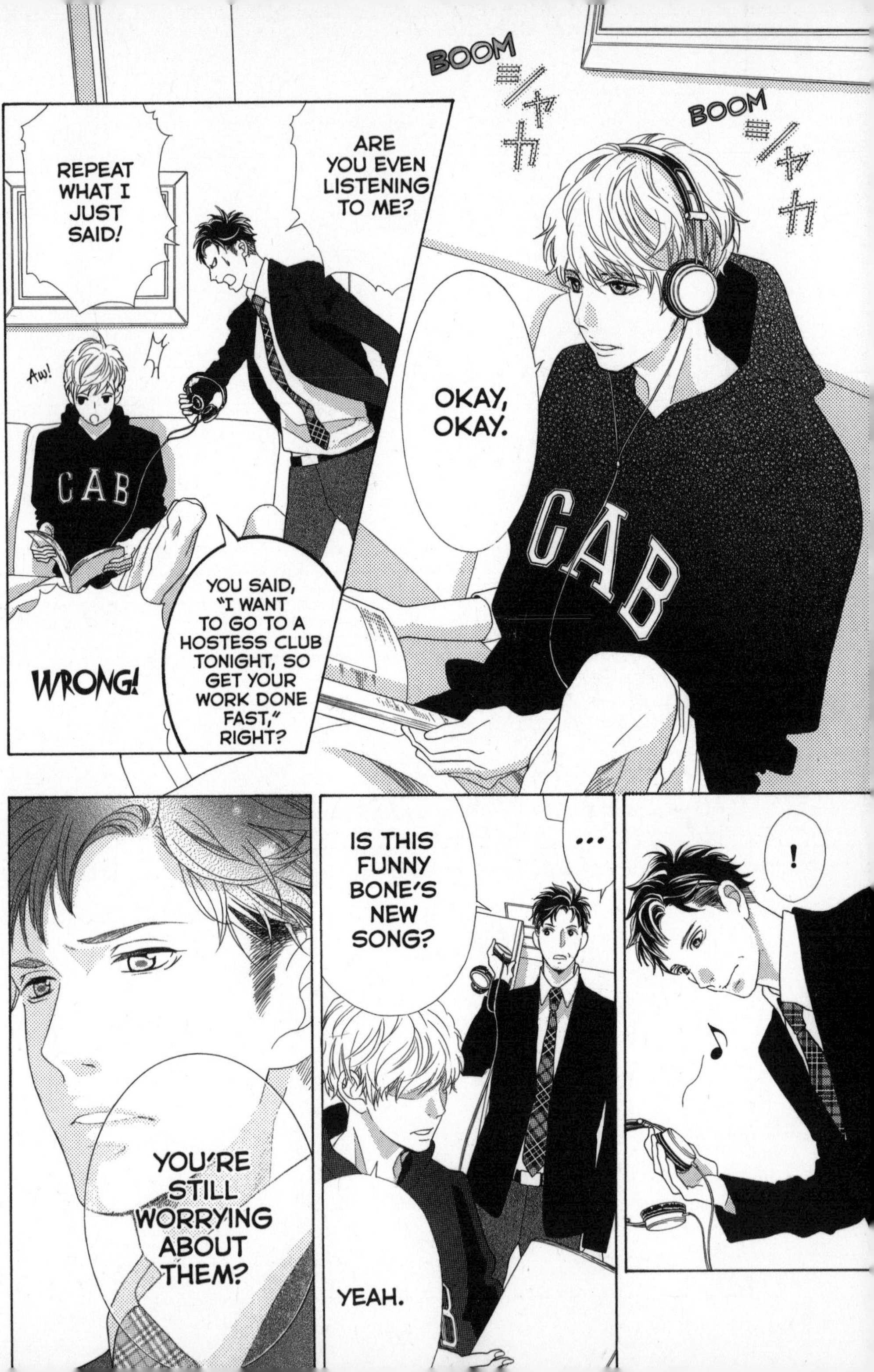
BOOM
BOOM
OKAY, OKAY.
ARE YOU EVEN LISTENING TO ME?
REPEAT WHAT I JUST SAID!
Aw!
YOU SAID, "I WANT TO GO TO A HOSTESS CLUB TONIGHT, SO GET YOUR WORK DONE FAST," RIGHT?
WRONG!
!
...
IS THIS FUNNY BONE'S NEW SONG?
YEAH.
YOU'RE STILL WORRYING ABOUT THEM?

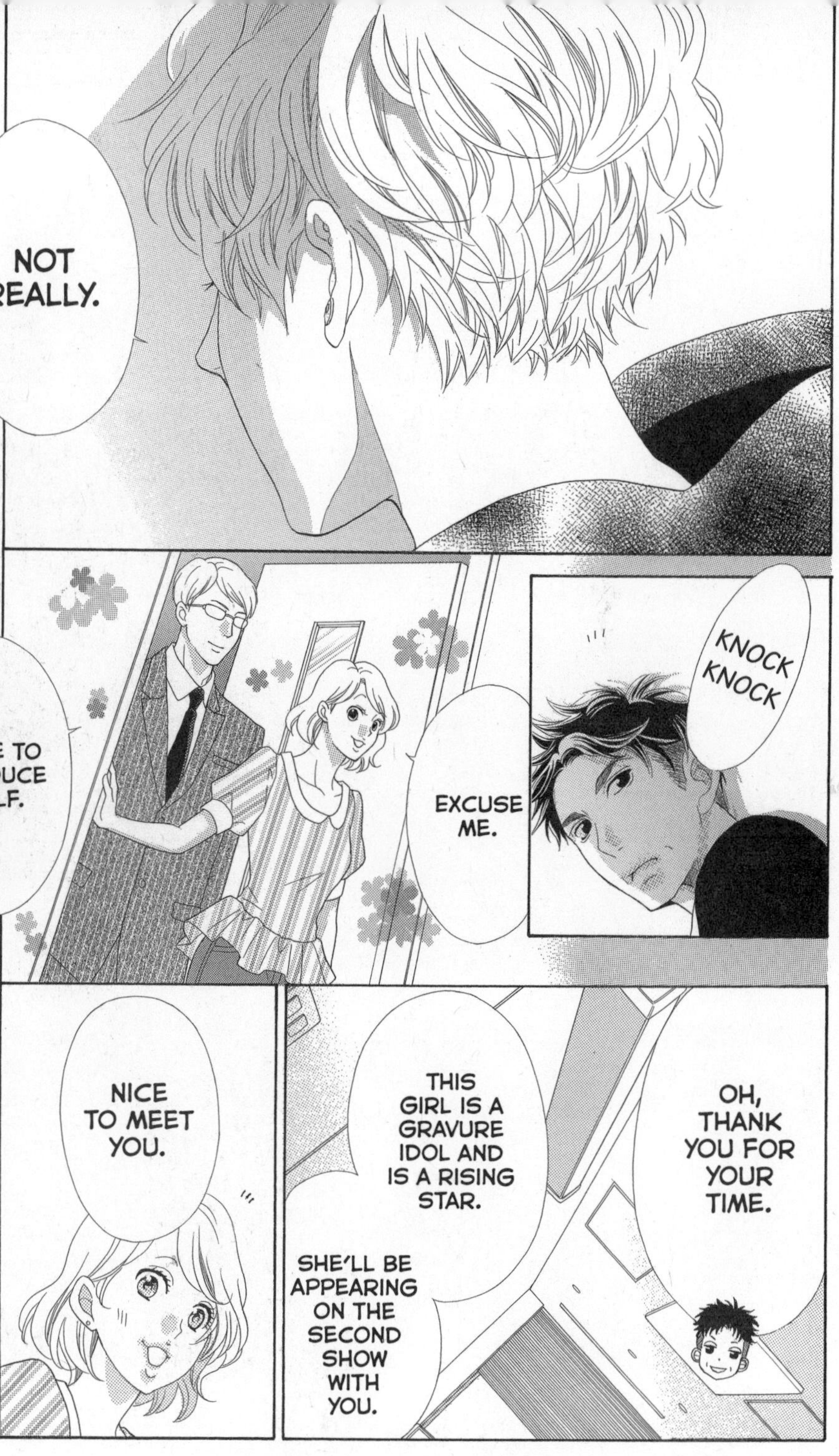
NOT REALLY.
KNOCK KNOCK
EXCUSE ME.
I CAME TO INTRODUCE MYSELF.
OH, THANK YOU FOR YOUR TIME.
THIS GIRL IS A GRAVURE IDOL AND IS A RISING STAR.
SHE'LL BE APPEARING ON THE SECOND SHOW WITH YOU.
NICE TO MEET YOU.

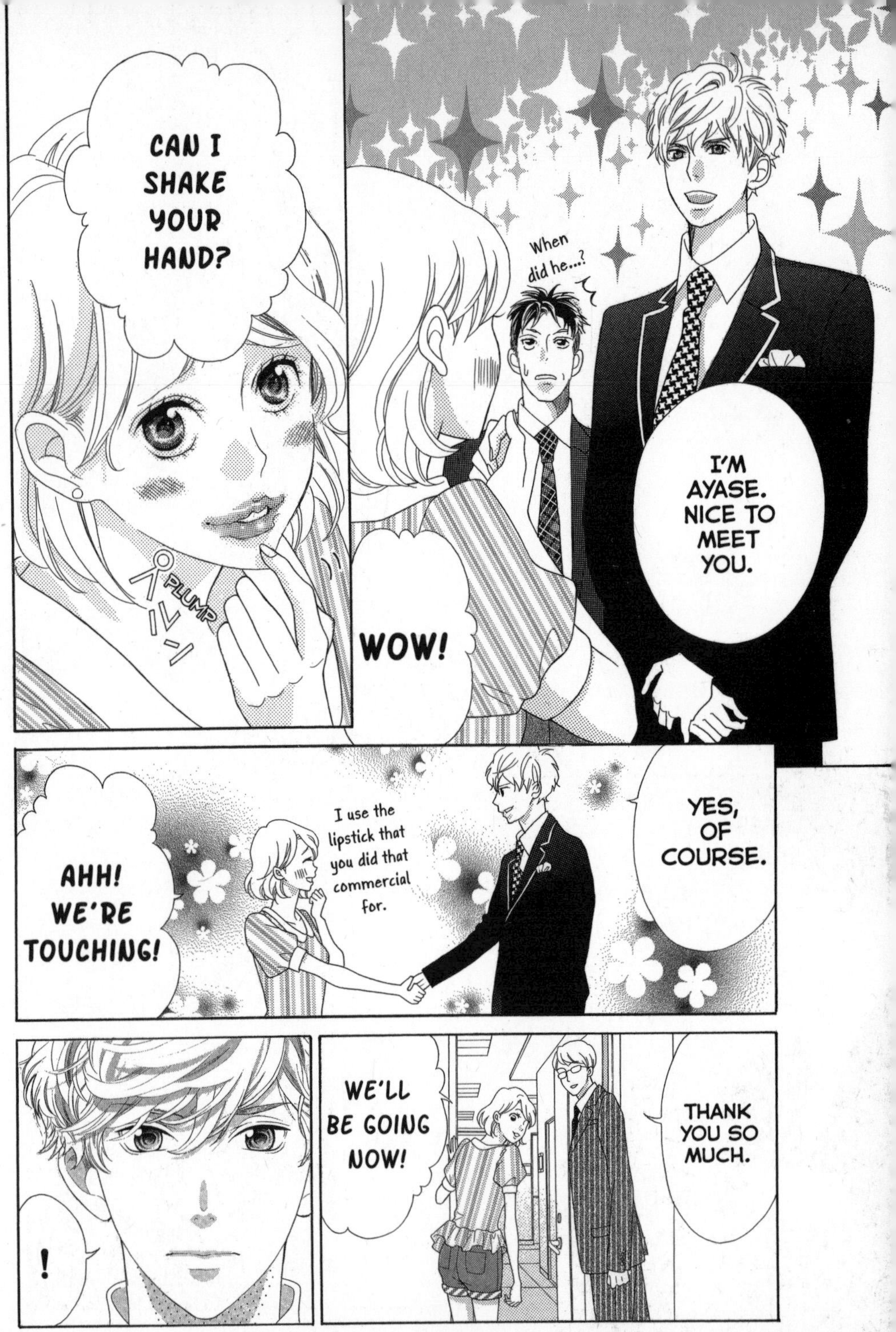
I'M AYASE. NICE TO MEET YOU.
When did he...?
WOW!
CAN I SHAKE YOUR HAND?
PLUMP
YES, OF COURSE.
I use the lipstick that you did that commercial for.
AHH! WE'RE TOUCHING!
THANK YOU SO MUCH.
WE'LL BE GOING NOW!
!

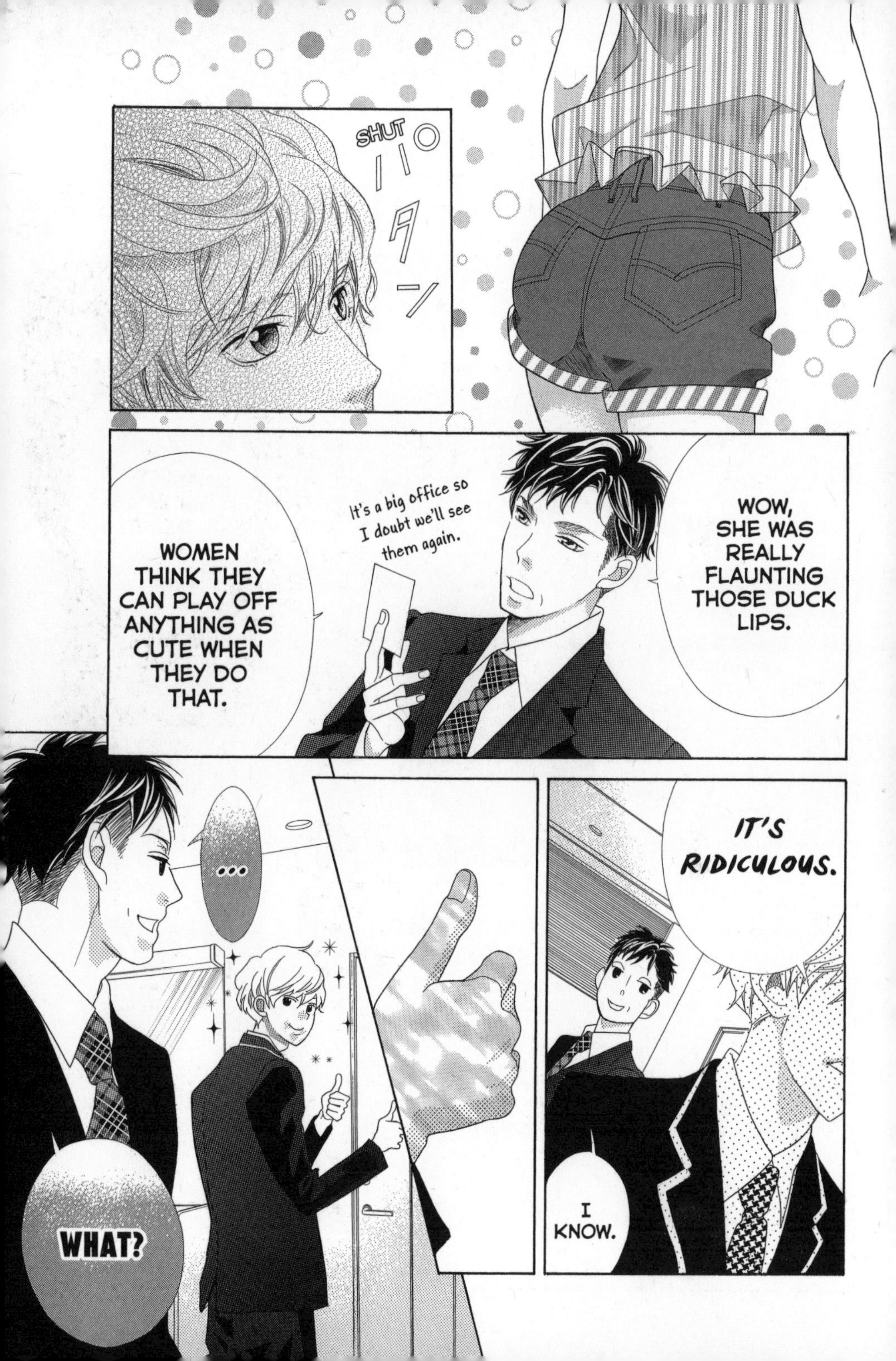
SHUT
WOW, SHE WAS REALLY FLAUNTING THOSE DUCK LIPS.
It's a big office so I doubt we'll see them again.
WOMEN THINK THEY CAN PLAY OFF ANYTHING AS CUTE WHEN THEY DO THAT.
IT'S RIDICULOUS.
I KNOW.
...
WHAT?

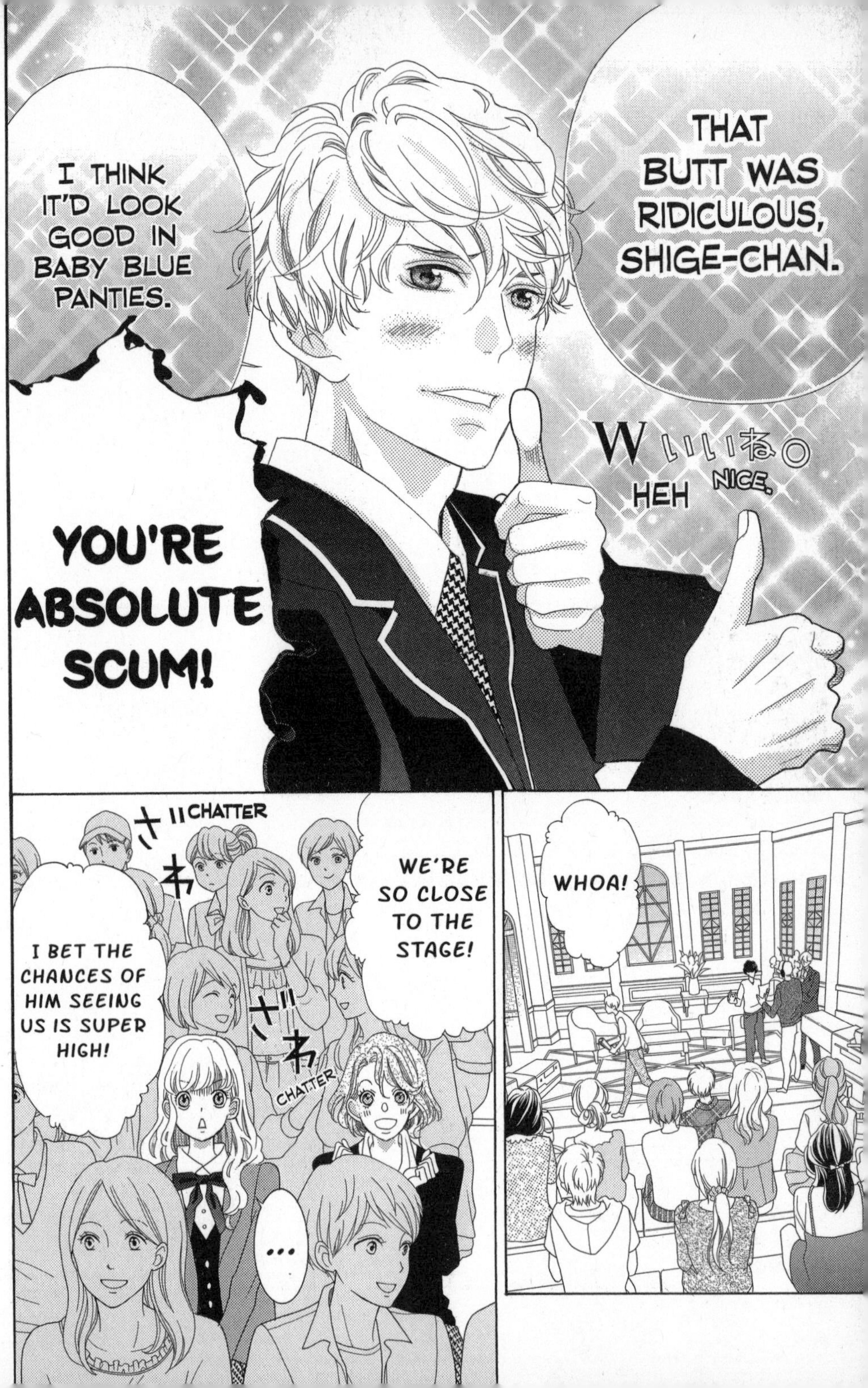
THAT BUTT WAS RIDICULOUS, SHIGE-CHAN.
I THINK IT'D LOOK GOOD IN BABY BLUE PANTIES.
W いいね○
HEH NICE.
YOU'RE ABSOLUTE SCUM!
WHOA!
さわ
CHATTER
WE'RE SO CLOSE TO THE STAGE!
I BET THE CHANCES OF HIM SEEING US IS SUPER HIGH!
ざわ
CHATTER
...

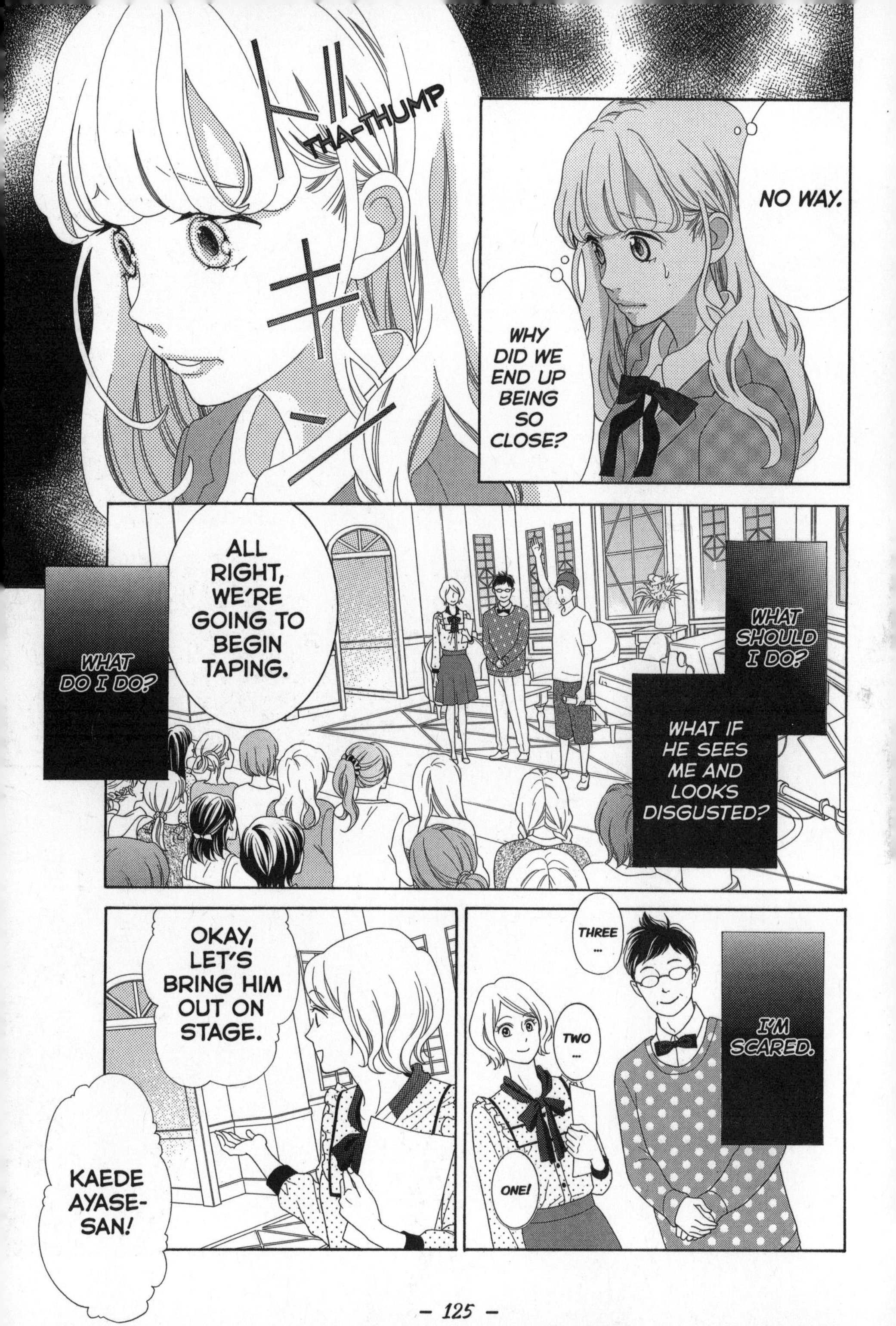
NO WAY.
WHY DID WE END UP BEING SO CLOSE?
THA-THUMP
WHAT SHOULD I DO?
WHAT IF HE SEES ME AND LOOKS DISGUSTED?
ALL RIGHT, WE'RE GOING TO BEGIN TAPING.
WHAT DO I DO?
THREE ...
I'M SCARED.
TWO ...
ONE!
OKAY, LET'S BRING HIM OUT ON STAGE.
KAEDE AYASE-SAN!

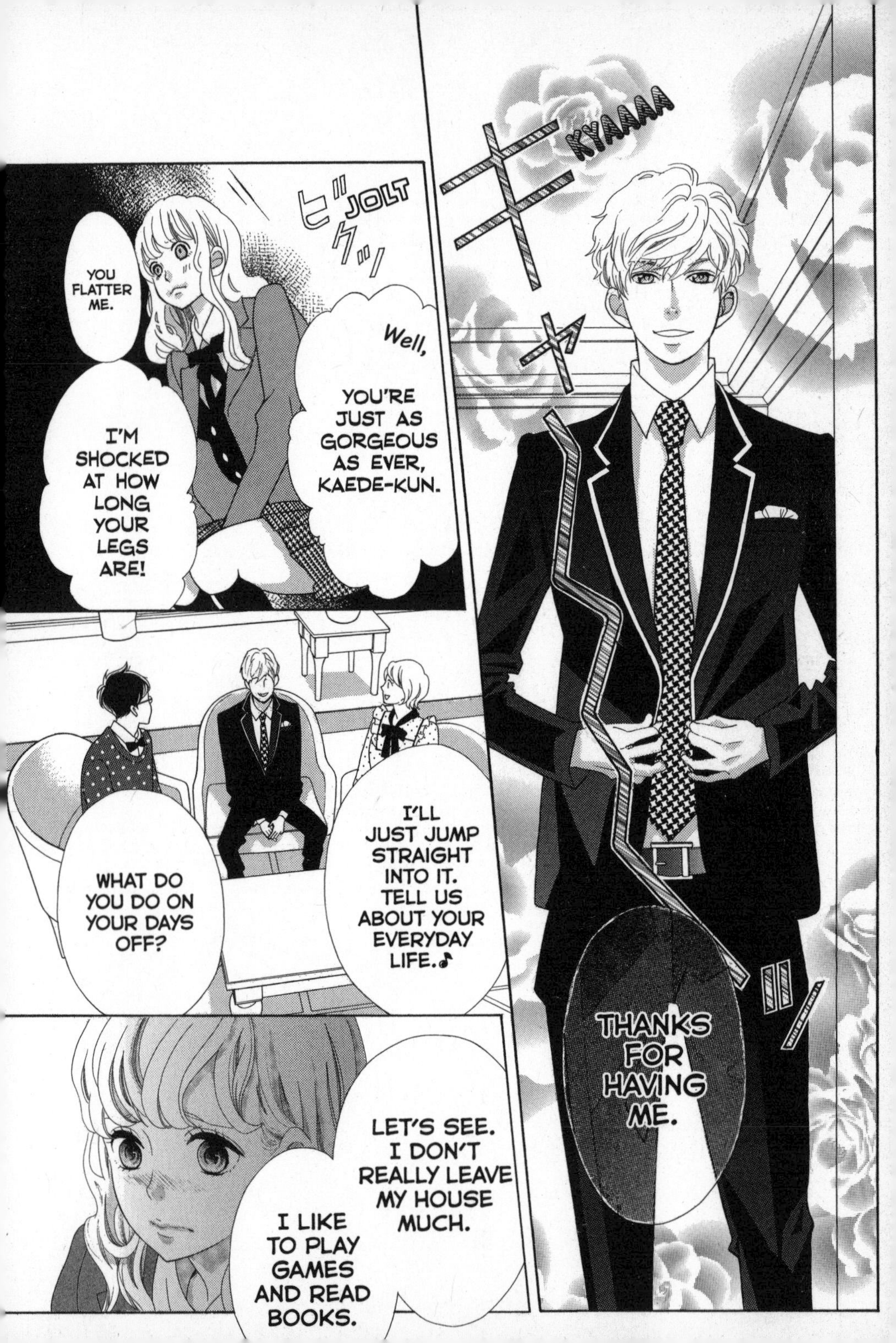
KYAAAA
THANKS FOR HAVING ME.
JOLT
Well,
YOU'RE JUST AS GORGEOUS AS EVER, KAEDE-KUN.
YOU FLATTER ME.
I'M SHOCKED AT HOW LONG YOUR LEGS ARE!
I'LL JUST JUMP STRAIGHT INTO IT. TELL US ABOUT YOUR EVERYDAY LIFE.♪
WHAT DO YOU DO ON YOUR DAYS OFF?
LET'S SEE. I DON'T REALLY LEAVE MY HOUSE MUCH.
I LIKE TO PLAY GAMES AND READ BOOKS.

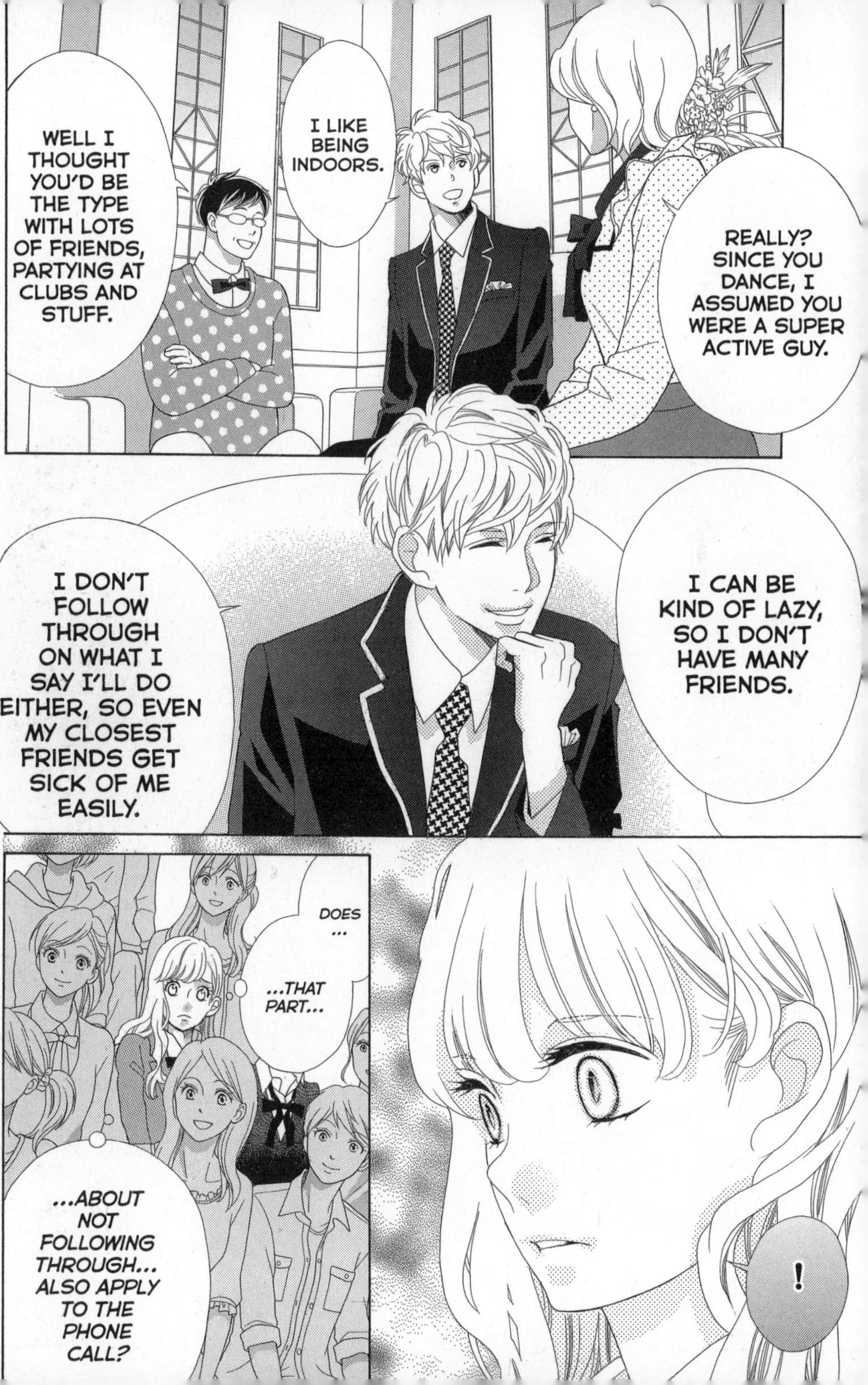
REALLY? SINCE YOU DANCE, I ASSUMED YOU WERE A SUPER ACTIVE GUY.
I LIKE BEING INDOORS.
WELL I THOUGHT YOU'D BE THE TYPE WITH LOTS OF FRIENDS, PARTYING AT CLUBS AND STUFF.
I CAN BE KIND OF LAZY, SO I DON'T HAVE MANY FRIENDS.
I DON'T FOLLOW THROUGH ON WHAT I SAY I'LL DO EITHER, SO EVEN MY CLOSEST FRIENDS GET SICK OF ME EASILY.
!
DOES ...
...THAT PART...
...ABOUT NOT FOLLOWING THROUGH... ALSO APPLY TO THE PHONE CALL?

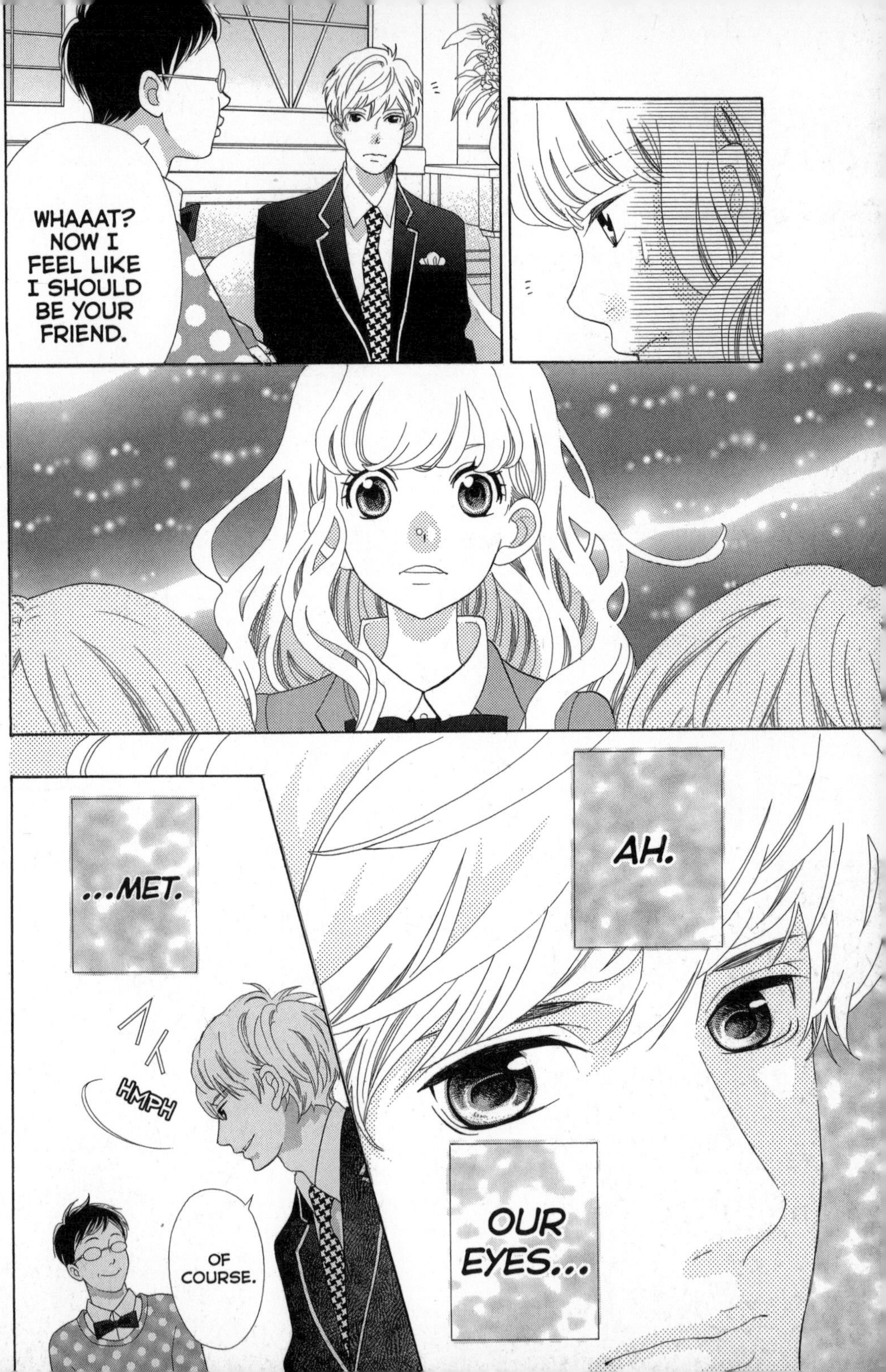
WHAAAT? NOW I FEEL LIKE I SHOULD BE YOUR FRIEND.
AH.
OUR EYES...
...MET.
HMPH
OF COURSE.

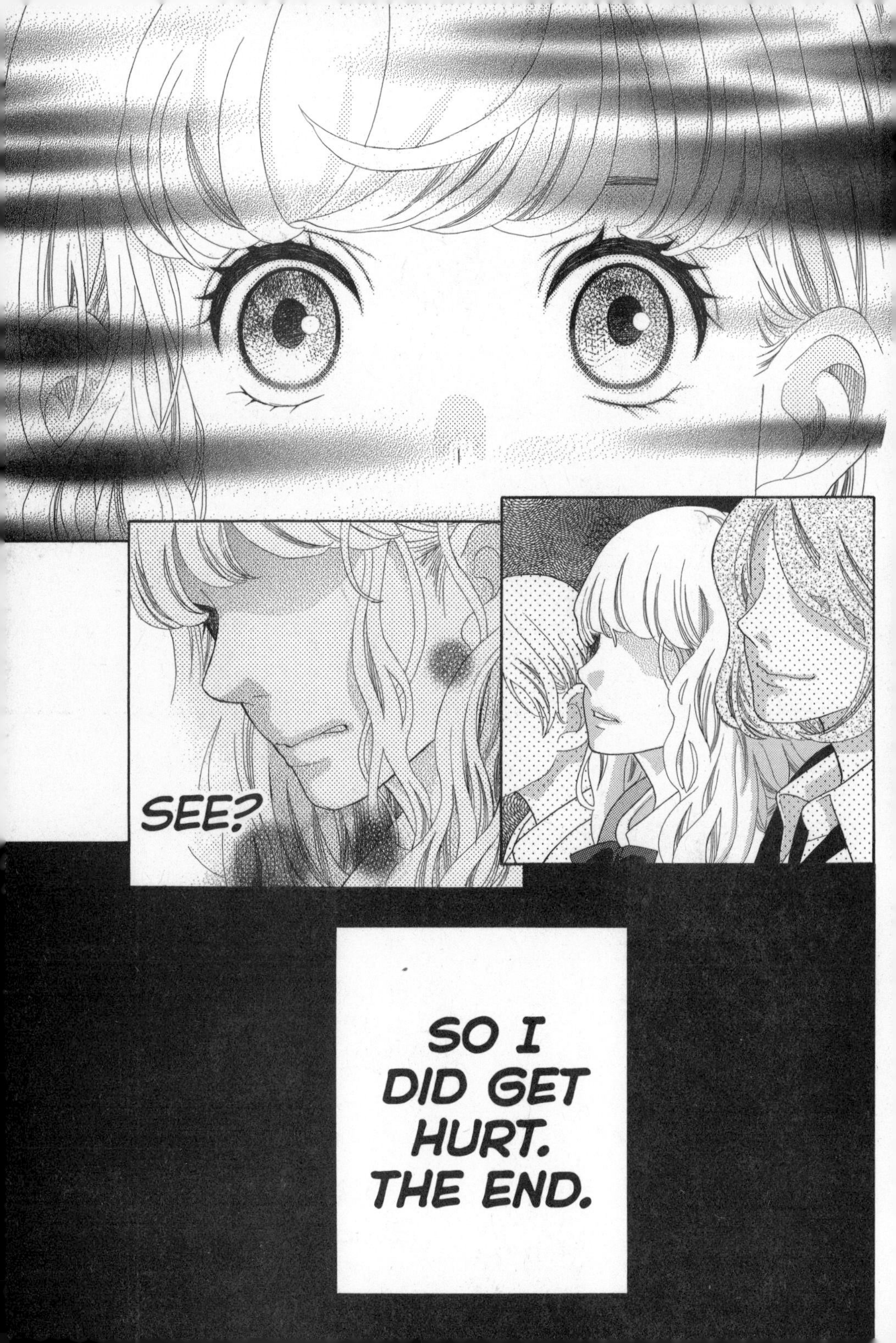
SEE?
SO I DID GET HURT. THE END.

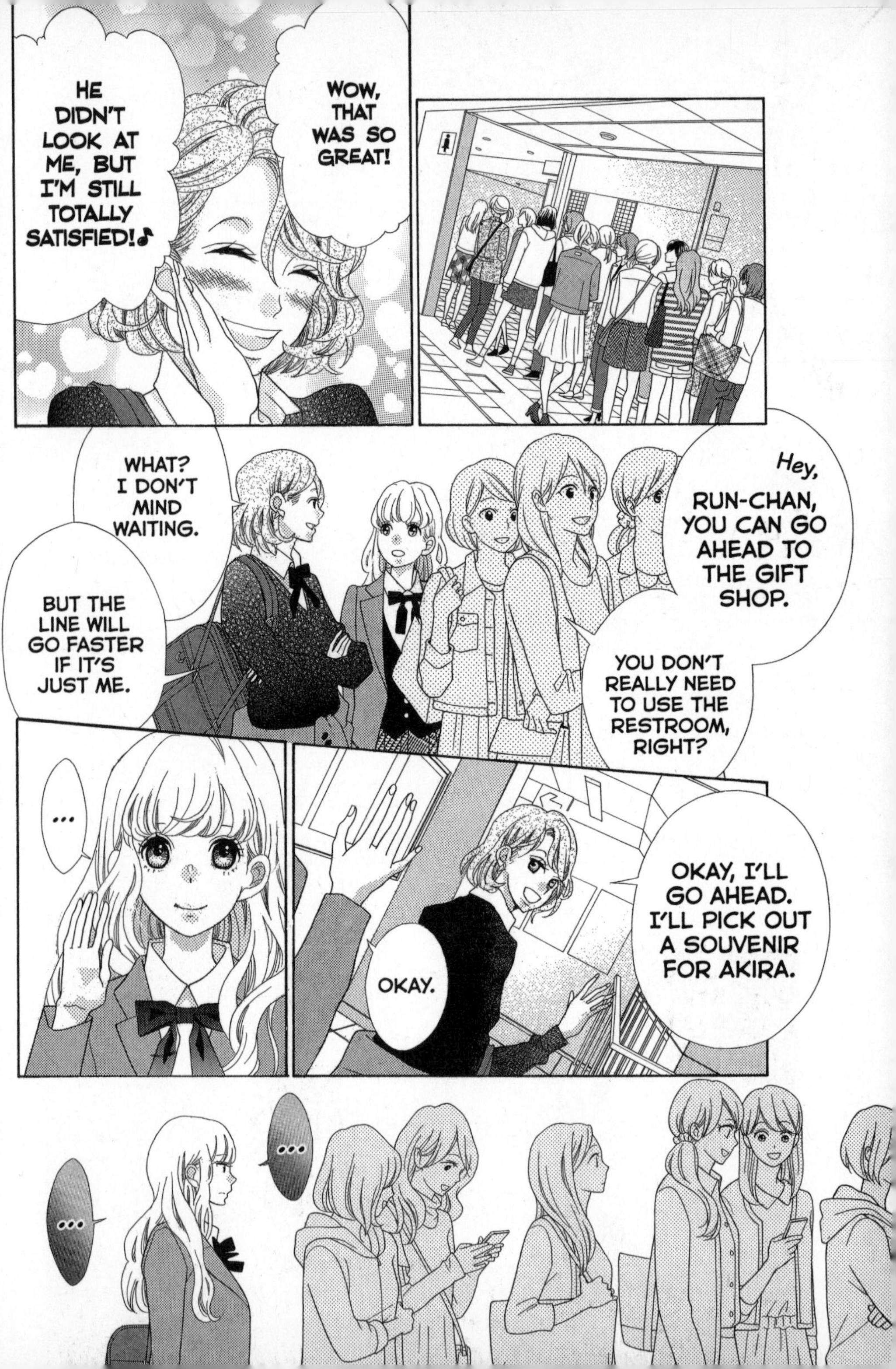
WOW, THAT WAS SO GREAT!
HE DIDN'T LOOK AT ME, BUT I'M STILL TOTALLY SATISFIED!♪
Hey, RUN-CHAN, YOU CAN GO AHEAD TO THE GIFT SHOP.
YOU DON'T REALLY NEED TO USE THE RESTROOM, RIGHT?
WHAT? I DON'T MIND WAITING.
BUT THE LINE WILL GO FASTER IF IT'S JUST ME.
OKAY, I'LL GO AHEAD. I'LL PICK OUT A SOUVENIR FOR AKIRA.
OKAY.
...
...
...

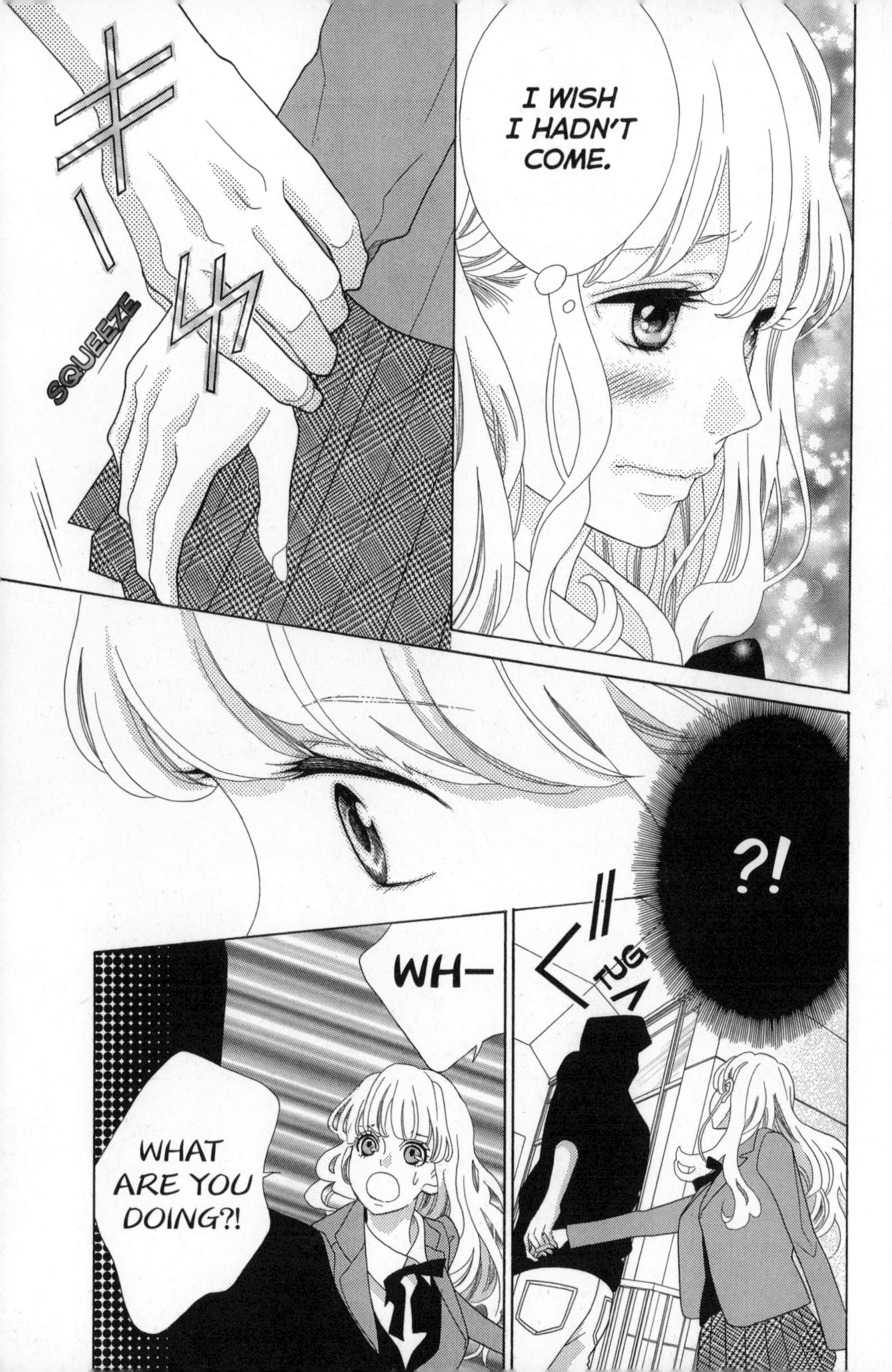
I WISH I HADN'T COME.
SQUEEZE
?!
TUG
WH–
WHAT ARE YOU DOING?!

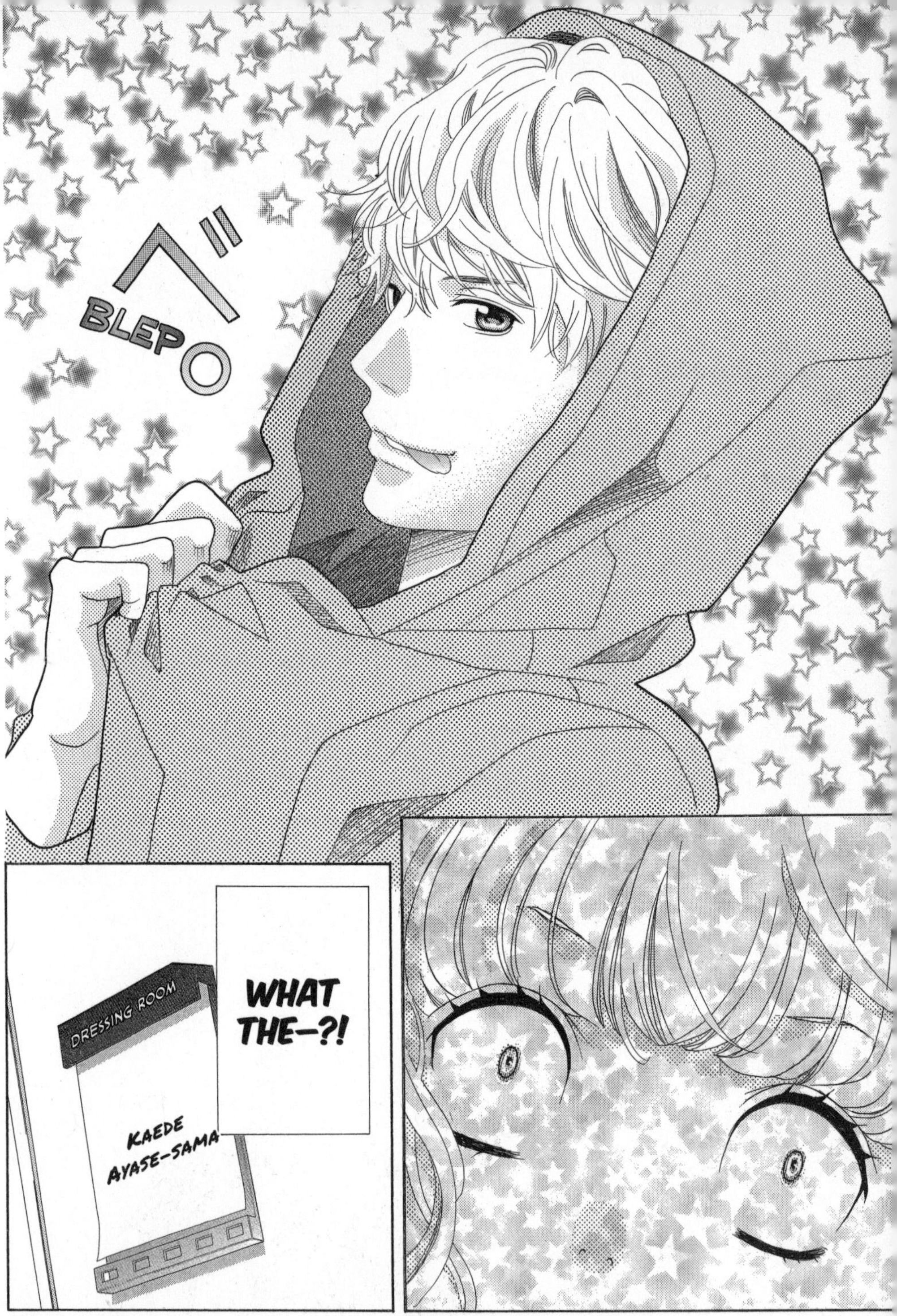
BLEPO
WHAT THE–?!
DRESSING ROOM
KAEDE AYASE-SAMA

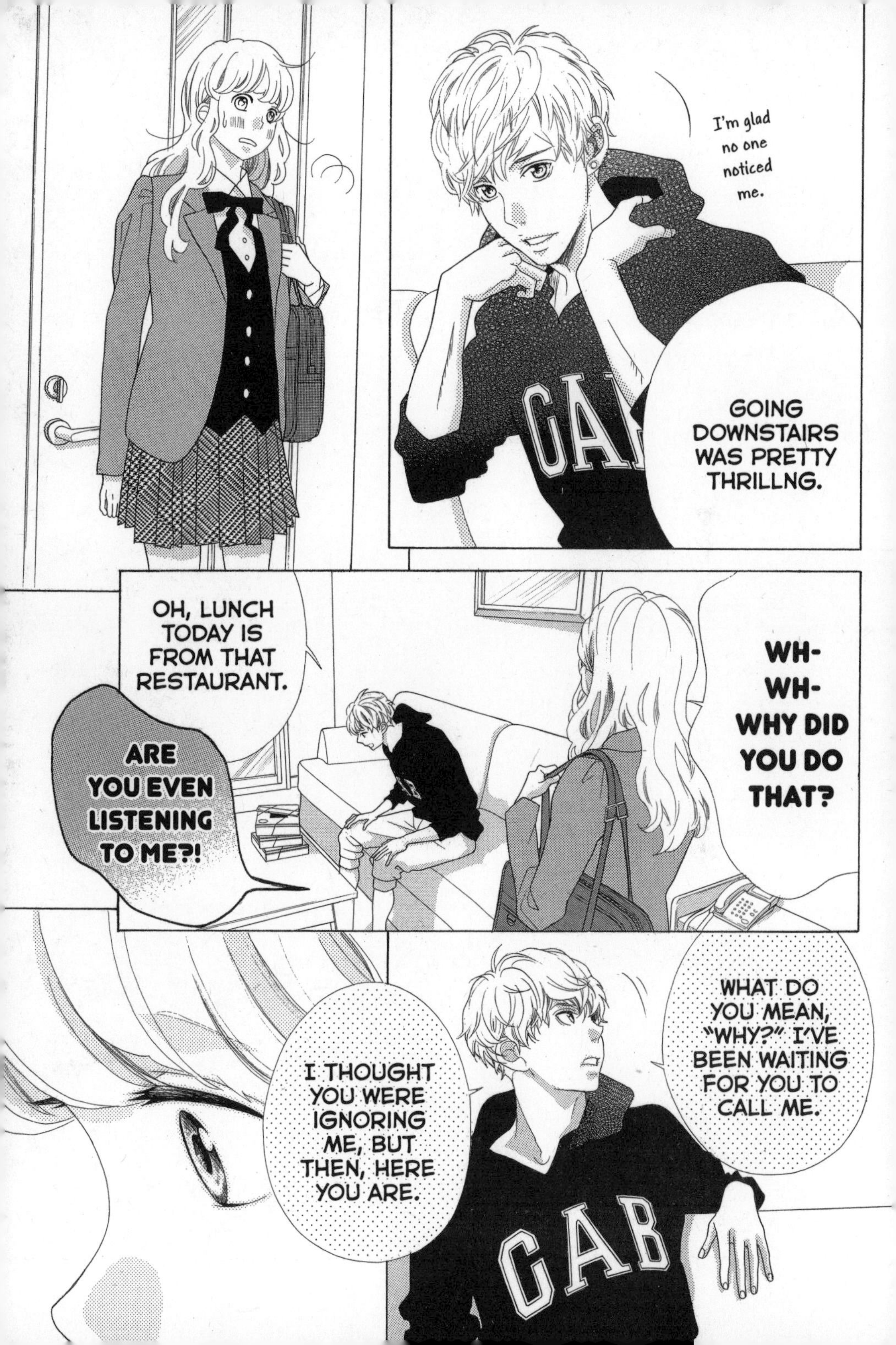
I'm glad no one noticed me.
GOING DOWNSTAIRS WAS PRETTY THRILLNG.
WH- WH- WHY DID YOU DO THAT?
OH, LUNCH TODAY IS FROM THAT RESTAURANT.
ARE YOU EVEN LISTENING TO ME?!
WHAT DO YOU MEAN, "WHY?" I'VE BEEN WAITING FOR YOU TO CALL ME.
I THOUGHT YOU WERE IGNORING ME, BUT THEN, HERE YOU ARE.

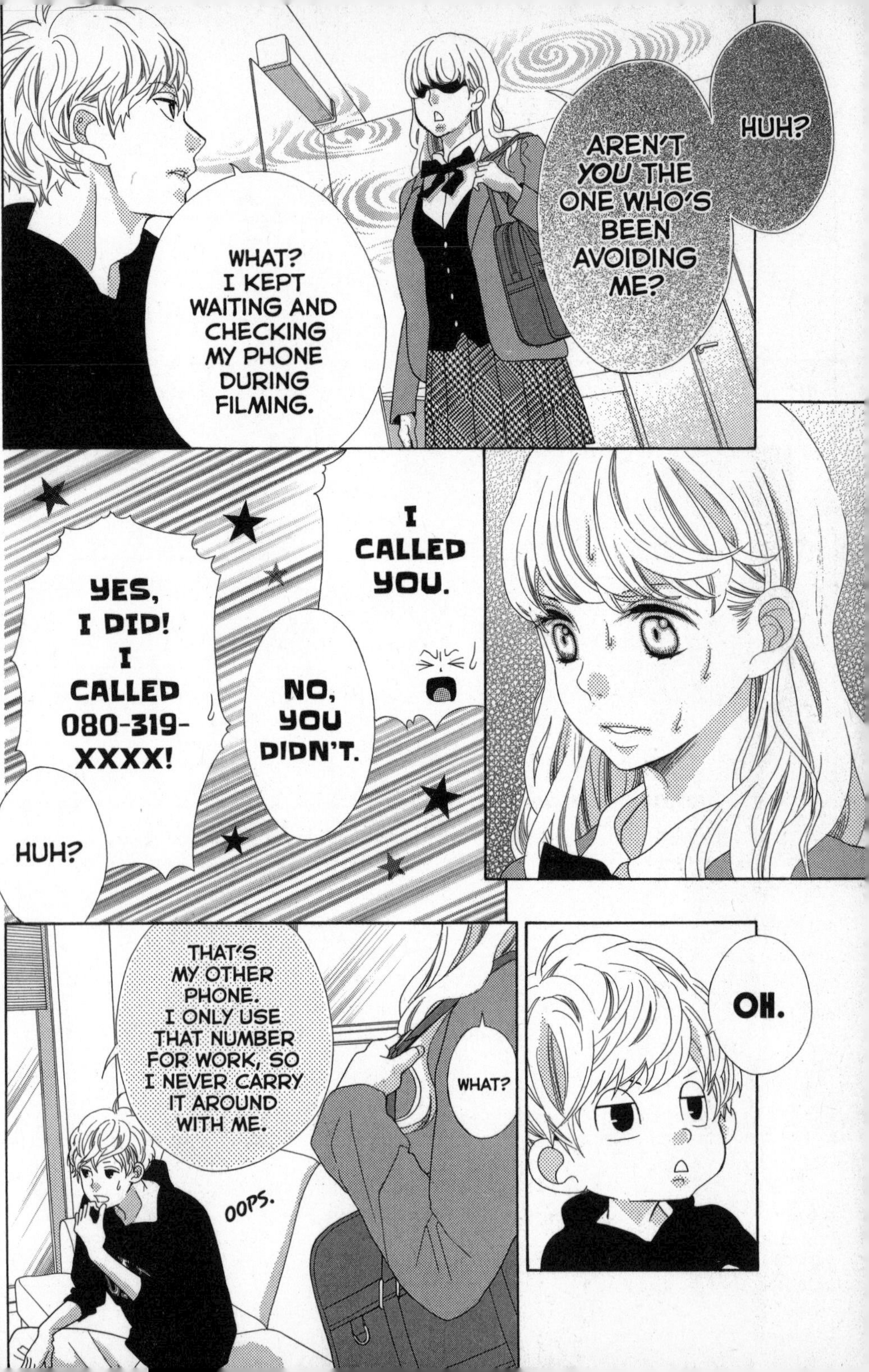
HUH?
AREN'T *YOU* THE ONE WHO'S BEEN AVOIDING ME?
WHAT? I KEPT WAITING AND CHECKING MY PHONE DURING FILMING.
I CALLED YOU.
NO, YOU DIDN'T.
YES, I DID! I CALLED 080-319-XXXX!
HUH?
OH.
THAT'S MY OTHER PHONE. I ONLY USE THAT NUMBER FOR WORK, SO I NEVER CARRY IT AROUND WITH ME.
WHAT?
OOPS.

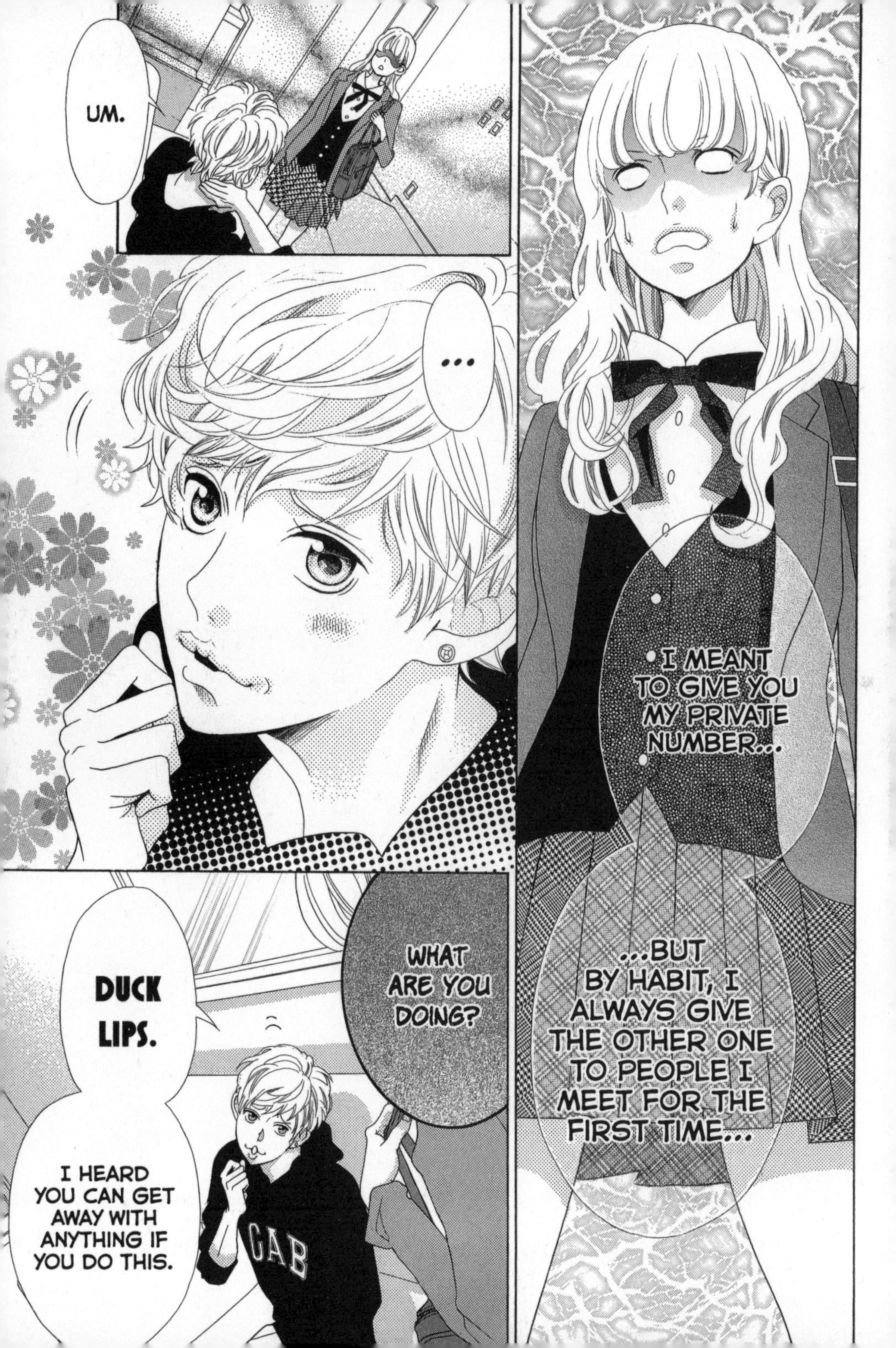

I MEANT TO GIVE YOU MY PRIVATE NUMBER...
...BUT BY HABIT, I ALWAYS GIVE THE OTHER ONE TO PEOPLE I MEET FOR THE FIRST TIME...
UM.
...
WHAT ARE YOU DOING?
DUCK LIPS.
I HEARD YOU CAN GET AWAY WITH ANYTHING IF YOU DO THIS.
GAB

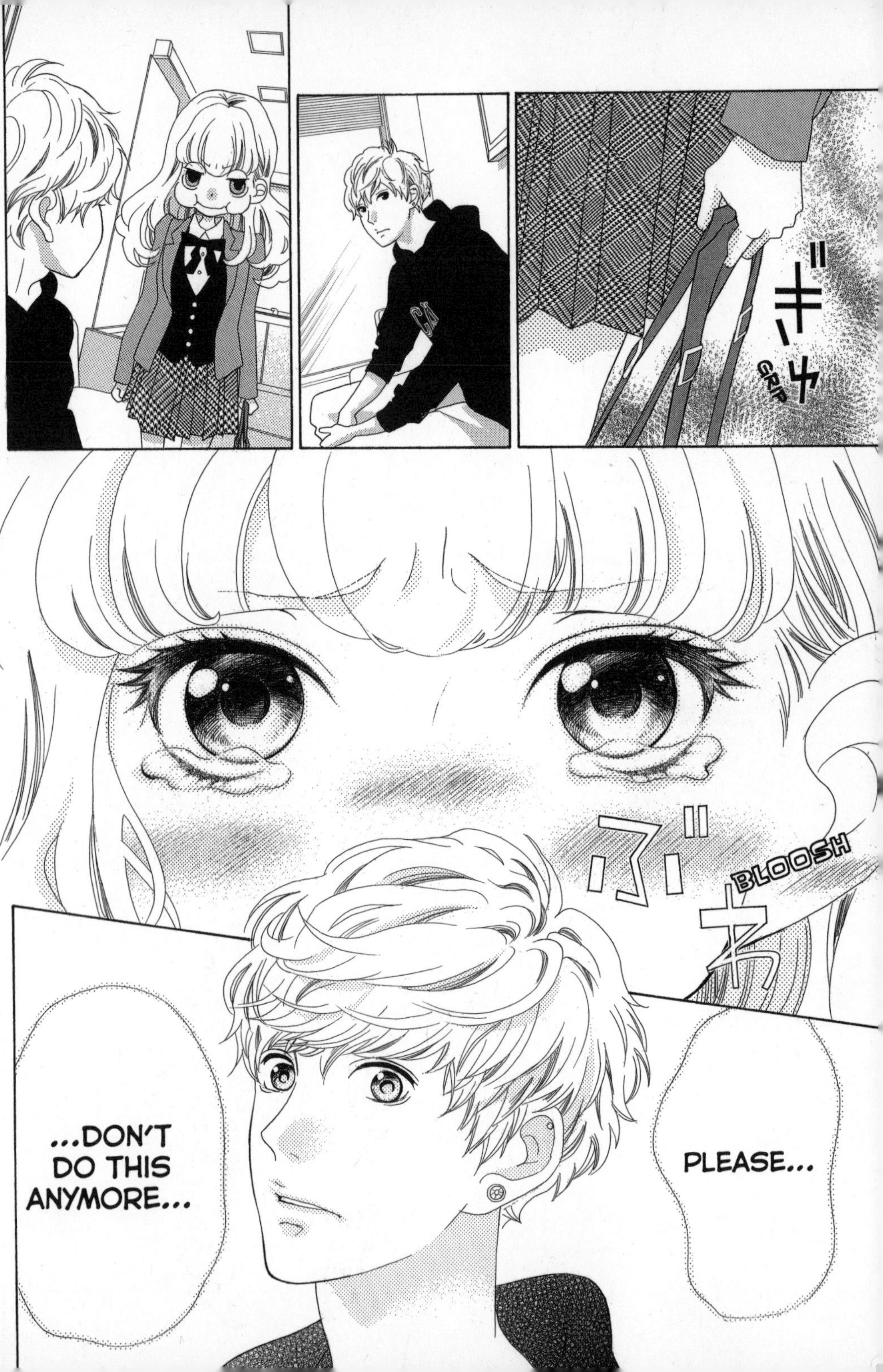
ギュッ
GRIP
ぶわ
BLOOSH
PLEASE...
...DON'T DO THIS ANYMORE...

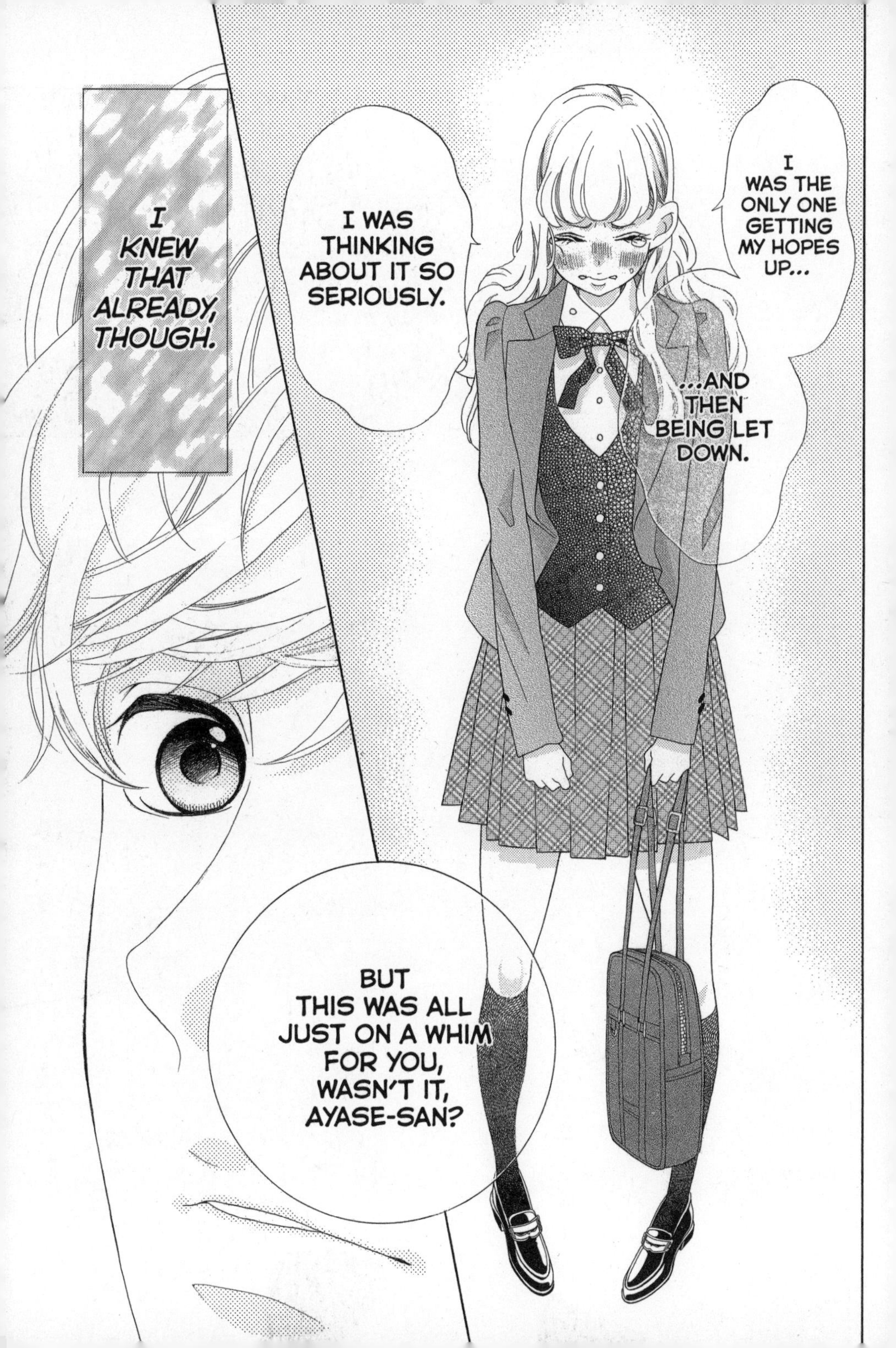
I WAS THE ONLY ONE GETTING MY HOPES UP...
...AND THEN BEING LET DOWN.
I WAS THINKING ABOUT IT SO SERIOUSLY.
BUT THIS WAS ALL JUST ON A WHIM FOR YOU, WASN'T IT, AYASE-SAN?
I KNEW THAT ALREADY, THOUGH.

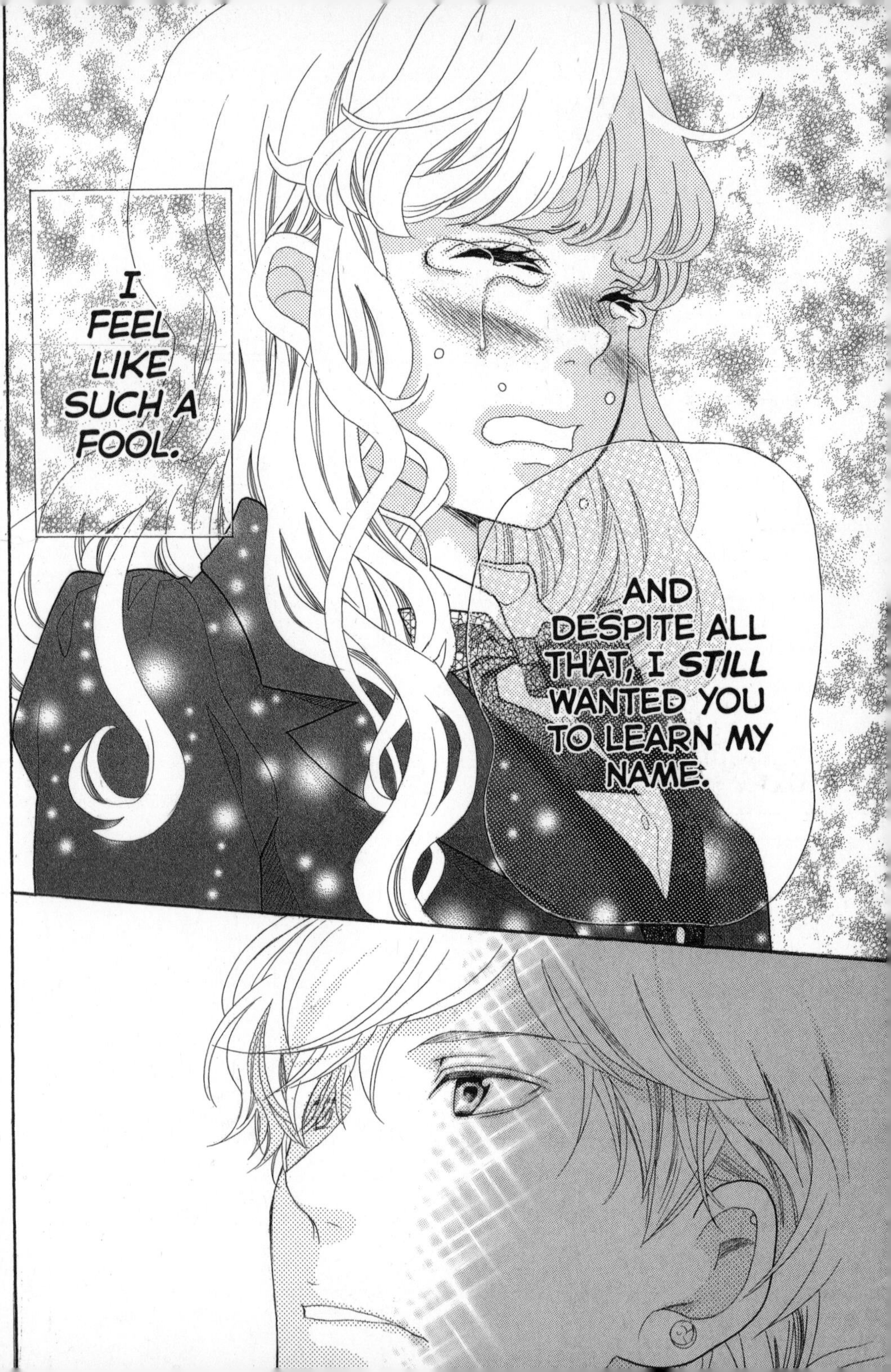
I FEEL LIKE SUCH A FOOL.
AND DESPITE ALL THAT, I STILL WANTED YOU TO LEARN MY NAME.

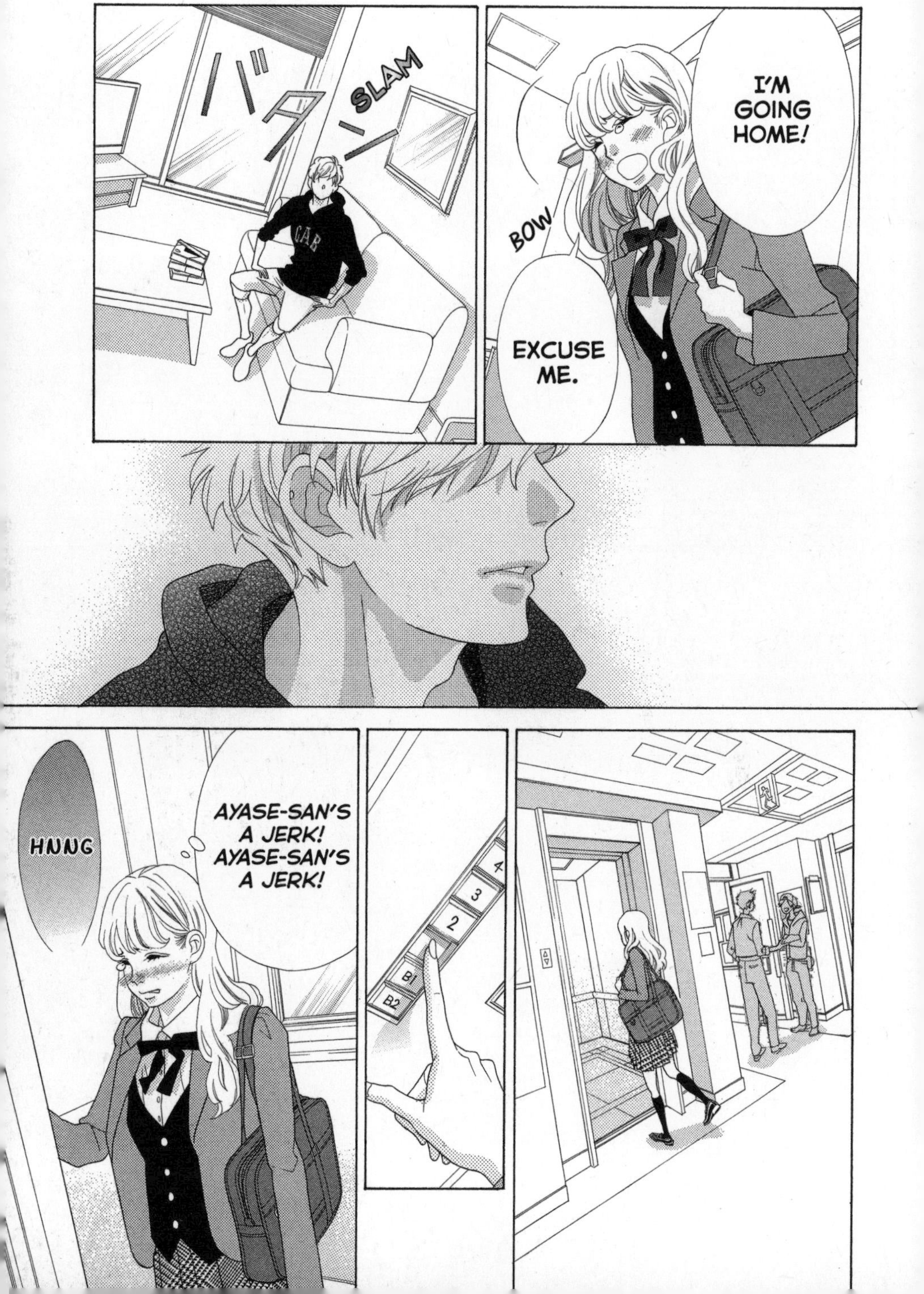
I'M GOING HOME!
BOW
EXCUSE ME.
バタ—
SLAM
4
3
2
B1
B2
AYASE-SAN'S A JERK! AYASE-SAN'S A JERK!
HNNG

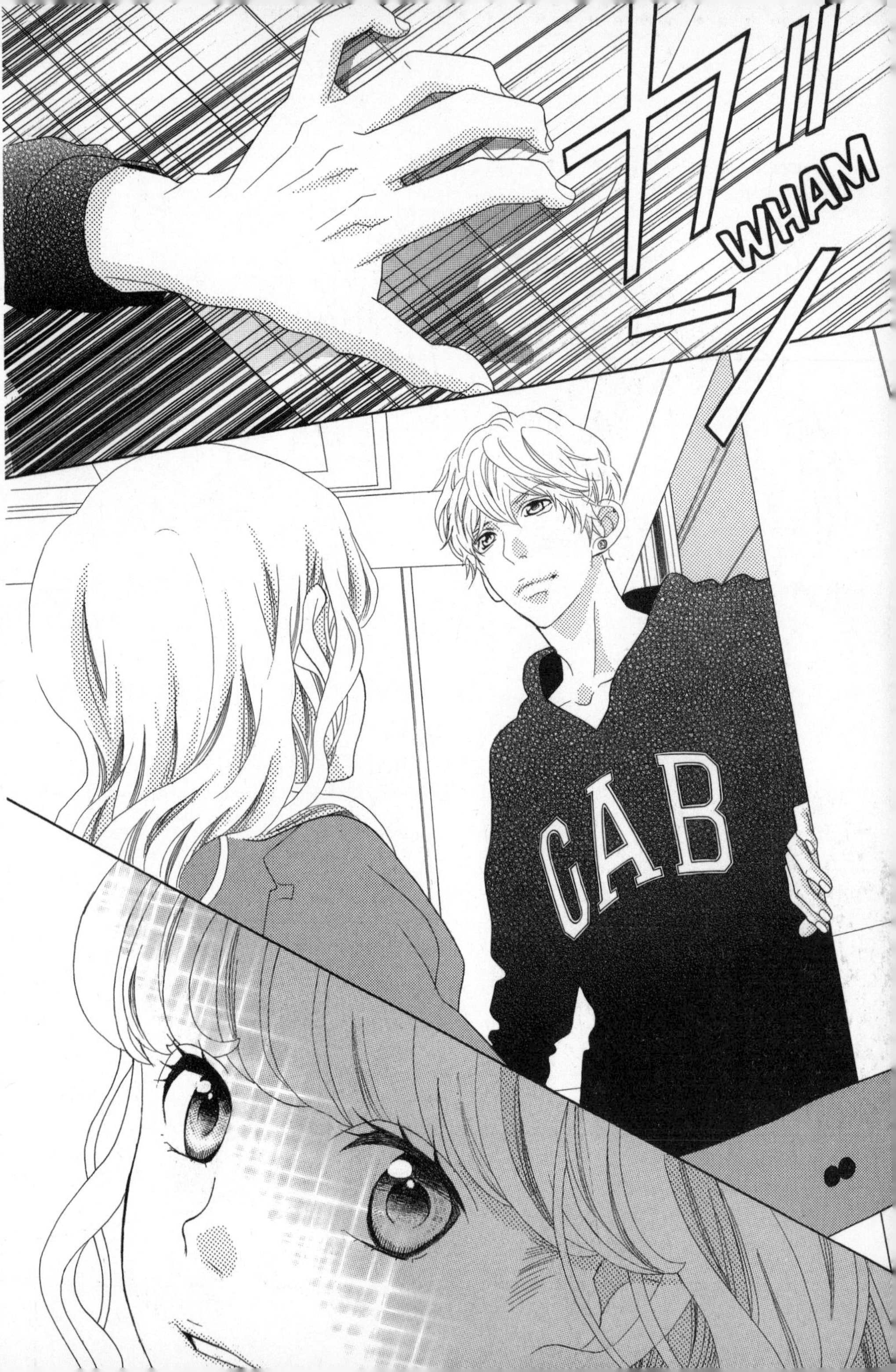
ガラ
WHAM
GAB

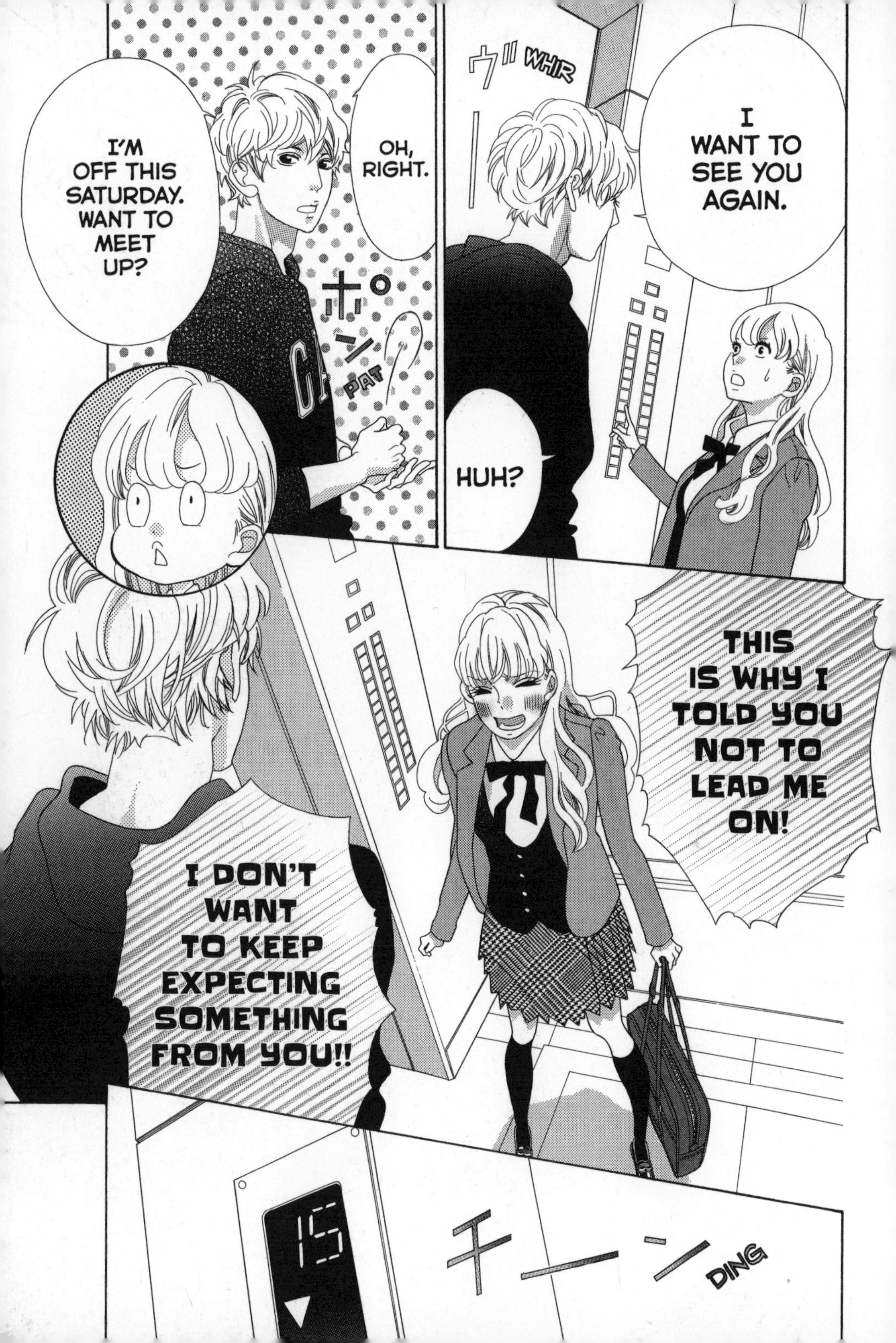
WHIR
I WANT TO SEE YOU AGAIN.
HUH?
OH, RIGHT.
I'M OFF THIS SATURDAY. WANT TO MEET UP?
PAT
THIS IS WHY I TOLD YOU NOT TO LEAD ME ON!
I DON'T WANT TO KEEP EXPECTING SOMETHING FROM YOU!!
15
DING

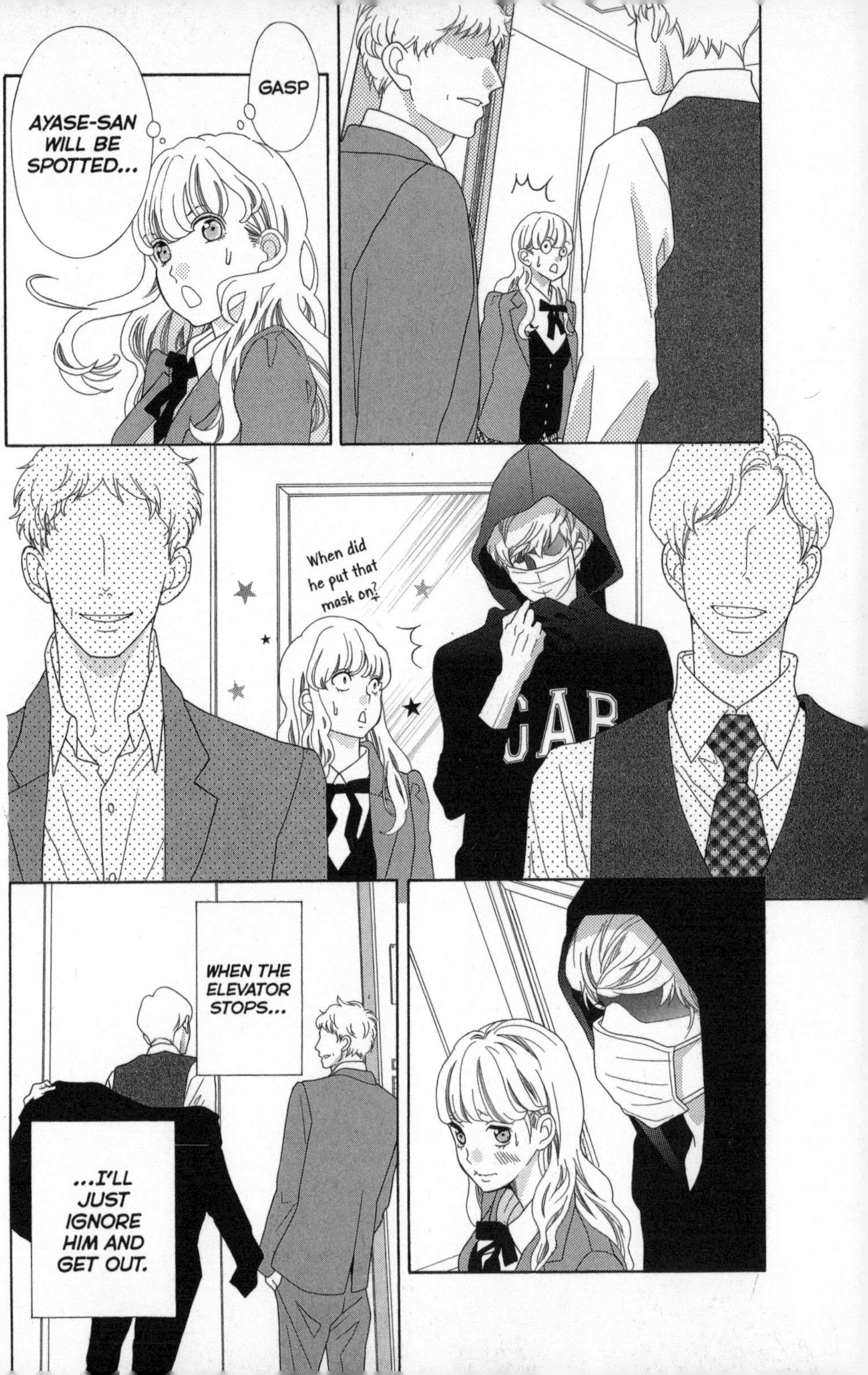
GASP
AYASE-SAN WILL BE SPOTTED...
When did he put that mask on?
WHEN THE ELEVATOR STOPS...
...I'LL JUST IGNORE HIM AND GET OUT.

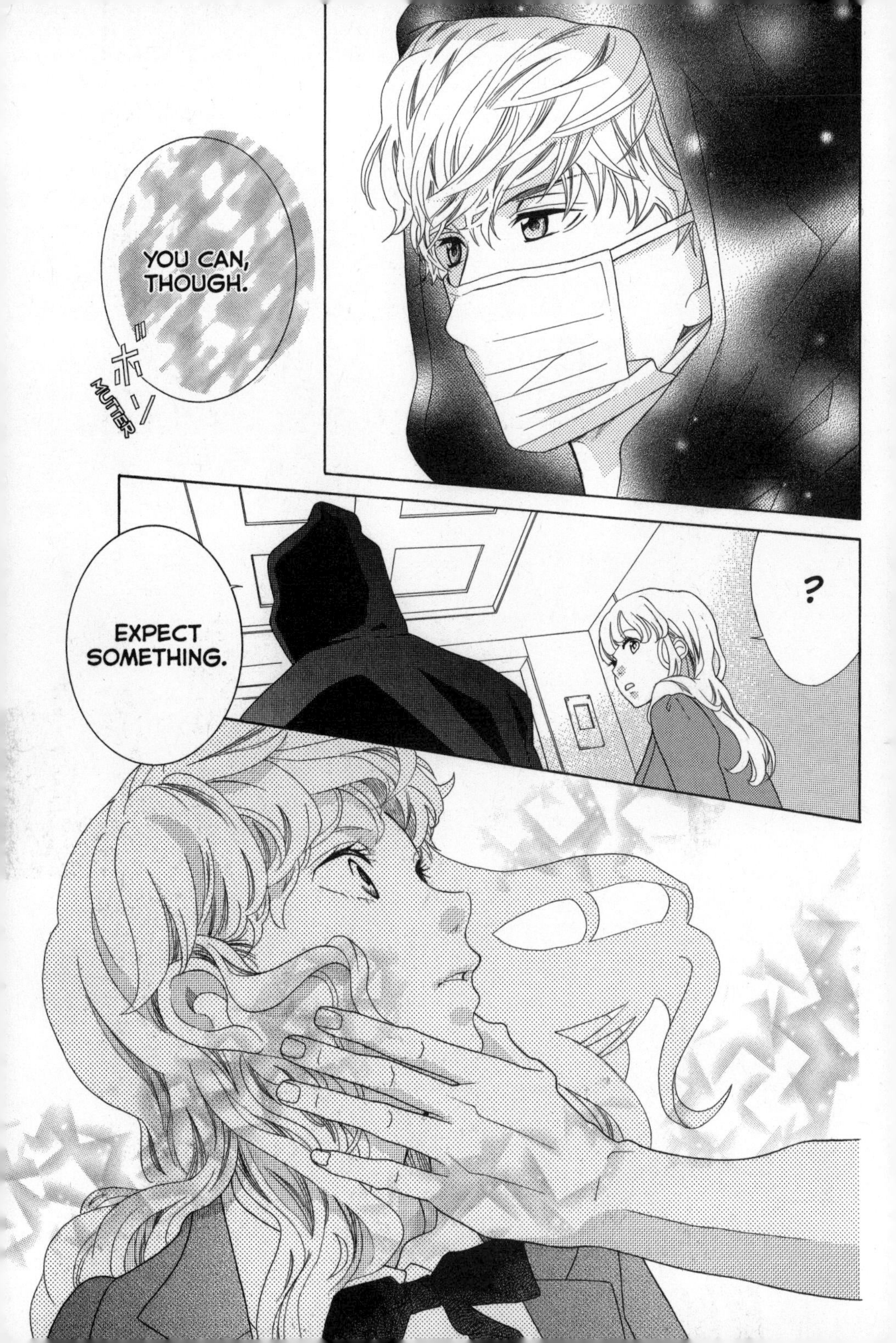
YOU CAN, THOUGH.
ボソ
MUTTER
?
EXPECT SOMETHING.

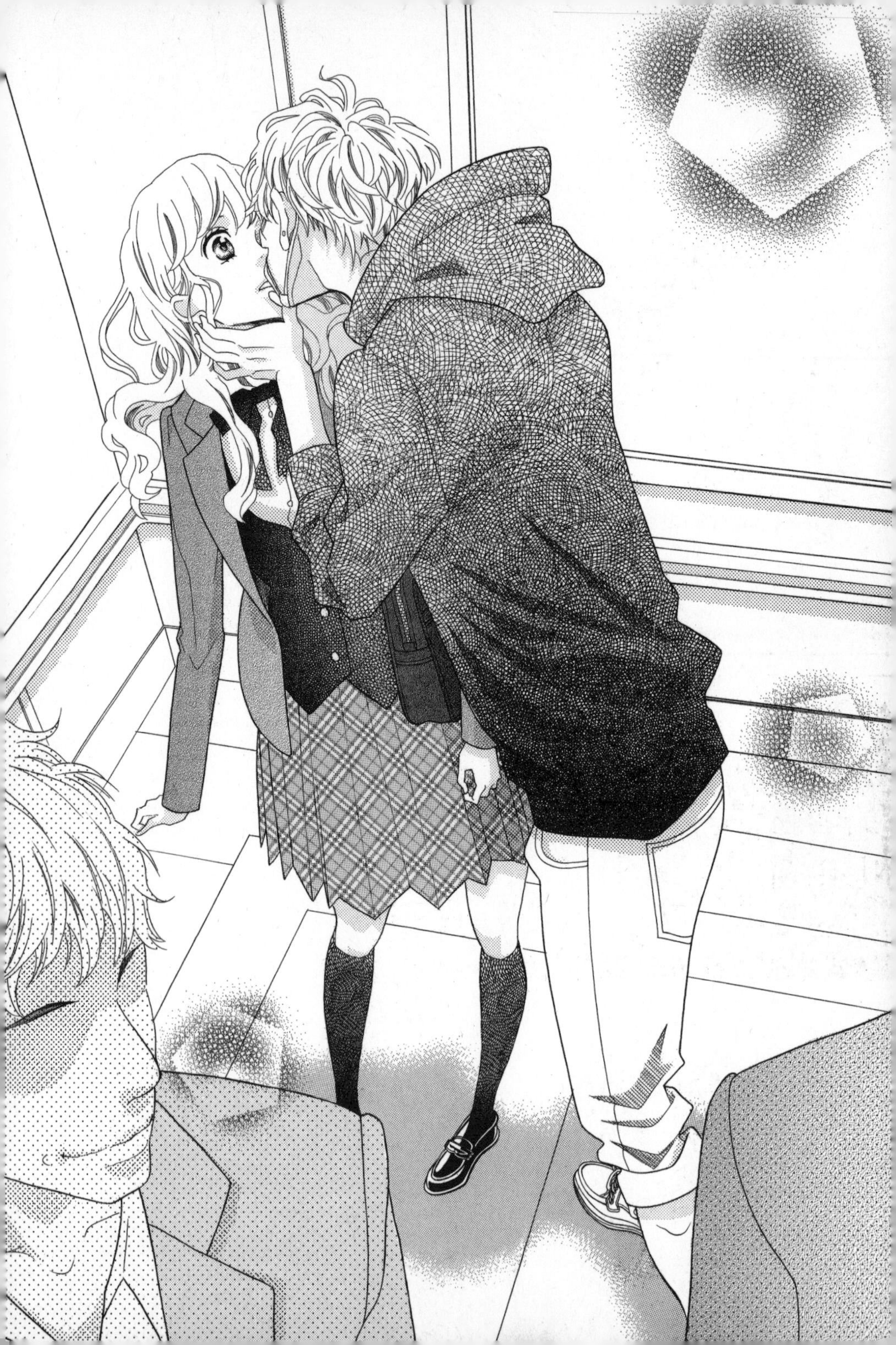

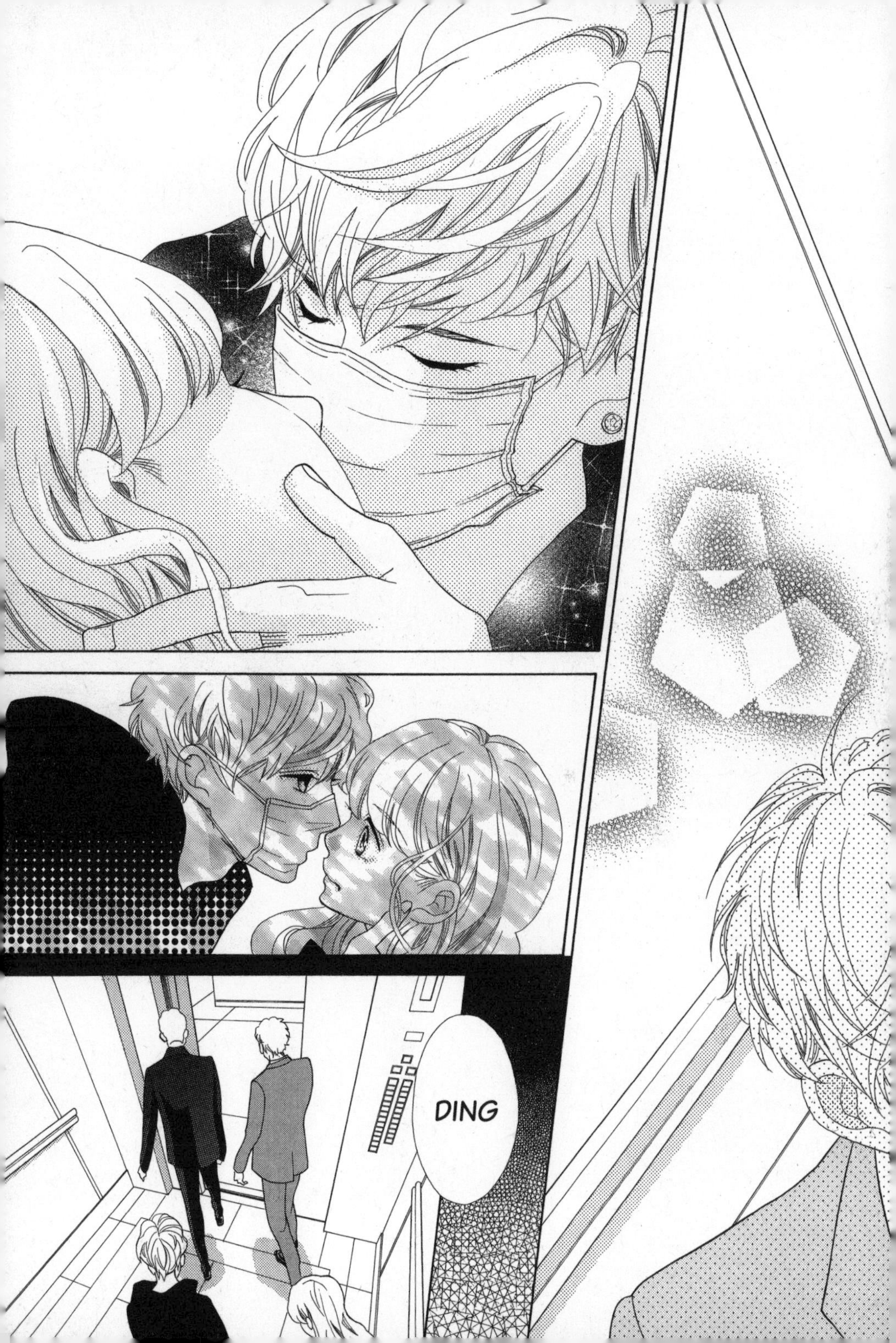
DING

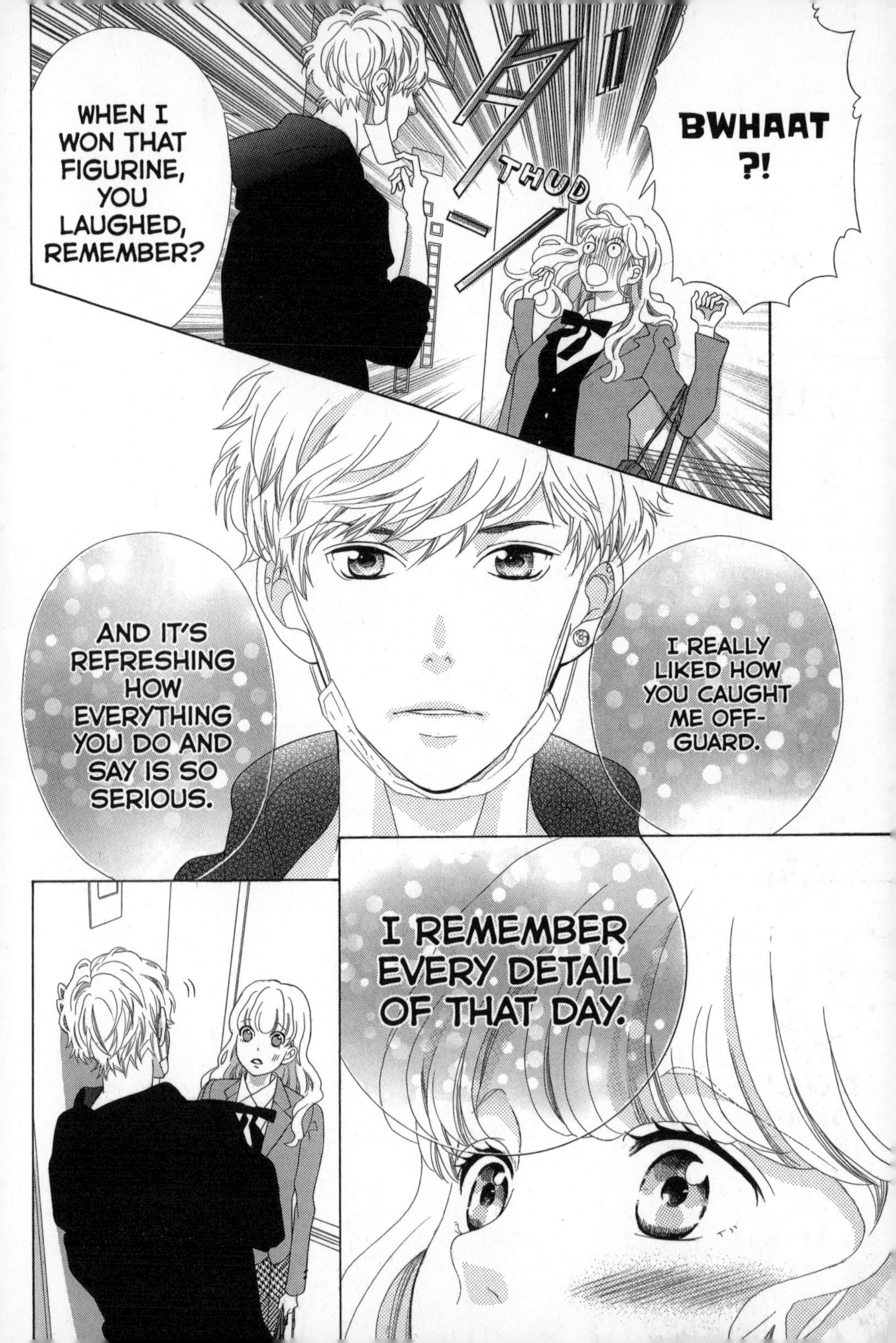
BWHAAT ?!
THUD
WHEN I WON THAT FIGURINE, YOU LAUGHED, REMEMBER?
I REALLY LIKED HOW YOU CAUGHT ME OFF-GUARD.
AND IT'S REFRESHING HOW EVERYTHING YOU DO AND SAY IS SO SERIOUS.
I REMEMBER EVERY DETAIL OF THAT DAY.

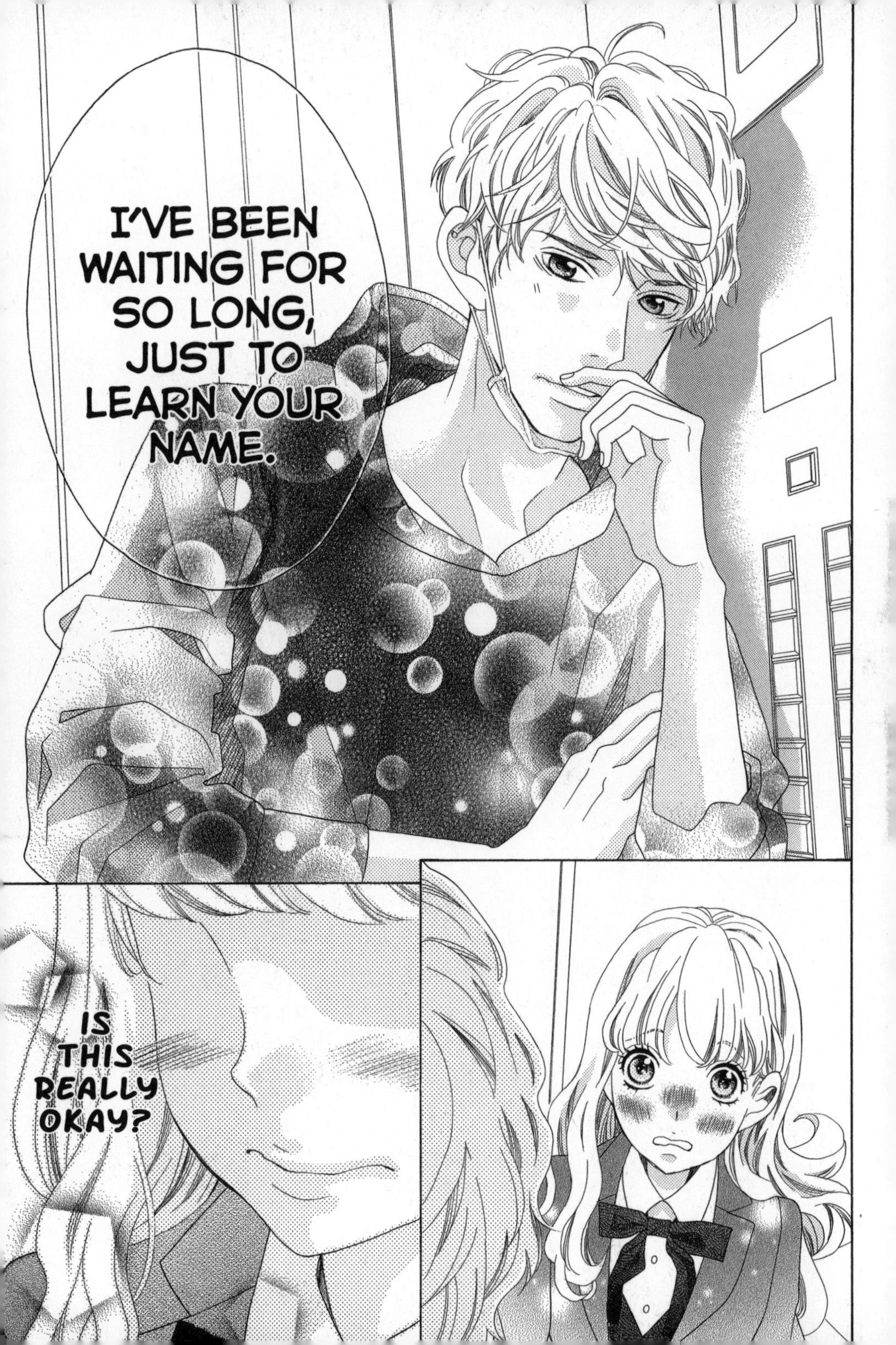
I'VE BEEN WAITING FOR SO LONG, JUST TO LEARN YOUR NAME.
IS THIS REALLY OKAY?

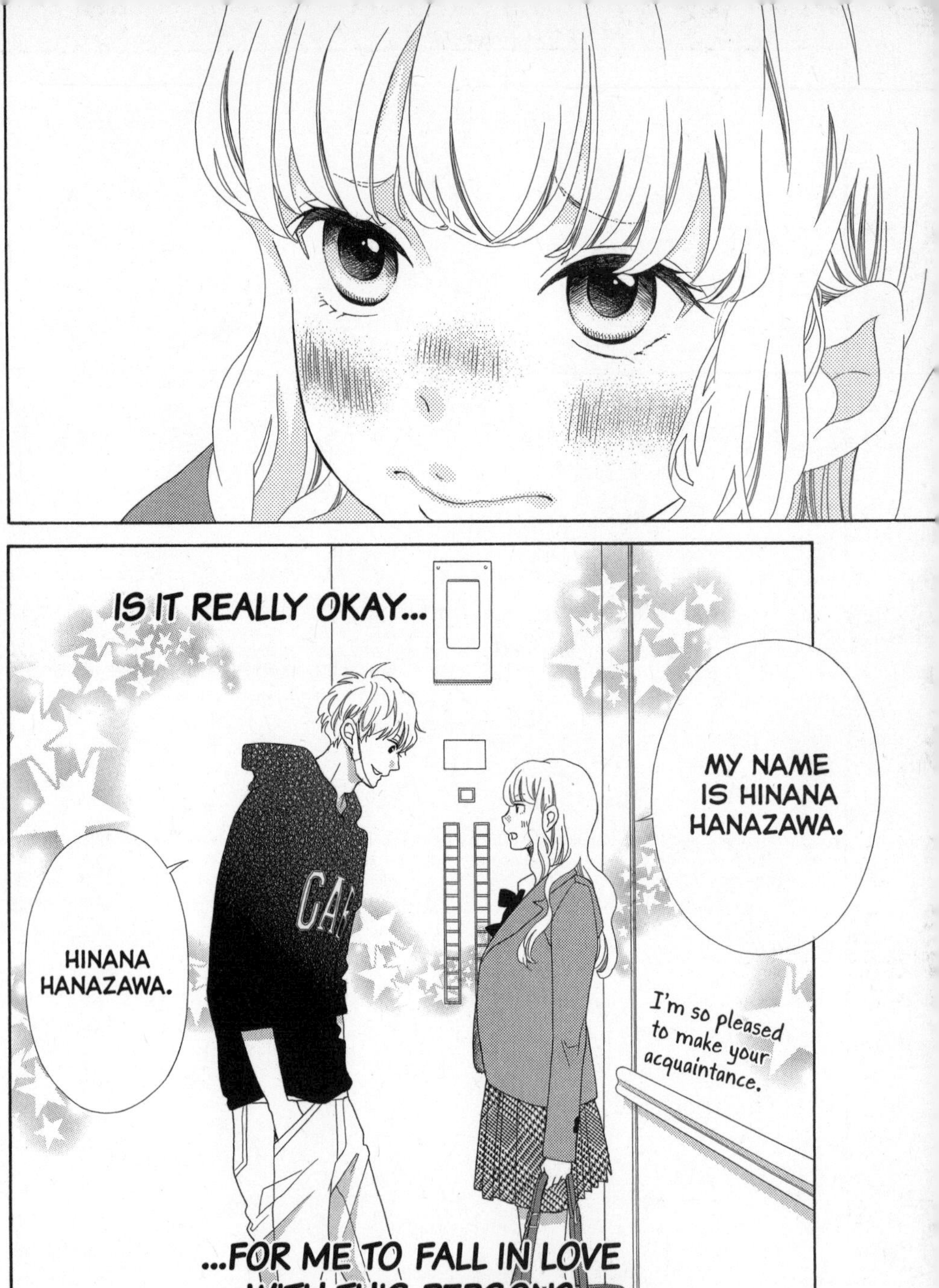
MY NAME IS HINANA HANAZAWA.
I'm so pleased to make your acquaintance.
HINANA HANAZAWA.
IS IT REALLY OKAY...
...FOR ME TO FALL IN LOVE WITH THIS PERSON?

E to Kiss
t 0:00 A.m.

STORY.3

Even Though You're Mine

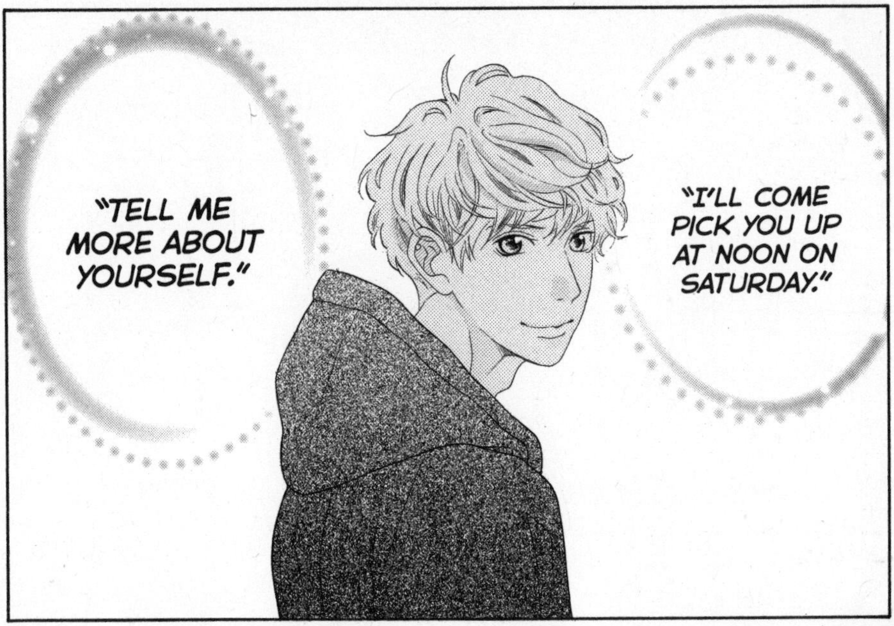
"I'LL COME PICK YOU UP AT NOON ON SATURDAY."
"TELL ME MORE ABOUT YOURSELF."

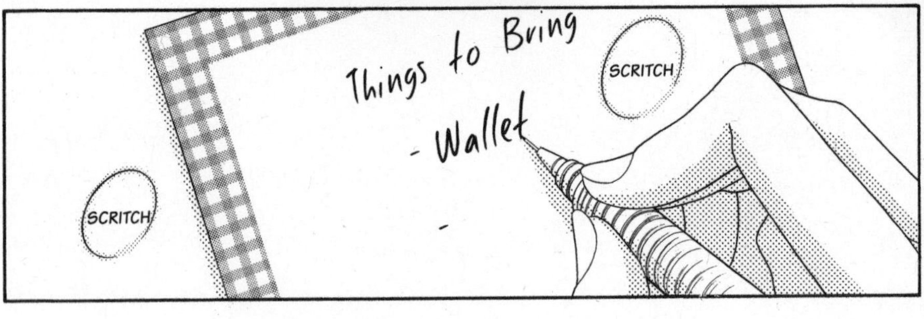
SCRITCH
Things to Bring
- Wallet
SCRITCH

Kiss Me at the Stroke of Midnight

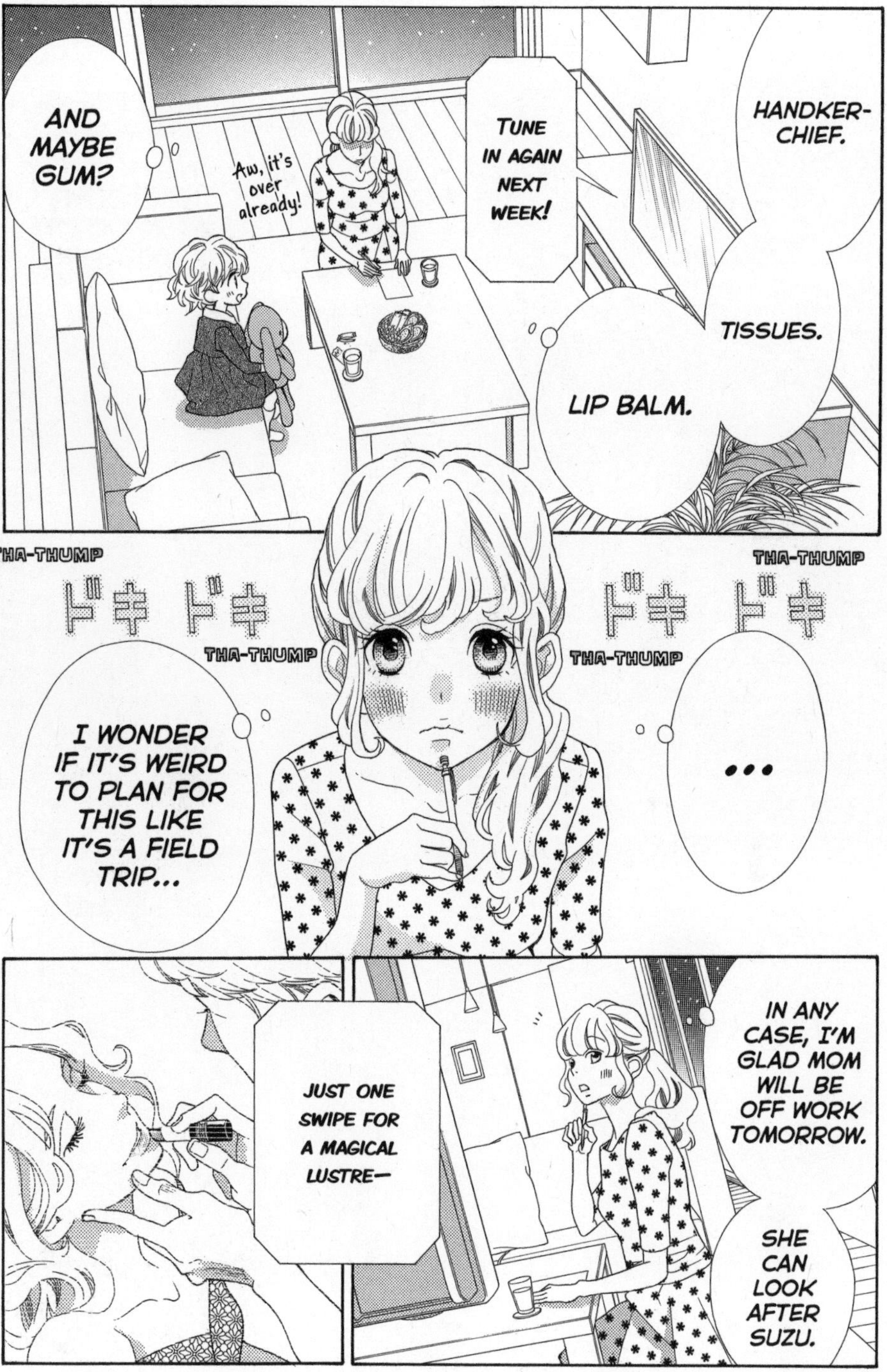
HANDKER-CHIEF.
TISSUES.
LIP BALM.
TUNE IN AGAIN NEXT WEEK!
Aw, it's over already!
AND MAYBE GUM?
THA-THUMP
ドキドキ
THA-THUMP
...
THA-THUMP
ドキドキ
THA-THUMP
I WONDER IF IT'S WEIRD TO PLAN FOR THIS LIKE IT'S A FIELD TRIP...
IN ANY CASE, I'M GLAD MOM WILL BE OFF WORK TOMORROW.
SHE CAN LOOK AFTER SUZU.
JUST ONE SWIPE FOR A MAGICAL LUSTRE—

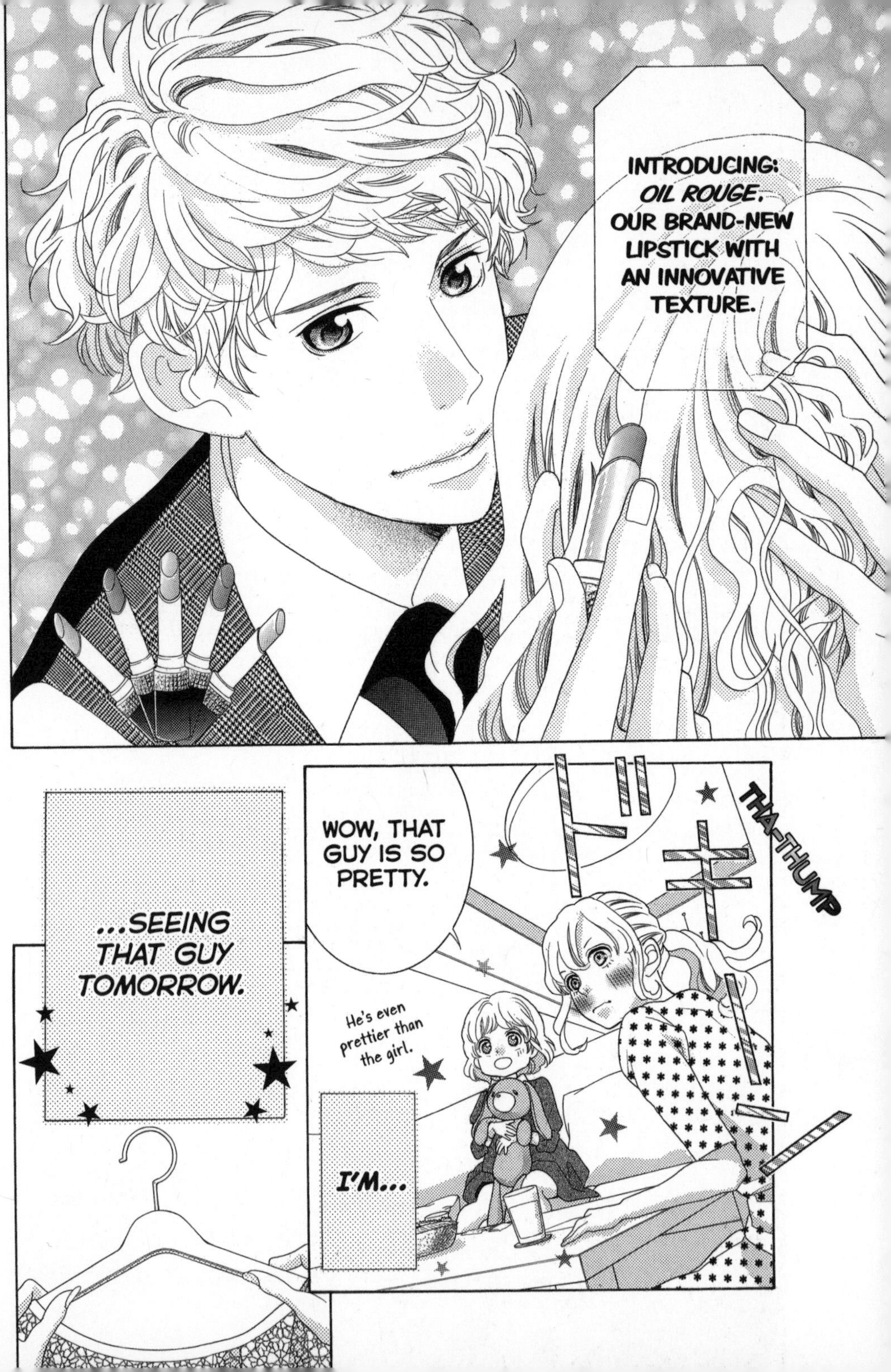
INTRODUCING: *OIL ROUGE*, OUR BRAND-NEW LIPSTICK WITH AN INNOVATIVE TEXTURE.
THA-THUMP
WOW, THAT GUY IS SO PRETTY.
He's even prettier than the girl.
I'M...
...SEEING THAT GUY TOMORROW.

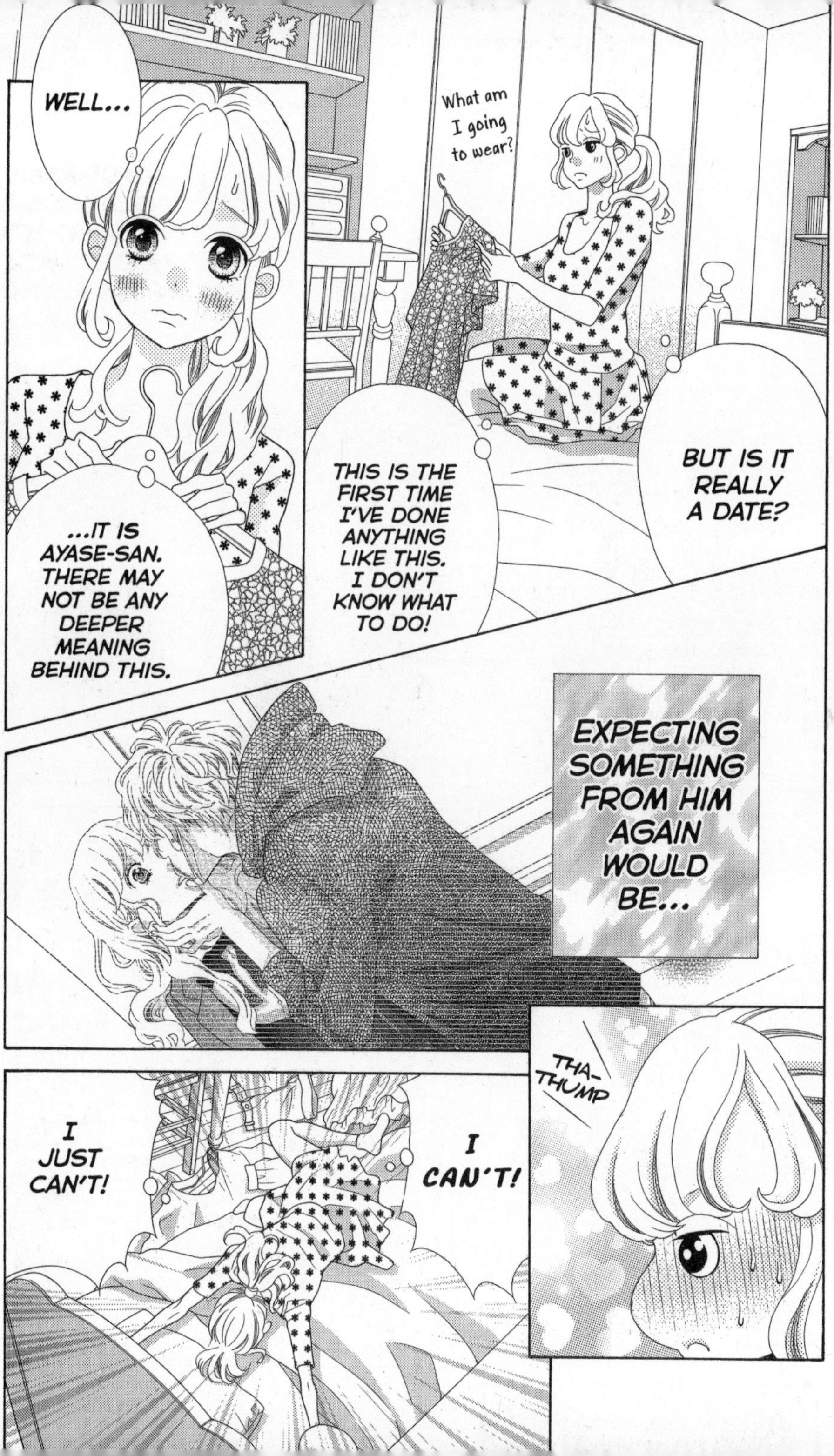
What am I going to wear?
BUT IS IT REALLY A DATE?
THIS IS THE FIRST TIME I'VE DONE ANYTHING LIKE THIS. I DON'T KNOW WHAT TO DO!
WELL...
...IT IS AYASE-SAN. THERE MAY NOT BE ANY DEEPER MEANING BEHIND THIS.
EXPECTING SOMETHING FROM HIM AGAIN WOULD BE...
THA-THUMP
I CAN'T!
I JUST CAN'T!

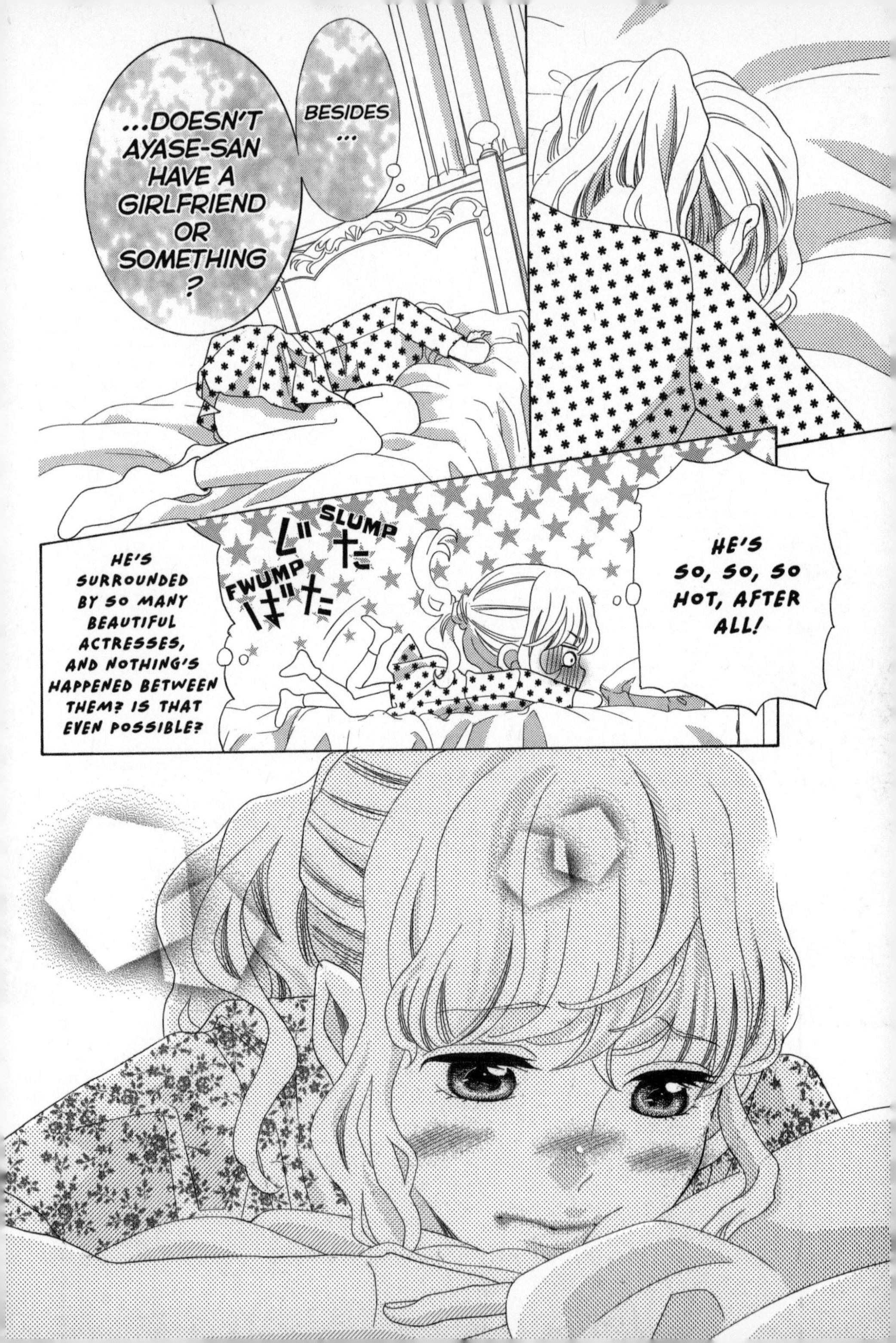
BESIDES ...
...DOESN'T AYASE-SAN HAVE A GIRLFRIEND OR SOMETHING ?
HE'S SO, SO, SO HOT, AFTER ALL!
じ SLUMP た
FWUMP ば た
HE'S SURROUNDED BY SO MANY BEAUTIFUL ACTRESSES, AND NOTHING'S HAPPENED BETWEEN THEM? IS THAT EVEN POSSIBLE?

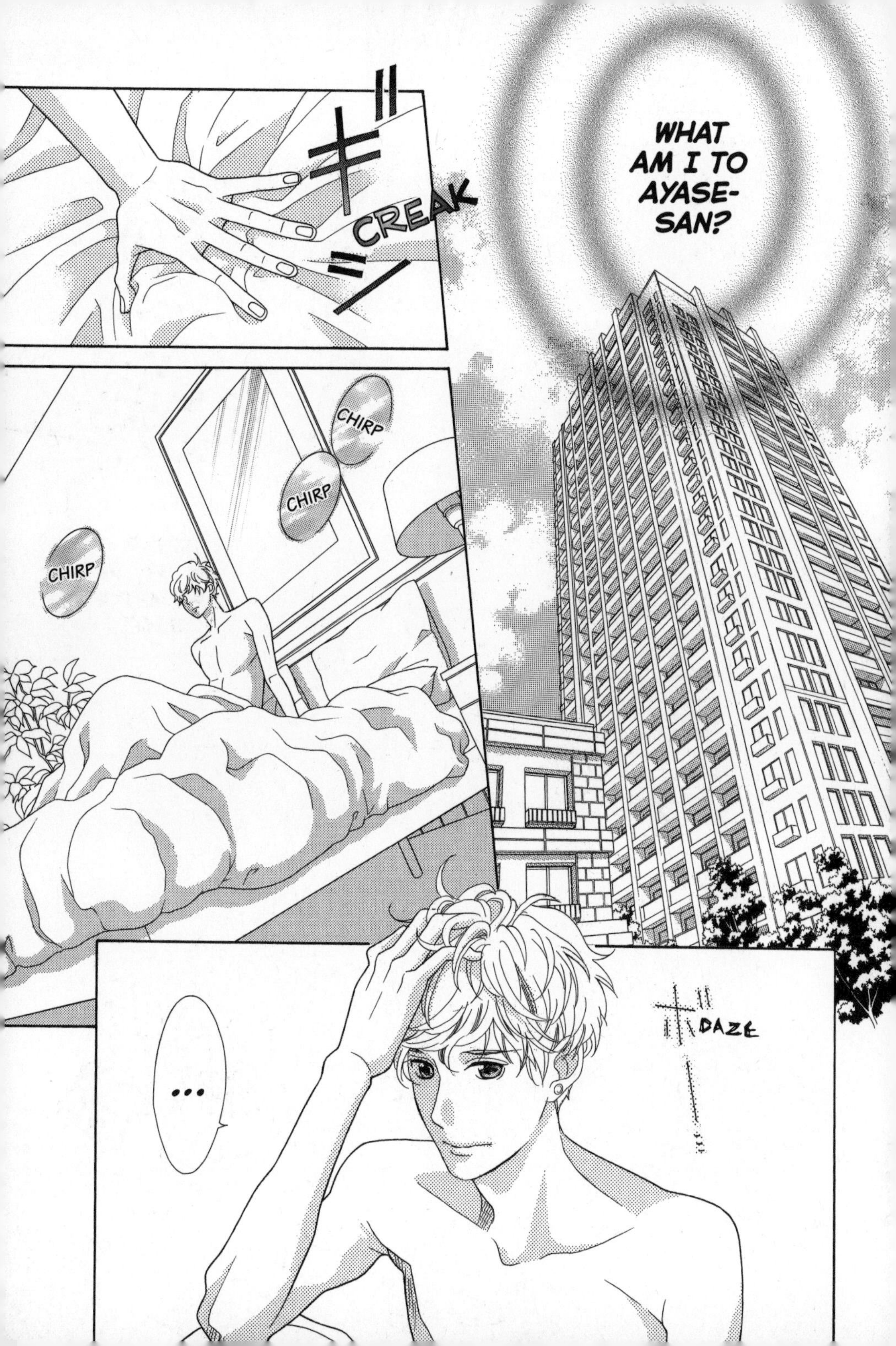
WHAT AM I TO AYASE-SAN?
CREAK
CHIRP
CHIRP
CHIRP
DAZE
...

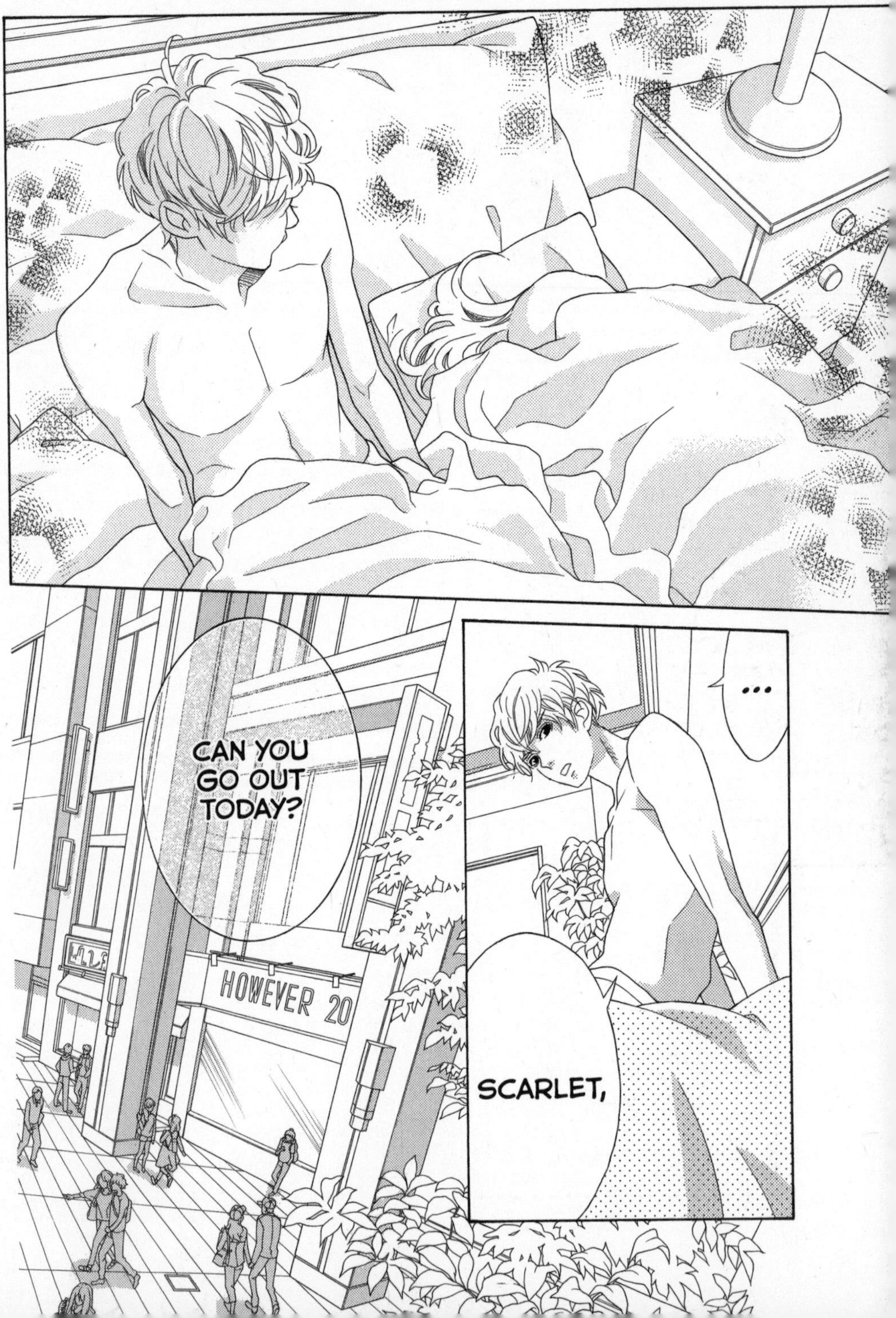
...
SCARLET,
CAN YOU GO OUT TODAY?
HOWEVER 20

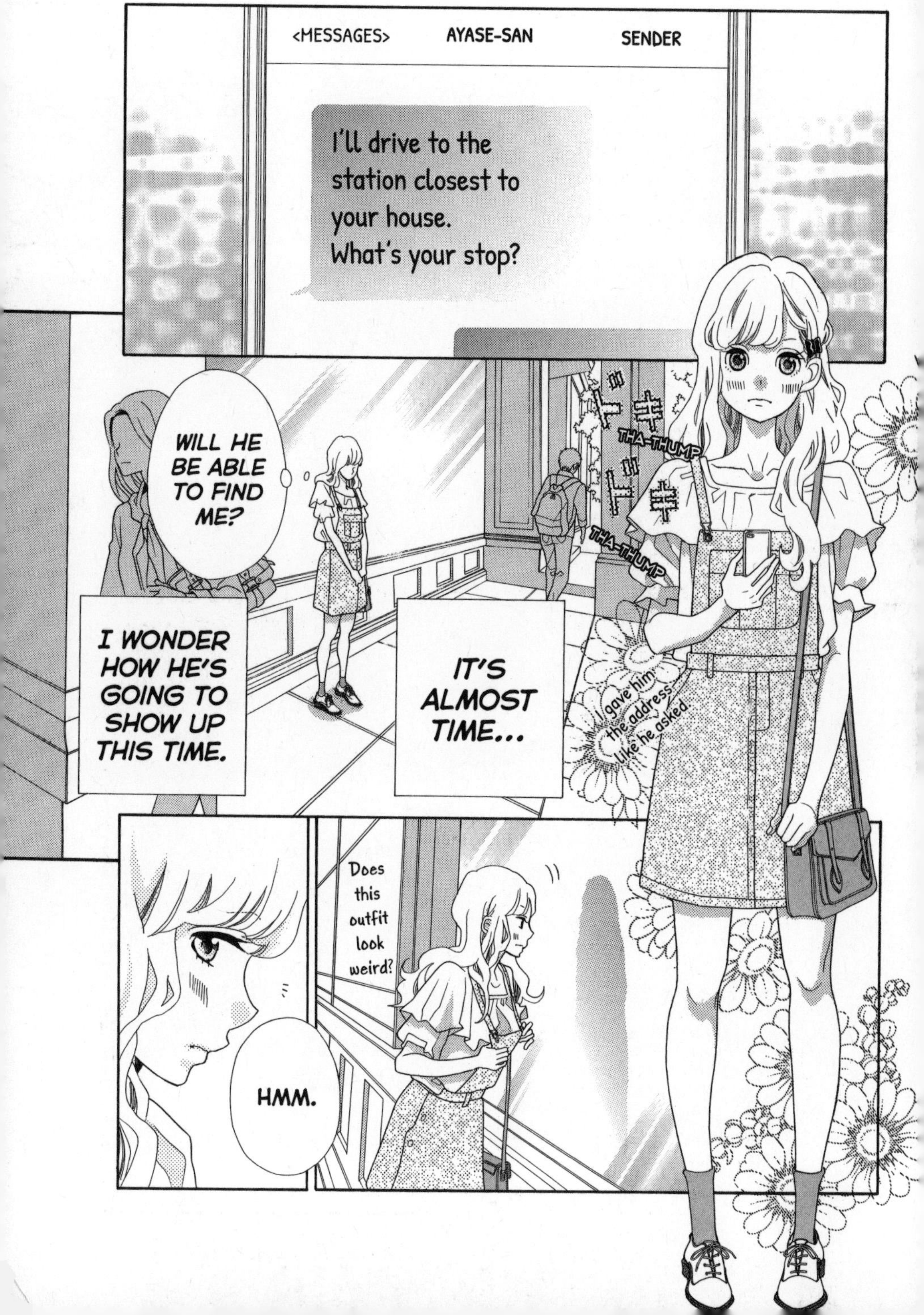
<MESSAGES> AYASE-SAN SENDER
I'll drive to the station closest to your house. What's your stop?
THA-THUMP
THA-THUMP
I gave him the address like he asked.
WILL HE BE ABLE TO FIND ME?
IT'S ALMOST TIME...
I WONDER HOW HE'S GOING TO SHOW UP THIS TIME.
Does this outfit look weird?
HMM.

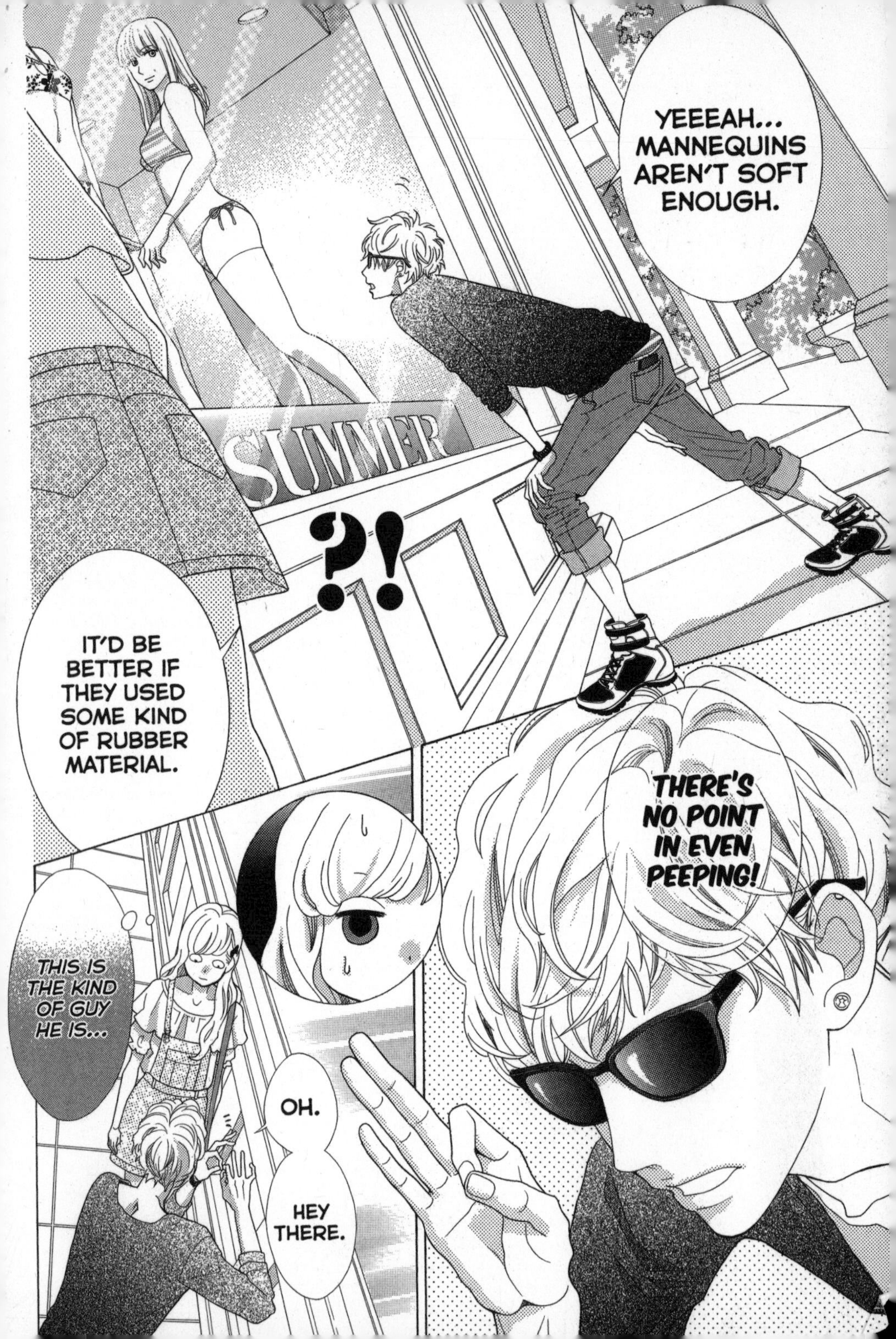
YEEEAH... MANNEQUINS AREN'T SOFT ENOUGH.
SUMMER
?!
IT'D BE BETTER IF THEY USED SOME KIND OF RUBBER MATERIAL.
THERE'S NO POINT IN EVEN PEEPING!
OH.
HEY THERE.
THIS IS THE KIND OF GUY HE IS...

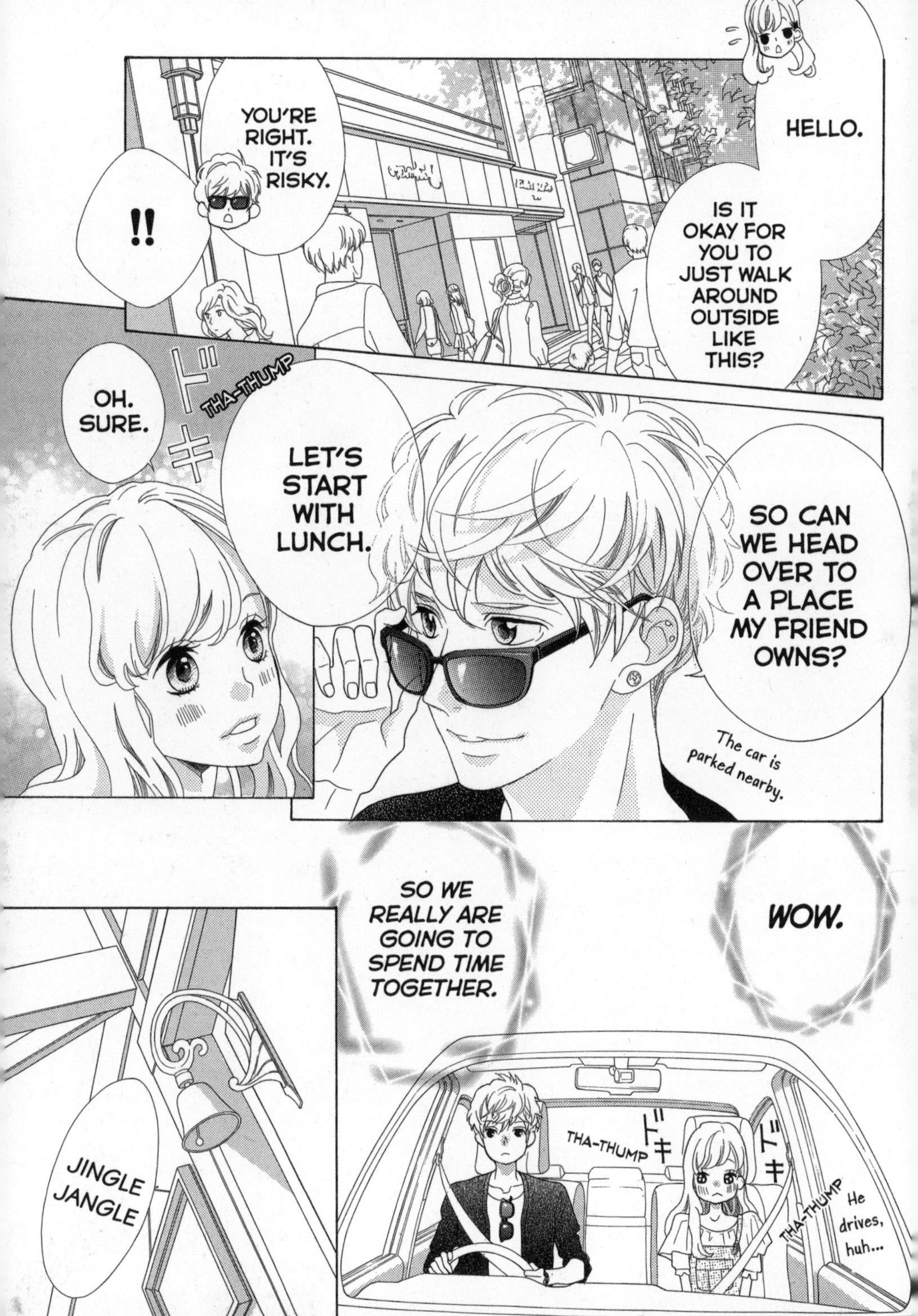
HELLO.
IS IT OKAY FOR YOU TO JUST WALK AROUND OUTSIDE LIKE THIS?
YOU'RE RIGHT. IT'S RISKY.
!!
SO CAN WE HEAD OVER TO A PLACE MY FRIEND OWNS?
The car is parked nearby.
LET'S START WITH LUNCH.
ドキ
THA-THUMP
OH. SURE.
WOW.
SO WE REALLY ARE GOING TO SPEND TIME TOGETHER.
ドキ
THA-THUMP
ドキ
THA-THUMP
He drives, huh...
JINGLE JANGLE

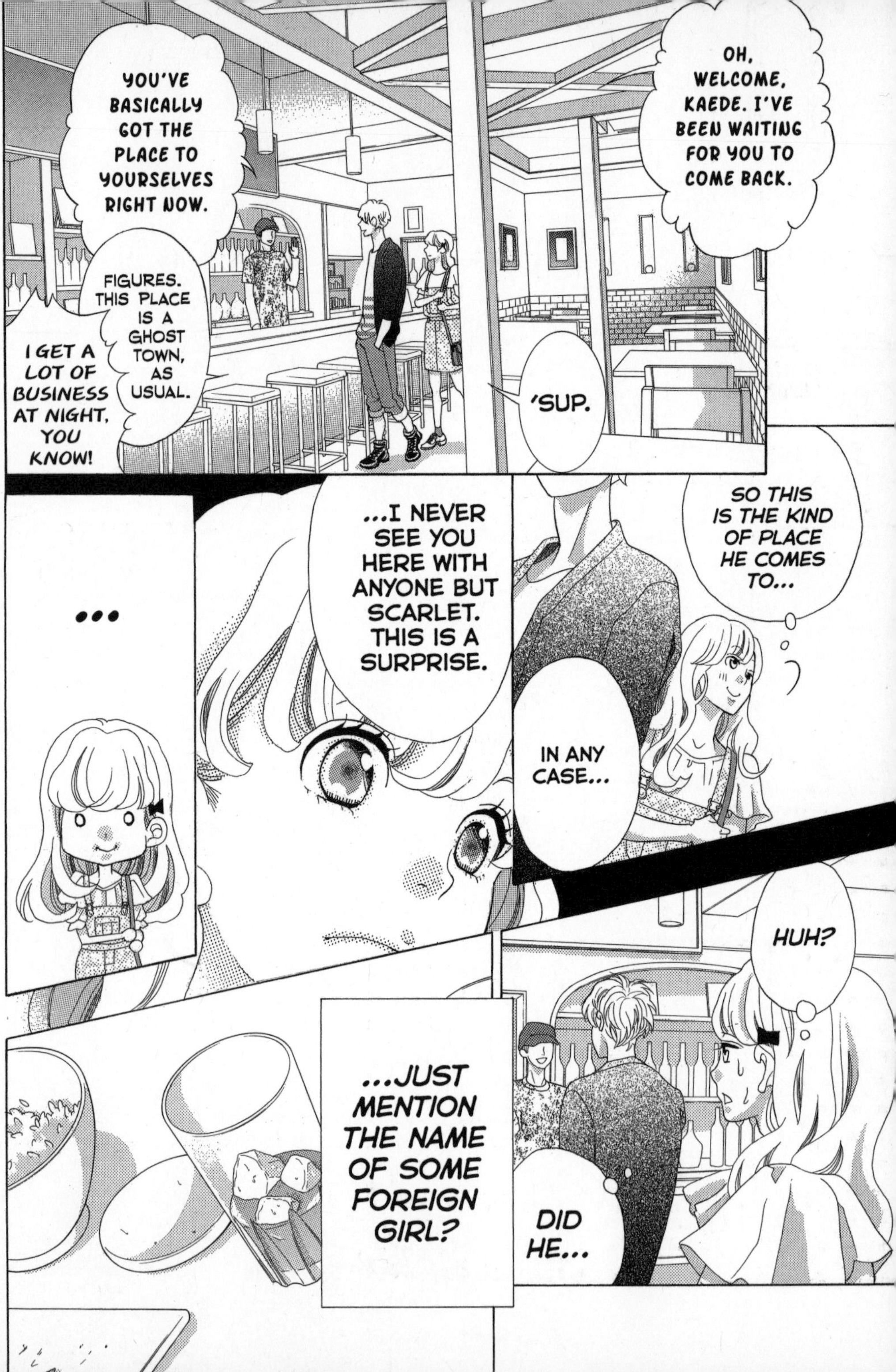
OH, WELCOME, KAEDE. I'VE BEEN WAITING FOR YOU TO COME BACK.
'SUP.
YOU'VE BASICALLY GOT THE PLACE TO YOURSELVES RIGHT NOW.
FIGURES. THIS PLACE IS A GHOST TOWN, AS USUAL.
I GET A LOT OF BUSINESS AT NIGHT, YOU KNOW!
SO THIS IS THE KIND OF PLACE HE COMES TO...
IN ANY CASE...
...I NEVER SEE YOU HERE WITH ANYONE BUT SCARLET. THIS IS A SURPRISE.
...
HUH?
DID HE...
...JUST MENTION THE NAME OF SOME FOREIGN GIRL?

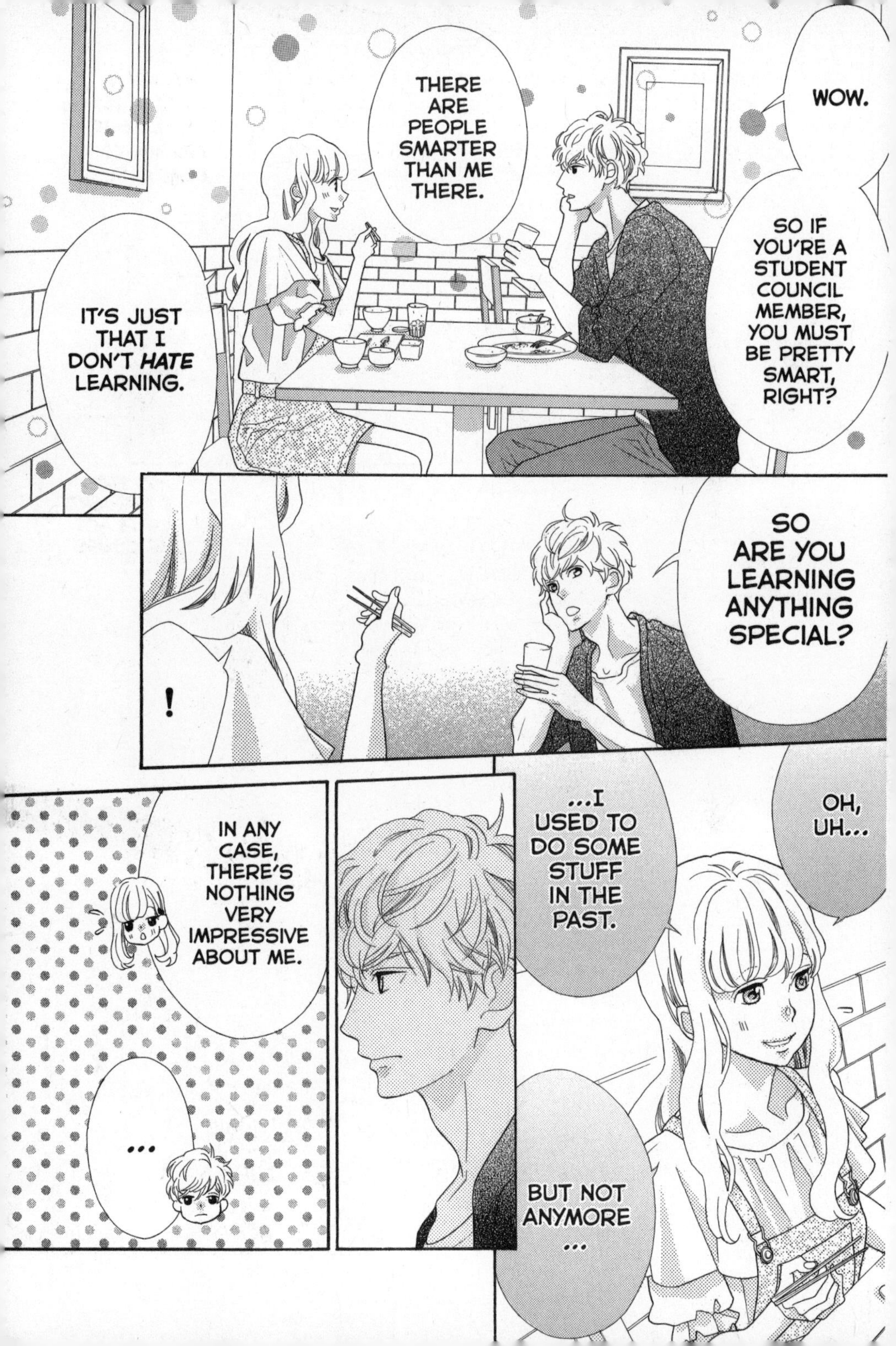
WOW.
SO IF YOU'RE A STUDENT COUNCIL MEMBER, YOU MUST BE PRETTY SMART, RIGHT?
THERE ARE PEOPLE SMARTER THAN ME THERE.
IT'S JUST THAT I DON'T *HATE* LEARNING.
SO ARE YOU LEARNING ANYTHING SPECIAL?
!
OH, UH...
...I USED TO DO SOME STUFF IN THE PAST.
BUT NOT ANYMORE ...
IN ANY CASE, THERE'S NOTHING VERY IMPRESSIVE ABOUT ME.
...

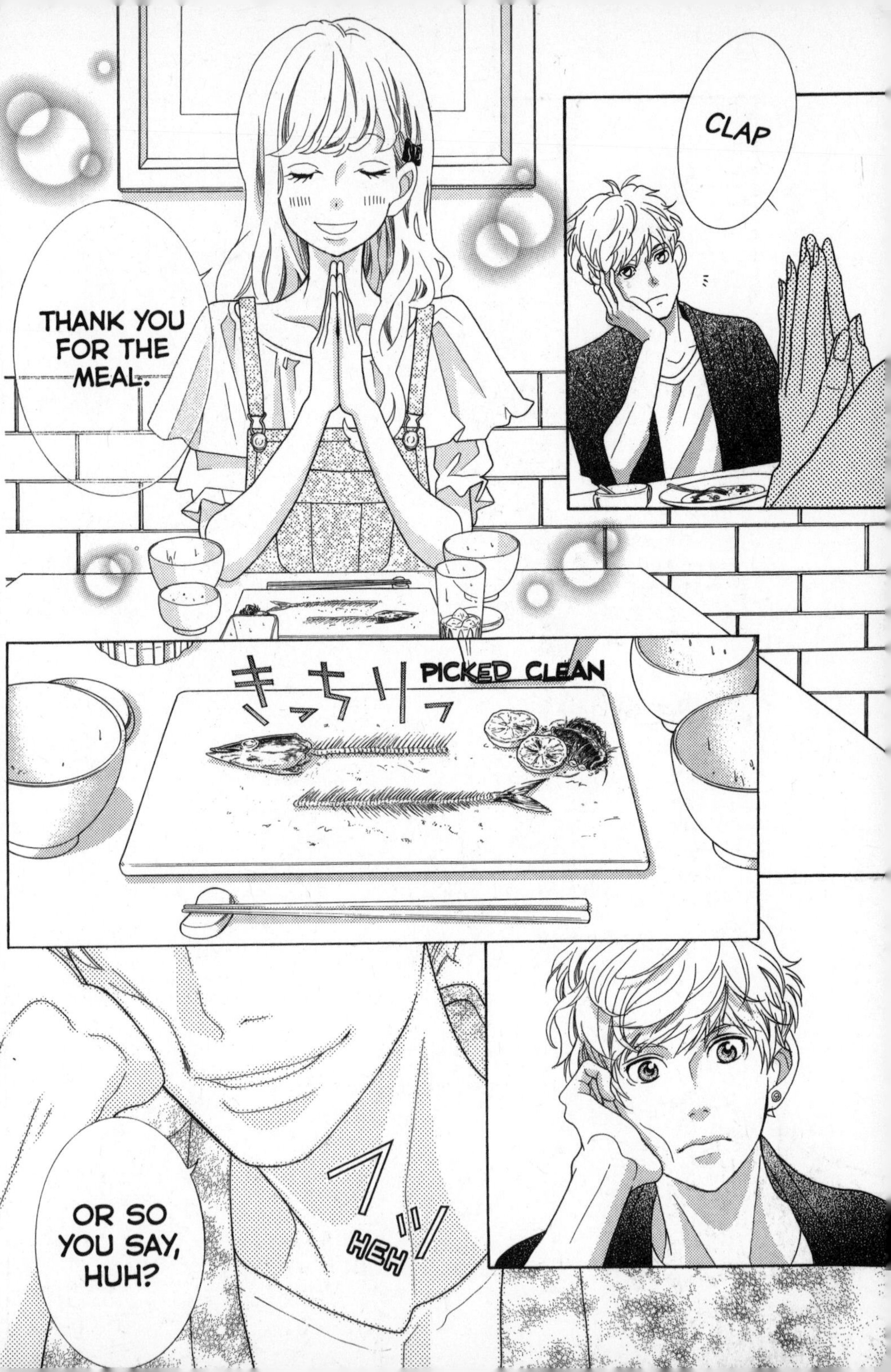

CLAP
THANK YOU FOR THE MEAL.
きっちりっ
PICKED CLEAN
HEH
OR SO YOU SAY, HUH?

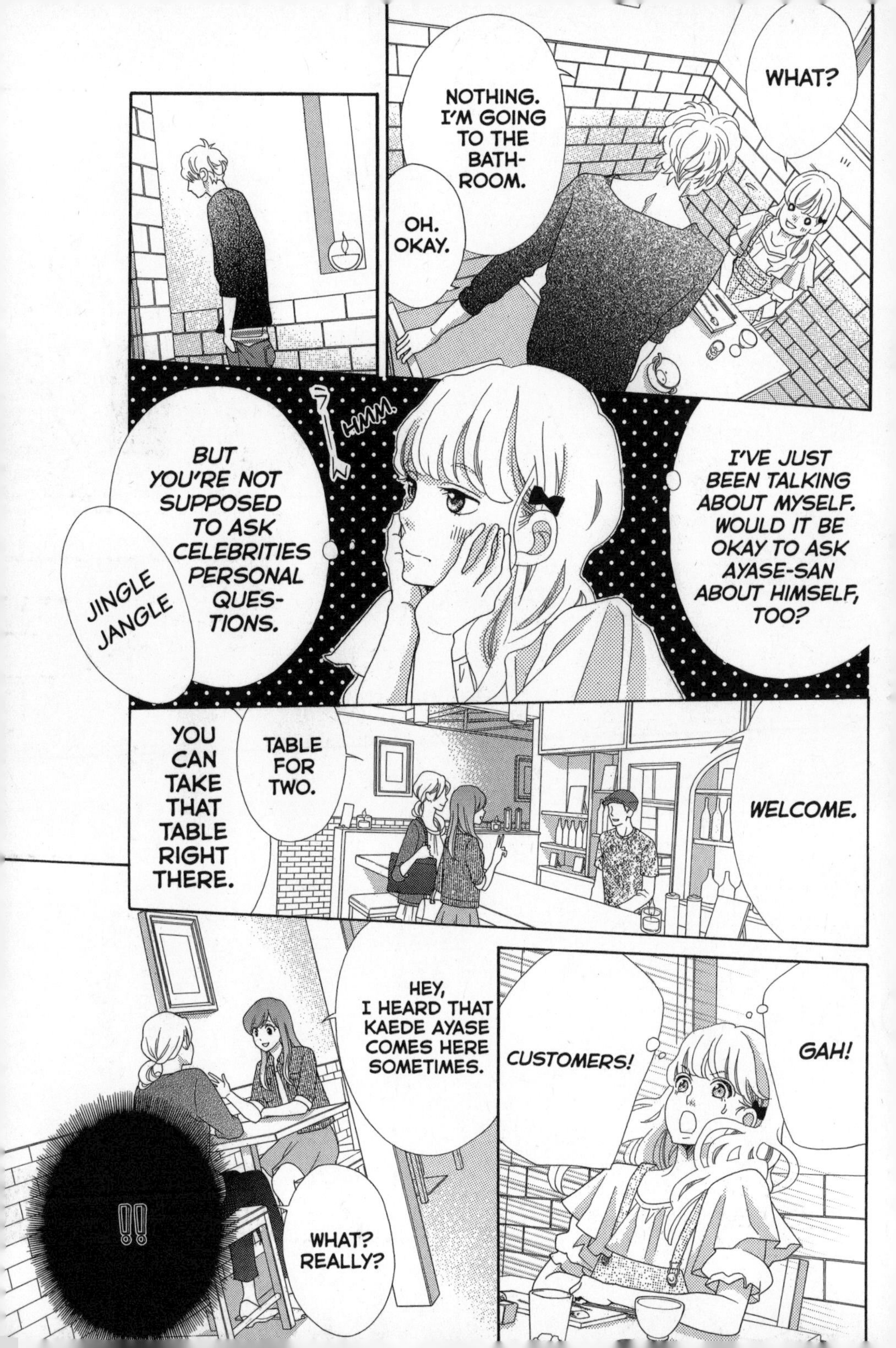
WHAT?
NOTHING. I'M GOING TO THE BATH-ROOM.
OH. OKAY.
I'VE JUST BEEN TALKING ABOUT MYSELF. WOULD IT BE OKAY TO ASK AYASE-SAN ABOUT HIMSELF, TOO?
HMM
BUT YOU'RE NOT SUPPOSED TO ASK CELEBRITIES PERSONAL QUES-TIONS.
JINGLE JANGLE
WELCOME.
TABLE FOR TWO.
YOU CAN TAKE THAT TABLE RIGHT THERE.
GAH!
CUSTOMERS!
HEY, I HEARD THAT KAEDE AYASE COMES HERE SOMETIMES.
WHAT? REALLY?
!!

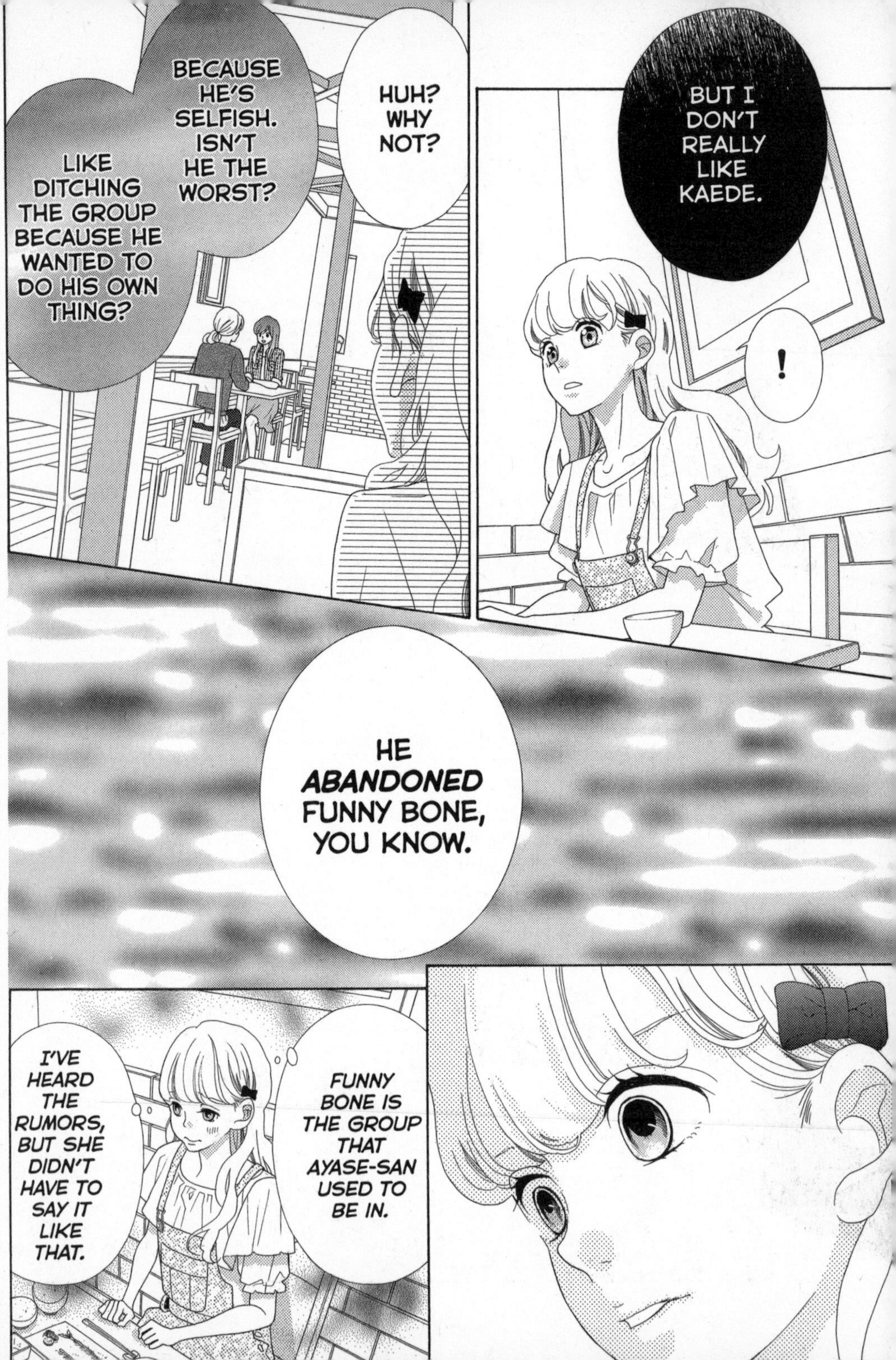
BUT I DON'T REALLY LIKE KAEDE.
!
HUH? WHY NOT?
BECAUSE HE'S SELFISH. ISN'T HE THE WORST?
LIKE DITCHING THE GROUP BECAUSE HE WANTED TO DO HIS OWN THING?
HE *ABANDONED* FUNNY BONE, YOU KNOW.
FUNNY BONE IS THE GROUP THAT AYASE-SAN USED TO BE IN.
I'VE HEARD THE RUMORS, BUT SHE DIDN'T HAVE TO SAY IT LIKE THAT.

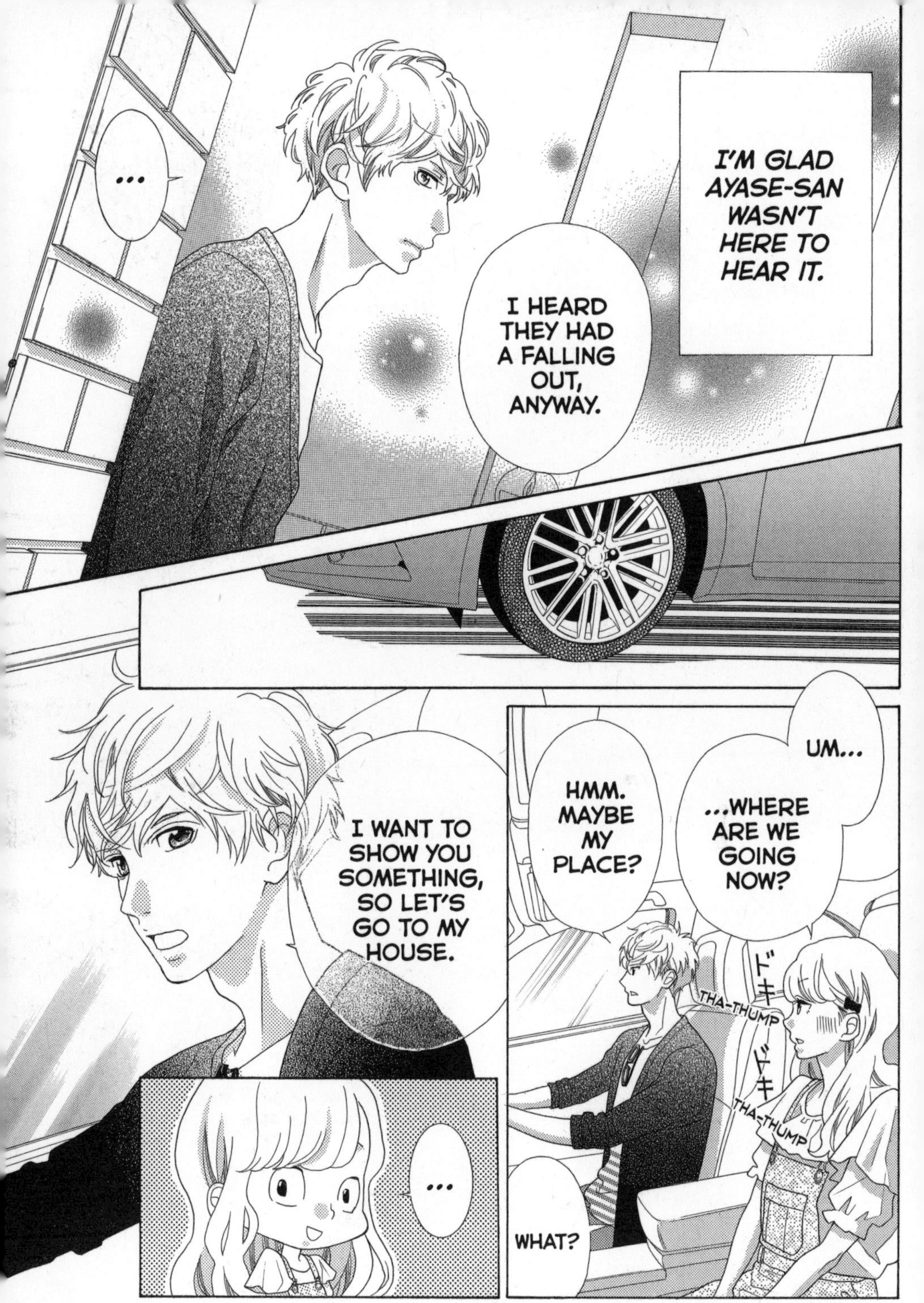
I'M GLAD AYASE-SAN WASN'T HERE TO HEAR IT.
I HEARD THEY HAD A FALLING OUT, ANYWAY.
...
UM...
...WHERE ARE WE GOING NOW?
HMM. MAYBE MY PLACE?
ドキ
THA-THUMP
ドキ
THA-THUMP
WHAT?
I WANT TO SHOW YOU SOMETHING, SO LET'S GO TO MY HOUSE.
...

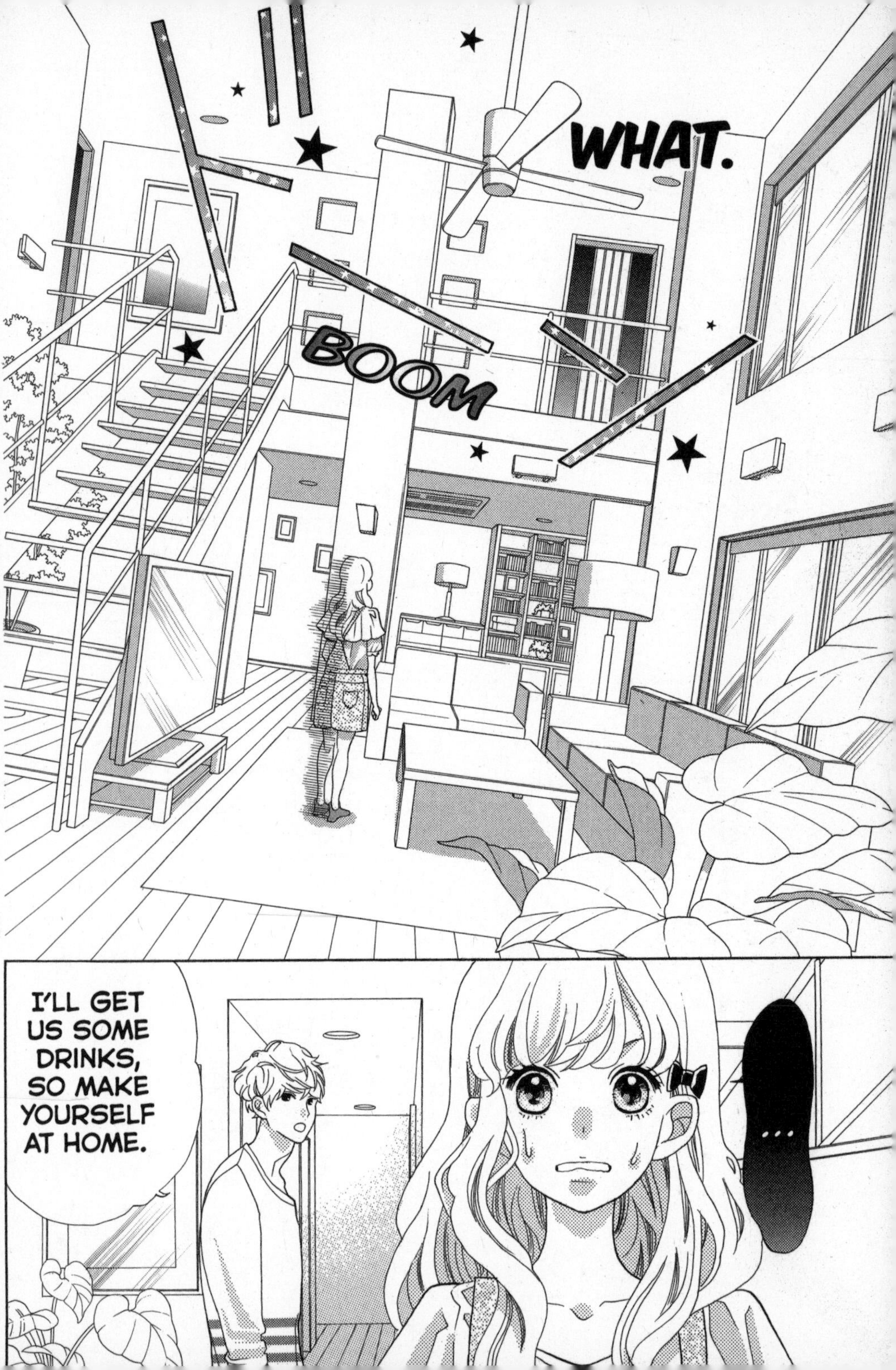
WHAT.
BOOM
...
I'LL GET US SOME DRINKS, SO MAKE YOURSELF AT HOME.

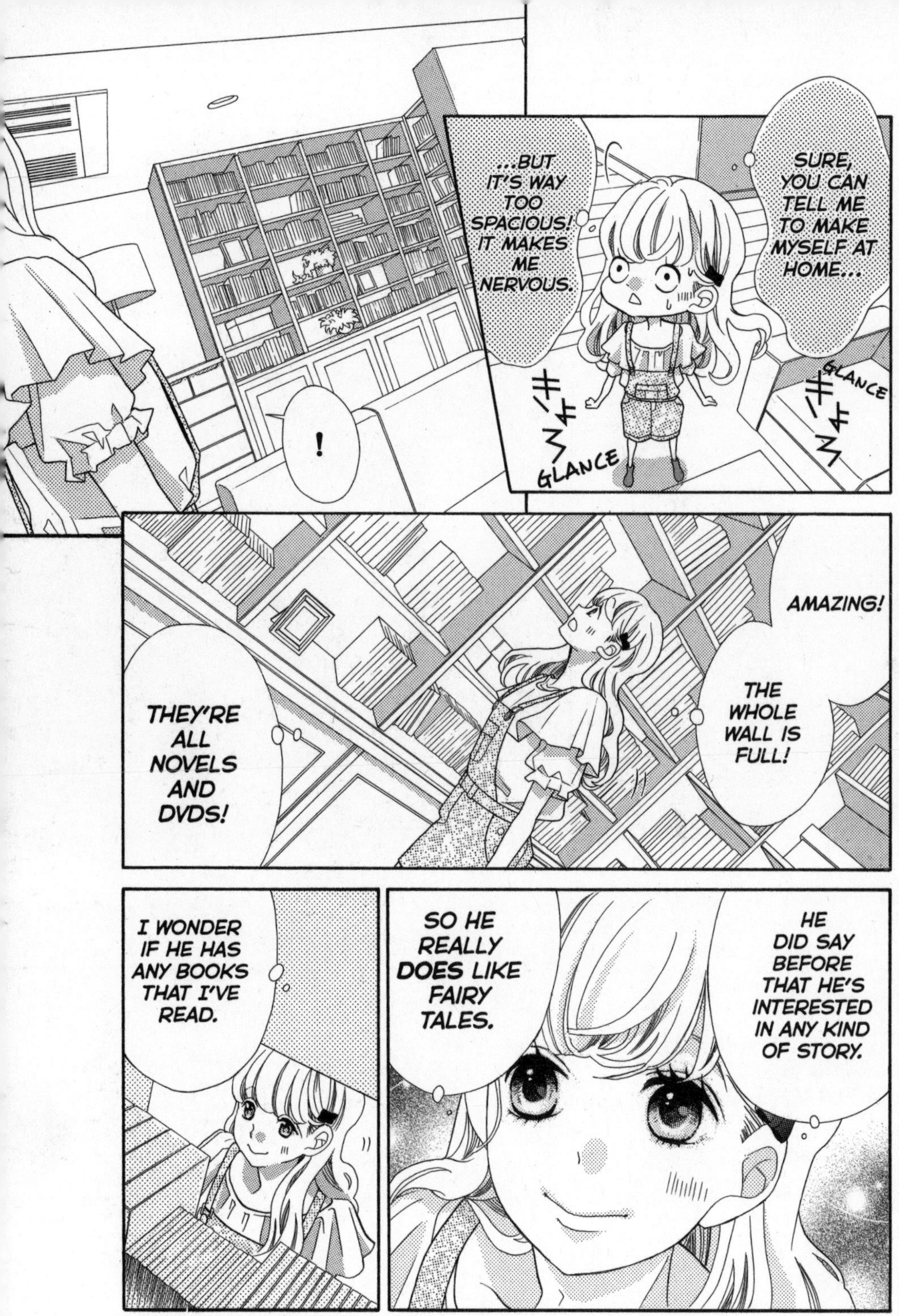
SURE, YOU CAN TELL ME TO MAKE MYSELF AT HOME...
...BUT IT'S WAY TOO SPACIOUS! IT MAKES ME NERVOUS.
GLANCE
GLANCE
!
AMAZING!
THE WHOLE WALL IS FULL!
THEY'RE ALL NOVELS AND DVDS!
HE DID SAY BEFORE THAT HE'S INTERESTED IN ANY KIND OF STORY.
SO HE REALLY **DOES** LIKE FAIRY TALES.
I WONDER IF HE HAS ANY BOOKS THAT I'VE READ.

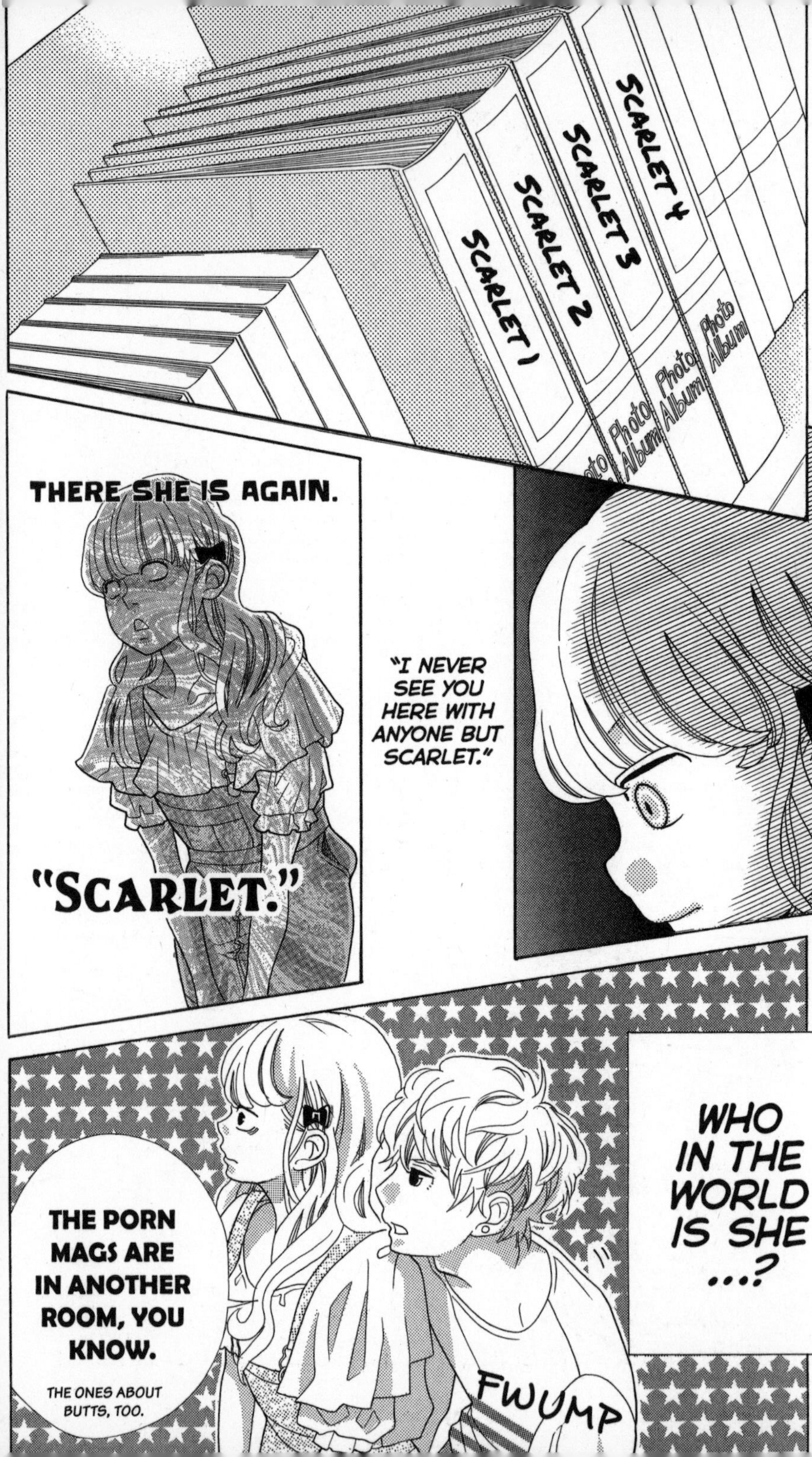
SCARLET 4
SCARLET 3
SCARLET 2
SCARLET 1
Photo Album
Photo Album
Photo Album
THERE SHE IS AGAIN.
"SCARLET."
"I NEVER SEE YOU HERE WITH ANYONE BUT SCARLET."
WHO IN THE WORLD IS SHE ...?
THE PORN MAGS ARE IN ANOTHER ROOM, YOU KNOW.
THE ONES ABOUT BUTTS, TOO.
FWUMP

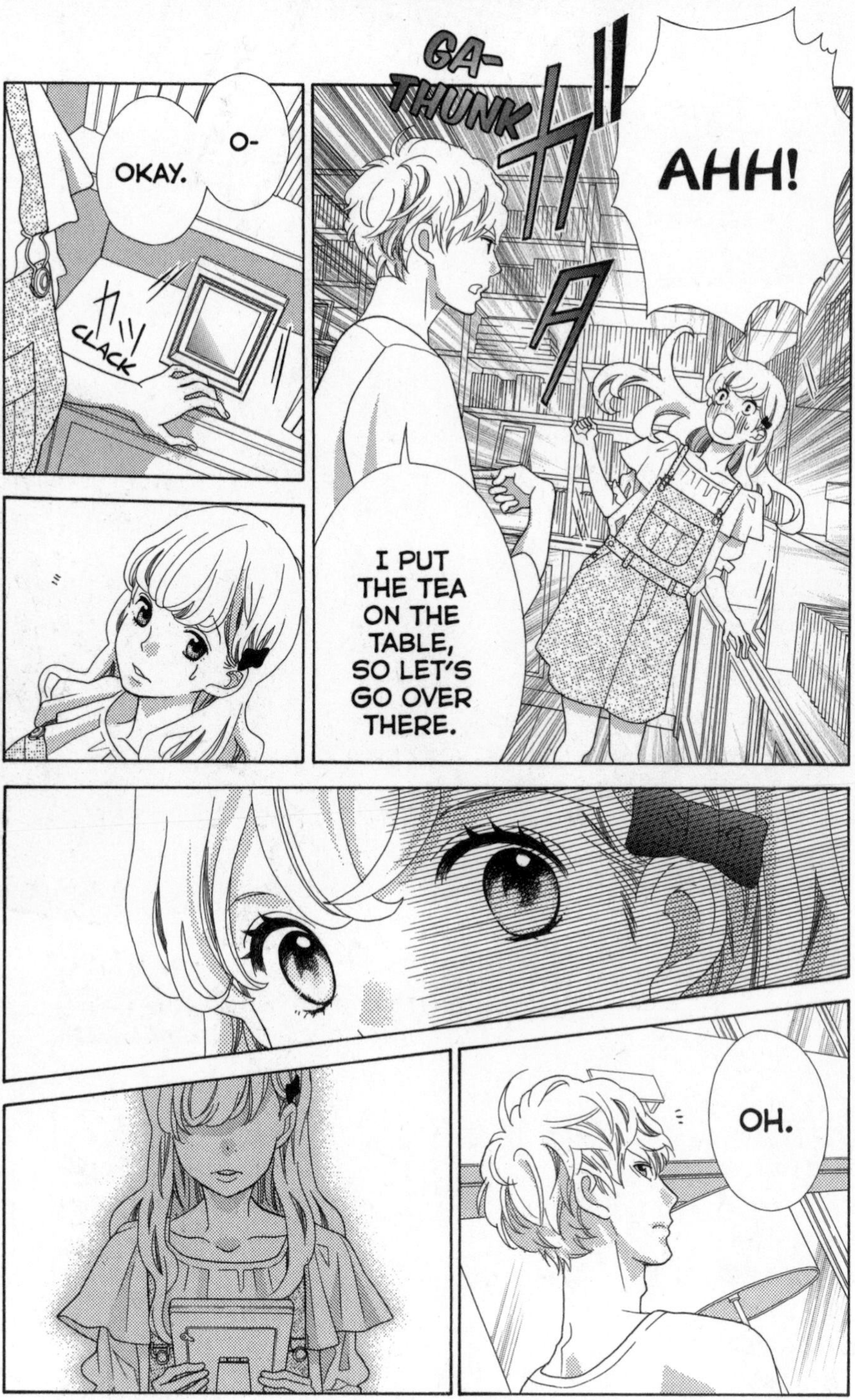
AHH!
GA-THUNK
I PUT THE TEA ON THE TABLE, SO LET'S GO OVER THERE.
O- OKAY.
CLACK
OH.

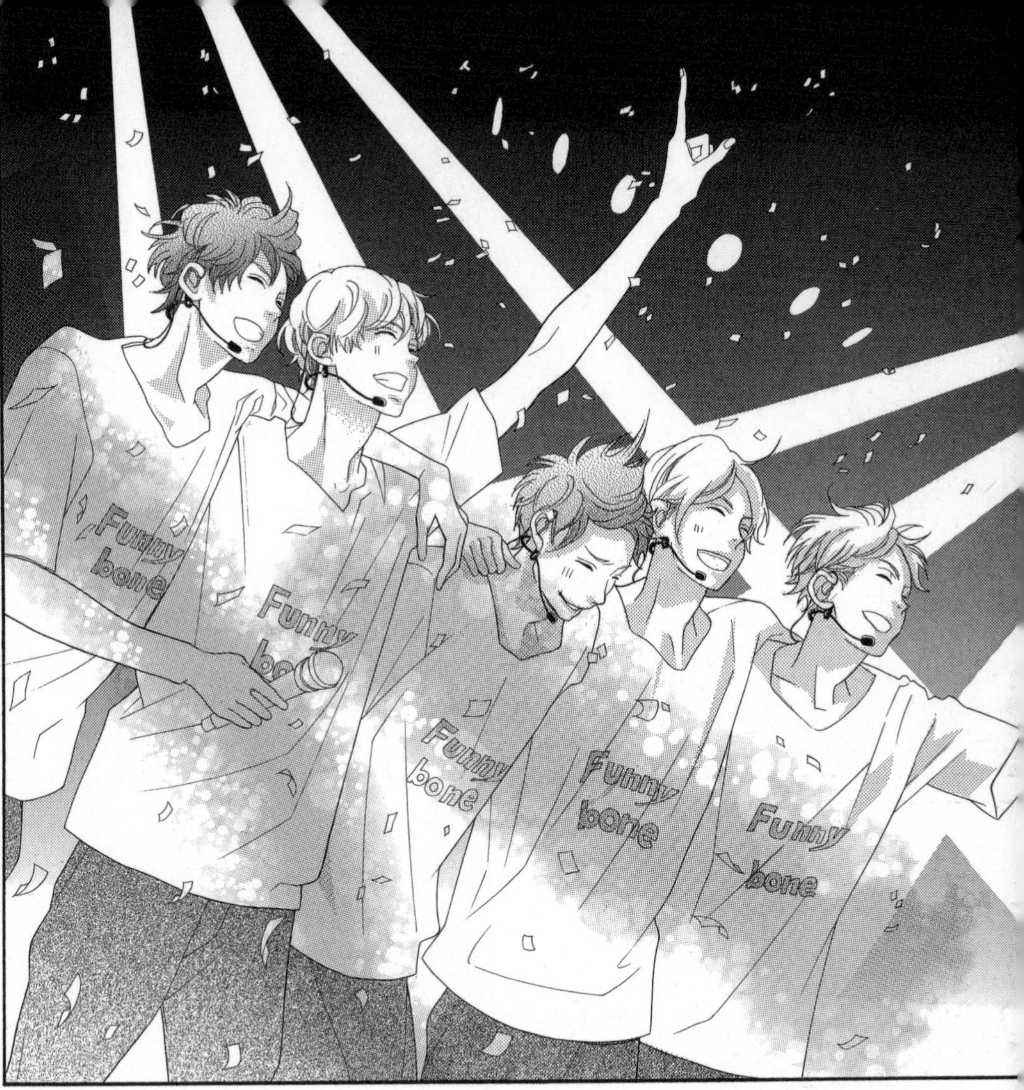
Funny bone
Funny bone
Funny bone
Funny bone
Funny bone
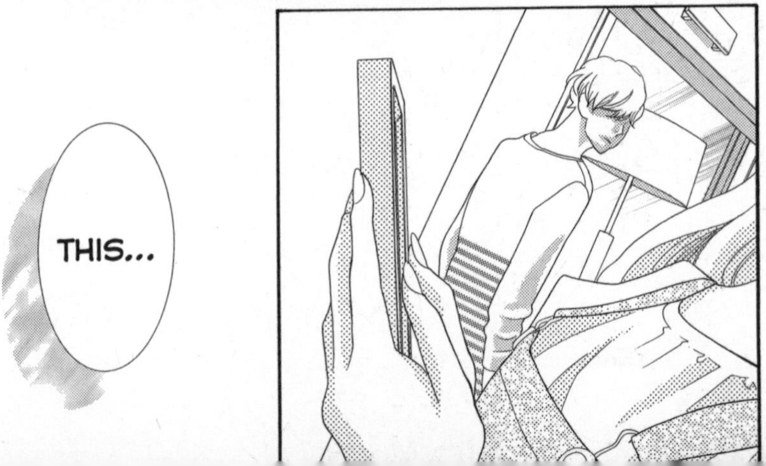
THIS...

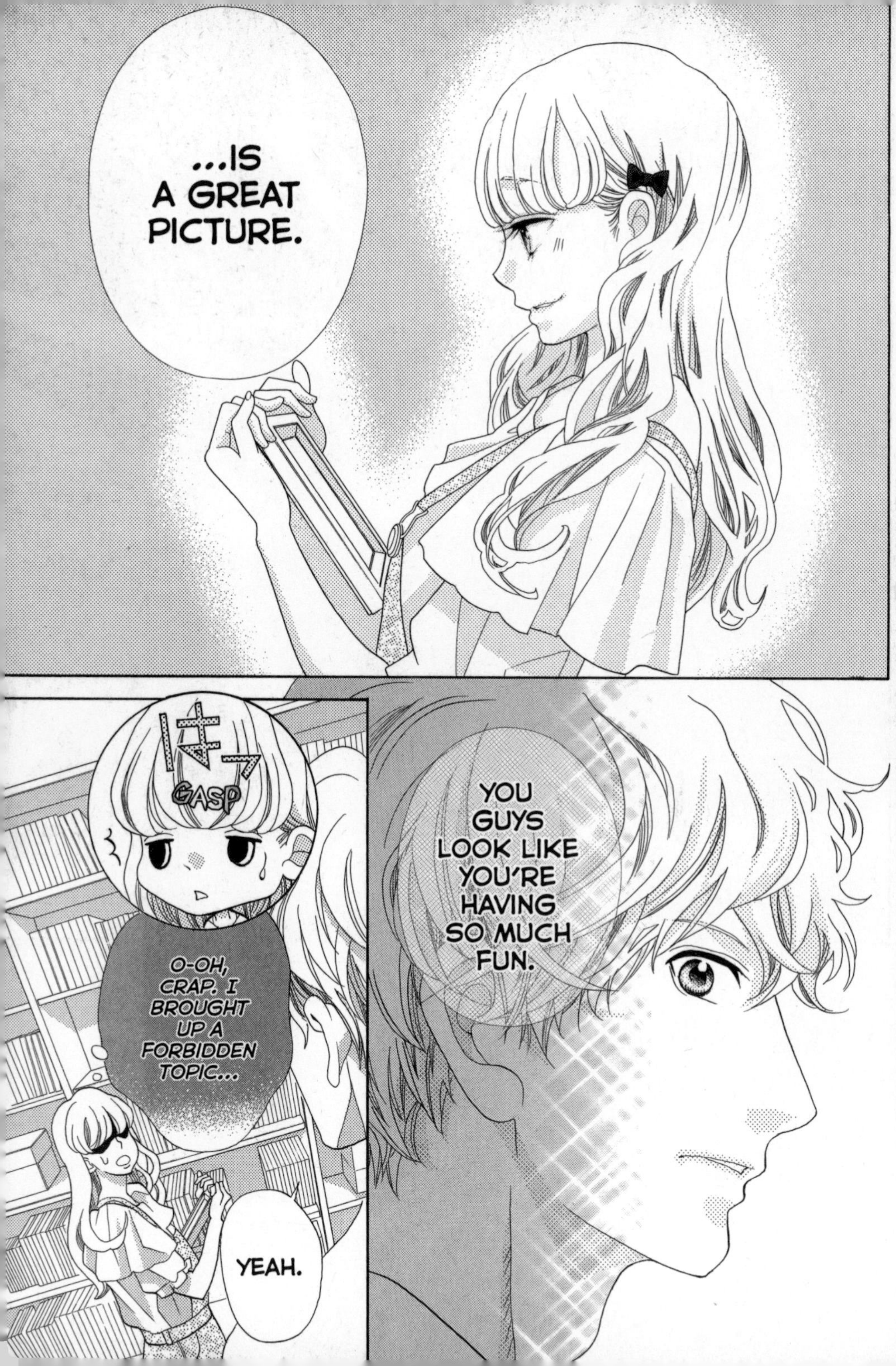
...IS A GREAT PICTURE.
YOU GUYS LOOK LIKE YOU'RE HAVING SO MUCH FUN.
GASP
O-OH, CRAP. I BROUGHT UP A FORBIDDEN TOPIC...
YEAH.

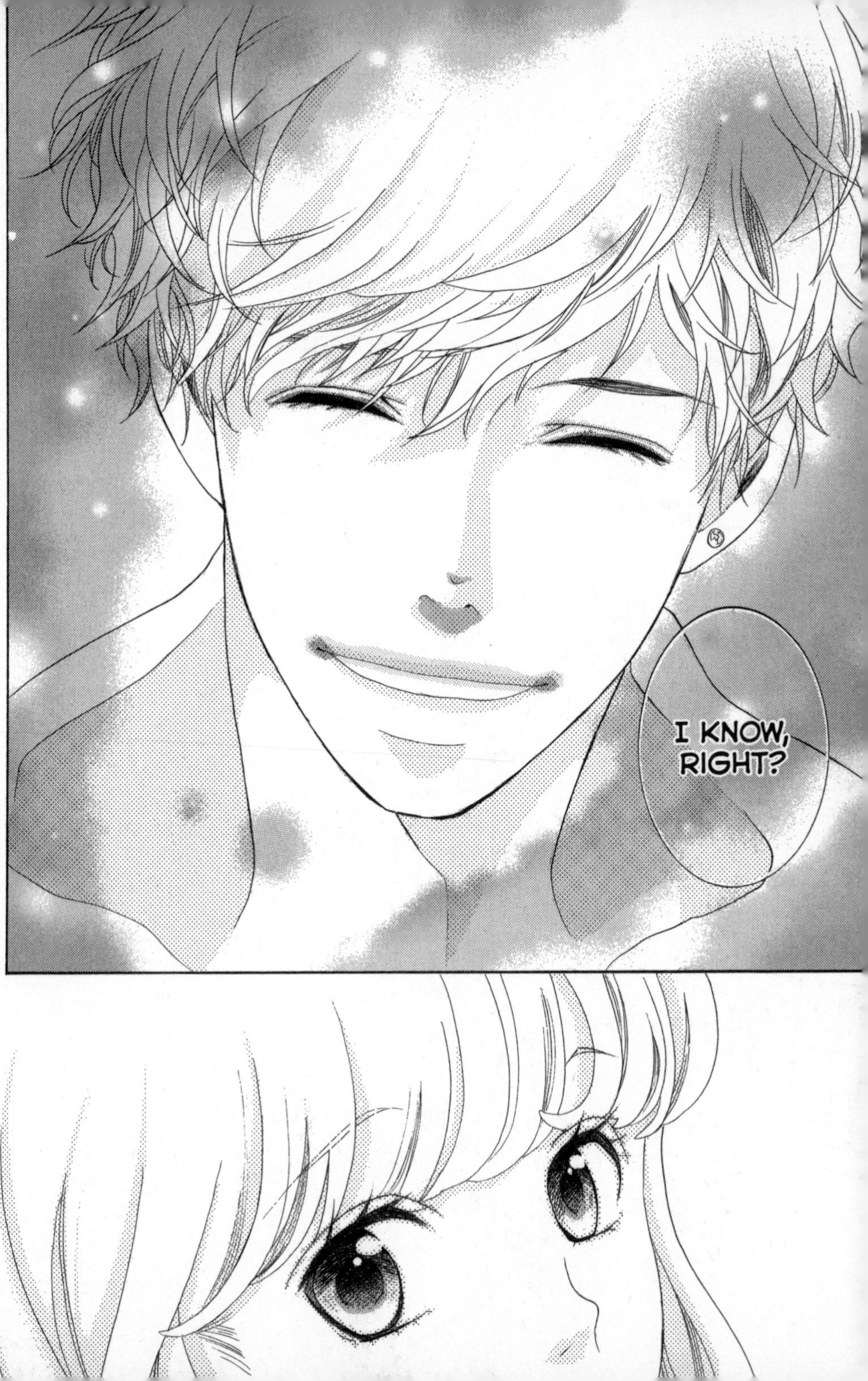
I KNOW, RIGHT?

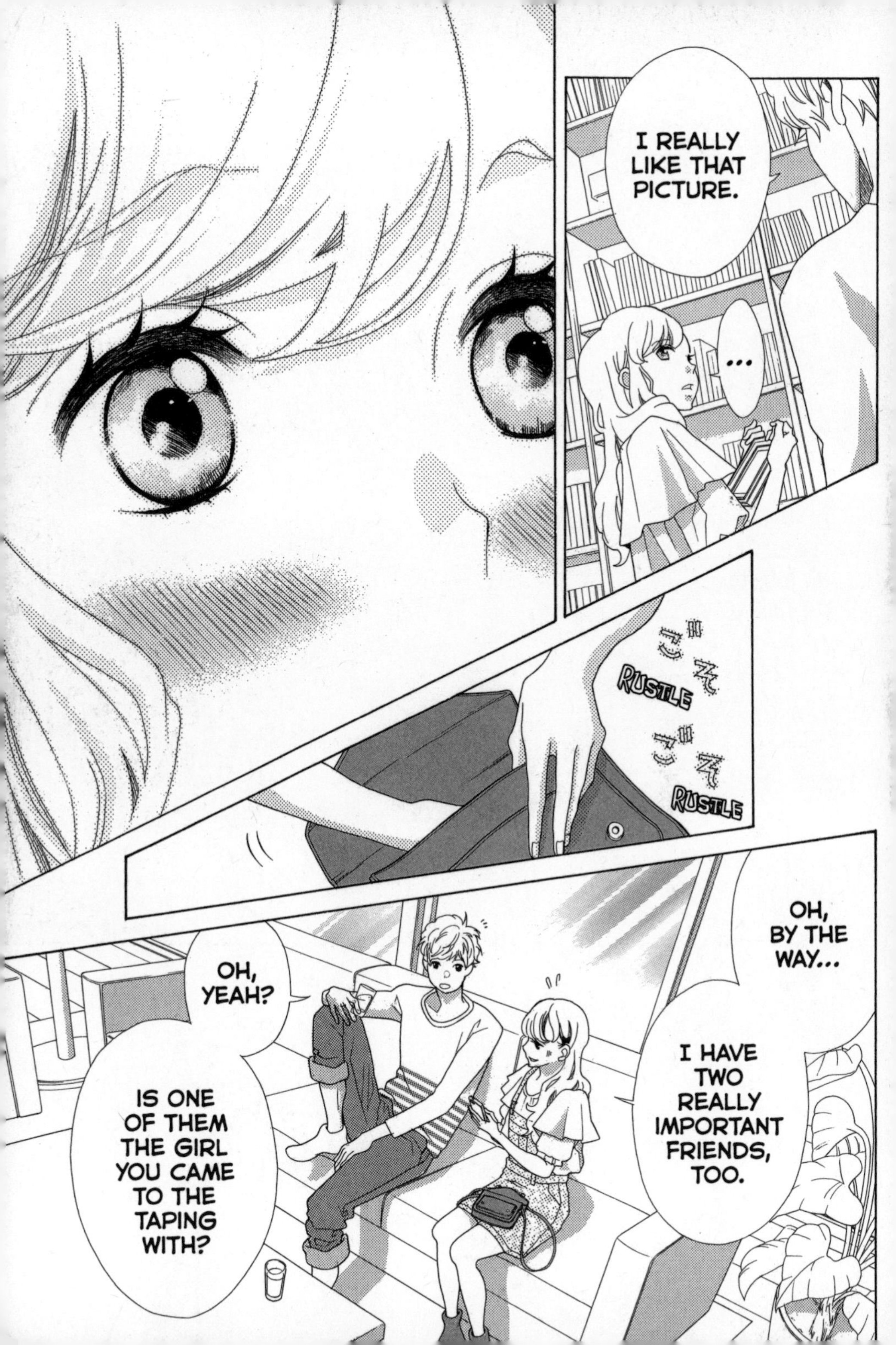
I REALLY LIKE THAT PICTURE.
...
RUSTLE
RUSTLE
OH, BY THE WAY...
I HAVE TWO REALLY IMPORTANT FRIENDS, TOO.
OH, YEAH?
IS ONE OF THEM THE GIRL YOU CAME TO THE TAPING WITH?

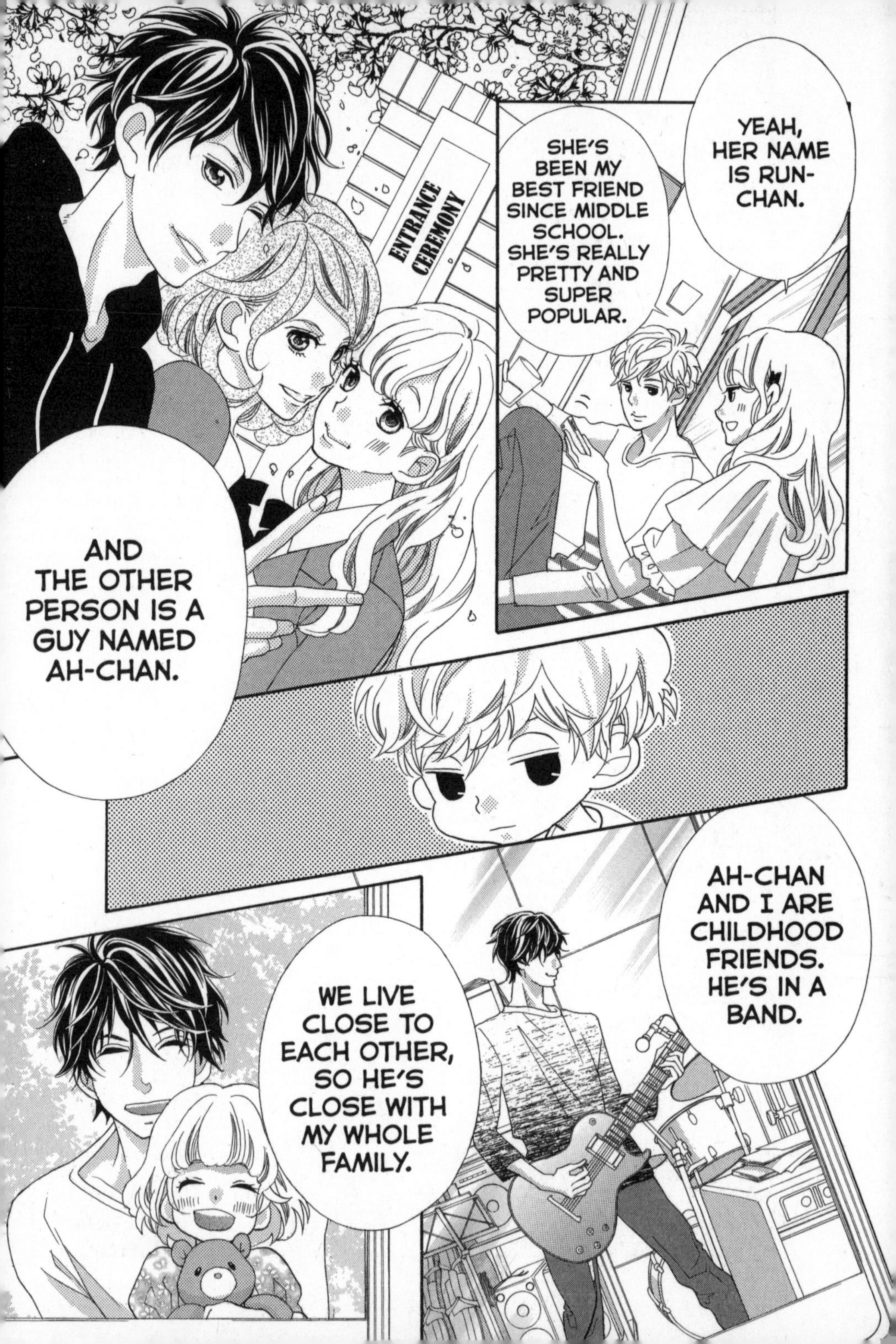

YEAH, HER NAME IS RUN-CHAN.
SHE'S BEEN MY BEST FRIEND SINCE MIDDLE SCHOOL. SHE'S REALLY PRETTY AND SUPER POPULAR.
ENTRANCE CEREMONY
AND THE OTHER PERSON IS A GUY NAMED AH-CHAN.
AH-CHAN AND I ARE CHILDHOOD FRIENDS. HE'S IN A BAND.
WE LIVE CLOSE TO EACH OTHER, SO HE'S CLOSE WITH MY WHOLE FAMILY.

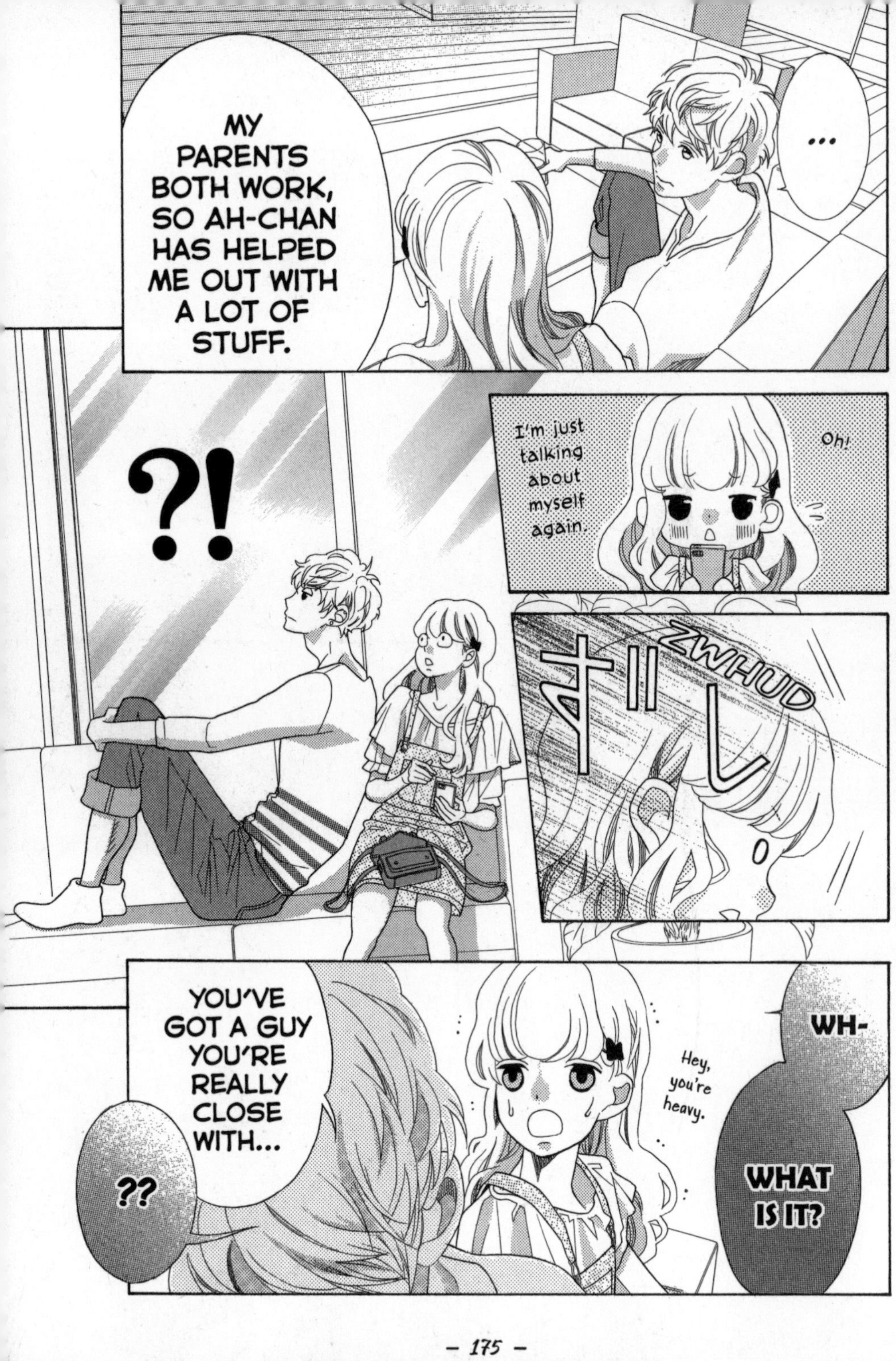
...
MY PARENTS BOTH WORK, SO AH-CHAN HAS HELPED ME OUT WITH A LOT OF STUFF.
Oh!
I'm just talking about myself again.
ZWHUD
?!
WH- WHAT IS IT?
Hey, you're heavy.
YOU'VE GOT A GUY YOU'RE REALLY CLOSE WITH...
??

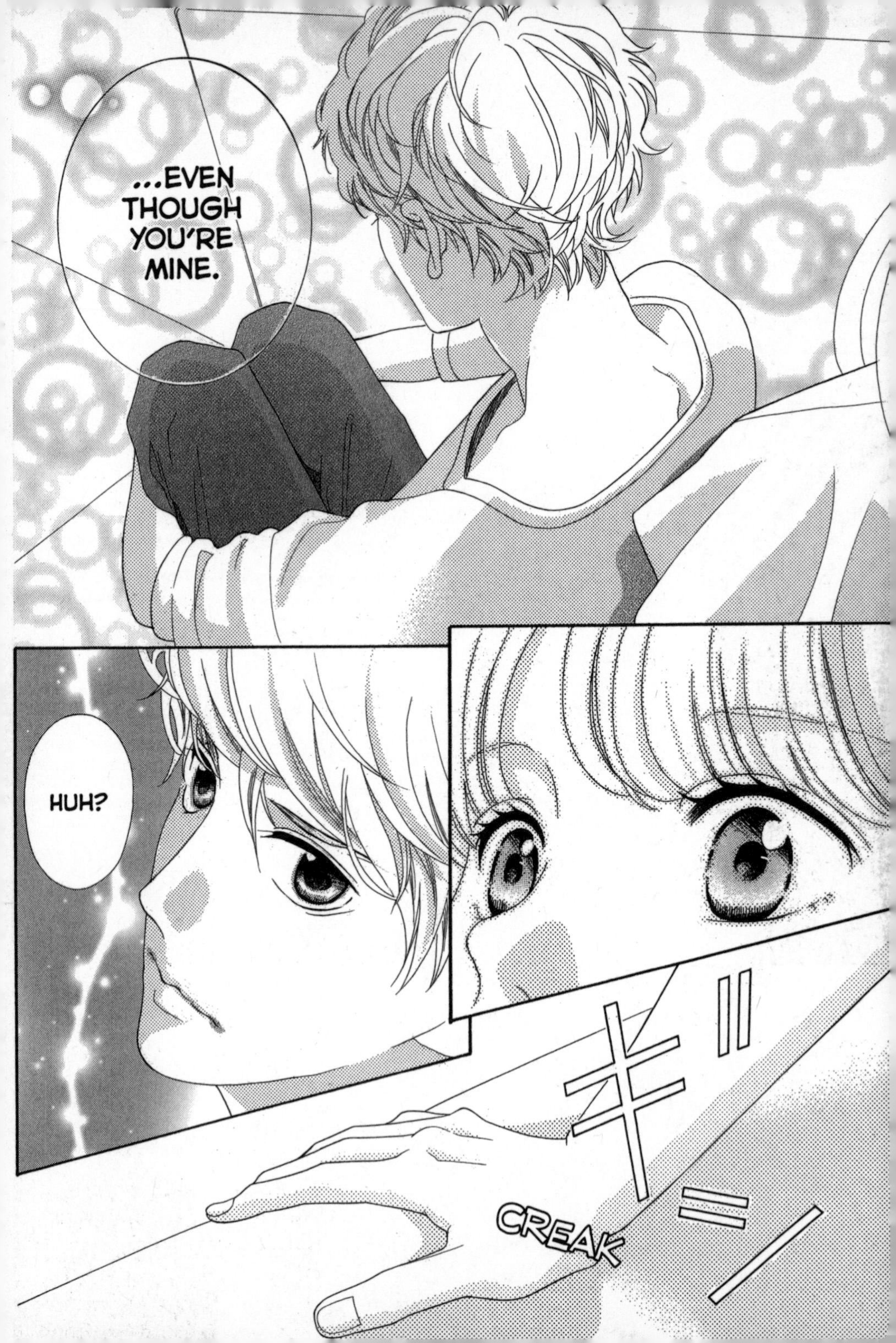
...EVEN THOUGH YOU'RE MINE.
HUH?
CREAK

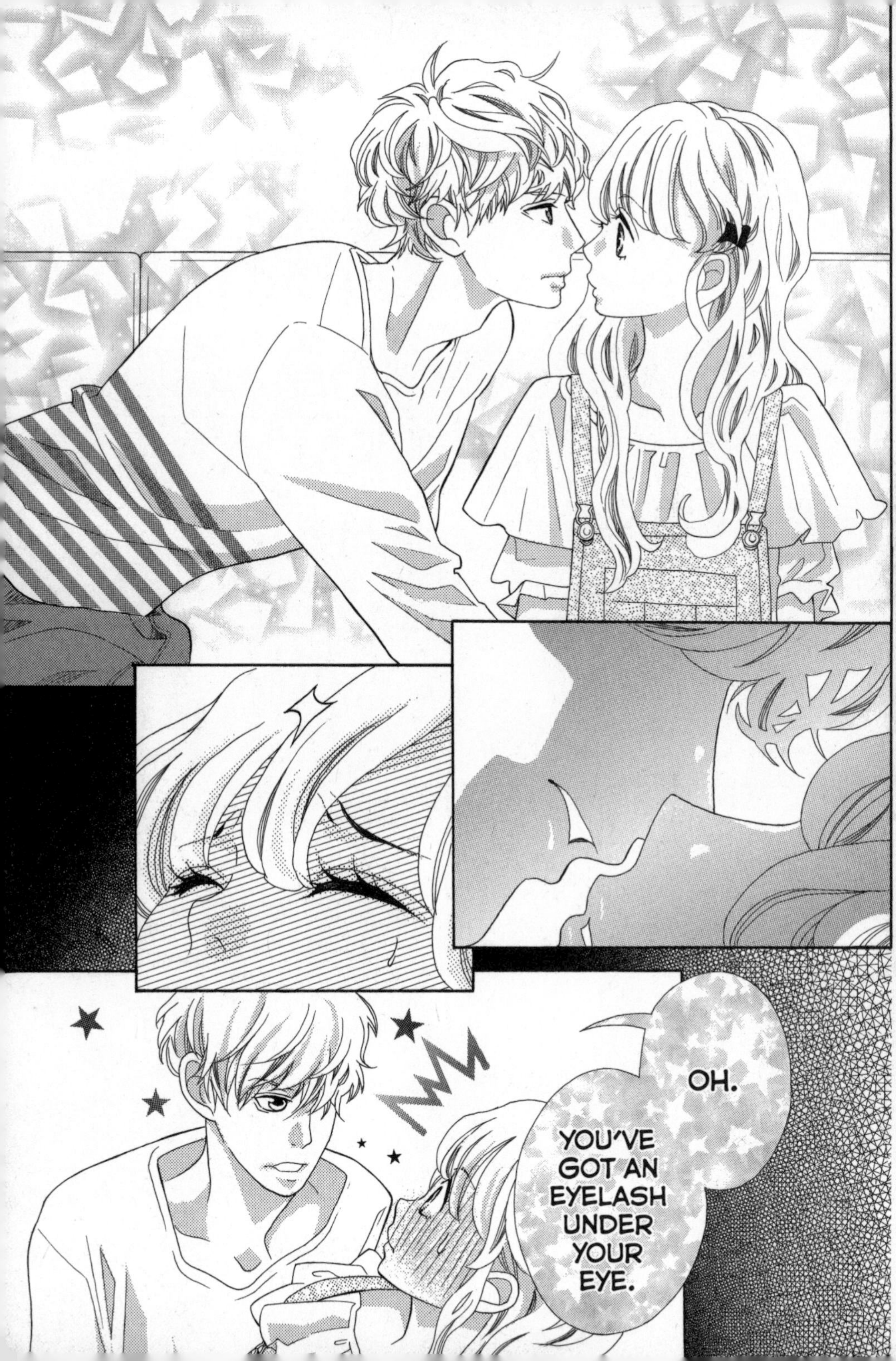
OH.
YOU'VE GOT AN EYELASH UNDER YOUR EYE.

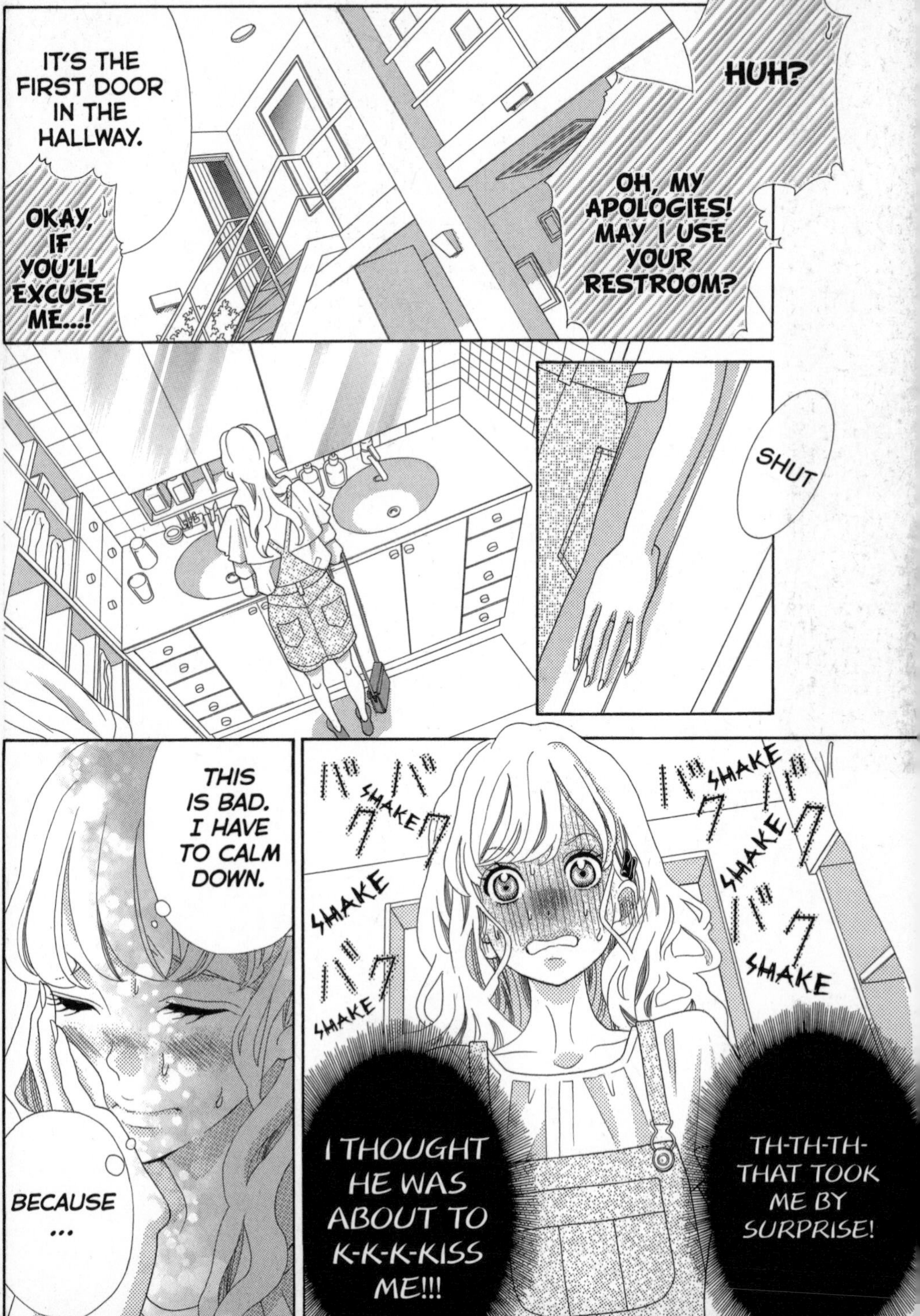
HUH?
OH, MY APOLOGIES! MAY I USE YOUR RESTROOM?
IT'S THE FIRST DOOR IN THE HALLWAY.
OKAY, IF YOU'LL EXCUSE ME...!
SHUT
SHAKE
SHAKE
SHAKE
SHAKE
SHAKE
SHAKE
SHAKE
TH-TH-TH-THAT TOOK ME BY SURPRISE!
I THOUGHT HE WAS ABOUT TO K-K-K-KISS ME!!!
THIS IS BAD. I HAVE TO CALM DOWN.
BECAUSE ...

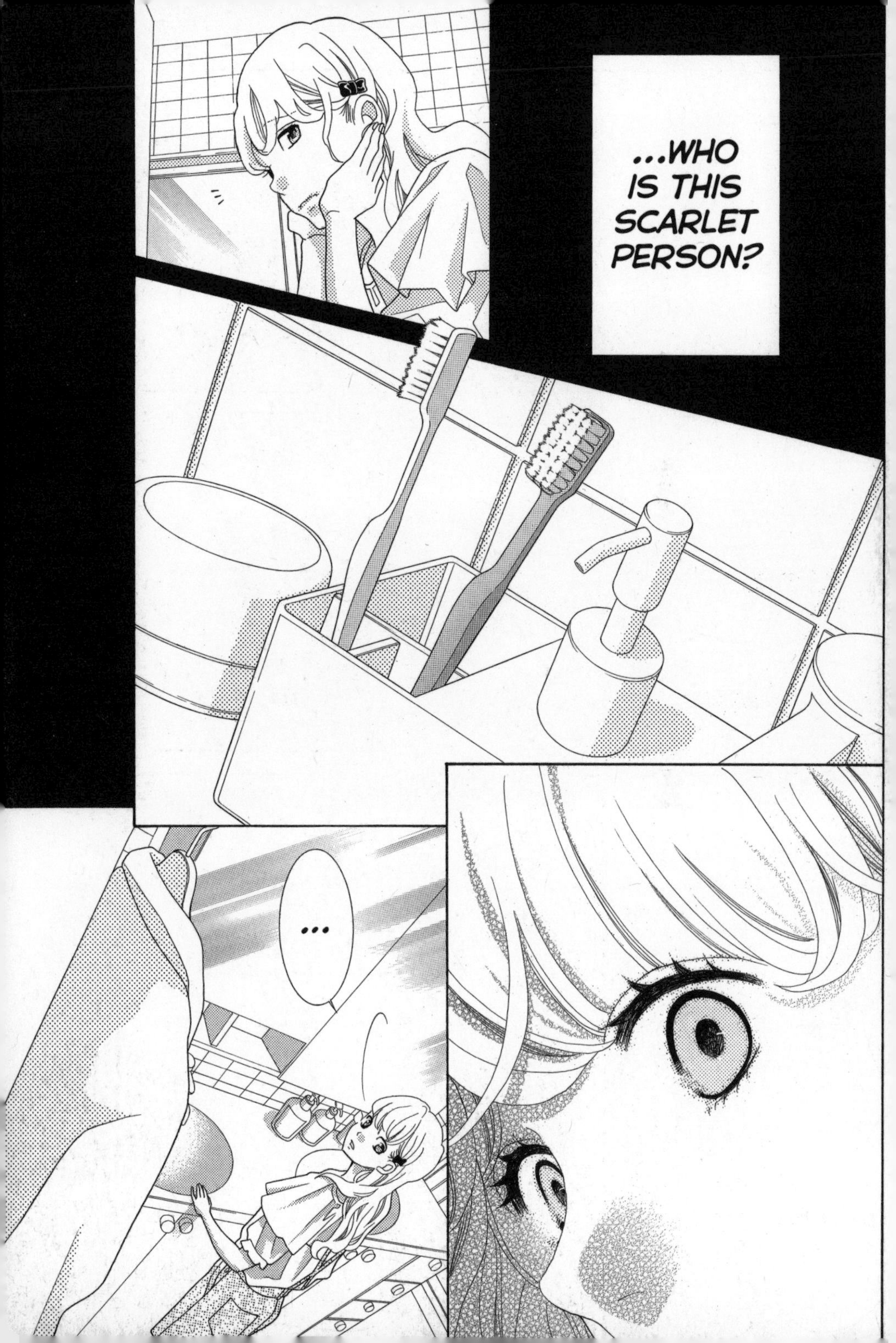
...WHO IS THIS SCARLET PERSON?
...

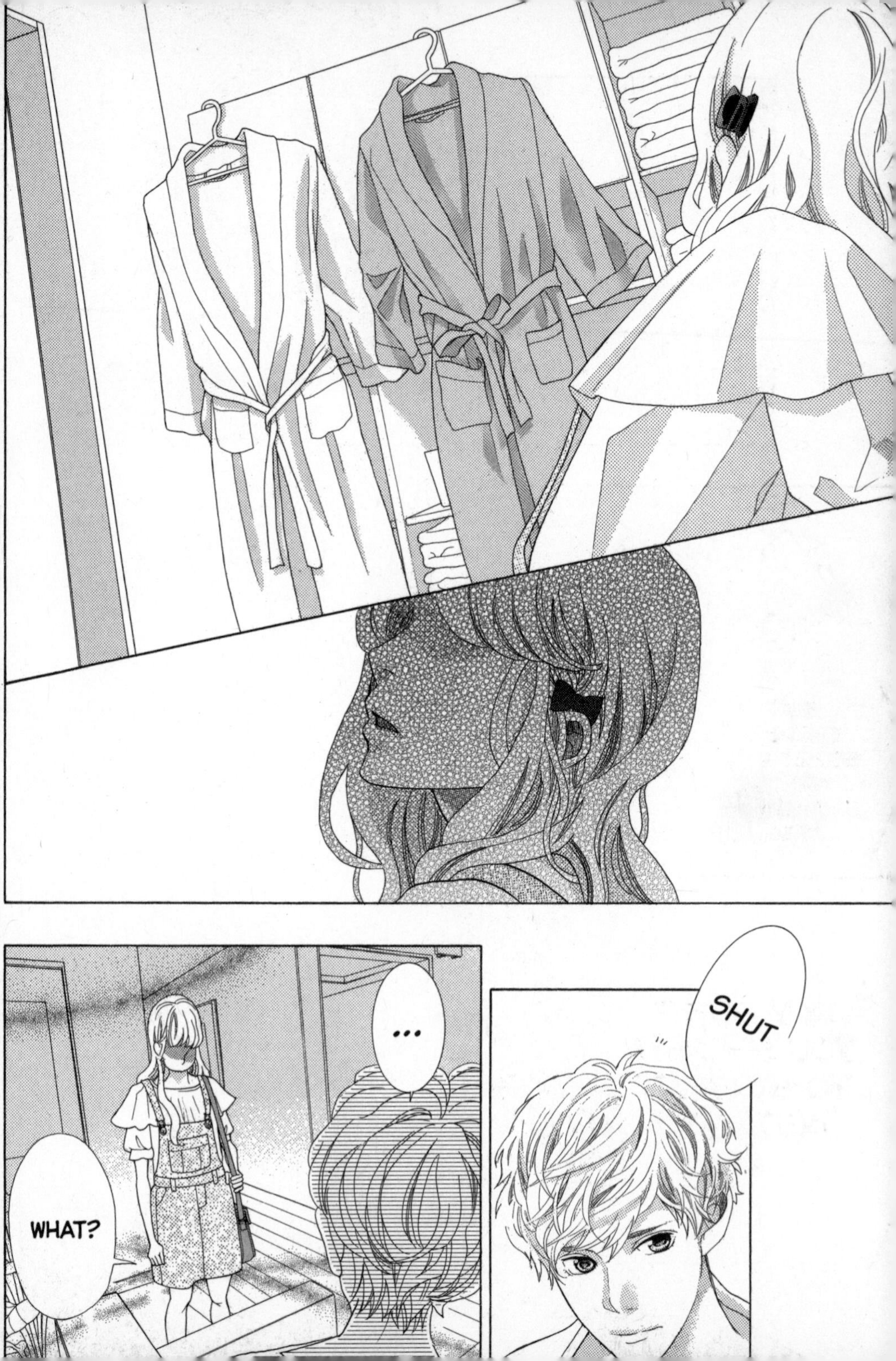
SHUT
...
WHAT?

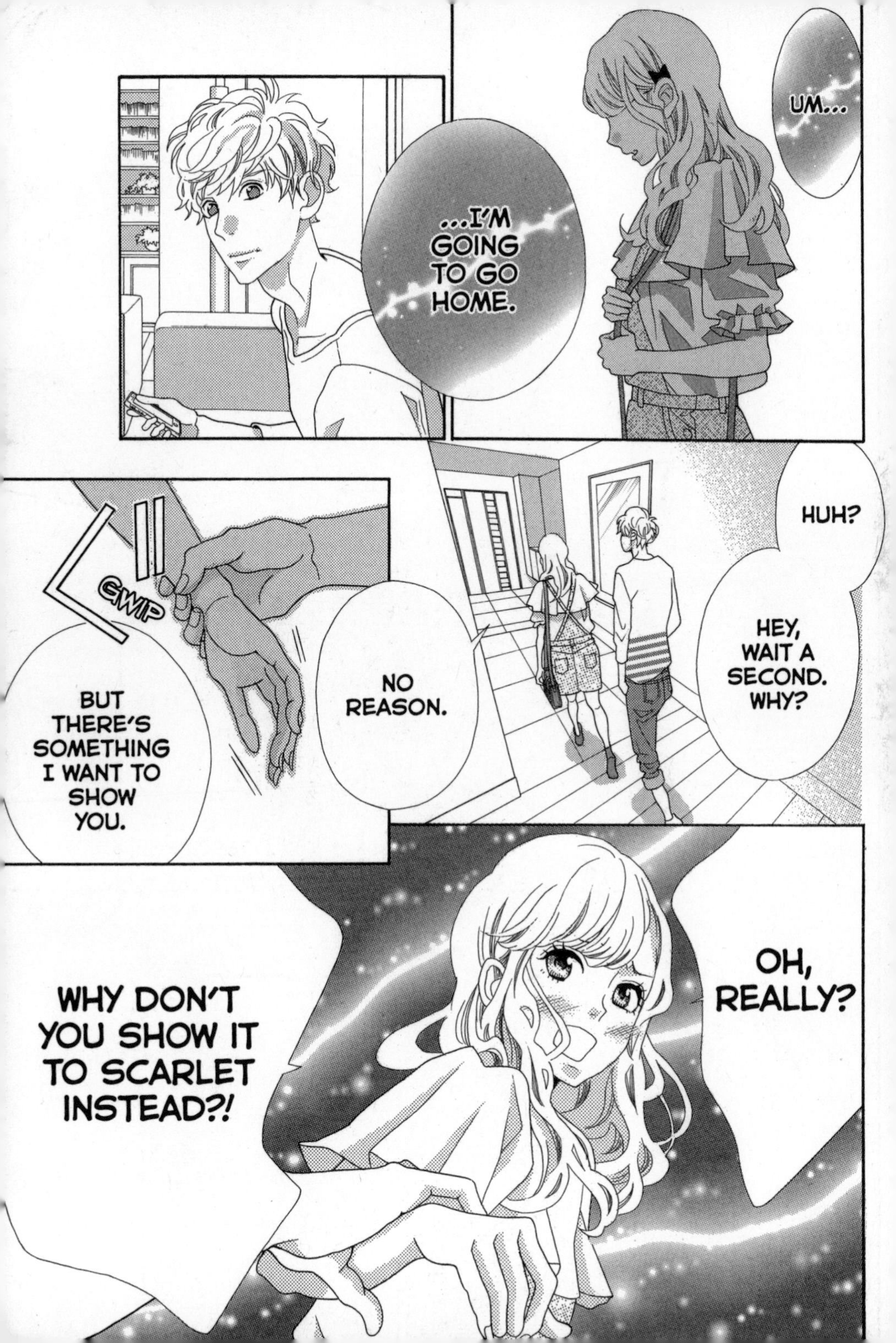
UM...
...I'M GOING TO GO HOME.
HUH?
HEY, WAIT A SECOND. WHY?
NO REASON.
GWIP
BUT THERE'S SOMETHING I WANT TO SHOW YOU.
OH, REALLY?
WHY DON'T YOU SHOW IT TO SCARLET INSTEAD?!

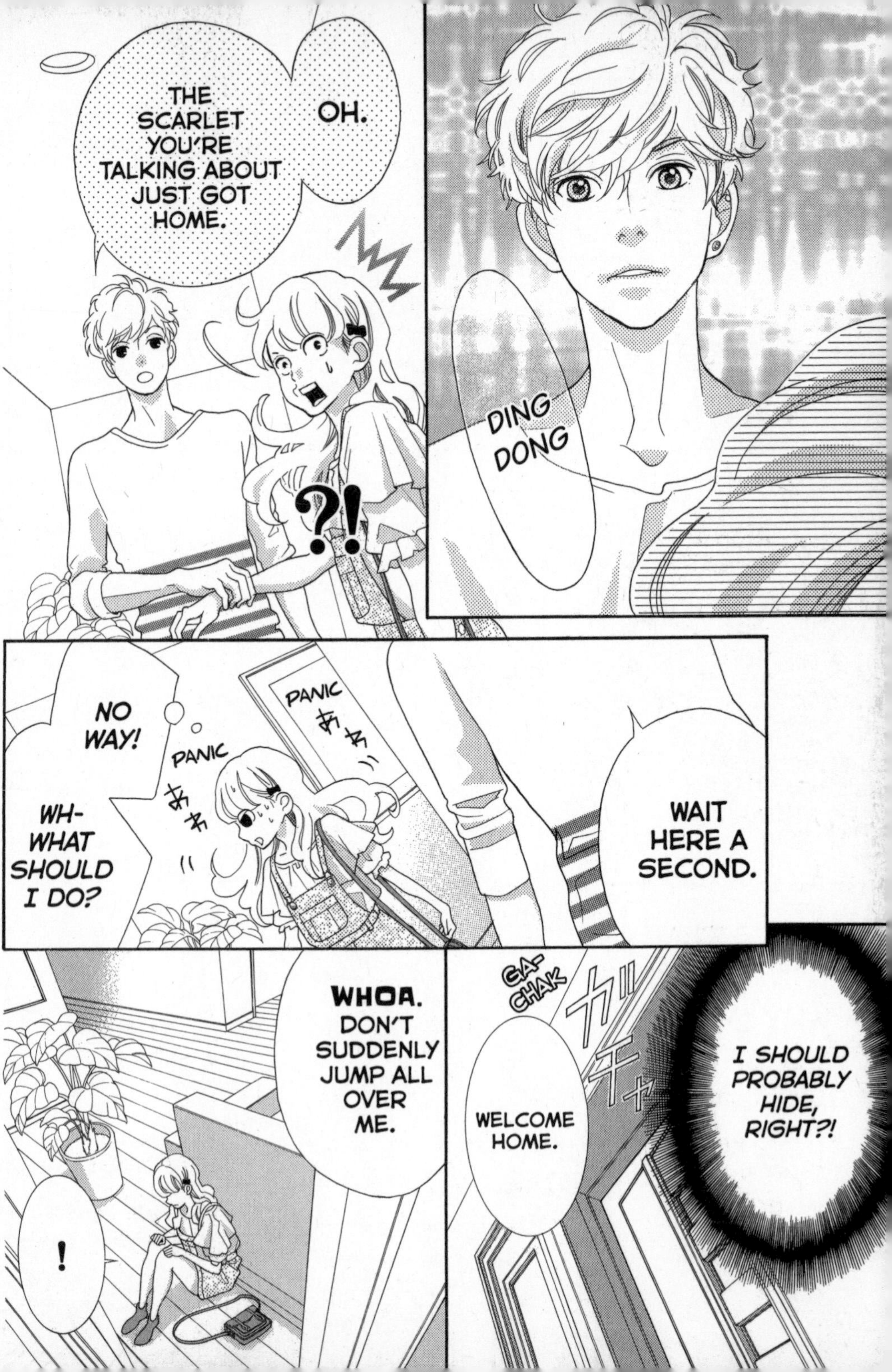
DING DONG
OH.
THE SCARLET YOU'RE TALKING ABOUT JUST GOT HOME.
?!
WAIT HERE A SECOND.
PANIC あわ
PANIC あわ
NO WAY!
WH- WHAT SHOULD I DO?
I SHOULD PROBABLY HIDE, RIGHT?!
GA-CHAK ガチャ
WELCOME HOME.
WHOA. DON'T SUDDENLY JUMP ALL OVER ME.
!

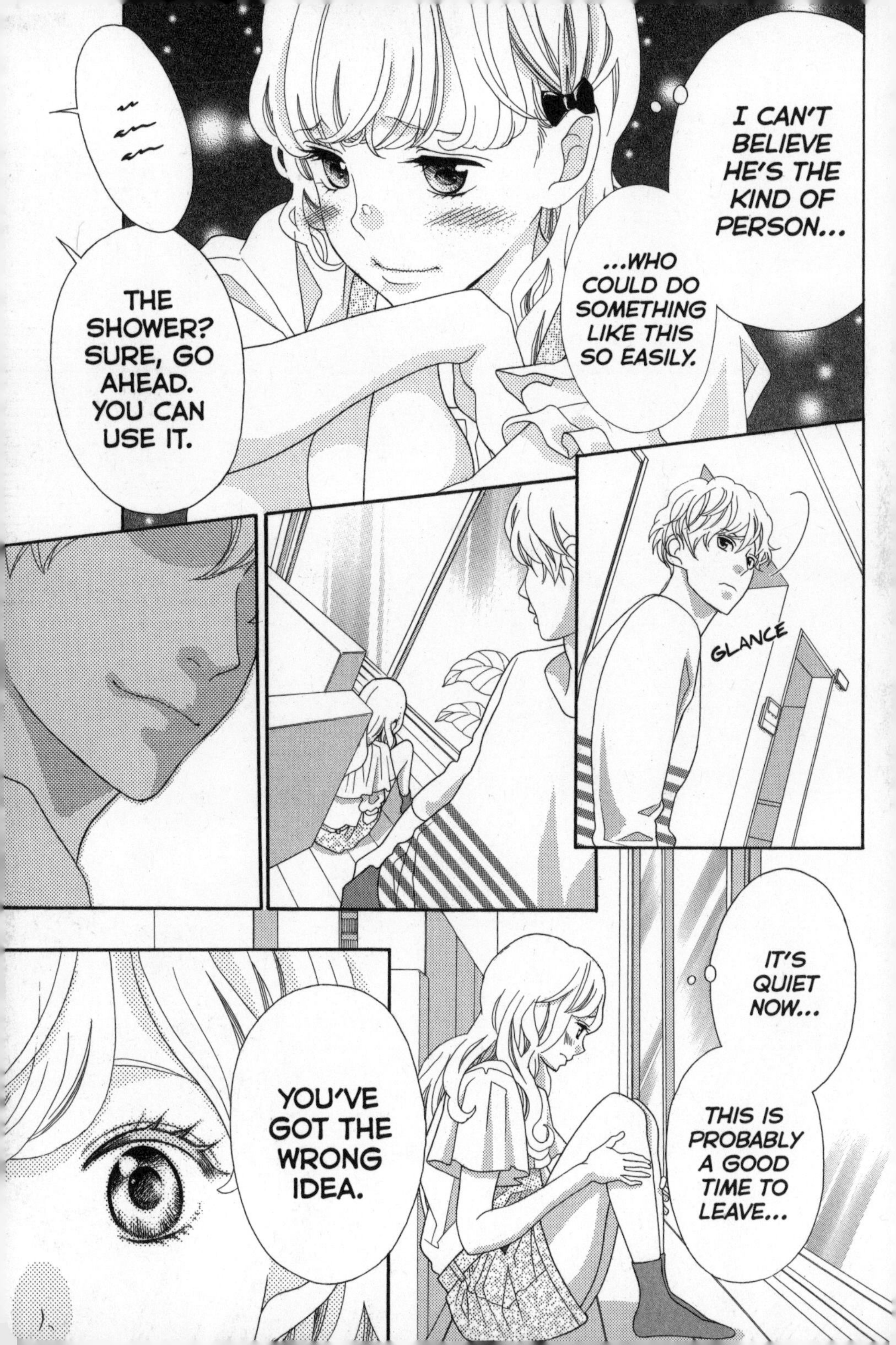
I CAN'T BELIEVE HE'S THE KIND OF PERSON...
...WHO COULD DO SOMETHING LIKE THIS SO EASILY.
THE SHOWER? SURE, GO AHEAD. YOU CAN USE IT.
GLANCE
IT'S QUIET NOW...
THIS IS PROBABLY A GOOD TIME TO LEAVE...
YOU'VE GOT THE WRONG IDEA.

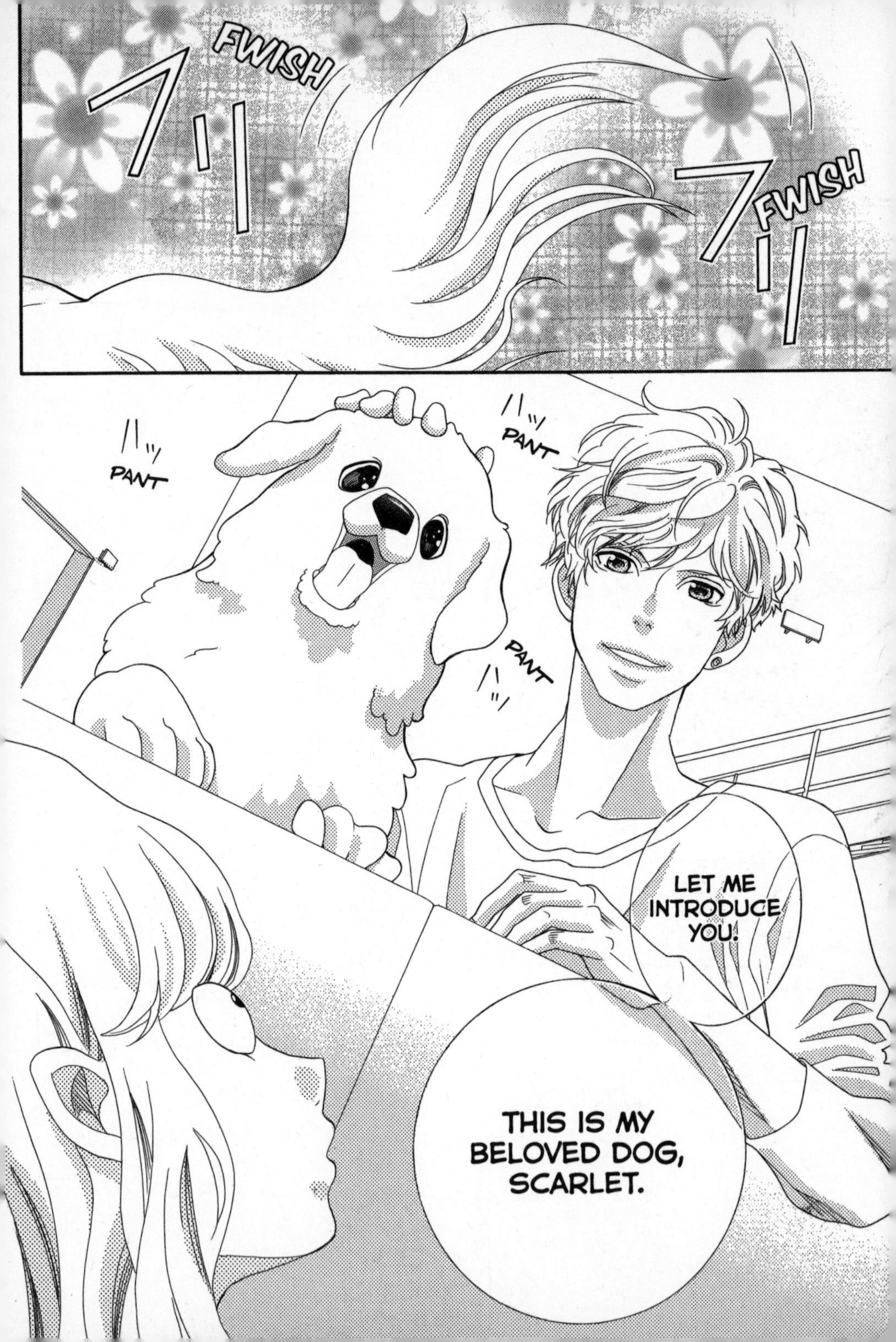
FWISH
FWISH
PANT
PANT
PANT
LET ME INTRODUCE YOU!
THIS IS MY BELOVED DOG, SCARLET.

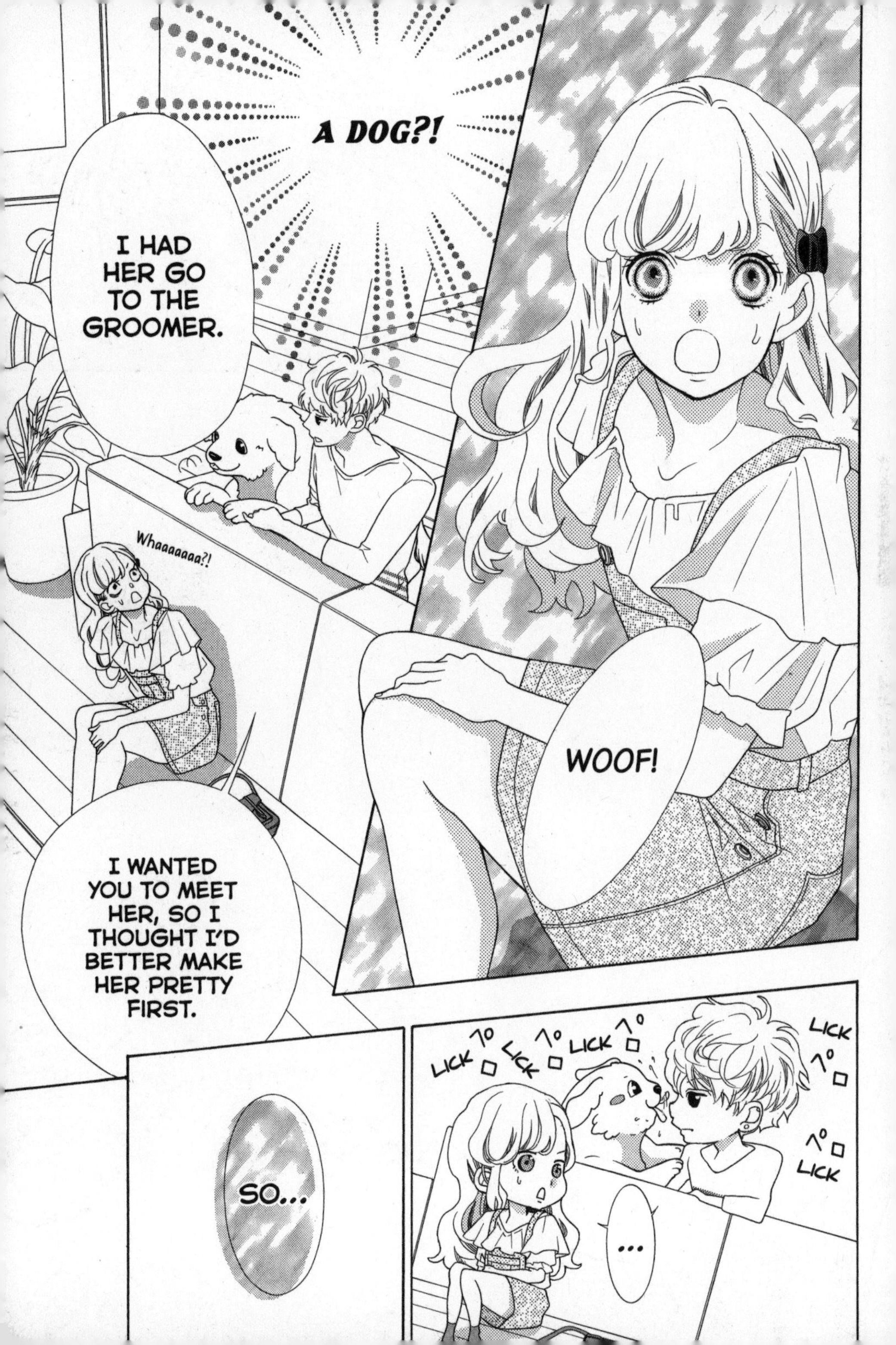
WOOF!
A DOG?!
I HAD HER GO TO THE GROOMER.
Whaaaaaaa?!
I WANTED YOU TO MEET HER, SO I THOUGHT I'D BETTER MAKE HER PRETTY FIRST.
LICK ペロ
LICK ペロ
LICK ペロ
LICK ペロ
LICK ペロ
...
SO...

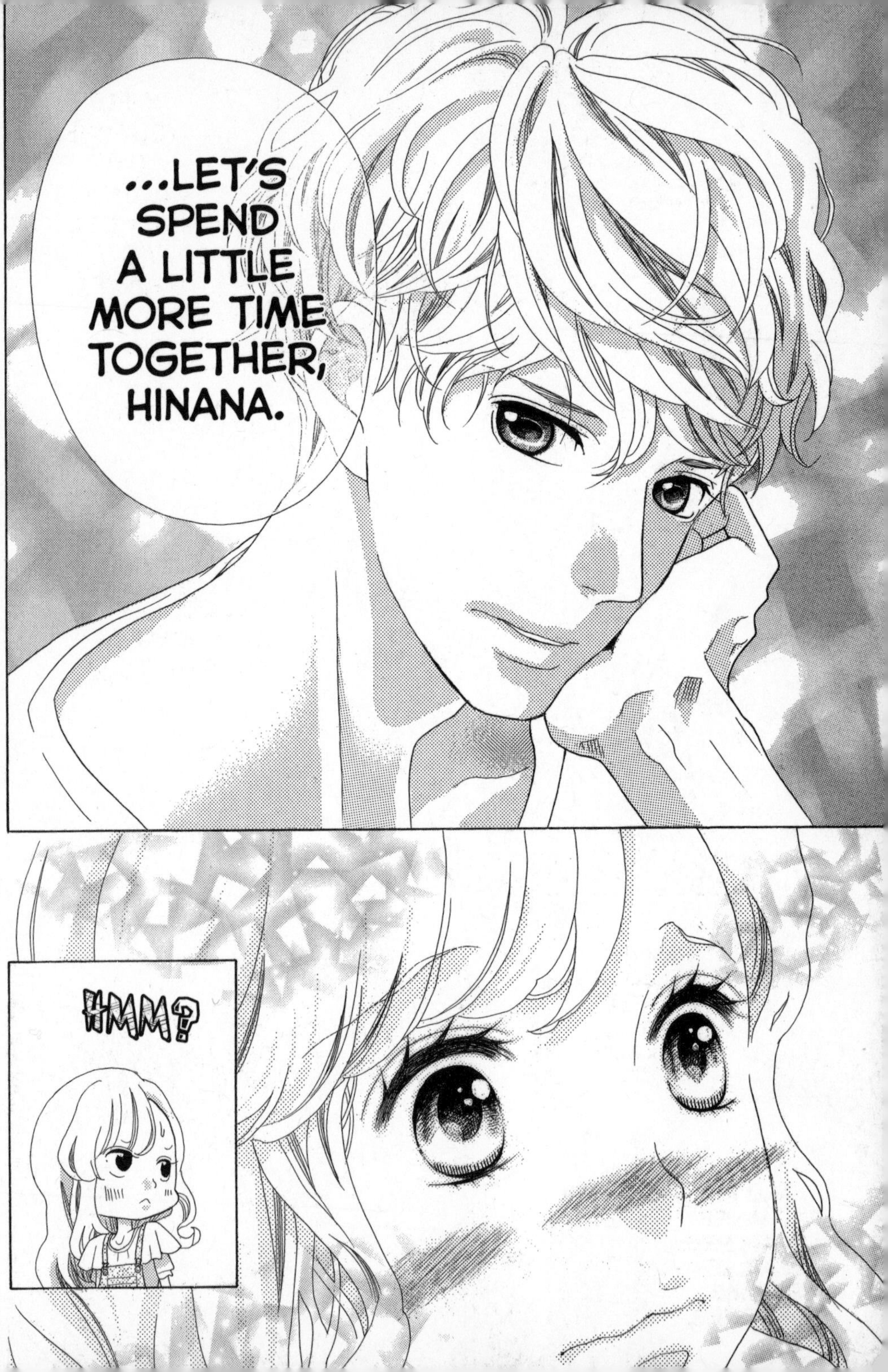
...LET'S SPEND A LITTLE MORE TIME TOGETHER, HINANA.
HMM?

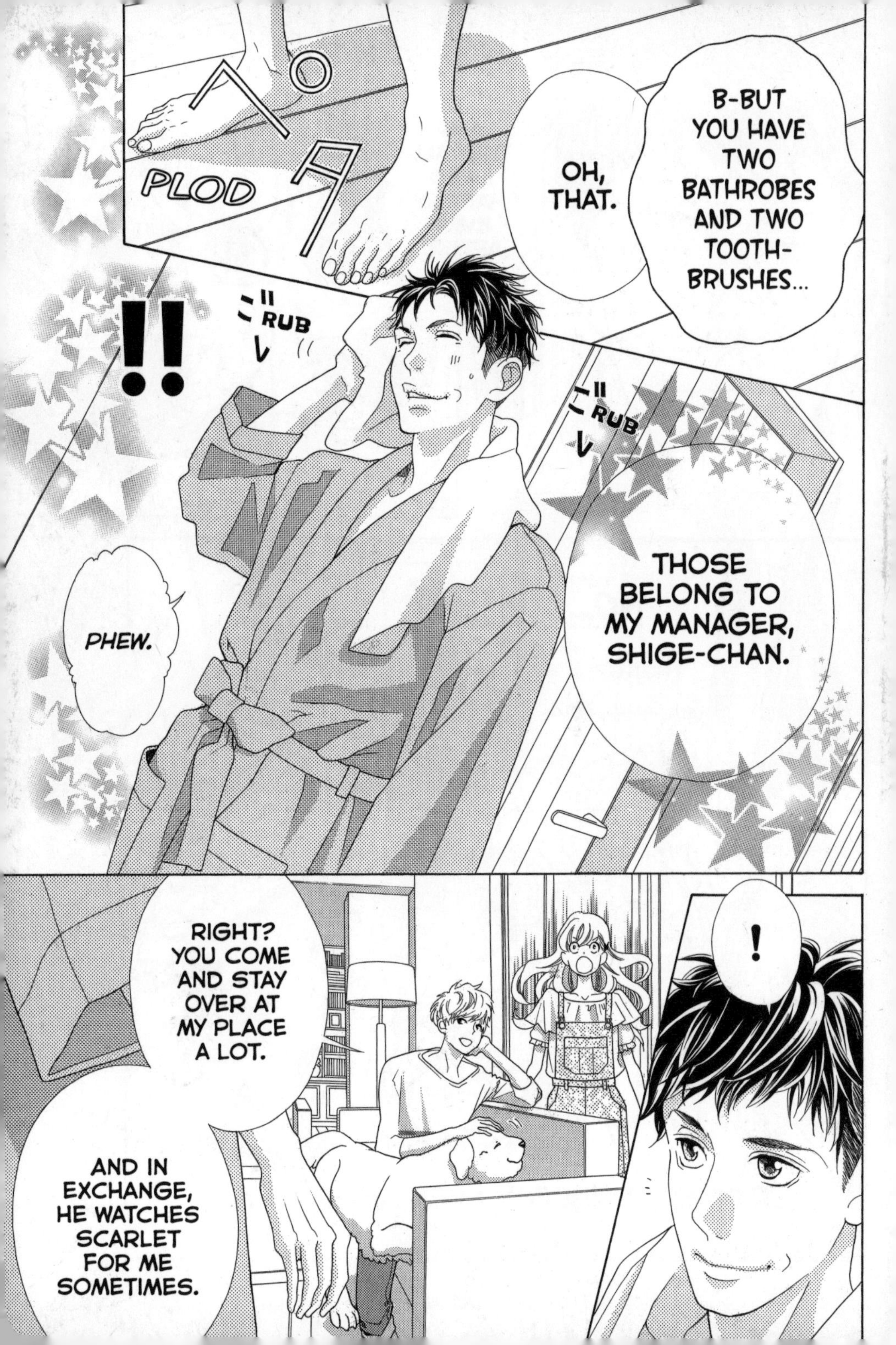
B-BUT YOU HAVE TWO BATHROBES AND TWO TOOTH-BRUSHES...
OH, THAT.
PLOD
!!
RUB
RUB
THOSE BELONG TO MY MANAGER, SHIGE-CHAN.
PHEW.
!
RIGHT? YOU COME AND STAY OVER AT MY PLACE A LOT.
AND IN EXCHANGE, HE WATCHES SCARLET FOR ME SOMETIMES.

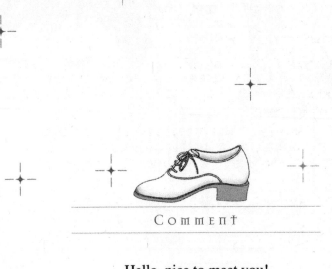

Comment

Hello, nice to meet you!
This time around, I decided
to take on the great challenge of
tackling a story purely focused on
Cinderella, nothing extra.
I really hope you have fun reading it!
Thank you for your ongoing support.

Rin Mikimoto

AFTERWORD

SO, HOW DID YOU LIKE IT?

NANA WASN'T MODELED AFTER ANOYONE IN PARTICULAR, BUT IF I HAD TO PICK SOMEONE, I'D SAY SHE WAS BASED ON PEOPLE—JUST LIKE YOU—WHO HAVE CELEBRITY CRUSHES!

OF COURSE, I ALSO HAVE CELEBRITY CRUSHES. SO GOING FORWARD, I'M GOING TO **REALLY** SUMMON MY FANGIRLING-FANTASIZING POWERS TO TRANSFORM KAEDE!

PLEASE LOOK AFTER DEAR NANA AND KAEDE IN THE FUTURE, TOO!

UNTIL WE MEET AGAIN IN VOLUME 2. FAREWELL!

6.2015   —RIN MIKIMOTO
                TWITTER: @RINMIKIRIN

Special thanx

S.sato   H.saijyo   M.kawai
M.takayashiki   K.kaneko
Every one of the staff,
everyone in the editorial department,
Horiuchi-sama,

Morita-san, Saiki-san,
arcoinc Kusume-sama

&U
I LOVE YOU

TRANSLATION NOTES

GOLDEN WEEK BREAK, P.17
In Japan, Golden Week is a holiday vacation from April 29th to early May.

BUTT ALIEN, P.32
In Japan, it is common to jokingly tack on "*-seijin*" ("-Alien") at the end of a word, in reference to a person who is obsessed with something beyond "regular people's" standards. The word "*seijin*" literally means "a being from another planet."

VARIETY SHOW, P.117
Variety shows are live TV shows that feature many segments. This can include interviews, musical numbers, games, skits, contests, quizzes, and much more. Shows like these are common in Japan, and are hosted by announcers and famous celebrities.

OSHARE *IZUMI* AND *SEKAI GYOTEN SCOOP*, P.119
Oshare Izumi is a reference to a famous Japanese variety and talk show called *Oshare Izumu*, which has been running since 2005. *Oshare* means "stylish" and *Izumu* is the transliteration of the English suffix "-ism." *Sekai Gyoten Scoop* is a reference to the documentary-style variety show called *The Sekai Gyoten News*, which has been on TV since 2001.

GRAVURE, P.121
In Japan, the usage of "gravure" comes from the English term "rotogravure," a printing process often used for printing images in magazines. Now, "gravure" in Japan most commonly refers to "gravure models/idols" and "gravure magazines" which feature suggestive photos of young women. Though the gravure industry is aimed at older audiences, it is mainly non-explicit in content. It centers on young women posing in swim suits, building an appealing public persona, and selling photobooks and merchandise. Gravure idols are just like any other celebrity in the entertainment industry, and the label itself is quite fluid.

THANK YOU FOR THE MEAL, P.162
Hinana says "*gochisousamadeshita*," in the original Japanese. When eating a meal in Japan, it is custom to say "*itadakimasu*" when beginning the meal, and "*gochisousama*" (or the more formal version that Hinana said) after finishing the meal. While "*itadakimasu*" has come to simply mean "let's eat," the original meaning translates to "I will gratefully accept this food" and by extension, "life." This is because every time someone eats food, it sustains them and gives them life, which was taken from another life (like plants and animals).

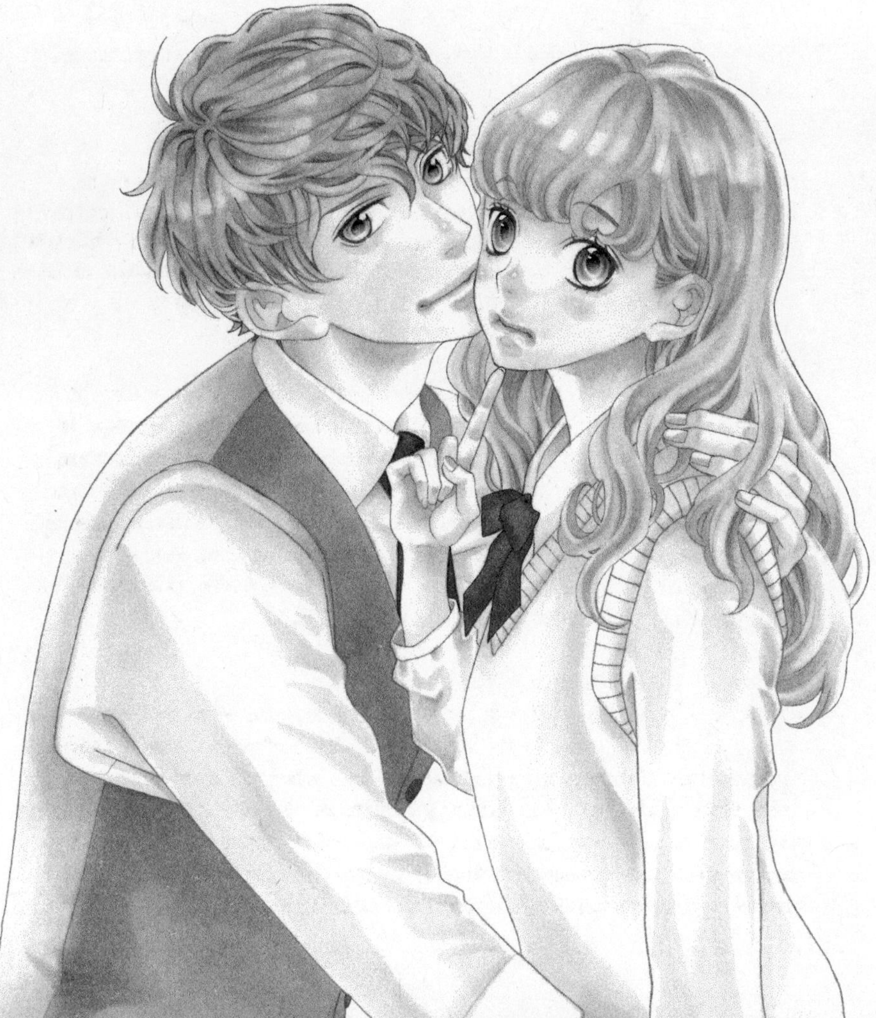

Having lost his wife, high school teacher Kōhei Inuzuka is doing his best to raise his young daughter Tsumugi as a single father. He's pretty bad at cooking and doesn't have a huge appetite to begin with, but chance brings his little family together with one of his students, the lonely Kotori. The three of them are anything but comfortable in the kitchen, but the healing power of home cooking might just work on their grieving hearts.

"This season's number-one feel-good anime!" —Anime News Network

"A beautifully-drawn story about comfort food and family and grief. Recommended." —Otaku USA Magazine

sweetness & lightning

By Gido Amagakure

"I'm pleasantly surprised to find modern shojo using cross-dressing as a dramatic device to deliver social commentary... Recommended."

-Otaku USA Magazine

The prince in his dark days

By **Hico Yamanaka**

A drunkard for a father, a household of poverty... For 17-year-old Atsuko, misfortune is all she knows and believes in. Until one day, a chance encounter with Itaru–the wealthy heir of a huge corporation–changes everything. The two look identical, uncannily so. When Itaru curiously goes missing, Atsuko is roped into being his stand-in. There, in his shoes, Atsuko must parade like a prince in a palace. She encounters many new experiences, but at what cost...?

KC
KODANSHA
COMICS

Japan's most powerful spirit medium delves into the ghost world's greatest mysteries!

Story by Kyo Shirodaira, famed author of mystery fiction and creator of *Spiral*, *Blast of Tempest*, and *The Record of a Fallen Vampire*.

Both touched by spirits called yôkai, Kotoko and Kurô have gained unique superhuman powers. But to gain her powers Kotoko has given up an eye and a leg, and Kurô's personal life is in shambles. So when Kotoko suggests they team up to deal with renegades from the spirit world, Kurô doesn't have many other choices, but Kotoko might just have a few ulterior motives...

IN/SPECTRE

STORY BY **KYO SHIRODAIRA**
ART BY **CHASHIBA KATASE**